Renate Luscher

deutsch kompakt neu

Selbstlernkurs Deutsch für Anfänger

A German Self-Study Course for Beginners

Zweisprachiges Arbeitsbuch

Bilingual Workbook

Englische Bearbeitung
John Stevens

Hueber Verlag

4. 3. 2. | Die letzten Ziffern
2018 17 16 15 14 | bezeichnen Zahl und Jahr des Druckes.
Alle Drucke dieser Auflage können, da unverändert,
nebeneinander benutzt werden.
1. Auflage
© 2013 Hueber Verlag GmbH & Co. KG, 85737 Ismaning, Deutschland
Redaktion: Hans Hillreiner, Hueber Verlag, Ismaning
Umschlaggestaltung: creative partners gmbh, München
Coverfotos von links: © Getty Images/Westend61; © Thinkstock/iStockphoto
Satz, Layout und Grafik: Martin Lange, Karlsfeld
Zeichnungen: Marlene Pohle, Stuttgart
Druck und Bindung: Auer Buch + Medien GmbH, Donauwörth
Printed in Germany
ISBN 978-3-19-627480-6

Contents

How to work with *deutsch kompakt*

Dear Learner of German,

You have acquired a German self-study course and are setting out to learn a language that is the mother tongue of 100 million people. To help you make rapid and solid progress, I'll give you a brief introduction to the course. In the package you'll find:
1. a Bilingual Workbook,
2. a Textbook and
3. three Audio-CDs.

The *Workbook* is your manual that will guide you step by step through the course. It is important that you always read the instruction in the Workbook first before you continue. Here's Lesson 1 as a model:

p. 5/6 + p. 5-7

Dialogue with exercises:
Work with the Textbook (= T) and the Workbook (= A) side by side. In the Workbook you'll find the pictograms of the listening texts and the translations of the instructions.

p. 7-8

Grammar – New Words – Exercises:
Continue working in the Workbook following the numbering. The Workbook contains thorough explanations of the grammar which is just sketched out on notepad sheets in the Textbook.

p. 9

Pronunciation
Also in the Workbook you'll find exercises on pronunciation features.

p. 8 + p. 9

Cultural Info:
To round off the lesson you'll do a game-like activity, for instance solving a puzzle. This is always on the last page of the lesson in the Textbook. You'll find translations and explanations in the Workbook.

p. 10

Test:
The Test at the end of each lesson will tell you whether you should go back and revise something or can continue.

The appendix contains the complete answer key and glossary. If you don't understand or have forgotten a word, look it up in the glossary. That's the quickest way to learn it. By the end of the course you'll know 1,500 words, and have learned enough to be able to communicate well in everyday situations, make phone calls and write simple letters.

So have fun now and enjoy yourself. And another final tip: don't listen to people who claim German is a difficult language to learn. We'll soon show you that the opposite is true!

With best wishes,
Renate Luscher

Guten Tag oder Hallo! – Hello and Hi

Four people – Jürgen Heinrich, Chris Bruckner, Rob Klein and Claudia Bergmann – are going to accompany you through this language course. At the beginning of Lesson 1 we're in Berlin, at the airport and at the station. Chris Bruckner has just arrived from Munich for a business meeting. Robert wants to have a look round Berlin. He's being met at the station by Claudia.

In Lesson 1 you'll learn how to greet somebody and say goodbye to them, and what the difference between *du* and *Sie* is, and also how you introduce somebody else.

1 *Please match.*
Please do exercise 1 in the textbook as preparation for the first dialogue: Guten Tag *is the standard form of greeting at any time of the day. Among friends people often just say* Hallo.

Guten Morgen!	*Good morning!*
Guten Abend!	*Good evening!*
(Gute Nacht!)	*(Good night)!*
Auf Wiedersehen!	*Goodbye!*
Tschüs!	*Bye!*

2 This is Jürgen Heinrich, Chris Bruckner, Robert and Claudia

1A
→ *Listen to how the four of them greet each other. Frau Bruckner and Herr Heinrich haven't met before, but Robert and Claudia already know each other of course. Listen to the conversation at least twice.*
→ *Read the dialogue in the textbook.*
→ *Listen to the text and read the dialogue at the same time.*
→ *Now underline the stressed syllables.*

Guten Tag. Sind Sie Herr Heinrich?
Ja, das bin ich.
Mein Name ist Bruckner, Chris Bruckner.
Guten Tag, Frau Bruckner. Herzlich willkommen.

→ *Read the dialogue out loud following your underlinings.*
→ *Then turn to the vocabulary section. Try to learn the meaning of the words and the sentences by heart.*

Guten Tag,	*Hello/Good morning/afternoon,*
sind Sie Herr Heinrich?	*are you Mr Heinrich?*
Ja, das bin ich.	*Yes, I am.*
ja	*yes*
ich bin	*I am*
Mein Name ist Bruckner.	*My name is Bruckner.*

Frau Bruckner	*Mrs Bruckner*
Guten Tag, Frau Bruckner.	*Hello, Frau Bruckner.*
Herzlich willkommen.	*Welcome.*

1B

→ *Listen to part 1B.*

→ *Read the dialogue in the textbook.*

→ *Listen to the text and read the dialogue at the same time.*

→ *Now underline the stressed syllables.*

Hallo, <u>Rob</u>.

etc.

→ *Read the dialogue out loud following your underlinings.*

→ *Then turn to the vocabulary section.*

Hallo, Rob/Claudia.	*Hi Rob/Claudia.*
Wie geht's dir/Ihnen?	*How are you? (informal/formal)*
Danke, gut.	*Fine, thanks.*

3 *Listen. What is the order?*

4 *What goes together?*
There is one answer for each sentence. Link the question and answer.

5 *Please complete.*
Complete the greetings when people say Sie *or* du *to each other.*

Sie or *du?*
When you address someone else you use *Sie* or *du*.
People use *du* when talking to relatives or friends, or when students are talking among themselves. Sometimes people who work together use it, too, but only in work-places where this is the normal thing to do. *Sie* is the polite and non-intrusive form of address and is the correct one to use in all other cases.

6 *Please complete.*
Fill in the forms of sein. *They are very important. The forms are unfortunately all irregular.*

7 *What fits? Listen and mark.*

8 *What fits? Please write.*

Now we're going to practise some grammar (grammar = Grammatik; exercises = Übungen).
As you do so, you'll also be extending your vocabulary (new words = Neue Wörter).

sein (be): Sie sind – du bist (both: you are)

Singular	1. Person	ich	**bin**	
	2. Person	du	**bist**	aus München, Berlin,
	3. Person	er/sie	**ist**	Köln, Stuttgart …
Plural	1. Person	wir	**sind**	
	2. Person	ihr	**seid**	
	3. Person	sie/Sie	**sind**	

	Sie/Sie	**du/ihr**
Singular	Sind Sie aus …?	Bist du aus …?
	(= Herr Heinrich)	(= Robert)
Plural	Sind Sie aus …?	Seid ihr aus …?
	(= Herr und Frau Heinrich)	(= Robert und Claudia)

9 *Please match.*

| Das bin | Das ist | Das sind | Das seid |

Sie   wir   ihr   sie (Sing.)

ich   er   sie (Pl.)

10 *Complete the sentences by writing in the missing forms.*

Ich _____ aus Barcelona.

_____ Sie aus Rom?

_____ du aus Warschau?

Herr Heinrich _____ aus Berlin.

Wir _____ aus Moskau.

_____ ihr aus London?

_____ Sie aus Rio?

11 *Wie geht's dir?*
There are three drawings. The people are talking. How do you think they greet each other?
Choose the correct answer.

Grüß Gott.

| Grüß Gott. | Danke, Frau Müller. | Tag auch. | Wie geht's? |

Hallo, Claudia, hallo, Evelyn, wie geht's?

| Grüß Gott, Nina. | Gut, und dir? | Aha. |

Grüezi.

| Grüezi, Nina. | Servus. | Gut, und dir? |

 Listen to the dialogues and check your answers.

12 *Revision*
Note these expressions. It would be best to learn them by heart.

Greeting someone / introducing yourself

Formal

Guten Tag, Frau / Herr + Nachname	*Good morning / afternoon / evening, Frau / Herr + surname*
Mein Name ist … (Bruckner / Heinrich).	*My name is … (Bruckner / Heinrich).*
Ich bin … (Chris Bruckner / Jürgen Heinrich).	*I am … (Chris Bruckner / Jürgen Heinrich).*
Ich heiße … (Bruckner / Heinrich).	*My name is … (Bruckner / Heinrich).*
Wie geht es Ihnen?	*How are you?*
Danke, gut. (Und Ihnen?)	*Fine, thanks. (And you?)*

 Here's a tip: The expression *Mein Name ist …* is very formal. Only use it with your surname: *Mein Name ist Bruckner.* The more common and informal expression is *Ich heiße* …, e.g. *Ich heiße Chris Bruckner.* And by the way: people don't usually say: *Ich heiße Frau Bruckner.*

Informal

Hallo + Vorname	*Hello + first name*
Ich bin … / Ich heiße …	*I'm … / My name's …*
Wie geht's? Wie geht's dir?	*How are you?*
Danke, gut. (Und dir?)	*Fine, thanks. (And you?)*

Introducing someone

Das ist Herr Berger.	*This is Herr Berger.*
Guten Tag, Herr Berger. Ich bin Klaus Nagel.	*Hello, Herr Berger. I'm Klaus Nagel.*

13 *Listen and repeat what you hear.*
You already know the words and phrases. Try and imitate the speaker's stress and
pronunciation as closely as you can.

Bruckner	Frau Bruckner	Guten Tag, Frau Bruckner.
Heinrich	Herr Heinrich	Guten Tag, Herr Heinrich.
Mein Name	Mein Name ist …	Mein Name ist Bruckner.
Ich	Ich heiße …	Ich heiße Heinrich.
Willkommen	Herzlich willkommen	Herzlich willkommen, Frau Bruckner.
Wie	Wie geht's?	Wie geht's Ihnen?
Danke	gut	Danke, gut.

14 *The Alphabet*
Now we're going to practise sounds. Listen and repeat. Try and copy the speaker's
pronunciation as closely as possible.

Aa	eF	Ka	Oo	eS	We
Be	Ge	eL	Pe	Te	iX
Ce	Ha	eM	Qu	Uu	Ypsilon
De	Ii	eN	eR	Vau	Zet
Ee	Jot				

15 *Special Sounds*
German has some special sounds – the umlauts ä, ö, ü, and ß (= eszet). Repeat the following
words and imitate the speaker as closely as possible.

Ö ö	schön	*(nice)*
Ü ü	Glück	*(luck)*
Ä ä	Geschäft	*(business)*
ß	ich heiße	

Try and spell your name. You won't have any trouble with that, will you?

Cultural info (Textbook page 8)

Here's a summary of how people greet each other and say goodbye in Northern and
Southern Germany, Austria and Switzerland. Of course there are many more regional
forms. But these can be heard very often.

Auf Wiedersehen.	*Goodbye.*
Tschüs.	*Bye/Cheerio/See you.*
Adieu.	*Goodbye/Bye.*
Ciao.	*See you.*

Listen and compare.

Vocabulary

1. Mark the right translation with a cross.

1. Guten Tag.
☐ Hello.
☐ Good afternoon.
☐ Good morning.

2. Guten Morgen.
☐ Hello.
☐ Good afternoon.
☐ Good morning.

3. Hallo.
☐ Hello.
☐ Good morning.
☐ Hi.

4. Wie geht's Ihnen?
☐ Where are you from?
☐ How are you?
☐ Who are you?

5. Danke, gut.
☐ Fine, thanks.
☐ And you, too.
☐ See you.

6. Auf Wiedersehen.
☐ Welcome.
☐ Goodbye.
☐ Hello.

2. Please complete.

1. Gute _____ !

2. Auf _____ !

3. _____ Tag!

4. _____ Abend!

5. _____ Morgen!

6. Tsch_____ !

Grammar

3. Fill in the forms of sein.

1. ich _____

2. du _____

3. er _____

4. sie (= Claudia) _____

5. Das _____ Robert.

6. _____ Sie Herr Bermann?

7. _____ Sie Frau Bergmann?

8. _____ Sie Herr und Frau Bergmann?

4. Please complete.

1. Ich _____ Julia.

2. _____ du Erik?

3. _____ Sie Herr Schmidt?

4. Ich _____ Wolfgang Schmidt.

5. Mein Name _____ Berger.

6. Das _____ Herr Berger.

Check your answers in the key at the back of the book and then add up your points.

Total:	1 – 13	Before you carry on, you really should do this lesson again.
	14 – 22	Quite good, but not perfect yet. Please go over the dialogues and the grammar again.
	23 – 26	Very good. You can carry straight on.

Woher kommen Sie? – Where do you come from?

Herr Heinrich takes Frau Bruckner to his office via the hotel. From their conversation on the way you find out more about them.
When you want to get to know somebody, you have to ask questions. So in Lesson 2 you are going to learn how to ask questions. That's relatively easy in German.

1 *To prepare for the conversation, have a look at the map (Textbook, page 8). Find the cities Berlin, München (Munich), Wien (Vienna), etc. and say out loud* Da ist … . *Three of the cities are mentioned in the dialogue.*

2 Herr Heinrich and Frau Bruckner in the car
→ *Listen to Herr Heinrich's and Frau Bruckner's conversation.*
→ *Listen to the conversation at least twice.*
→ *Read the dialogue in the textbook.*
→ *Listen to the text and read the dialogue at the same time.*
→ *Now underline the stressed syllables.*

Sind Sie aus Berlin, Herr Heinrich?
etc.

→ *Then read the dialogue out loud following your underlinings.*
→ *Then turn to the vocabulary section. Try to learn the meaning of the words and the sentences by heart.*

Sind Sie …?	Are you …?
aus Berlin	from Berlin
Kommen Sie …?	Do you come …?
Wohnen Sie …?	Do you live …?
Leben Sie …?	Do you live …?
Ja, klar.	Yes, of course.
Und Sie,	And you,
woher kommen Sie?	where do you come from?
Aus Österreich,	From Austria,
ich bin aus Wien.	I am from Vienna.
aber	but
ich lebe	I live
ich komme	I come
ich kenne	I know
in München	in Munich
schon lange	a long time
Sind Sie gern in …?	Do you like it in …?
sehr gern	like (doing something) a lot
ich wohne	I live

schon fünf Jahre	for five years
dort	there
Kennen Sie …?	Do you know …?
Ja, aber nicht gut.	Yes, but not well.

3 *Mark the verb.*

4 *What fits?*
Now listen to the text again und check your answers.

5 *Questions put to Chris Bruckner. Mark the right answer.*

6 *Please answer. What is correct?*

7 *We ask – you answer*
Imagine somebody asks you personally how you are. Listen, then select your answer and say it out loud.

If you say *Na ja*, people know immediately that you don't feel too good.
If you start with *Ach*, it's a sign that you're going to say you don't feel good at all.

8 *Write the verbs.*
The Sie *form is always the same as the infinitive.*

Please write. What is the question / answer?

lebt	Pierre	Paris	in	_____ ?
in	Paris	ja	er	lebt	_____ .
aus	Paris	er	ist	_____ .

kennen	Paris	Sie	_____ ?
nicht	ja	gut	aber	_____ .
kenne	London	ich	gut	_____ .

These grammar explanations include information on the differences between German and English usage, whenever relevant.

Verbs in the present – Verben im Präsens

Singular	1. Person	ich	komm**e**	
	2. Person	du	komm**st**	aus München, Berlin, Köln,
	3. Person	er / sie	komm**t**	Stuttgart …
Plural	1. Person	wir	komm**en**	
	2. Person	ihr	komm**t**	
	3. Person	sie / Sie	komm**en**	

- Unlike in English, the ending of the verb changes with the person (*ich, du, er* etc.), though some persons share the same ending (*wir kommen, sie kommen*).
- Other verbs that have the same ending as *kommen* are: *kennen, leben, wohnen, heißen* (Note: *du heißt*).
- The infinitive has the ending *-(e)n*. This is the form you find in a dictionary. It is also the form you know from the instructions: *Hören Sie. Schreiben Sie* etc.

9 *Underline the infinitives.*

| bist | heiße | sein | kenne | seid | lebe | wohnen |

| lebt | kennst | komme | heißen | wohnt | kennen |

10 *Complete the table by writing in the missing forms.*

		kennen	**leben**	**wohnen**	**heißen**
Singular	ich	kenne	lebe	wohne	
	du		lebst		heißt
	er / sie	kennt	lebt		heißt
Plural	wir	kennen	leben		heißen
	ihr		lebt	wohnt	heißt
	sie / Sie	kennen		wohnen	

11 *Fill in the forms of* heißen.

Ich heiße _____ _____ (= Ihr Name).

Wie _____ du?   Wir _____ Knut und Boris.

Er _____ Boris.   Wie _____ ihr?

Wie _____ Sie? Neumann?   Karla und Fritz _____ Sauter.

Questions with and without question words – Fragen mit und ohne Fragewort

There are questions with and without question words. *Woher* is a question word.

Woher **kommen Sie**?	–	**Aus** Berlin / England / Italien.
Woher **kommst du**?	–	**Aus** München / Polen / Frankreich.

Kommen Sie aus Italien?	–	Ja, ich komme **aus** Italien.
Kommst du aus Polen?	–	Nein, ich komme **aus** Frankreich.

Questions are easy to form in German. You just turn the subject (= the person doing the action) and the verb round. So *Sie kommen* becomes *Kommen Sie* in a question.

12 *Here are lots of questions and answers. Write the correct form of the verb in the gap.*

Woher _____ (kommen) Andrea?

Aus Berlin. Sie _____ (kommen) aus Berlin.

_____ (leben) Pierre in München?

Nein, in Paris. Pierre _____ (leben) in Paris.

Woher _____ (kommen) Graziella
und Paolo? Aus Verona?

Ja, sie _____ (kommen) aus Verona.

_____ (wohnen) Juan auch in Verona?

Nein, Juan _____ (wohnen) in Madrid.

_____ (kennen) Sie Warschau?

Ja, ich _____ (kennen) Warschau gut.

_____ (wohnen) Elsbeta in Warschau?

Ja, sie _____ (wohnen) in Warschau.

13 *Revision*
Note these expressions. It would be best to learn them by heart.

Asking where someone comes from

Woher sind / kommen Sie? Woher bist / kommst du?	*Where are you from? / Where do you come from?*
Ich bin / komme aus … (Berlin / München / Österreich).	*I am / come from … (Berlin / Munich / Austria).*
Aus … (Berlin / München / Österreich).	*From … (Berlin / Munich / Austria).*
Sind Sie aus … (München / Österreich)? Bist du aus … (München / Österreich)?	*Are you from … (Munich / Austria)?*
Ja, ich bin aus …	*Yes, I'm from …*
Nein, ich bin aus …	*No, I am from …*
Leben / Wohnen Sie in … (Berlin / München)?	*Do you live in … (Berlin / Munich)?*
Ja, ich lebe / wohne in …	*Yes, I live in …*
Nein, ich lebe / wohne in …	*No, I live in …*
Ich bin schon fünf Jahre in …	*I have been in … for five years.*
Kennen Sie … (Berlin / München)?	*Do you know … (Berlin / Munich)?*
Ja, aber nicht gut.	*Yes, but not well.*

14 *Listen and repeat.*
You already know the words and phrases. Try and imitate the speaker's stress and pronunciation as closely as you can.

Aus Berlin.	Sind Sie aus Berlin?
Aus Wien.	Ich bin aus Wien.
In München.	Aber ich lebe in München.
schon fünf Jahre	Ich wohne schon fünf Jahre dort.
kennen	Kennen Sie Berlin?
nicht gut	Ja, aber nicht gut.

15 *Repeat the names of the cities and countries.*

Zürich	Leipzig	Salzburg
Frankfurt	Hamburg	Augsburg
Berlin	Wien	Paris
Köln	Bern	Graz
Deutschland	Österreich	die Schweiz

16 a. *Listen.*
Three young people – Nina, Achim and Christian – are greeting each other.

Nina:	Hallo, ich bin Nina, und du?
Achim:	Ich heiße Achim. Hallo!
Nina:	Kommst du auch aus Berlin?
Achim:	Nein, aus München, ich bin schon lange in München.
Christian:	Ich bin Christian.
Achim:	Tag, Christian.
Christian:	Tag.
Achim:	Woher bist du?
Christian:	Aus Hamburg.
Achim:	Aha.

16 b. *Now listen to the dialogue a second time and read the sentences at the same time. Try and imitate the speaker's stress as closely as you can.*

Cultural info: City quiz (Textbook page 12)

In addition to the capital cities Berlin and Vienna, here are some other important cities. You can look and see on the map where they are.
Auerbach's Cellar: One of the ten most famous restaurants in the world. Made famous by Goethe's Faust.

What's the name of the city?
Write the names of the cities.

Vocabulary

1. *Mark the right translation.*

1.
Wie geht's?
☐ How are you?
☐ Where are you from?
☐ How do you do?

2. (Kommen Sie aus Berlin?)
– Ja, klar.
☐ Yes, I am from Berlin.
☐ Yes, of course.
☐ Really?

3. (Sind Sie Herr / Frau …?)
– Ja, das bin ich.
☐ I'm …
☐ Yes, I am.
☐ Yes, please.

2. *Give the correct translation.*

1. to come _____

2. to live _____

3. to be called _____

4. to be _____

5. to know _____

| kennen |
| kommen |
| leben / wohnen |
| heißen |
| sein |

Grammar

3. *Underline the correct form.*

1. Kommst du auch [in] [aus] [im] Berlin?
2. [Kommst] [Kommen] [Kommt] Sie aus England?
3. Ich [wohne] [leben] [komme] schon lange in München.
4. Und woher kommen [Sie] [er] [ich]?
5. [Kennst] [Kennen] [Kenne] Sie Hamburg?
6. [Kommt] [Kommen] [Kommt] Sie auch aus Norddeutschland?

4. *What's the question?*

1. [Sie] [kommen] [woher] _____?
2. [Sie] [aus Hamburg] [sind] _____?
3. [in München] [wohnen] [Sie] _____?
4. [Berlin] [Sie] [kennen] _____?
5. [Sie] [sind] [Herr Müller] _____?
6. [geht es] [wie] [Ihnen] _____?

Check your answers in the key at the back of the book and then add up your points.

Total:
1 – 10	It would be a good idea to do this lesson again straightaway.
11 – 17	Pretty good. But it wouldn't hurt to go over the dialogues and the grammar again.
18 – 20	Excellent. If you like, you could go over the vocabulary again, otherwise you can carry straight on.

Im Hotel – At the Hotel

Frau Bruckner checks in at her hotel. She has to fill in the registration form and supply her personal details.
In this lesson you're going to learn a lot about nouns. A special feature of German is the fact that all nouns are written with a capital letter. There is also a capital letter at the beginning of a sentence, and proper names are also written with a capital: *Mein Name ist Müller.*

1 *Please match.*
Please do exercise 1 as preparation for the lesson. Here is a summary of nouns that are important when giving personal details. Match the terms.
If you want to make things a bit easier, you can start with the following translation exercise. Please match the terms and their translations.
Note: postcodes in Berlin start with a 1...

der Name	country
der Vorname	postcode / zipcode
der Geburtsort	address
die Adresse	name
der Ort	place
die Postleitzahl	street / road
die Straße	signature
das Land	first name
die Unterschrift	place of birth

Do you notice anything? Yes, of course. There are words in German and English that have the same root: *the name – der Name, the address – die Adresse* and many more.

2 Checking in at the hotel
This is Frau Bruckner's business card. First listen to the words and then fill in the hotel registration form.

3 *What's your name? Fill in the registration form for yourself.*
You are now the hotel guest.

4 *Ask and answer: What fits?*
Maybe the receptionist has asked for your personal details. Match the questions to the details on the form.

5 *What belongs together? Write the noun with its article.*
All nouns have an article. In German there are three different articles: der, die, das.

Always learn nouns together with their article, so learn *der Name*, not just *Name*. Store article and noun in your memory as a unit that belongs together. That will help you avoid a lot of mistakes.

6 *What's the word?*
This requires a good memory. So let's relax a bit with a little puzzle.

7 *A form – Please fill in.*

Familienname	*family name, surname*
Vorname / Vornamen	*first name / first names*
Geburtsname	*maiden name, name at birth*
Geburtsland	*country of birth*
Geburtsdatum	*date of birth*
Tag	*day*
Monat	*month*
Jahr	*year*
Familienstand	*marital status*
ledig	*single*
verheiratet	*married*
geschieden	*divorced*
Geschlecht	*sex*
männlich	*male*
weiblich	*female*
Nationalität	*nationality*
Platz	*place*
Nummer	*number*
Stadt	*town*
Pass-Nummer	*passport number*
Ausweis-Nummer	*identity card number*
Datum	*date*

8 *What belongs together?*
Draw lines.

9 *Write your name, where you come from and where you live.*
Try and say the sentence out loud. You're bound to be asked sometime.

10 aus *and* in
aus *and* in *are used in combination with certain verbs. Fill in the appropriate preposition.*

There are certain points to note about the names of countries if you want to avoid mistakes.

Ländernamen – Names of countries

without an article	with an article		
	der	die	Plural
China	der Libanon	die Schweiz	die Niederlande
Japan	der Sudan	die Türkei	die USA
Österreich	(der) Irak		
Polen	(der) Iran		
Spanien	(der) Jemen		
Deutschland usw.			

Most names of countries don't have an article. It's easiest if you just note the exceptions.

11 *Please complete.*
A lot of names of countries end in -ien. Is your country one of them? Write the name in English next to each country.

Arg _ _ _ _ _ ien   _____

Austr _ _ ien   _____

Bel _ _ en   _____

Bra _ _ _ ien   _____

Bul _ _ rien   _____

Groß _ _ _ _ _ nien   _____

I _ dien   _____

Ind _ _ esien _____

Ita _ ien   _____

Kro _ _ _ en _____

Molda _ ien   _____

Rum _ nien   _____

Sl _ _ enien   _____

Woher kommen Sie / kommst du?	– **Aus** Österreich / Deutschland / Spanien / Russland / Japan / Australien. Aber: **Aus der** Schweiz/**Aus den** USA. **Aus (dem)** Irak / **Aus (dem)** Iran / **Aus dem** Sudan.
Wo wohnen Sie / wohnst du?	– **In** Österreich/Deutschland/Spanien/ Russland / Japan / Australien. Aber: **In der** Schweiz/**In den** USA. **Im/In** Irak / **Im/In** Iran / **Im** Sudan.

12 *Complete the name of the country.*
You can see from the name where the person comes from.

Woher kommt ...

... Tatjana?   Aus R _ _ _ land.   ... Paul?   Aus

_ _ _ _ _ _ _ _ _ _ _ .

... Michel?   Aus F _ _ _ _ reich.   ... Urs?   Aus der _ _ _ _ _ _ _ .

... Susan?   Aus den _ _ _ .   ... Eri Enaba?   Aus J _ _ _ _ .

Numbers – Zahlen

0 null	**3** drei	**6** sechs	**9** neun
1 eins	**4** vier	**7** sieben	**10** zehn
2 zwei	**5** fünf	**8** acht	

13 *Start at 0 and draw a line to the next number until you get to 10. Then write the numbers down in the right order.*

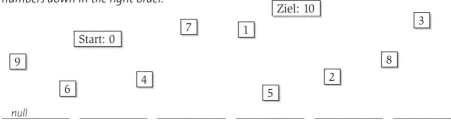

null _____ _____ _____ _____ _____ _____

_____ _____ _____ _____ _____

14 *Write down the postcodes. Then listen and compare.*

sieben null eins neun null	_ _ _ _ _	Stuttgart
acht null acht null fünf	_ _ _ _ _	München
sieben sechs eins drei sieben	_ _ _ _ _	Karlsruhe
sechs null drei eins drei	_ _ _ _ _	Frankfurt am Main
sechs neun eins eins acht	_ _ _ _ _	Heidelberg
zwei null eins vier drei	_ _ _ _ _	Hamburg

15 *Revision*
Here are some important questions and requests:

Entschuldigung, ich habe eine Frage.	*Excuse me, I have a question.*
Was bedeutet das?	*What does this mean?*
Was bedeutet das Wort?	*What does the word mean?*
Was bedeutet der Satz?	*What does the sentence mean?*
Wie heißt das auf Deutsch?	*What is that in German?*
Bitte buchstabieren Sie.	*Please spell it.*
Bitte langsam.	*Slowly please.*
Bitte sprechen Sie langsam.	*Please speak slowly.*
Bitte sprechen Sie nicht so schnell.	*Please don't speak so fast.*
Bitte wiederholen Sie.	*Please repeat.*

In German these phrases don't sound as abrupt as in English.

16 *Listen and repeat what you hear.*
You already know the words and phrases. Try and imitate the speaker's stress and pronuncia-tion as closely as you can.

Woher	Woher kommst du?
Wo	Wo bist du geboren?
Wo	Wo wohnst du?
Wie	Wie heißt du?
Wie	Wie geht's dir?
Was	Was ist das?

17 *Listen and repeat.*
Numbers 0 – 10: You'll find the numbers on page 20.

18 *For bright sparks.*
If you're good in working things out, you'll have no problems with this. Read the four numbers in each line, then fill in the last number.

eins	zwei	drei	vier	_____
zehn	acht	sechs	vier	_____
acht	sieben	sechs	fünf	_____
eins	drei	fünf	sieben	_____

19 *Postcodes. Repeat the question.*

Wo ist 20103?	Das ist in Hamburg.
Wo ist 69317?	Das ist in Frankfurt.
Wo ist 69118?	Das ist in Heidelberg.
Wo ist 10117?	Das ist in Berlin.
Wo ist 80637?	Das ist in München.

Cultural info (Textbook page 16)

People who look as though they're foreigners often aren't. Often they were born in Germany and have a German passport.

What does the reporter say? What does the man say?
Write the dialogue.

Now listen and compare.

Vocabulary

1. *Mark the right translation.*

1. Wie ist Ihr Name?
☐ How are you?
☐ What's your name?
☐ Tell me your name.

2. Wo sind Sie geboren?
☐ When were you born?
☐ Where were you born?
☐ What's your place and date of birth?

3. Bitte buchstabieren Sie.
☐ Please repeat.
☐ Please spell it.
☐ Please don't speak so fast.

4. Ich bin geschieden.
☐ I'm married.
☐ I'm divorced.
☐ I'm single.

5. Woher …?
☐ Where … from?
☐ Who …?
☐ Where …to?

6. Die Pass-Nummer bitte.
☐ Your passport number, please.
☐ The date of issue of your passport, please.
☐ The password, please.

2. *Supply the article.*

1. _____ Land   3. _____ Adresse   5. _____ Pass

2. _____ Stadt   4. _____ Ort   6. _____ Visum

Grammar

3. *Please complete.*

1. Sind Sie _____ ?

2. Wo _____ _____ ?

3. Wie ist _____ _____ ?

4. Woher _____ _____ ?

5. Ist das _____ _____ ?

6. Kommen Sie _____ _____ ?

| wohnen Sie |
| kommen Sie |
| aus Österreich |
| Ihre Adresse |
| verheiratet |
| die Pass-Nummer |

Listening Comprehension

1|25

4. *Listen to the short dialogue and mark the right answers.*

1. Der Mann heißt
☐ Müller.
☐ Janssen.

2. Die Frau heißt
☐ Janssen.
☐ Müller.

3. Die Frau kommt aus
☐ Berlin.
☐ Hamburg.

Check your answers in the key at the back of the book and then add up your points.

Total: | 1 – 11 | Oh dear, it's a pity. Please do this unit again.
12 – 18 | Not so bad. But even so, it would be a good idea to go over the vocabulary and the grammar again.
19 – 21 | Excellent. There's nothing to stop you carrying on.

Smalltalk

We are now in Herr Kühne's office. Chris Bruckner has an appointment with him. You'll hear some small talk about a journey and the weather, and will learn how to ask "how are you?" and to reply to this.

1 *Please do exercise 1 in the textbook as preparation for the dialogue. Are you missing some vocabulary items? Here are the translations.*

Wie geht's?	How are you?
Wie ist das Wetter?	What's the weather like?
Wie ist das Hotel?	What's the hotel like?
Wie war die Reise?	How was the trip?
Gut, danke. / Es geht.	Fine, thanks. / Not too bad.
Nicht sehr gut. Leider.	Not very good, I'm afraid.
Das ist prima.	That's great.

2 Frau Bruckner and Herr Kühne in the office   1|26

4A

→ *Now listen to Herr Kühne greeting Frau Bruckner. They talk about her journey and the weather of course. Listen to the conversation at least twice.*

→ *Read the dialogue in the textbook.*

→ *Listen to the text and read the dialogue at the same time.*

→ *Underline the stressed syllables.*

Guten Tag, Frau Bruckner. Wie geht's?   Auch gut. Und nicht weit.
Wie war die Reise?   Sie sind ja direkt im Zentrum.
Guten Tag, Herr Kühne. Danke, gut.   Ja, das ist sehr praktisch.
Und wie ist das Hotel?

→ *Read the dialogue out loud following your underlinings.*

→ *Then turn to the vocabulary section. Try to learn the meaning of the words and the sentences by heart.*

Reise (die)	trip, journey
weit	far
Sie sind ja direkt im Zentrum.	You're right in the centre.
Zentrum (das)	centre
praktisch	handy, practical

The question: *Wie war die Reise?* is a frequent expression and a good one for starting a conversation.

4B

→ Listen to part 4B.
→ Read the dialogue in the textbook.
→ Listen to the text and read the dialogue at the same time.
→ Now underline the stressed syllables.
→ Read the dialogue out loud following the stressed syllables.
→ Then turn to the vocabulary section.

Das Wetter ist auch prima.	The weather's great, too.
Wetter (das)	weather
prima – schön – warm	fine, great – fine, beautiful – warm
Wie ist es denn in München?	What's it like in Munich?
Leider schlecht.	Bad, I'm afraid.
schlecht	bad
Es regnet schon zwei Tage.	It's been raining for two days.
regnen – es regnet	rain
Da haben Sie hier Glück.	You're lucky here.
Glück (das)	luck
Dann machen wir eine Stadtrundfahrt.	Then we'll do a city tour.
machen – er / sie macht	do, make
Stadtrundfahrt (die)	city tour
Vielleicht morgen?	Maybe / Perhaps tomorrow?
Ja, gerne.	Gladly. / I'd like that.

3 Listen to the dialogue. Mark the person.

4 What's right? What's wrong? Mark accordingly.

5 Read the dialogue.

6 What's right?

7 An interview – First read the answers. Then listen and answer accordingly.
As preparation please do the following exercise, then exercise 7 in the textbook will be no problem. Please complete.

Positiv					Negativ
sehr gut	gut	nicht so gut	nicht (sehr) gut	schlecht	sehr schlecht
sehr schön	_____	_____	_____	schlecht	_____

8 Listen, and write the adjectives.

24

Now we're going to do a bit of grammar practice. We're going to concentrate on nouns and articles that are very typical of German.

Article + Noun – Artikel + Nomen
Every noun has its article.

People	Article + Noun		Personal Pronoun
Jürgen Heinrich	**der** Name	→	er
Chris Bruckner	**die** Adresse	→	sie
	das Land	→	es

In German all nouns are written with a capital letter. That makes it easy to spot them. Unlike English, German has three different articles. Unfortunately there's no hard and fast rule that says which article goes with which noun.

9 *Note down all the nouns from Dialogue 4.*

_____ _____ _____ _____

_____ _____ _____ _____

_____ _____ _____

10 *Fill in the article.*

_____ Reise   _____ Land   _____ Stadt   _____ Stadtrundfahrt

_____ Zentrum   _____ Name   _____ Hotel   _____ Glück

_____ Adresse   _____ Tag   _____ Wetter

11 *Fill in the right personal pronoun. The article will help you.*
For example: das Wetter → es

das Geschäft – _____   der Euro – _____   das Auto – _____

der Tag   – _____   die Reise – _____   die Zeit   – _____

die Stadt   – _____   das Haus – _____   die Adresse – _____

yes / no questions – Negation with *nicht*   **Ja / Nein-Fragen – Die Verneinung mit *nicht***

Ist das Frau Bruckner?	–	**Ja**, das ist Frau Bruckner.
Ist das Herr Heinrich?	–	**Nein**, das ist **nicht** Herr Heinrich.
Wie ist das Wetter in München?	–	Es ist sehr **schön**.
Wie ist das Wetter in Berlin?	–	Es ist **nicht schön**.
Kennen Sie Berlin gut?	–	**Ja**, ich kenne Berlin **gut**.
Kennen Sie München gut?	–	**Nein**, ich kenne München **nicht gut**.
Regnet es?	–	**Ja**, es regnet.
	–	**Nein**, es regnet **nicht**.

- *nicht* is placed in front of the part of sentence that is being negated: *nicht gut, nicht schön, nicht Herr Heinrich.*
- When a whole sentence is negated, *nicht* is placed at the end: *Nein, es regnet nicht.*

12 *What adjectives do you know now? Write them down from memory.*

13 *Simply say* NEIN.

Das Hotel ist prima.	–	Nein, das Hotel ist nicht prima.
Das Wetter ist schön.	–	Nein, _____
Es regnet.	–	Nein, _____
Das Zentrum ist weit.	–	_____
Das Hotel ist praktisch.	–	_____
Die Reise ist prima.	–	_____

14 *Revision*
Note these expressions. It would be best to learn them by heart.

Asking how someone is

Guten Tag, Frau/Herr + Nachname	*Hello/Good morning/afternoon, Frau/Herr + surname*
Guten Morgen, Frau/Herr + Nachname	*Good morning, Frau/Herr + surname*
Guten Abend, Frau/Herr + Nachname	*Good evening, Frau/Herr + surname*
Wie geht's?	*How are you? (informal)*
Wie geht es Ihnen?	*How are you? (formal)*
Danke, sehr gut/gut/nicht schlecht/es geht.	*Very well/Fine/Not bad/OK, thank you.*
Danke, nicht so gut.	*Thanks for asking, not so good.*

Small talk: Travel and weather

Wie war die Reise?	*How was the journey/your trip?*
– Danke, gut.	*– Fine, thanks.*
Wie ist das Wetter? –	*What's the weather like? –*
Es regnet./Es ist nicht so schön./	*It's raining./It's not so nice./*
Es ist schön/warm/kalt.	*It's nice/fine/warm/cold.*
Das Wetter ist prima/gut/sehr gut/	*The weather's great/good/very good/*
schön/schlecht.	*nice/fine/bad.*
Die Sonne scheint.	*The sun is shining.*
Es schneit.	*It's snowing.*
Es ist windig.	*It's windy.*

15 *Listen and repeat.*

Tag	Guten Tag.	schön	Es ist schön.
Wie	Wie geht's?	schlecht	Es ist schlecht.
Wetter	Wie ist das Wetter?	windig	Es ist windig.
Sonne	Die Sonne scheint.	schneien	Es schneit.

16 *Add* sehr. *First listen, then repeat.*

schön	sehr schön	weit	sehr weit
gut	sehr gut	warm	sehr warm
schlecht	sehr schlecht	kalt	sehr kalt

17 *Supply the article, and then repeat.*

_____ Name   _____ Adresse

_____ Land   _____ Geburtsland

_____ Familienstand   _____ Nationalität

18 *Listen to the names of countries.*

Brasilien	Frankreich	Österreich
China	Italien	Russland
Deutschland	Korea	Türkei
England	Neuseeland	

19 *Listen and read at the same time.*
Look up exercise 5 (Textbook page 18).

Cultural info (Textbook page 20)

Before you do the test, open the textbook. Do you recognize the countries at first sight?

Supply the names of countries and find all the names that end in -land. *How many are there?*
Do you recognize the country? Match the country names.

Vocabulary

1. *Mark the correct translation.*

1. Wie geht's?
☐ Where are you from?
☐ How are you?
☐ What's the weather like?

2. Sehr gut.
☐ Very badly.
☐ Very well.
☐ Not very well.

3. Leider schlecht.
☐ Great.
☐ You're lucky.
☐ Bad, I'm afraid.

2. *What's the weather like? Please match.*

◯ Es ist sehr warm.

◯ Es ist windig.

◯ Es ist kalt.

◯ Die Sonne scheint.

◯ Es regnet.

◯ Es schneit.

Grammar

3. *Supply the article.*

1. _____ Name
2. _____ Stadt
3. _____ Land
4. _____ Adresse
5. _____ Hotel
6. _____ Zentrum

4. *What is positive? Mark with a cross.*

1. ☐ Das Wetter ist schön.
2. ☐ Ich kenne die Stadt nicht gut.
3. ☐ Das Hotel ist nicht weit.
4. ☐ Das ist sehr praktisch.

5. ☐ Sie haben Glück.
6. ☐ Es regnet schon zwei Tage.
7. ☐ Das Wetter ist nicht schön.
8. ☐ Aber die Reise ist prima.

5. *Please negate.*

1. Das ist weit.   Nein, _____ .

2. Das ist schön.   _____ .

3. Es ist kalt.   _____ .

4. Es ist windig.   _____ .

5. Es regnet.   _____ .

6. Es schneit.   _____ .

Check your answers in the key at the back of the book and then add up your points.

Total:
1 – 15   Before you carry on, you really should do this unit again.
16 – 25   Quite good, but not perfect yet. Please go over the dialogues and the grammar again. It'll be worth it.
26 – 29   Very good. You can carry straight on.

Wie lange fahren wir denn? – How long will it take us?

Claudia and Robert take the S-Bahn to Claudia's place. Claudia shares a flat with her friend Niki Bat in the north of Berlin.

Here are a lot of different questions that all start with a W-question word. This will also give you a chance to learn how to thank somebody, and some colloquial expressions that you can use in many different situations.

1 *Who says it?*
Please do exercise 1 as preparation. These are common responses in everyday speech. Note the gestures and head movement.

Aha, ich verstehe.	*Ah, I understand.*
Na ja, das ist nicht schlimm.	*Never mind.*

2 Claudia and Robert take the S-Bahn

5A

→ *First listen to the dialogue 5A at least twice.*
→ *Read the dialogue in the textbook.*
→ *Listen to the text and read the dialogue at the same time.*
→ *Now underline the stressed syllables.*
→ *Then read the dialogue following your underlinings.*
→ *Then turn to the vocabulary section. Try to learn the meaning of the words and the sentences by heart.*

Was kostet …?	*What does … cost? How much is …?*
kosten – er/sie kostet	*cost*
Fahrkarte (die), die Fahrkarten	*ticket*
zwei Euro	*two euros*
Euro (der), die Euro(s)	*euro*
Das habe ich.	*I've got that.*
Wo ist der Automat?	*Where is the ticket machine?*
Automat (der), die Automaten	*(ticket) machine*
Ich mache das.	*I'll do it.*
nett	*kind, nice*
Vielen Dank.	*Thank you very much.*
Wie lange fahren wir denn?	*How long does it take?*
fahren – er/sie fährt	*go, drive*
Stunde (die), die Stunden	*hour*
Wie bitte?	*Sorry?*
Minute (die), die Minuten	*minute*
Großstadt (die) (groß + die Stadt)	*city (groß = big)*
Kleinstadt (die) (klein + die Stadt)	*small town (klein = small)*

Compound nouns sometimes consist of an adjective and a noun:
groß + die Stadt = die Großstadt.

5B

→ *Listen to part 5B.*
→ *Read the dialogue in the textbook.*
→ *Listen to the text and read the dialogue at the same time.*
→ *Underline the stressed syllables.*
→ *Read the dialogue following the stress marks.*
→ *Then turn to the vocabulary section.*

Morgen haben wir das Auto.	*We'll have the car tomorrow.*
Auto (das), die Autos	*car*
mit der S-Bahn	*by S-Bahn*
S-Bahn (die), die S-Bahnen	*S-Bahn (city and suburban railway)*
Wann kommt Niki denn nach Hause?	*When does Niki get home?*
Wann?	*When?*
nach Hause	*home*
Heute kommt er spät.	*He's coming late today.*
heute / spät	*today / late*
Er arbeitet wieder furchtbar viel.	*He's working terribly hard again.*
arbeiten – er / sie arbeitet	*work*
wieder	*again*
furchtbar viel / wenig	*terribly much / hard / little*
Hast du ein Glück!	*You're lucky!*

3 *Read the text and fill in the right question word. Do you still remember which it is?*
Listen to the dialogue again and check your answers.

4 *That's wrong!*
Write the correct sentence.

5 Wie bitte? *Read and complete.*
Two people are having problems communicating. The complete sentence is not so elegant, but clearer.
Now listen and compare.

6 *A few questions. – Give a brief answer. Write.*
When you give an answer, you can do it in a short sentence or a long one. Read the question and the long sentence. Then find the matching short answer. The short version is used in everyday speech.

7 *Write the singular.*

New Verbs – Neue Verben

		haben	**arbeiten**	**fahren**
Singular	ich	habe	arbeite	fahre
	du	**hast**	arbei**test**	fährst
	er/sie/es	**hat**	arbei**tet**	fährt
Plural	wir	haben	arbeiten	fahren
	ihr	habt	arbeitet	fahrt
	sie/Sie	haben	arbeiten	fahren

The verb has a different ending for each person, but some verbs change the stem, too, in the second and third person:

• *hast* and *hat* are irregular.
• *a* becomes *ä: fahren – du fährst, er/sie/es fährt.*
• After a *-t* or *-d* an extra *-e-* is inserted. This makes pronunciation easier: du *arbeitest, er arbeitet/du findest, er findet.*

8 *All the special forms are missing in the following table. Fill them in.*

		haben	**arbeiten**	**fahren**
Singular	ich	habe	arbeite	fahre
	du			
	er/sie/es			
Plural	wir	haben	arbeiten	fahren
	ihr	habt		fahrt
	sie/Sie	haben	arbeiten	fahren

9 *Match the right article.*

_____ Minute   _____ Großstadt   _____ Kleinstadt   _____ S-Bahn

_____ Fahrkarte   _____ Euro   _____ Stunde   _____ Auto

Nomen im Plural – Nouns in the plural

Singular	Plural
der Tag	die Tag**e**
das Jahr	die Jahr**e**
die Stadt	die St**ä**dt**e**
das Land	die L**ä**nd**er**
das Wort	die W**ö**rt**er**
der Name	die Name**n**
die Fahrkarte	die Fahrkarte**n**
die Minute	die Minute**n**

Note: *die* = feminine singular (**die** Minute) and plural (der Tag, **die** Tage/die Minute, **die** Minuten/das Jahr, **die** Jahre)

10 *What are they? Write the answers.*

1 Das sind zwei _____

2   fünf _____

3   drei _____

4   drei _____

5   zwei _____

6   zwei _____

1

6 Name
   Adresse

Polen

2

3

5 Spanien

4 Markus Graf
   Steffi Sommer
   Toni Koch

11 *Please complete.*
For example: ein Jahr *– drei* Jahre

_____ Minute   – drei _____   _____ Kleinstadt – drei _____

_____ Stunde   – drei _____   _____ Geschäft – drei _____

_____ Stadt   – drei _____   _____ S-Bahn   – drei _____

_____ Großstadt – drei _____   _____ Auto   – drei _____

The number one: - We count *eins – zwei – drei – vier* etc.
- *ein-* changes when used in combination with a noun: **ein** *Tag (der Tag) –* **zwei** *Tage;*
eine *Stunde (die Stunde) –* **zwei** *Stunden; ein* Wort *(das Wort) –* **zwei** *Wörter*

12 *Revision*
Note these expressions. It would be best to learn them by heart.

Thanking

Danke. / Vielen Dank. – Bitte.	*Thank you. / Thank you very much. – That's OK. /*
	You're welcome. / Not at all. / Don't mention it.
Das ist nett (von dir).	*That's nice / kind (of you). (informal)*
Das ist nett (von Ihnen).	*That's nice / kind (of you). (formal)*

Colloquial expressions

(Das ist) super. (Das ist) prima.	*(That's) super. (That's) great.*
Furchtbar viel / wenig / alt / schlecht.	*Terribly hard / much / little / old / bad.*
Wie bitte?	*Sorry?*

Furchtbar viel is sehr sehr viel.
You can also say: furchtbar lange *or* furchtbar alt …

13 *a or ä, o or ö. Fill in and then repeat.*

1|40

die St__ dt – die St__ dte

das L__ nd – die L__ nder

das W__ rt – die W__ rter

der S__ tz – die S__ tze

der P__ ss – die P__ sse

14A *Who is that man?*
→ *Listen to the dialogue.*
→ *Complete the following text.*

1|41

Herr Binder arbeitet i__ B__ __ __ __ __ .

Er ist s__ __ __ __ ein J__ __ __ dort.

Er k__ __ __ __ Frau Antes.

14B
→ *And now repeat. Try to imitate the speaker's stress and pronunciation as closely as possible. This is naturally spoken everyday speech.*
→ *If you're not sure whether you've understood everything, you can read the text here:*

1|42

Frau Antes:	Wer ist der Herr da?
Herr Meyer:	Das ist Herr Binder. Er arbeitet jetzt in Bremen.
Frau Antes:	Hallo, Herr Binder! Was machen Sie denn hier?
Herr Binder:	Ja Frau Antes, guten Tag. Wie geht's Ihnen denn?
Frau Antes:	Danke, gut. Und Ihnen?
Herr Binder:	Auch gut.
Frau Antes:	Sind Sie schon lange hier?
Herr Binder:	Ja, schon ein Jahr.

Cultural info (Textbook p. 24)

1|43

Germany is at the heart of Europe. It has nine neighbouring countries. There is access to the sea in the north, to the North Sea and Baltic Sea.

Which countries are they?
Listen to the country names. Note down the answers.

Write the country names on the map.

Vocabulary

1. *Mark the correct translation.*

1. Danke.
☐ Please.
☐ Thank you.
☐ Sorry.

2. Was kostet das?
☐ How much is it?
☐ When do you get home?
☐ How long does it take?

3. nach Hause
☐ to work
☐ from work
☐ home

4. wenig Zeit
☐ little time
☐ a lot of time
☐ one hour

5. furchtbar viel
☐ terribly little
☐ terribly hard
☐ very small

6. Wie bitte?
☐ How do I ask?
☐ Sorry?
☐ Who is it, please?

2. *Write the singular.*

1. die Städte _____

2. fünf Minuten   eine _____

3. zehn Stunden eine _____

4. die Fahrkarten _____

5. die Wörter _____

6. zwei Länder   ein _____

Grammar

3. *Fill in the verb.*

1. _____ du zu Hause? (arbeiten)

2. _____ du heute Zeit? (haben)

3. Wir _____ sehr viel. (arbeiten)

4. _____ ihr mit dem Auto? (fahren)

5. Wir _____ mit der S-Bahn. (fahren)

6. Was _____ die Fahrkarte? (kosten)

4. *Supply the article.*

1. _____ Wörter
2. _____ S-Bahn

3. _____ Fahrkarten
4. _____ Automat

5. _____ Großstadt
6. _____ Auto

Which words are plural? Note down the numbers: _____ .

5. *Fill in* a, ä, o *or* ö.

1. die St__ dt
2. die W__ rter

3. die S__ tze
4. das L__ nd

5. der P__ ss
6. die P__ sse

Check your answers in the key at the back of the book and then add up your points.

Total:	1 – 15	It would be a good idea to do this unit again straightaway.
	16 – 26	Pretty good. But it wouldn't hurt to go over the dialogues and the grammar again.
	27 – 30	Excellent. If you like, you could go over the vocabulary again, otherwise you can carry straight on.

Wer ist Claudia? Wer ist Robert? – Who is …?

Now it really is time to find out a bit more about Claudia and Robert. You want to get to know them a bit better, don't you?

You will learn how to make statements about people and ask the corresponding questions. There is a lot about numbers and figures. And at the end we'll introduce you to a special sight.

1 *Who is who? Please match.*
What do you think the people look like? Please match. You know some of them, but not yet others. If you don't know all the words, please look them up in the glossary at the back of the workbook.

2 Claudia and Robert   1|44
→ *Listen to the text 6A at least twice.*
→ *Read the text in the textbook.*
→ *Listen and read the text at the same time.*
→ *Underline the stressed syllables.*
→ *Read the text following your underlinings.*
→ *Then turn to the vocabulary section. Try to learn the meaning of the words and the sentences by heart.*

6A

Claudia ist in Berlin geboren.	*Claudia was born in Berlin.*
Sie ist 23 Jahre alt.	*She is 23 years old.*
Sie ist Medien-Designerin von Beruf.	*She works as a media designer.*
Sie ist … (Designerin / Stewardess) von Beruf.	*She works as a … (designer / flight attendant).*
Beruf (der), die Berufe	*job, profession*
Sie arbeitet bei …	*She works for …*
Ihre Hobbys sind Reisen und Sprachen.	*Her hobbies are travel and languages.*
Hobby (das), die Hobbys	*hobby*
Sprache (die), die Sprachen	*language*
Ihre Handy-Nummer ist …	*Her mobile (phone) number is …*
Handy-Nummer (die), die Handy-Nummern	*mobile (phone) number*

6B

→ *Listen to part 6B.*   1|45
→ *Read the text in the textbook.*
→ *Listen and read the text at the same time.*
→ *Underline the stressed syllables.*
→ *Then turn to the vocabulary section.*

eine Kleinstadt in Bayern	*a small town in Bavaria*
Sie liegt südlich von München.	*It is situated south of Munich.*
liegen – er/sie liegt	*lie, be situated/located*
südlich von	*south of*
Robert studiert Informatik.	*Robert is studying computer science.*
studieren – er/sie studiert	*study*
Student (der), -en /die Studentin, -innen	*student*
Er hat viele Hobbys und immer	*He has a lot of hobbies and always*
wenig Zeit.	*little time.*
immer	*always*
Seine Handy-Nummer ist …	*His mobile (phone) number is …*
Seine Telefonnummer ist …	*His telephone number is …*
Telefonnummer (die), -n	*telephone number*
(das Telefon + die Nummer)	
Er findet Claudia sehr sympathisch.	*He likes Claudia a lot.*
sympathisch	*nice*

Er studiert **X** Informatik.
Sie studiert **X** Sprachen.
Nanni Köhler ist **X** Ärztin.
X = no article.

3 *Where does Robert come from? Where is he studying? Where is he now?*
Complete the sentences.

4 *What's missing?*

5 *We ask – you answer*
Write complete sentences.

6 *What do you think of it?*
Match the sentences to the drawings.

7 *Sorry? Ask questions as in the example.*
You are having a conversation, but you don't understand everything and have to ask a question to check. Listen to the sentence and ask. Then listen to the right question.

8 *What do you think of them? Fill in the person and the adjective.*
Have you already formed an impression of the people you've met so far?

wh-questions – W-Fragen

Wer ist Claudia?	**Wie** alt ist sie?
Woher kommt sie?	**Was** ist sie von Beruf?
Wo wohnt sie?	**Wie** lange kennt sie Robert?

- Question words begin with a *W*.
- Be careful with *wer* and *wo*. They look like „where" and „who" – but it's exactly the other way round: *wer?* = who? ↔ *wo?* = where?
- wh-questions usually include *denn*. This makes them sound more personal:
  Wer ist *denn* Claudia? Woher kommt sie *denn*? Wo wohnt sie *denn*?

9 *You are a bit curious and would like to find out a bit more about Robert. Find the matching answer.*

1. Wie heißt Robert denn mit Nachnamen?   a. Nein, nicht so viel.
2. Wo wohnt er denn?   b. Sehr sympathisch.
3. Wo liegt denn Bayern?   c. Er heißt Klein.
4. Wo studiert er?   d. Er studiert Informatik.
5. Was studiert er denn?   e. In Rosenheim in Bayern.
6. Arbeitet Robert viel?   f. Im Süden von Deutschland.
7. Wie findet er Claudia?   g. In München.

Numbers – Zahlen

You learned numbers 0 to 10 in lesson 3.

10 **zehn**	17 sieb**zehn**	30 drei**ßig**	200 zwei**hundert**
11 **elf**	18 ach**tzehn**	40 vier**zig**	300 drei**hundert**
12 **zwölf**	19 neun**zehn**	50 fünf**zig**	400 vier**hundert**
13 drei**zehn**		60 sech**zig**	500 fünf**hundert**
14 vier**zehn**	20 zwan**zig**	70 sieb**zig**	600 sechs**hundert**
15 fünf**zehn**	21 **einundzwanzig**	80 ach**tzig**	700 sieben**hundert**
16 **sechzehn**	22 **zweiundzwanzig**	90 neun**zig**	800 ach**thundert**
	…		900 neun**hundert**

100 **hundert**
101 hundert**eins**   1000 **tausend**
102 hundert**zwei**   2000 zwei**tausend**
…   1000 000 **eine Million**

Read numbers 13-99 – with the exception of the tens – from right to left:
13 = *dreizehn*, 21 = *einundzwanzig*.

10 *Write the numbers out in full.*

150 Euro	_____ Euro	15 Euro	_____ Euro
25 Euro	_____ Euro	5 Euro	_____ Euro
73 Euro	_____ Euro	99 Euro	_____ Euro

11 *Listen and note down the missing numbers.*

1. 089 – __ . __ 37 49.   Das ist in München.

2. 040 – 77 8__ 90.   Das ist in Hamburg.

3. 030 – 30__ 26 5__ .   Das ist in Berlin.

4. 069 – __ 2 __ 6 __ 0.   Das ist in Frankfurt am Main.

Phone numbers consist of a dialling code, e.g. 089 for Munich or 030 for Berlin, and the personal phone number. The numbers are usually spoken individually as in English, so you say, for example, 3 – 4 – 6 – 5 – 8 – 3.

12 *Revision*

Note these expressions. It would be best to learn them by heart.

Asking about Places & Countries

Wo liegt … (+ Ort/Stadt/Land)?	Where is … (+ place/city/country)?
Im Norden/Süden/Osten/Westen von …	In/To the north/south/east/west of …
Nördlich/Südlich/Östlich/Westlich von …	North/South/East/West of …

Personal Questions

Wie heißen Sie? – (Ich heiße …) …	What's your name? – My name is …
(Vorname + Zuname)	(first name + surname)
Wie ist Ihr Name? – … Ich buchstabiere.	What's your name? – … I'll spell it.
Woher sind Sie? – Aus …	Where are you from? – From …
Wo arbeiten Sie?	Where do you work?
– Bei … (Firmenname)	– For … (company name)
Wo sind Sie geboren? –	Where were you born?
– In … (Land/Stadt/Ort)	– In … (country/city/place)
Wo wohnen Sie? – In … (Stadt/Ort)	Where do you live? – In … (city/place)
Wie alt sind Sie? – Ich bin … (24) Jahre alt.	How old are you? – I'm … (24) years old.
Was sind Sie von Beruf?	What do you do?
– Ich bin … (Designerin/Ingenieur)	– I'm a … (designer/engineer)
Wie ist Ihre Adresse?	What's your address?
Wie heißt du?	What's your name?
Woher bist du?	Where are you from?
Was studierst du?	What are you studying?

13 *Repeat these numbers.*

zwei	zwanzig	zweihundert
drei	dreißig	dreihundert
vier	vierzig	vierhundert
fünf	fünfzig	fünfhundert
sechs	sechzig	sechshundert
sieben	siebzig	siebenhundert

14 *I'll spell it.*

If you've got an easy name, you're lucky and don't have a lot of problems. But if you've got a complicated one, you often have to spell it.
Spell your name and say your phone number.
Start with: Ich heiße ... Ich buchstabiere: ... Meine Telefonnummer ist: ...

Here's the alphabet for spelling something over the phone:

A wie Anton	**J** wie Julius	**S** wie Samuel
B wie Berta	**K** wie Kaufmann	**T** wie Theodor
C wie Cäsar	**L** wie Ludwig	**U** wie Ulrich
D wie Dora	**M** wie Martha	**V** wie Viktor
E wie Emil	**N** wie Nordpol	**W** wie Wilhelm
F wie Friedrich	**O** wie Otto	**X** wie Xanthippe
G wie Gustav	**P** wie Paula	**Y** wie Ypsilon
H wie Heinrich	**Q** wie Quelle	**Z** wie Zacharias
I wie Ida	**R** wie Richard	

Cultural info Neuschwanstein (Textbook, page 28)

Southern Germany is a tourist centre. No federal state has as many tourists as Bavaria and Munich, and the numbers are rising all the time. Bavaria is the most popular holiday area among both Germans and tourists from all over the world.
The castles built by the Bavarian King Ludwig II in the 19th century are just an hour's drive from Munich. He was the fairytale king who loved castles and music, especially Wagner, whom he brought to Munich. The fact that the king, towards the end of his life, was a very lonely figure, and that he died rather mysteriously in Lake Starnberg means he is shrouded with a fairytale cloak of magic and mystery.

Answer the questions.

Vocabulary

1. Write the word or words.

1. K _ ei _ st _ dt
2. v _ _ l _ n D _ _ k
3. T _ _ _ fonnum _ _ _
4. n _ _ _ Hau _ _
5. Ho _ _ y
6. i _ t _ ress _ _ _

2. Write the sentences.

1. erstudiert
2. siestudiertinhamburg
3. eristindeutschlandgeboren
4. eristdreijahrealt
5. woarbeitensie
6. wassindsievonberuf

Grammar

3. Underline the right form.

1. Wo [arbeiten] [arbeitest] [arbeite] du?
2. Wer [studieren] [studiert] [studiere] Informatik?
3. Ich [fahre] [fährst] [fahren] immer mit der S-Bahn.
4. Wann [kommst] [kommt] [kommen] du nach Hause?
5. Wann [habe] [hast] [hat] du Zeit?

4. Here are some important questions that you're bound to be able to use in a conversation. Underline the right question word.

1. [Wer] [Wo] [Was] sind Sie geboren?
2. [Was] [Wer] [Wie lange] sind Sie von Beruf?
3. [Wie] [Wie lange] [Wo] arbeiten Sie? (Firma)
4. [Was] [Wie] [Wo] finden Sie die Arbeit?
5. [Wie] [Wie lange] [Wo] arbeiten Sie schon dort?
6. [Wer] [Wie] [Was] sind Ihre Hobbys?

Listening Comprehension

1|51

5. Listen to the short dialogue and mark the right answers.

1. Der Mann
☐ ist in Deutschland geboren.
☐ ist nicht in Deutschland geboren.

2. Er
☐ arbeitet.
☐ studiert.

3. Er ist
☐ ein Jahr da.
☐ schon fünf Jahre da.

Check your answers in the key at the back of the book and then add up your points.

Total:		
	1 – 14	Oh dear, it's a pity. Please do this unit again.
	15 – 23	Not so bad. But even so, it would be a good idea to go over the dialogues and the grammar again.
	24 – 26	Excellent. There's nothing to stop you carrying on.

Entschuldigung! – Sorry!

Before getting down to work, Herr Heinrich offers his guest something to drink. In this dialogue you learn how to express a wish and how to ask somebody what they wish to have. The modal verbs *möchten* and *können* play an important part.

1 *Please complete.*
Please do exercise 1 as preparation.
The question you use when you ask someobody what they wish to have is Möchten
Sie ... / Möchtest du ...? – Would you like ...? *If you don't know all the words, please look them up in the glossary.*

2 Drinking coffee in the office
→ *First listen to what Herr Heinrich and Frau Bruckner say. Something seems to have happened. Listen to the conversation at least twice.*
→ *Read the dialogue.*
→ *Listen and read at the same time. If you like, you can underline the stressed syllables.*
→ *Now learn the vocabulary.*

Möchten Sie etwas trinken?	*Would you like something to drink?*
möchten – er / sie möchte	*would like*
etwas	*something*
trinken – er / sie trinkt	*drink*
Kaffee (der)	*coffee*
Haben Sie auch Tee?	*Do you have tea, too?*
Tee (der)	*tea*
Ja, natürlich.	*Yes, of course.*
tut mir leid	*sorry*
Der Tee ist schon kalt.	*The tea is (already) cold.*
Dann nehme ich Kaffee.	*Then I'll take coffee.*
Milch (die)	*milk*
Zucker (der)	*sugar*
Nur Milch, bitte.	*Just milk, please.*
nur	*just, only*
Macht nichts.	*That's OK. Never mind.*
	[literally: it makes nothing]
nichts	*nothing*
Hier ist eine Serviette.	*Here is a serviette.*
Serviette (die), die Servietten	*serviette*
Wir arbeiten jetzt bis Mittag.	*We'll work now till lunchtime/midday.*
Mittag (der), die Mittage	*lunchtime, midday*
Dann machen wir eine Stunde Pause	*Then we'll take an hour's break*
Pause (die), die Pausen	*break*

und gehen in die Kantine.	and go to the canteen.
gehen – er / sie geht	go
Kantine (die), die Kantinen	canteen
Einverstanden.	OK. Fine.

Do you know now what happened? Herr Heinrich spilt some coffee, but luckily only into the saucer. That's why he's bringing a napkin.

3 *What is the right order? Note down the numbers.*

4 *You ask.*
How does the sentence continue? Find the most suitable continuation. Note down the letters.

We say *Entschuldigung*:
• when we've had a mishap (= sorry)
• or when we make a polite request (= excuse me): *Entschuldigung, wie ist Ihr Name?*

5 *Crossword*
Can you do the crossword? Senkrecht means Down, waagerecht means Across.
Now find the solution – a word that you need all the time.
Take:
1. the fourth letter
2. the fifth letter
3. the fourth letter
4. the first letter
5. the third letter.   _ _ _ _ _

6 *Listen to the question. Answer politely. Then listen to the answer.*
You are the guest and are being asked what you would like. Select a polite response from the suggestions given.

7 *What doesn't fit?*
Write down the word that doesn't fit the group.

8 *Chris Bruckner's note*
Notes from the first day of the visit.

Articles: definite and indefinite – Artikel: bestimmt und unbestimmt:
der, die, das und *ein/eine*

Singular	masculine	feminine	neuter
personal pronoun	er	sie	es
definite article	der Name	die Adresse	das Land
indefinite article	**ein** Name	**eine** Adresse	**ein** Land

The definite article has three different forms, the indefinite article has two: *der/die/das* and *ein/eine*.

Careful: indefinite amounts don't need an article, or a word corresponding to English "some": *Möchten Sie Kaffee?/Tee, bitte, mit Milch.*

9 *Fill in the indefinite article (*ein/eine*).*

Was ist das?

Wasserburg	Das ist _____ Kleinstadt.
0170 – 82 73 47	Das ist _____ Handy-Nummer.
Andy	Das ist _____ Vorname.
Lettland	Das ist _____ Land in Nordeuropa.
81825	Das ist _____ Postleitzahl.
etwas	Das ist _____ Wort.

Verbs – Verben: e → i(e)/möchten/können

		nehmen	**möchten**	**können**
Singular	ich	nehme	möchte	**kann**
	du	nimmst	möchtest	**kannst**
	er/sie	nimmt	möchte	**kann**
Plural	wir	nehmen	möchten	können
	ihr	nehmt	möchtet	könnt
	sie/Sie	nehmen	möchten	können

- Some strong verbs change: *e* to *i* or *ie (nehmen: du nimmst, er/sie nimmt; lesen: du liest, er/sie liest; sprechen: du sprichst, er/sie spricht; geben: es gibt)*
- *möchten* expresses a wish. It's a modal verb: *Ich **möchte** noch etwas Kaffee.*
- *können* is also a modal verb. It is used to express a wish in the form of a question: ***Kann** ich bitte die Milch **haben**?*

When you use *möchten*, you are expressing yourself politely. So you can omit additional terms of politeness such as *bitte* or *gern*. Example: *Möchten Sie Kaffee oder Tee?*

10 *Which form is missing?*

| möchtet | kannst | kann | möchte | können | nimmt | kann | nimmst | möchtest |

		nehmen	**möchten**	**können**
Singular	ich	nehme		
	du			
	er/sie		möchte	
Plural	wir	nehmen	möchten	können
	ihr	nehmt		könnt
	sie/Sie	nehmen	möchten	

11 *Fill in* möchten *or* können.

_____ Sie Kaffee oder Tee?

_____ ich etwas Milch haben?

_____ ich eine Serviette haben?

_____ Sie telefonieren?

_____ ich bitte telefonieren? *(make a phone call)*

_____ Sie ein Hotelzimmer? *(hotel room)*

_____ Sie das wiederholen? *(repeat)*

_____ Sie mir helfen? *(help)*

12 *Fill in:* wer * wann * wo * wie * was * woher.

Können Sie mir sagen, … *(Could you tell me …)*

_____ das Hotel ist?　　　　_____ die Fahrkarte kostet?

_____ der Bus kommt?　　　　_____ Herr Bünzli kommt? Aus der Schweiz?

_____ der Herr heißt?　　　　_____ Herr Heinrich ist?

13 *Revision*

Apologizing

Tut mir leid.	*Sorry.*
Entschuldigung.	*Sorry/Excuse me.*
Entschuldige/Entschuldigen Sie.	*Sorry/Excuse me. (informal/formal)*
(Das) macht nichts./Bitte.	*(That's) OK/alright./Never mind.*

Asking what someone would like/Offering

Möchten Sie …/Möchtest du … (Kaffee)?	*Would you like … (coffee)?*

14 *Mark with a cross.*
The vowels a, e, i, o, u can be either short or long in German. The difference is very important
for a good pronunciation. So try and imitate the speaker's pronunciation as exactly as
possible. Listen and mark with a cross whether the vowels are long or short, then repeat.

	kurz (short)	lang (long)		kurz (short)	lang (long)
haben	☐	☐	schlecht	☐	☐
hat	☐	☐	schon	☐	☐
da	☐	☐	kommt	☐	☐
dann	☐	☐	Sie	☐	☐
Stadt	☐	☐	sind	☐	☐
Jahr	☐	☐	nur	☐	☐
Tee	☐	☐	eine Stunde	☐	☐

15 *Link the English expressions to the German equivalents. Listen, then read out loud.*

Who is that please? This is (Meier/Beate Meier).	Ist dort Meier? Nein, hier ist Keller. Haben Sie 34 57? Nein, 34 77. Entschuldigung. Auf Wiederhören.
Is that Meier? Speaking. / Yes, this is Meier.	
Is that Meier? No, this is Keller. Is your number 34 57? No, 34 77. Goodbye.	Wer ist dort bitte? Hier ist Meier. / Hier ist Beate Meier. Ist dort Meier? Ja, hier Meier.

Cultural info (Textbook, page 32)

You can be taken by surprise in a café. In Germany espresso and cappuccino from Italy
are popular drinks alongside coffee with milk. There's nowhere that has so many different sorts of coffee as Austria. There's black coffee (black without milk or sugar), brown
coffee (black coffee with whipped cream), a "Kapuziner" (small black coffee with whipped cream), mocca (strong black coffee, mocca is an Arabic word), a double mocca
(double portion of mocca), "Melange" (made of equal portions of coffee and milk),
"Viennese Melange" (like Melange, but with foamy milk) and "Fiaker" (black coffee with
rum or cognac). Completely confusing if you're a stranger.
And it's not always so easy in Switzerland either. If you ask for a "Schale" (bowl), you'll
get a coffee with milk.

45

Vocabulary

1. Please complete.

1. Kaffee oder _____ ?

2. Tee mit Z_____

3. Entschuldigung. – Macht _____ .

4. Mann und _____

5. Hobby und _____

6. im Norden und im S_____

2. What's right?

1. Macht nichts.
☐ That's OK.
☐ That's all I need.
☐ That's kind of you.

3. Ich möchte …
☐ I'd like …
☐ I take …
☐ I have …

5. Tut mir leid, …
☐ I'm fine.
☐ I'm sorry.
☐ That's OK.

2. Kann ich bitte …?
☐ I'll take …
☐ Can I please …?
☐ Do you have …?

4. Einverstanden?
☐ OK?
☐ How much?
☐ What would you like?

6. Ja, natürlich.
☐ OK, fine.
☐ Right.
☐ Yes, of course.

Grammar

3. Fill in.

1. Möchte___ Sie Tee?

2. Ich möcht___ gern Kaffee.

3. Ich nehm___ Zucker und Milch.

4. Wir arbeit___ bis Mittag.

5. Wer geh___ in die Kantine?

6. Mach___ Sie auch eine Pause?

7. Könn___ wir jetzt eine Pause machen?

8. Wer k_____ mir helfen?

4. Fill in ein / eine.

1. _____ Person

2. _____ Hotel

3. _____ Straße

4. _____ Übung

5. _____ Großstadt

6. _____ Ort

7. _____ Reise

8. _____ Hobby

Check your answers in the key at the back of the book and then add up your points.

Total:		
	1 – 16	Before you carry on, you should do this unit again.
	17 – 23	Quite good, but not perfect yet. Please go over the dialogue and the grammar again.
	24 – 28	Excellent. There's nothing to stop you carrying on.

Zu Hause – At home

Claudia and Robert have finally got home after an hour's journey. Claudia's friend Niki is already there.

Niki tells them what he has prepared. He talks about something in the past.

From here on you'll learn to talk about something that is over.

1 *There's something missing here. Please complete.*

Do exercise 1 as preparation. All the vowels are missing. Does anything strike you? There are a lots of es, especially in the endings: hör**e**n, hör**e**, ess**e** *etc.*

2 At Claudia and Niki's place

→ *Now listen to how the story continues.*

→ *Read and listen.*

→ *Learn the words.*

Du bist ja zu Hause!	*Oh, you're home.*
zu Hause	*(at) home*
Na klar.	*Yes, of course.*
Ich bin extra früher gegangen.	*I left early on purpose.*
extra	*on purpose, specially*
früher	*earlier*
gehen – er / sie geht, ist gegangen	*go, leave*
Alles bestens.	*Everything's just great.*
Claudia sagt, du arbeitest viel.	*Claudia says you work a lot.*
sagen – er / sie sagt, hat gesagt	*say*
Ach was!	*Not at all.*
Von nichts kommt nichts. (Sprichwort)	*Nothing comes of nothing. (proverb)*
sagt man	*people say*
man	*one, people, they*
Die Arbeit macht auch Spaß.	*Work is fun.*
Spaß (der)	*fun*
Du hast recht.	*You're right.*
recht haben – er / sie hat recht	*be right*
Und jetzt essen wir was.	*And now we'll have something to eat.*
essen – du isst, er / sie isst, hat gegessen	*eat*
was = etwas	*something*
Nun bin ich dran.	*Now it's my turn.*
nun	*now*
dran sein – er / sie ist dran	*be someone's turn*
Ich habe nämlich eine Überraschung.	*I have a surprise.*
nämlich	*namely, in fact*
Überraschung (die), die Überraschungen	*surprise*

Es gibt heute Spaghetti und Salat.	*There's spaghetti and salad.*
geben – es gibt, hat gegeben	*give – there is/are*
Spaghetti (die Pl.)	*spaghetti [always plural]*
Salat (der), die Salate	*salad, lettuce*
Ich habe gekocht.	*I've cooked.*
kochen – er/sie kocht, hat gekocht	*cook*
klasse	*great*

3 *Please complete.*
Select the right expression. Then check your answers by listening to the text again.

4 *Jumbled letters.*
Find two words that are hidden in the puzzle. They are words you've already learned:

H_____ and D_____ .

5 *What do Robert, Niki and Claudia say? Mark the right answers.*
You remember what Robert, Claudia and Niki said, don't you?

6 *Please complete.*
The forms of sein *and* haben *are missing. They are part of the perfect tense used to talk about the past.*

7 *What do you say?*
Here you can check how good your reactions are. Reply with the appropriate expression.

8 *Robert's diary*

Perfect tense 1 – Das Perfekt 1

			kochen			**gehen**
Singular	ich	habe	**ge**kocht	ich	bin	**ge**gangen
	du	hast		du	bist	
	er/sie	hat		er/sie	ist	
Plural	wir	haben		wir	sind	
	ihr	habt		ihr	seid	
	sie/Sie	haben		sie/Sie	sind	

- When you talk about something in the past, you use the perfect.
  For example: *Gestern habe ich gekocht. Heute gehen wir essen.*
- The perfect is also possible in cases where you would use the simple past tense in English.
- The perfect consists of two parts: *Gestern habe* ich Spaghetti *gekocht.* You need the conjugated form of *haben* or *sein* (*ich habe, du hast* etc.) and the past participle (*gekocht*).
- The past participle usually starts with *ge-* and ends in *-(e)t* (*gearbeitet, gekocht*) or *-en* (*gegangen*). It is placed at the end of the sentence, and the form doesn't change.
- In German as in English there are weak and strong verbs. Weak ones have the ending *-(e)t*, strong ones *-en*.

9 *What is happening in the present? What happened in the past?*
*Mark with **G** (= Gegenwart = present) or **V** (= Vergangenheit = past).*

_____ Was hast du heute gemacht?   _____ Ich habe schon gegessen.

_____ Wo bist du geboren?   _____ Hast du gearbeitet?

_____ Fahrt ihr in die Stadt?   _____ Du hast recht.

_____ Was heißt das?   _____ Ich bin früh nach Hause gegangen.

_____ Hast du Hunger?   _____ Wohin fährt die Bahn?

Verbs with a vowel change – Verben mit Vokalwechsel

		fahren	**sprechen**	**lesen**
Singular	ich	fahre	spreche	lese
	du	f**ä**hrst	spr**i**chst	l**ie**st
	er/sie	f**ä**hrt	spr**i**cht	l**ie**st
Plural	wir	fahren	sprechen	lesen
	ihr	fahrt	sprecht	lest
	sie/Sie	fahren	sprechen	lesen

Some strong verbs change the stem vowel: $a \to ä$, $i \to i(e)$.
du and *er/sie* forms that are special are given in the vocabulary lists.

49

10 *Note down the verbs with special* du *and* er / sie *forms.*

| lesen | machen | essen | haben | gehen |

| sein | geben | trinken | fahren | nehmen | sprechen |

Infinitiv	du	er / sie	Infinitiv	du	er / sie

11 *What's the opposite?*

etwas	nichts
jemand (somebody)	niemand *(nobody)*
viel	wenig
früher	später

Ich habe heute nichts gekocht.   Ich _____.

Ist da jemand?   Da ist _____.

Du arbeitest zu wenig.   Nein, ich _____.

Wir sind extra später gegangen.   Ich bin extra _____.

12 *Revision*
Note the sentences. It would be best to learn them by heart.

Agreeing / Disagreeing

Du hast / Sie haben (nicht) recht.	*You're (not) right.*
Ja. / Nein. / Einverstanden.	*Yes. / No. / OK / Fine.*

Colloquial Expressions 2

Du bist ja zu Hause! – Na klar.	*You're at home! – Of course.*
Einverstanden? – Einverstanden.	*OK? – OK.*
(= Sind Sie / bist du einverstanden?	*(= Are you in agreement?*
– Ich bin einverstanden.)	*– I am in agreement.)*
was = etwas	*something*
extra: Ich bin extra früher gegangen.	*specially: I left early specially.*
Das ist prima / klasse.	*That's great.*
Ich bin / Du bist / Sie sind dran.	*It's my / your turn.*

A lot of endings have an -e- in German. But this -e- is toned down and not spoken like a full -e-. The way you speak the endings is a good sign of how well you can already speak German.

13 *So listen carefully and repeat.*

essen	kochen	gehen
sagen	fragen	lesen
der Name	die Straße	die Adresse
die Tage	die Städte	die Berufe
der Hunger	das Wetter	die Nummer
die Studenten	die Minuten	die Verben

14 *Stress*
Here are a few perfect forms that you've already met. The stress is always on the second syllable. Try repeating them.

geboren   gemacht   gegessen   gearbeitet   gefahren   gegangen

15 *Write a dialogue. Complete the following seven sentences.*

Hallo.
Hier / Meyer.
Nein / hier / … Meyer / Telefon 46 77 11.
Bitte / sehr.

Wer / … / dort / bitte?
… / dort Meyer / Telefon 46 88 11?
Oh, Entschuldigung.

Now listen and repeat.

Cultural info (Textbook page 36)

Proverbs and the images in them are a lot of fun. They're very typical of a language. Think about whether there's a similar proverb or saying in your language, and what image is used to express it.

Fill in the words.

To help you understand the proverbs here is a paraphrase or example.

If you take your time, you'll find a solution.
For example: The son who has turned out badly (= the apple) takes after his father (= the tree trunk).
It's often better to try something out than to think about it for a long time.
For example: If you are friendly (= the sound), you will get a friendly answer (= the music).
Someone who has a lot of worries comforts himself with a good vintage (= liqueur).

You'll find the translation in the glossary.

Vocabulary

1. *Please complete.*

| recht | was | Hunger | nichts | Spaß | dran |

1. Du hast _____ .

2. Du bist _____ .

3. Hast du _____ ?

4. Das macht _____ .

5. Von nichts kommt _____ .

6. Ach _____ !

2. *Write the sentence.*

1. er | gegangen | extra | früher | ist   _____

2. arbeitet | er | viel   _____

3. recht | sie | hat   _____

4. eine | Überraschung | das | ist   _____

5. hat | wer | gekocht   _____

6. er | Spaghetti | hat | gekocht   _____

Grammar

3. *Fill in the forms of* haben *or* sein.

1. Was _____ du gekocht? (haben)

2. _____ Petra schon nach Hause gegangen? (sein)

3. _____ ihr in die Stadt gefahren? (sein)

4. Wir _____ um zwölf gegessen. (haben)

5. Er _____ viel gearbeitet. (haben)

6. Was _____ du heute gemacht? (haben)

4. *Write the 3rd person singular.*

1. fahren   er / sie _____

2. essen   er / sie _____

3. nehmen   er / sie _____

4. geben   es _____

5. sein   er / sie _____

6. sprechen   er / sie _____

Check your answers in the key at the back of the book and then add up your points.

Total:	1 – 12	It would be a good idea to do this unit again straightaway.
	13 – 20	Pretty good. But it wouldn't hurt to go over the dialogue and the grammar again.
	21 – 24	Excellent. If you like, you could go over the vocabulary again, otherwise you can carry straight on.

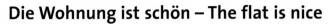
Die Wohnung ist schön – The flat is nice

Claudia and Niki only found their flat a short time ago. You'd probably like to find out how they live.

As you do so, you'll find out quite a lot about flats, rents and adverts, and you'll be able to say what you think of something. Adjectives of course have an important part of play in all this.

1 *What is where?*
Please do exercise 1 as preparation.

das Wohnzimmer	*livingroom*
das Schlafzimmer	*bedroom*
die Küche	*kitchen*
das Bad	*bathroom*
die Toilette	*toilet*
der Flur	*hall(way)*
der Balkon	*balcony*

2 Two rooms, kitchen and bath
→ *Read the text.*
→ *If you need help with unknown words, have a look at the vocabulary list.*

Die Wohnung von Claudia und Niki ist nicht groß.	*Claudia and Niki's flat isn't big.*
Wohnung (die), die Wohnungen	*flat*
von	*of, from*
Sie ist aber sehr gemütlich.	*But it's very cosy.*
gemütlich	*cosy, comfortable*
Ein Zimmer mit Bad	*One room with a bath*
Zimmer (das), die Zimmer	*room*
Bad (das), die Bäder	*bath(room)*
das reicht, hat Niki immer gesagt.	*that's all I need, Niki always said.*
reichen – es reicht, hat gereicht	*be enough, be all you need*
sagen – er/sie sagt, hat gesagt	*say*
Und jetzt haben sie zwei Zimmer,	*And now they have two rooms,*
eine Küche und ein Bad.	*a kitchen and a bathroom.*
Küche (die), die Küchen	*kitchen*
Auch für Besuch ist Platz.	*There's room for visitors, too.*
für	*for*
Besuch (der)	*visit, visitor*
Platz (der)	*room, space*
Robert schläft im Wohnzimmer.	*Robert sleeps in the livingroom.*

schlafen – du schläfst, er/sie schläft, hat geschlafen	*sleep*
Claudia hat lange zu Hause gewohnt	*Claudia lived at home for a long time*
wohnen – er/sie wohnt, hat gewohnt	*live*
und die Miete gespart.	*and saved the rent.*
Miete (die), die Mieten	*rent*
sparen – er/sie spart, hat gespart	*save*
Dann haben sie die Wohnung im Norden von Berlin gefunden.	*Then they found a flat in the north of Berlin.*
finden – er/sie findet, hat gefunden	*find*
Claudia hat die Anzeige gelesen.	*Claudia read the advert.*
Anzeige (die), die Anzeigen	*ad, advert*
lesen – du liest, er/sie liest, hat gelesen	*read*
Dachwohnung (die), die Dachwohnungen	*penthouse*
45 qm (= Quadratmeter)	$45m^2$ *(= square metres)*
550 Euro monatlich, warm	*550 euros a month, including heating for*
ab sofort frei	*immediate occupation, available immediately*

 You can listen to the text. Then read the text yourself out loud.

3 *What's right? Please mark the answer.*
You remember everything, don't you? Mark the correct statements.

4 *Now pretend you are Claudia talking about your flat. Say* ich und wir.

5 *Rents, rents, rents. Please match.*
Match the rents to the flats or houses. They are from the Munich area. Munich is the most expensive city in Germany.

6 *Some sums.*

7 *Fill in the verbs.*

 8 *What do you think of this?*
First listen to the example. Then we'll ask and you reply. Listen to the correct solution.

sein *is followed by the nominative,* finden *by the accusative. A lot of verbs take the accusative.*

9 *Fill in the adjective.*
Adjectives to the left of a noun have an ending: das **schöne** Bad.
Adjectives to the right of a noun have no ending: Das Bad ist **schön**.

Perfect tense 2 – Das Perfekt 2

			kochen	wohnen	sparen	finden	lesen
Singular	ich	habe	gekocht	gewohnt	gespart	gefunden	gelesen
	du	hast					
	er/sie	hat					
Plural	wir	haben					
	ihr	habt					
	sie/Sie	haben					

In the text they talk about the past. There are some more perfect forms with *haben*.

10 *Note down the answer that fits.*

1. Wohnt er in Hamburg? _____
2. Spart sie? _____
3. Geht Peter nach Hause? _____
4. Findet Claudia eine Wohnung? _____
5. Liest sie die Anzeige? _____
6. Kochst du? _____

a. Sie hat gespart.
b. Er hat in Hamburg gewohnt.
c. Sie hat schon eine Wohnung gefunden.
d. Er ist schon nach Hause gegangen.
e. Sie hat die Anzeige schon gelesen.
f. Ich habe schon gekocht.

Articles: definite and indefinite – Artikel: bestimmt und unbestimmt – Nominativ und Akkusativ: *der, ein – den, einen*

Singular		masculine	feminine	neuter
definite article	*nom.*	der Balkon	die Küche	das Bad
indefinite article		ein Balkon	eine Küche	ein Bad
definite article	*acc.*	den Balkon	die Küche	das Bad
indefinite article		einen Balkon	eine Küche	ein Bad

11 *Fill in the indefinite article* (ein / eine).

Was ist das?

1. Das ist _____ Kantine.
2. Das ist _____ Bad.
3. Das ist _____ Wohnzimmer.
4. Das ist _____ Balkon.
5. Das ist _____ Küche.
6. Das ist _____ Schlafzimmer.

12 *Now fill in the definite article* (der/die/das).

_____ Kantine ist sehr groß.   _____ Balkon ist schön.

_____ Bad ist klein.   _____ Küche ist praktisch.

_____ Wohnzimmer ist gemütlich.   _____ Schlafzimmer ist nicht groß.

13 *Fill in the definite article* (den, die, das).

Wie finden Sie _____ Kantine?   Wie finden Sie _____ Balkon?

Wie finden Sie _____ Bad?   Wie finden Sie _____ Küche?

Wie finden Sie _____ Wohnzimmer?   Wie finden Sie _____ Schlafzimmer?

14 *Fill in the indefinite article* (einen, eine, ein).

Wir haben _____ Wohnung gefunden. Sie ist sehr schön.

Wir haben _____ Anzeige gelesen. Sie ist sehr interessant.

Wir haben _____ Lösung gefunden. Sie ist richtig.

Wir haben _____ Salat gemacht. Er ist sehr gut.

Wir haben _____ Büro im Zentrum gefunden. Das ist sehr praktisch.

15 *Some revision, and new words that belong to the topic.*

Living

wohnen – er / sie wohnt, hat gewohnt	*live*
die Wohnung, die Wohnungen	*flat, apartment*
das Haus, die Häuser	*house*
das Wohnzimmer	*livingroom*
das Schlafzimmer	*bedroom*
die Küche, die Küchen	*kitchen*
das Bad, die Bäder	*bathroom*
der Balkon, die Balkone	*balcony*
der Flur, die Flure	*hall(way)*
die Toilette, die Toiletten	*toilet*
die Terrasse, die Terrassen	*terrace / patio*
der Garten, die Gärten	*garden*
die Tür, die Türen	*door*
die Garage, die Garagen	*garage*
die 2-Zimmer-Wohnung	*two-roomed flat*
die Mieten, die Mieten	*rent*
monatlich kalt / warm	*basic rent per month without / with heating etc.*
der Platz (viel / wenig Platz)	*room, space (lot of / litte room)*
gemütlich – alt – neu	*cosy, comfortable – old – new*

16 *Say the numbers. Imitate the speaker's pronunciation as precisely as you can.*
Pay special attention to z- and the ending -zig.

zehn	zwanzig	dreißig	siebzig
elf	einundzwanzig	vierzig	achtzig
zwölf	zweiundzwanzig	fünfzig	neunzig
dreizehn	dreiundzwanzig	sechzig	hundert
…	…		

17 *Now listen to a few prices. Note down the numbers.*

Kaffee: _____ €

Fahrkarte: _____ €

Wohnung: _____ €

Haus: _____ €

1-Zimmer-Wohnung München: _____ €

1-Zimmer-Wohnung Norddeutschland: _____ €

18 *Listen and repeat.*
A couple are looking for a flat. The husband is phoning the landlord.

Herr Bergmann:	Bergmann.
Paul Fischer:	Guten Tag, Herr Bergmann. Hier Fischer.
	Wir haben Ihre Anzeige gelesen.
	Ist die Wohnung noch frei?
Herr Bergmann:	Ja, da haben Sie Glück. Die ist noch frei.
Paul Fischer:	Prima. Wir – hm – meine Frau und ich – kommen sofort. Geht das?
Herr Bergmann:	Ja. Es ist jetzt 3 Uhr. Wann sind Sie dann hier?
Paul Fischer:	So um 5. Nicht später.
Herr Bergmann:	Gut, also dann bis 5.
Paul Fischer:	Bis 5. Vielen Dank. Auf Wiedersehen.

Cultural info (Textbook page 40)

The solution is something you can wish somebody, an expression you can use in many different situations. To go with it, there are some symbols of good luck.

Fill in the numbers.
Write the letters.

das Hufeisen	*horseshoe*
der Fliegenpilz	*fly agaric [toadstool]*
der Schornsteinfeger	*chimney sweep*
das Kleeblatt	*cloverleaf*

Vocabulary

1. Mark the correct translation.

1. die Wohnung
- ☐ flat
- ☐ hallway
- ☐ living room

2. die Anzeige
- ☐ advert
- ☐ time
- ☐ newspaper

3. die Garage
- ☐ garden
- ☐ garage
- ☐ patio

4. 500 € monatlich kalt
- ☐ 500 euros a month with heating
- ☐ 500 euros a month basic rent
- ☐ 500 euros a week

5. ab sofort frei
- ☐ available immediately
- ☐ available from the end of the month
- ☐ no deposit

6. Die Wohnung ist gemütlich.
- ☐ The flat is big.
- ☐ It's a nice flat.
- ☐ The flat is cosy.

Grammar

2. Fill in the article.

1. Die Wohnung hat 2 Zimmer: _____ Wohnzimmer und _____ Schlafzimmer.

2. Sie hat natürlich auch _____ Flur, _____ Küche und _____ Bad.

3. Sie hat k_____ Terrasse.

4. Aber sie hat _____ Balkon.

5. _____ Bad ist nicht sehr groß.

6. _____ Toilette ist extra.

3. Fill in: gewohnt, gefunden, gespart, gesagt, gelesen, gemietet.

1. Wir haben eine Wohnung _____. (finden)

2. Was hast du _____?

3. Ich habe Geld _____. Ich habe zu Hause _____.

4. Wir haben die Anzeige _____.

5. Wir haben eine Dachwohnung _____. (mieten)

Listening Comprehension

1|66

4. Listen to two people flat-hunting. What did you understand? Mark the right answers.

1. Die Wohnung hat	2. Sie ist	3. Die Miete ist	4. Die Telefonnummer ist
☐ 1 Zimmer mit Bad.	☐ 35 qm groß.	☐ 600 Euro kalt.	☐ 0911 – 62524.
☐ 2 Zimmer.	☐ 46 qm groß.	☐ 850 Euro warm.	☐ 0211 – 62424.
☐ 3 Zimmer.	☐ 55 qm groß.	☐ 850 Euro kalt.	☐ 0911 – 62424.

Check your answers in the key at the back of the book and then add up your points.

Total:	1 – 11	Oh dear, it's a pity. Please do this unit again.
	12 – 18	Not so bad. But evens o, it would be a good idea to go over the vocabulary and the grammar again.
	19 – 21	Excellent. There's nothing to stop you carrying on.

58

Viel Verkehr! – A lot of traffic!

Next morning Frau Bruckner takes a taxi from her hotel to the Europartner office. She arrives a bit late. This is your chance to learn how to tell the time.

1 *Clocks – please match.*
Please do exercise 1 as preparation. The clocks all show different times. Match the times and clocks. Indicate whether the clock is right or wrong, fast or slow.

Armbanduhr	*watch*
Taschenuhr	*pocket watch*
Digitaluhr	*digital clock/watch*
Kuckucksuhr	*cuckoo clock*
Küchenuhr	*kitchen clock*
Bahnhofsuhr	*station clock*

Die Uhr geht …	*The clock/watch is …*
… richtig.	*… right.*
… falsch.	*… wrong.*
… vor.	*… fast.*
… nach.	*… slow.*

2 Chris Bruckner takes a taxi to the Europartner offices

→ *She is in a hurry and takes a taxi. Listen to what she says to the taxi driver. Listen to the conversation at least twice.*

→ *To help you understand what's going on, you can check up on some vocabulary via the vocabulary list.*

Bitte in die Potsdamer Straße Nummer 205.	*(To) Potsdamer Straße number 205, please.*
Nummer (die), die Nummern	*number*
Heute ist viel Verkehr.	*There is a lot of traffic today.*
Verkehr (der)	*traffic*
Haben Sie es sehr eilig?	*Are you in a great hurry?*
es eilig haben – er/sie hat es eilig	*be in a hurry*
Ja, ich habe einen Termin um 10 Uhr.	*Yes, I have an appointment at 10 o'clock.*
Termin (der), die Termine	*appointment*
um 10 Uhr	*at 10 o'clock*
Uhr (die), die Uhren/die Uhrzeit	*clock/time*
Kein Problem.	*No problem.*
Problem (das), die Probleme	*problem*
Wie weit ist es?	*How far is it?*
Wie lange brauchen wir?	*How long do we need/does it take?*
brauchen – er/sie braucht, hat gebraucht	*need*
Ungefähr vierzig Minuten.	*About forty minutes.*
ungefähr	*about*
Wir nehmen die Stadtautobahn.	*We'll take the (urban) motorway/freeway.*
Stadtautobahn (die), die Stadtautobahnen	*urban motorway/freeway*
Berlin hat viel Wasser.	*Berlin has a lot of water.*
Wasser (das)	*water*
Man sieht viele Häfen und Kanäle.	*You see a lot of docks and canals.*

sehen – du siehst, er / sie sieht, hat gesehen	*see*
Hafen (der), die Häfen	*docks, harbour, port*
Kanal (der), die Kanäle	*canal*
Wie in Venedig.	*Like in Venice.*
fast	*almost*
Ich komme leider eine Viertelstunde später.	*I'm afraid I'm going to be a quarter of an hour late. [literally: … come … later.]*
Viertelstunde (die)	*quarter of an hour*
Bis gleich.	*See you soon / later.*
Morgens ist immer Stau.	*In the mornings there's always a tailback.*
morgens	*in the morning(s)*
Stau (der), die Staus	*tailback, traffic jam*
mittags	*at lunchtime*
abends	*in the evening(s)*
Schrecklich!	*Awful! Terrible!*
Da sind wir.	*Here we are.*
Und bitte eine Quittung.	*And a receipt please.*
Quittung (die), die Quittungen	*receipt*

 The word *Stadtautobahn* is made up of *die Stadt* and *die Autobahn*. There are a lot of compound nouns in German.

 morgen**s** um acht = **immer** morgens um acht
heute Morgen = **nur** heute Morgen

3 *Who said it? Frau Bruckner or the taxi driver?*

4 *Please complete.*
Some of the nouns have disappeared from the text. Choose the right noun and complete the dialogue.

5 *What's the time?*

 6 *Speaking exercise.*
Now you're in a hurry and take a taxi. First you'll hear the example. Then you speak, using the prompt words. We'll correct you.

 7 *I'd like to …*
If you want to go to a specific place, you say nach.
Look at the photos. You want to go there. Write down the sentence you would say.
Then practise orally. First listen to the example. Then give the answers yourself.

The plural – Der Plural

In German there are 9 different ways of forming the plural. Here is an overview.
Look closely at the various plural forms, and learn the plural with each noun. Careful:
There are of course some nouns that don't have a plural, such as *das Wetter* or *der Verkehr* or *der Norden, der Süden*.

Singular		Plural
das Zimmer		die Zimmer
der Tag	⊕ -e	die Tage
die Stadt	umlaut ⊕ -e	die Städte
der Hafen	umlaut	die Häfen
das Kind	⊕ -er	die Kinder
das Land	umlaut ⊕ -er	die Länder
das Auto	⊕ -s	die Autos
die Frage	⊕ -n	die Fragen
die Bahn	⊕ -en	die Bahnen

The definite article is always *die* in the plural.

Always remember two things about each noun: the article in the singular and the plural form, so: *das Auto, die Autos*.

8 *Listen to a series of nouns. Tick on whether you hear the singular or the plural form.*

	1.	2.	3.	4.	5.	6.	7.	8.
Singular	☐	☐	☐	☐	☐	☐	☐	☐
Plural	☐	☐	☐	☐	☐	☐	☐	☐

9 *Fill in the singular or plural.*

Singular	Plural
	die Hobbys
die Adresse	
	die Kinder
das Hotel	
	die Namen
der Tag	
das Auto	
die Nummer	
	die Stunden
	die Länder
die Frage	

Telling the time (informally and officially) – Die Uhrzeit (informell und offiziell)

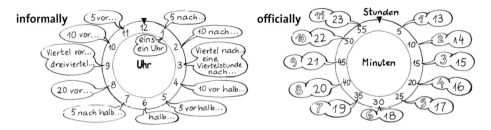

10 *Imagine you hear the exact time on the radio. "Translate" them into the form normally used in speech. Complete the sentence.*

Example: Es ist jetzt neunzehn Uhr. → Es ist sieben.

Es ist jetzt elf Uhr dreißig. Es ist _____ _____.

Es ist jetzt sechzehn Uhr fünfzehn. Es ist _____ nach _____.

Es ist jetzt zehn Uhr fünfundvierzig. Es ist _____ vor _____.

Es ist jetzt dreizehn Uhr. Es ist _____.

Es ist jetzt neun Uhr zehn. Es ist _____ nach _____.

Es ist jetzt neun Uhr vierzig. Es ist _____ vor _____.

11 *Revision*

Asking the time

Wie spät ist es?	*What time is it?*
Es ist … (3 Uhr).	*It's … (3 o'clock).*
Ungefähr … 3	*About … 3.*
… (5) Minuten vor / nach … 3.	*… (5) minutes to/past … 3.*
Viertel vor / nach … (4).	*(a) quarter to/past (4).*
halb drei, halb vier	*half past <u>two</u>, half past <u>three</u>*
	(halb refers forward to the next full hour.)

In the taxi

Sind Sie frei? Zum Flughafen bitte.	*Are you free? To the airport, please.*
Bitte in die …	*To …*
(Potsdamer Straße Nummer 205).	*(Potsdamer Straße number 205), please.*
Bitte nach … (Tegel / Siemensstadt).	*To … (Tegel / Siemensstadt), please.*
Ich habe es eilig / sehr eilig.	*I'm in a hurry/great hurry.*
Ich habe einen Termin um … (10 Uhr).	*I have an appointment at … (10 o'clock).*
Wie lange brauchen wir?	*How long do we need/does it take?*
Bitte eine Quittung.	*A receipt, please.*

Short and long vowels – Die kurzen und die langen Vokale

12 *Listen and repeat.*
Now you're going to hear some words that have either a long or a short vowel. Mark with a
cross what you hear, and repeat the word.

	viel	links	abends	fast	Problem	Kanal	schrecklich	morgens
lang	☐	☐	☐	☐	☐	☐	☐	☐
kurz	☐	☐	☐	☐	☐	☐	☐	☐

13 *Listen and repeat.*

Zum Flughafen bitte.   Wie spät ist es?
Bitte nach Siemensstadt.   Viertel vor drei.
Bitte eine Quittung.   Ungefähr drei.

14 *Listen and repeat.*
Now we're going to practise vowels. Try to imitate the speaker's pronunciation as accurately
as you can.

eilig   Ich habe es eilig.
weit   Wie weit ist es?
ungefähr   Ungefähr vierzig Minuten.
später   Ich komme später.
heute Abend   Haben Sie heute Abend Zeit?

Cultural info (Textbook page 44)

This page is of special interest to those of you who don't live in Europe. It's easy to
misjudge distances. For everybody else it's a good exercise.
It shows you how to make comparisons:
… weiter als …: Oslo ist von Frankfurt weiter als Warschau. (… further away than …:
Oslo is further from Frankfurt than Warsaw.)

How far is that from Frankfurt?
6 countries – 6 capitals
Note down the capital cities.
Please complete.

Vocabulary

1. *Fill in the missing word.*

1. Hallo, _____ Sie frei?

2. Wohin _____ Sie?

3. _____ Siemensstadt.

4. Wie _____ brauchen wir?

5. Nicht lange. Eine halbe _____.

6. Wir sind da. – Bitte eine _____.

2. *Mark the correct translation*

1. Die Uhr geht falsch.
☐ The clock is fast.
☐ The watch is slow.
☐ The clock is wrong.

2. Die Uhr geht vor.
☐ The watch is right.
☐ The clock is fast.
☐ The clock is wrong.

3. Die Uhr geht nach.
☐ The watch is fast.
☐ The clock is slow.
☐ The clock is right.

4. Ungefähr 20 Minuten.
☐ About 20 minutes.
☐ After 20 minutes.
☐ 20 minutes past.

5. Viertel nach drei
☐ Quarter to three.
☐ Quarter past three.
☐ 14 minutes past three.

6. Viertel vor sieben
☐ 7.40.
☐ 14 minutes to seven.
☐ Quarter to seven.

Grammar

3. *Write the official time.*

1. 10 nach 3 (nachmittags)   Es ist _____.

2. 5 Minuten vor 5 (nachmittags)   Es ist _____.

3. Viertel nach sechs (abends)   Es ist _____.

4. Viertel vor 8 abends   Es ist _____.

5. 7 nach halb 10 (vormittags)   Es ist _____.

6. 5 vor 12 (mittags)   Es ist _____.

4. *Write the plural.*

1. die Stadt   _____

2. das Taxi   _____

3. die Quittung   _____

4. der Termin   _____

5. das Büro   _____

6. die Anzeige   _____

7. das Haus   _____

8. die Nummer   _____

Check your answers in the key at the back of the book and then add up your points.

Total:	
	1 – 13 Before you carry on, you should really do this unit again.
	14 – 22 Quite good, but not perfect yet. Please go over the dialogue and the grammar again. It'll be worth it.
	23 – 26 Very good. You can carry straight on.

Die Firmenbesichtigung, Teil 1 –
Guided tour of the company, Part 1

Before lunch there is a guided tour of the company building.
You'll learn how to extend an invitation, and have a look at how a company is structured.

1 *Mark with a cross.*
Please do exercise 1 as preparation. You have your preferences when choosing a means of transport, don't you?
Maybe you'd like to explain why you prefer a particular means of transport. That's why we've suggested some phrases for giving reasons.
People use der Zug *when talking about journeys between cities,* die Bahn *more when talking about transport within a town or city.*

teuer – billig	*expensive – cheap*
schnell – langsam	*quick – slow*

2 An invitation to dinner and a guided tour
11A

→ *Listen to what Frau Bruckner gets to see. First though, Herr Kühne has a special sugges-tion. Listen to the text at least twice.*
→ *To help you understand what's going on, you can check up on some vocabulary via the vocabulary list.*

Es ist 11 Uhr.	*It's 11 o'clock.*
Mein Vorschlag …	*My suggestion …*
Vorschlag (der), die Vorschläge	*suggestion*
Wir machen jetzt eine Firmenbesichtigung.	*We'll do a tour of the company now.*
Firmenbesichtigung (die) (die Firma + die Besichtigung)	*(guided) tour of a company*
Und um zwölf gehen wir in die Kantine.	*And at twelve we'll go to the canteen.*
Eine Frage, …	*Can I ask you something? [literally: A question, …]*
Haben Sie heute Abend Zeit?	*Are you free/Do you have time this evening?*
Wir möchten Sie zum Essen einladen.	*We'd like to invite you to dinner.*
Essen (das)	*meal, dinner*
einladen – du lädst ein, er/sie lädt ein, hat eingeladen	*invite*
Ist sieben Uhr in Ordnung?	*Is seven o'clock OK?*
in Ordnung	*OK*
Ordnung (die)	*order*
Geht auch halb acht?	*Is half past seven OK, too?*

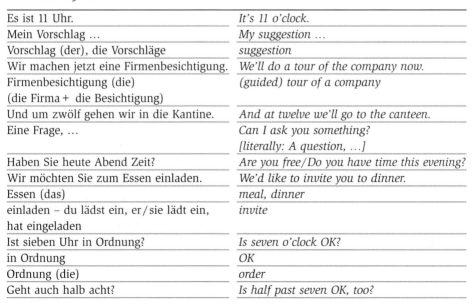

Wann fliegen Sie zurück?	*When do you fly back?*
zurückfliegen	*fly back*
– er / sie fliegt zurück, ist zurückgeflogen	
Das heißt, ich fahre mit dem Zug.	*Actually I'm going by train.*
das heißt	*actually, in fact*
mit dem Zug	*by train*
Zug (der), die Züge	*train*
Das sind nur 6 einhalb Stunden.	*It's only six and a half hours.*

11B

So, hier ist also der Vertrieb.	*Right, this is the sales department.*
Die Geschäftsleitung und das Sekretariat sind hier geradeaus.	*The management and secretaries' office is straight ahead.*
Geschäftsleitung (die)	*management*
Sekretariat (das)	*secretaries' office*
geradeaus	*straight ahead / on*
Wir nehmen jetzt den Aufzug.	*We'll take the lift now.*
Aufzug (der), die Aufzüge	*lift*
Keller (der), die Keller	*cellar, basement*
Einen Moment …	*Just a moment …*
Archiv (das), die Archive	*filing room, storeroom*

Here's a tip for learning vocabulary. Learn 5 to 10 words, then another 5 to 10 the next time. Mark the words that are important to you.

3 *Complete the text. The time expressions are missing.*
All the expressions of time have disappeared. Read the text and complete it with the right expressions.

4 *What's right? Mark with a cross.*
You remember what they said, don't you? We're going to ask you some questions.

5 *Answer with* Nein.

6 *What doesn't fit?*
These verbs take the accusative. Underline the accusative form in each case that doesn't fit.

 7 *Practise the dialogue as in the example. Then listen.*

8 *Chris Bruckner's notes*

The accusative – Der Akkusativ

		masculine	feminine	neuter
personal pronoun		er	sie	es
definite article	*nom.*	der Balkon	die Wohnung	das Bad
indefinite article		ein Balkon	eine Wohnung	ein Bad
negative article		**kein** Balkon	**keine** Wohnung	**kein** Bad
definite article	*acc.*	**den** Balkon	die Wohnung	das Bad
indefinite article		ein**en** Balkon	eine Wohnung	ein Bad
negative article		**keinen** Balkon	**keine** Wohnung	**kein** Bad

Nominative and accusative

sein is followed by the nominative: *Das ist eine Dachwohnung. Die Wohnung ist schön.*
Most verbs are followed by the accusative: *Wir möchten einen Balkon.*
Only the masculine accusative singular has a different form from the nominative:
Ich möchte keinen Tee.

Definite and indefinite article

- When you first mention something, you use the indefinite article:
  *Das ist **eine** Dachwohnung.*
- Then you use the definite article because the thing is now known:
  ***Die** Wohnung finde ich schön.*

Negative article

- *kein-* is the negative of *ein-* and means 'no' or 'not any':
  *Wir haben **keinen** Balkon.*
- *ein-* and *kein-* are always placed in front of a noun.

9 *Fill in* den, die, das *and* der, die, das.

Nehmen Sie _____ Bus?　　　– Nein, _____ Bus ist schon weg.

Nehmen Sie _____ Bahn?　　– Nein, _____ Bahn ist schon weg.

Nehmen Sie _____ Zug?　　　– Nein, _____ Zug ist schon weg.

Nehmen Sie _____ Flugzeug?　– Nein, _____ Flugzeug ist schon weg.

Nehmen Sie _____ Auto?　　　– Nein, _____ Auto ist kaputt.

10 *Fill in the article.*

Wir haben _____ Kantine.　　　– Aber _____ Kantine ist nicht gut.

Gibt es hier _____ Aufzug?　　　– Ja, _____ Aufzug ist da geradeaus.

Machen wir _____ Pause?　　　– Ja, _____ Pause ist um zwölf.

Haben Sie schon _____ Hotel?　– Ja, _____ Hotel liegt direkt im Zentrum.

Wir haben _____ Dachwohnung.　– _____ Wohnung ist sehr gemütlich.

11 *Fill in the missing part of the sentence in the accusative.*

Wir haben _____ _____ (ein Termin).

Wir nehmen _____ _____` und _____ _____. (der Bus, die Bahn)

Möchten Sie _____ _____? (ein Kaffee)

Kennen Sie _____ _____? (der Hafen)

Wir möchten _____ _____ (der Reichstag) besichtigen.

Wir möchten _____ _____ (ein Ausflug) machen.

12 *Fill in* kein- *and* ein-.

Ist das Tee? — Nein, das ist _____ Tee, das ist Kaffee.

Ist das eine Pension? — Nein, das ist _____ Pension, das ist _____ Hotel.

Ist das eine Telefonnummer? — Nein, das ist _____ Telefonnummer, das ist _____ Fax-Nummer.

Ist das ein Vorname? — Nein, das ist _____ Vorname, das ist _____ Nachname.

Ist Australien ein Land? — Nein, Australien ist _____ Land, es ist _____ Erdteil.

Ist das eine Vorwahlnummer? — Nein, das ist _____ Vorwahlnummer, das ist _____ Postleitzahl.

13 kein- + *noun or* nicht + *verb – Please negate.*

Ich habe ein Auto.   Ich habe _____ Auto.

Ich fliege.   Ich fliege _____.

Ich fliege gern.   Ich fliege _____ _____.

Ich fahre mit dem Auto.   Ich fahre _____ mit dem Auto.

Ich habe Zeit.   Ich habe _____ Zeit.

Ich komme.   Ich komme _____.

Ich habe eine Frage.   Ich habe _____ Frage.

14 *Revision*

Inviting someone

Haben Sie …	*Are you free/Do you have time …*
(heute Abend/morgen/…) Zeit?	*(this evening/tomorrow/…)?*
Wir möchten Sie zum Essen einladen.	*We'd like to invite you to dinner.*
Gerne. Vielen Dank.	*Fine./I'd like that. Thank you very much.*
Ist … (sieben Uhr) in Ordnung?	*Is … (seven o'clock) OK?*
– Ja natürlich./Geht auch halb acht?	*– Yes, of course./Would half past seven be OK too?/Is half past seven OK too?*

Stress

15 *Mark with a cross, and repeat.*
A very large number of words in German are stressed on the first syllable, as in English. Listen closely. Mark with a cross which syllable is stressed. Then repeat the word.

2|4

1st	2nd	syllable	1st	2nd	syllable	1st	2nd	syllable	1st	2nd	syllable
☐	☐	Straße	☐	☐	morgens	☐	☐	Geschäft	☐	☐	München
☐	☐	Verkehr	☐	☐	Reise	☐	☐	Besuch	☐	☐	Norden
☐	☐	Quittung	☐	☐	machen	☐	☐	Zimmer	☐	☐	gestern
☐	☐	Nummer	☐	☐	Beruf	☐	☐	Mittag	☐	☐	Frage
☐	☐	Termin	☐	☐	Handy	☐	☐	Berlin	☐	☐	Vorschlag

16 *Mark with a cross, and repeat.*
Now here are some three-syllable words. First listen, then mark with a cross which syllable of the word is stressed. At the end, repeat the words.

2|5

1st	2nd	3rd	syllable	1st	2nd	3rd	syllable
☐	☐	☐	Stadtrundfahrt	☐	☐	☐	Fahrkarte
☐	☐	☐	Anzeige	☐	☐	☐	sympathisch
☐	☐	☐	Telefon	☐	☐	☐	Kantine
☐	☐	☐	arbeiten	☐	☐	☐	Geburtsort
☐	☐	☐	Adresse	☐	☐	☐	Grammatik

17 *An exercise for experts. Mark with a cross.*
Don't worry if the stress is new for you. The more you hear and speak German texts, the more you'll get into the swing of it.
Listen and mark the stressed syllable with a cross.

2|6

1st	2nd	3rd	4th	syllable	1st	2nd	3rd	4th	syllable
☐	☐	☐	☐	buchstabieren	☐	☐	☐	☐	besichtigen
☐	☐	☐	☐	interessant	☐	☐	☐	☐	geradeaus
☐	☐	☐	☐	Informatik	☐	☐	☐	☐	Entschuldigung
☐	☐	☐	☐	Information					

Cultural info (Textbook page 48)

There's a surprise waiting for you. Start at START. Find the way through to the end.
The letters make up two sentences. What are the sentences?
Have fun!

Weg (der)   *way*
Ziel (das)   *destination, goal*

Vocabulary

1. Mark the correct translation with a cross.

1. die Einladung
□ guided tour
□ invitation
□ suggestion

2. mit dem Zug
□ by plane
□ on the motorway
□ by train

3. Das macht Spaß.
□ It's terrible.
□ It's fun.
□ There's no room here.

4. zum Essen einladen
□ have an appointment
□ be late
□ invite someone to dinner

5. heute Abend
□ this evening
□ later today
□ in the evening

6. der Vorschlag
□ water
□ meal
□ suggestion

2. Fill in the right verb.

1. Zeit _____

2. zum Essen _____

3. ein Taxi _____

4. mit dem Zug _____

5. zu Fuß _____

6. einen Termin _____

Grammar

3. ein- or kein-? – Please complete

1. Gibt es hier _____ Telefon?   – Nein, hier gibt es _____ Telefon.

2. Gibt es hier _____ Aufzug?   – Nein, hier gibt es _____ Aufzug.

3. Gibt es hier _____ Kantine?   – Nein, hier gibt es _____ Kantine.

4. Gibt es hier _____ Vertrieb?   – Nein, hier gibt es _____ Vertrieb.

5. Gibt er hier _____ Firmen-   – Nein, hier gibt es _____ Firmenbesichtigung?   besichtigung.

6. Gibt es hier _____ Chef?   – Nein, hier gibt es _____ Chef.

4. The accusative is missing. Please complete.

1. der Hafen   – Wir besichtigen heute _____ _____.

2. der Bus   – Wir nehmen _____ _____.

3. der Stau   – Siehst du _____ _____?

4. der Zug   – Wir nehmen _____ _____ um achtzehn Uhr.

5. der Aufzug   – Nehmen Sie _____ _____?

6. die Kantine   – Gehen wir in _____ _____?

7. der Raum   – Wir haben _____ _____ Nummer 3.

8. die Arbeit   – Wer macht _____ _____?

Check your answers in the key at the back of the book and then add up your points.

Total:	1 – 13	It would be a good idea to do this unit again straightaway.
	14 – 22	Pretty good. But it wouldn't hurt to go over the dialogues and the grammar again.
	23 – 26	Excellent. If you like, you could go over the vocabulary again, otherwise you can carry straight on.

Die Firmenbesichtigung, Teil 2 –
Guided tour of the company, Part 2

1 *What do you see? Please match.*
The names of various departments are mentioned on the company tour. Before you listen to the text mark the German words that come from English. There are actually quite a few.

die Buchhaltung	*accounts (department)*
das Controlling	*controlling (department)*
die IT-Abteilung	*IT department*
die Redaktion, die Redaktionen	*editorial department*
die Herstellung/Produktion	*production (department)*
die Marketing-Abteilung	*marketing department*
der Vertrieb	*sales (department)*
der Versand	*despatch department*
das Lager	*warehouse, stock-room*

2 Left, right, straight on

12A

→ *Now follow us round the rooms and departments on the ground floor. At the end we'll meet up in the canteen. First listen to the dialogue.*

→ *To help you understand what's going on, you can check up on some vocabulary via the vocabulary list.*

Wir sind jetzt im Erdgeschoss.	*We're now on the ground floor.*
Erdgeschoss (das)	*ground floor*
Hier links ist das Informationszentrum.	*Here on the left is the information centre.*
links – rechts – geradeaus	*(on the) left – (on the) right – straight on*
Informationszentrum (das), die Informations-zentren (die Information + das Zentrum)	*information centre*
Konferenzraum (der), die Konferenzräume (die Konferenz + der Raum)	*conference room*
Da macht die Arbeit Spaß.	*Work is fun there.*
Den Empfang und die Redaktionen haben Sie schon gesehen.	*You've already seen reception and the editorial departments.*
gegenüber	*opposite*
Ich verstehe.	*I see/understand.*
verstehen – er/sie versteht, hat verstanden	*understand*
besichtigen – er/sie besichtigt, hat besichtigt	*look round, see*
Das ist eine Viertelstunde zu Fuß.	*It's a quarter of an hour's walk/quarter of an hour on foot.*
glauben – er/sie glaubt, hat geglaubt	*believe, think*
Raum (der), die Räume	*room*

12B

At the entrance to the canteen there is a sign. Read what it says. If you don't understand everything, you can look up the words here.

Selbstbedienung (die)	*self-service*
Geöffnet von … bis	*Open from … to*
Gäste-Casino (das)	*visitors' canteen*
Gast (der), die Gäste	*visitor, guest*
Anmeldung (die)	*booking, reception*
Kantinenleitung (die)	*canteen management*
(die Kantine + die Leitung)	

Now listen to the text. Then read it out loud to yourself.

3 *What's the right order?*
Listen again to the order in which the departments are visited. Note down the order of the departments from B to F. We've already done the information centre (A) for you.

4 *This is Europartner. Read the text and draw the route on the sketch.*
If you take the right route, you'll soon get there and be able to sit down and enjoy your lunch.

5 *Frau Bruckner tells Herr Kühne what she's seen. Write the correct form.*

6 *Please match.*
The opening times of shops and public buildings in Germany are fixed by law, and regulations are only gradually becoming more flexible. Opening times give you a pretty good idea of where you are at a particular time. Read the signs and match the drawings to them. If you don't understand all the words, here is the vocabulary:

Montag	*Monday*	Freitag	*Friday*
Dienstag	*Tuesday*	Sonnabend / Samstag	*Saturday*
Mittwoch	*Wednesday*	Sonntag	*Sunday*
Donnerstag	*Thursday*		

Sprechstunde (die)	*Surgery*
geöffnet / geschlossen (von … bis …)	*open / closed (from … to …)*
(Montag) geschlossen … bis …	*closed (on Monday) … till …*

7 *Speaking exercise. What would you like to see? First listen to the example, then answer.*

8 *Please write.*
Some important information is missing in this calendar. Write in the days of the week.

Word order I – Satzstellung I

I	II		I	II		
Wir	**arbeiten**	bis 11.	Dann	**machen**	wir	Pause.
Wir	**machen**	Pause.	Um zwölf	**gehen**	wir	in die Kantine.
Wir	**gehen**	in die Kantine.	Geradeaus	**ist**		die Kantine.

- In German, sentences often begin with a word or expression giving information about the time or place. Often, too, there is a link back to the preceding sentence (for example *Dann* …). The verb is nevertheless always in position 2. The noun or pronoun come after it.
- Statements and questions starting with a question word: The verb is always in position II. Questions without a question word: The verb is in position I.
  Wann **gehen** *wir in die Kantine?*
  Gehen *wir in die Kantine?*

9 *What's the sentence?*
This is all about word order. We ask you a question. You have part of the reply. Write the answer.

- Was machen wir um 10 Uhr? ► Wir │ bis 11 Uhr │ arbeiten

- Und dann?   ► eine Pause │ wir │ Dann │ machen

- Und was machen wir dann? ► machen │ Um 11 Uhr 15 │ wir │ eine Firmenbesichtigung

---

- Wie lange machen wir   ► die Firmenbesichtigung │ bis 12 │ dauert
  die Firmenbesichtigung?

- Was machen wir um 12?   ► in die Kantine │ wir │ Um 12 │ gehen

---

- Wie lange essen wir?   ► Wir │ essen │ bis eins

- Und dann?   ► wir │ Dann │ arbeiten │ bis 3

- Was machen wir um 3?   ► machen │ Um 3 │ wir │ eine Stadtrundfahrt

---

- Wann sind wir zurück?   ► im Hotel │ zurück │ wir │ sind │ Um 7

---

10 *What's the sentence?*

jetzt	Wir machen eine Firmenbesichtigung. Jetzt machen _____
um 12 Uhr	Ich komme in die Kantine. _____
heute Abend	Ich habe Zeit. _____
morgen	Ich fahre zurück nach München. _____
vielleicht	Ich nehme den Zug. _____
dann	Ich rufe an. _____

11 *Das* Krankenzimmer - *The sickbay*
First read the dialogue. Then listen to the words.

der Kopf	*head*
das Haar	*hair*
das Auge, die Augen	*eye*
der Mund	*mouth*
der Zahn, die Zähne	*tooth*
der Hals	*neck*
die Hand, die Hände	*hand*
der Arm, die Arme	*arm*
der Bauch	*stomach*
das Bein, die Beine	*leg*

Frau Bruckner:	Was haben Sie hier?
Herr Heinrich:	Das ist das Krankenzimmer. Deshalb das Plakat.
Frau Bruckner:	Ah ja. Haben Sie einen Notarzt im Haus?
Herr Heinrich:	Nein, nein, den rufen wir.
	Tut Ihnen was weh? Ich hoffe nicht.
Frau Bruckner:	Nein, zum Glück, ich bin ganz gesund.

12 *Revision and extension*

The sickbay

krank – gesund	*ill – well, healthy*
Krankheit (die)	*illness, disease*
Gesundheit (die)	*health*
wehtun	*hurt*
Notarzt (der), die Notärzte	*emergency doctor*
Schmerzen (die Plural)	*pain, ache*
Zahnschmerzen (die Plural) (der Zahn + die Schmerzen)	*toothache*

13 *Which syllable is stressed? Listen closely and underline.*

1	2	3	4	5	6
Emp	fang				
Re	dak	tion			
Erd	ge	schoss			
ge	ra	de	aus		
ge	gen	ü	ber		
Kon	fe	renz	räu	me	
In	for	ma	tions	zen	trum
Fir	men	be	sich	ti	gung

Cultural info (Textbook page 52)
What do I do? What do I say? – Some little tips

Hello and goodbye
People usually shake hands when saying *Guten Tag or Auf Wiedersehen*. But when do you do it, and when don't you?
Handshaking is always rather formal. You greet business partners like this. Good friends or colleagues see each other daily, and they of course don't shake hands. They just say *Hallo, Guten Tag* or *Grüß Gott* (in the south), often adding the person's name, and that's it. On special occasions and when it's someone's birthday, friends and colleagues are also more formal and shake the person's hand.

„Mahlzeit"
At work you often hear people saying *Mahlzeit* (literally: "mealtime") to each other around the middle of the day. You say *Mahlzeit*, and the reply is *Mahlzeit* too. Then you go to the canteen or have something to eat in your office. People only say *Mahlzeit* at work, never at home or in a restaurant.

Help! I'm going to be late!
Punctuality is important in Germany. People who are repeatedly late for business meetings make a bad impression. But it can happen of course. Then you can phone and say: *Ich komme leider eine halbe Stunde später*. Or you can apologize with the sentence: *Tut mir leid, dass ich zu spät komme*.

Vocabulary

1. What's the word?

1. [fe] [renz] [kon] [raum]   2. [ti] [kan] [ne]   3. [dung] [la] [ein]

4. [ger] [la]   5. [trum] [zen] [tions] [infor] [ma]   6. [dak] [re] [tion]

2. Write correctly.

1. hieristkeinplatz _____   4. dasmachtspaß _____

2. ichglaubenicht _____   5. ichverstehe _____

3. dageradeaus _____

Grammar

3. Write the sentence.

1. Wir besichtigen den Hafen. - Heute _____

2. Wir nehmen den Bus. - Um eins _____

3. Wir haben Raum 3. - Morgen _____

4. Das Casino ist geöffnet. - Bis 18 Uhr _____

5. Wir besichtigen die Firma. - Am Vormittag _____

6. Ich fahre wieder zurück. - Mittwoch _____

4. Note down the verbs with special forms in the singular.

	sehen	du siehst	er / sie sieht

glauben	fahren
verstehen	nehmen
mögen	schlafen
besichtigen	wohnen
geben	möchten
fliegen	

1. _____ _____ _____

2. _____ _____ _____

3. _____ _____ _____

4. _____ _____ _____

5. _____ _____ _____

Listening Comprehension

5. First listen to the dialogue between a taxi driver and a tourist. Then answer the questions.

1. Wo ist der Tourist? In _ _ _ _ _ _ .

2. Wie viel kostet die Fahrt? Circa _ _ _ _ _ _ _ Euro.

3. Wohin möchte er? Ins _ _ _ _ _ _ _ .

4. Wie fährt er? Mit der _ _ _ _ _ _ _ .

5. Hat er einen Stadtplan? _ _ , natürlich.

Check your answers in the key at the back of the book and then add up your points.

Total:	1 - 14	Oh dear, that's a pity. Please do this unit again.
	15 – 23	Not so bad. But even so, it would be a good idea to go over the dialogues and the grammar again.
	24 – 27	Excellent. There's nothing to stop you carrying on.

Das Frühstück – Breakfast

In this lesson you're going to learn something about a typical part of German life:
breakfast. Claudia talks about her family over breakfast. As she does so, the possessive
articles *mein* and *dein* are used.

1 *Please match.*
Listen to how the items on the breakfast table are pronounced, and repeat out loud.

Brötchen (das), die Brötchen	*roll*	Marmelade (die)	*jam*
Butter (die)	*butter*	Messer (das), die Messer	*knife*
Brot (das), die Brote	*(slice of) bread*	Löffel (der), die Löffel	*spoon*
Ei (das), die Eier	*egg*	Gabel (die), die Gabeln	*fork*
Teller (der), die Teller	*plate*	Käse (der)	*cheese*
Tasse (die), die Tassen	*cup*	Obst (das)	*fruit*
		Serviette (die), die Servietten	*napkin*

2 Breakfast is ready
*It's all right for Robert. He doesn't have to go to work or to the university. He gets up late and
goes into the kitchen. Claudia has laid the breakfast table there.*
*Now listen to how Claudia greets Robert and what there is for breakfast. Listen to the text at
least twice. And here's some help with the vocabulary again.*

Hast du gut geschlafen?	*Did you sleep well?*
schlafen – du schläfst, er/sie schläft, hat geschlafen	*sleep*
Niki ist schon weg.	*Niki has already left.*
weg sein – er/sie ist weg	*be gone*
Es gibt gleich Frühstück.	*Breakfast won't be a minute.*
gleich	*in a minute, straightaway*
Keinen Tee. (= Ich möchte keinen Tee.)	*No tea. (= I don't want tea.)*
Ich mag lieber Kaffee.	*I prefer coffee.*
mögen – er/sie mag, hat gemocht	*like*
lieber mögen	*prefer*
Und dann ein Brötchen mit Butter und Marmelade.	*And then a roll with butter and jam.*
Eier sind auch da.	*There are some eggs, too.*
Sag mal, Claudia, deine Eltern, wo wohnen die eigentlich?	*Tell me, Claudia, your parents, where do they live actually?*
Eltern (die Plural)	*parents*
eigentlich	*actually, in fact, really*
Ganz in der Nähe.	*Very nearby.*
Übrigens, meine Schwester ist da.	*By the way, my sister is here.*

mein, meine	*my*
Schwester (die), die Schwestern	*sister*
Sie ist gestern aus Sydney gekommen.	*She came from Sydney yesterday.*
gestern	*yesterday*
Sie hat dort ein paar Monate gearbeitet.	*She's been working there for a few months.*
Regisseurin (die) – Regisseur (der)	*director, producer*
Mein Bruder Ralf geht noch zur Schule.	*My brother Ralf is still in school.*
Bruder (der), die Brüder	*brother*
zur Schule gehen	*go to school, be in school*
Schule (die), die Schulen	*school*
Er wohnt natürlich zu Hause.	*He lives at home of course.*
Wir besuchen heute meine Eltern.	*We'll visit my parents today.*
besuchen – er/sie besucht, hat besucht	*visit*
Was meinst du?	*What do you think?*
meinen – er/sie meint, hat gemeint	*think*
dann lerne ich endlich deine Geschwister kennen	*then I'll get to know your brothers and sisters at last*
kennen lernen – er/sie lernt kennen, hat kennen gelernt	*get to know*
Geschwister (die Plural)	*brothers and sisters*

3 *Please complete.*
These questions and sentences can all be spoken at the breakfast table. Fill in the gaps.

4 *Reconstruct the text .*
Find the most suitable word. And remember: the meaning must fit, not just the form.

 Unspecific quantities have no article: *Ich möchte Brot mit Butter und Marmelade.*
The article is used with a specific quantity and in the negative: *Ich möchte ein Brötchen, kein Brot.*

5 *Please complete.*
This is all about the modal verb mögen, möchten *is used in polite questions and answers.*

6 *Please complete. Here you practise* mein *and* dein *in the nominative.*

 7 *Speaking exercise*
Now you can decide what you would like. Listen to the question. Then read the prompts and reply. The picture gives you the answer.

8 *Robert's diary – Some important words are missing.*

Verbs – Verben: mögen

		mögen
Singular	ich	**mag**
	du	**magst**
	er / sie	**mag**
Plural	wir	mögen
	ihr	mögt
	sie / Sie	mögen

mögen:
There are special forms in the singular: *mag, magst, mag.*
Notice the difference between *ich mag* (I like) and *ich möchte* (I'd like):
Möchten Sie Kaffee?
Nein danke, ich möchte lieber Tee. (= Bitte einen Tee.)
Ich mag keinen Kaffee. (= Ich trinke keinen Kaffee.)

Ralf mag Katrin. Aber Katrin mag Guido.

9 *What doesn't fit? Please cross out.*

Ich mag …

| Test | keinen Tee | Müsli | Ei | das Brot | Dachwohnung | Eltern | Christine | Wort |

| meinen Beruf | Sidney | Australien | Berlin | die Übungen | deinen Bruder | Sprache |

Article *kein*; possessive articles *mein / dein* – Artikel *kein*; Possessivartikel *mein / dein*

		masculine		**feminine**		**neuter**	
Personal pronouns	nom. sing.	**er**		**sie**		**es**	
indefinite article		ein	Bruder	ein**e**	Schwester	ein	Haus
negative article		kein		kein**e**		kein	
possessive article		mein		mein**e**		mein	
		dein		dein**e**		dein	
indefinite article	acc. sing.	ein**en**	Bruder	ein**e**	Schwester	ein	Haus
negative article		kein**en**	Bruder	kein**e**	Schwester	kein	Haus
possessive article		mein**en**	Bruder	mein**e**	Schwester	mein	Haus
		dein**en**		dein**e**		dein	

The possessive articles *mein-* and *dein-* have the same endings as *kein-*.

10 *Please complete.*
You can make something negative with nicht *and* kein. kein- *is always placed before a noun.*

Haben Sie ein Auto?   – Nein, ich habe _____ Auto.

Haben Sie eine Uhr?   – Nein, ich habe _____ Uhr.

Haben Sie Geschwister?   – Nein, ich habe _____ Geschwister.

Haben Sie Zeit?   – Nein, ich habe _____ Zeit.

Haben Sie Semesterferien?   – Nein, ich habe _____ Semesterferien.

Haben Sie Hunger?   – Nein, ich habe _____ Hunger.

11 mein *and* dein. *Fill in.*

Markus, ist das _____ Fahrkarte?

Nina, ist das _____ Handy?

Klaus, ist das _____ Kaffee?

Ralf, ist das _____ Frühstück?

Das ist _____ Bruder. – Kennst du _____ Bruder?

Das ist _____ Schwester. – Kennst du _____ Schwester?

12 *Please complete.*
Somebody here is not very friendly. He says very clearly what is his. Careful when you get to the last sentence.

Das ist nicht _____ Frühstück, das ist _____ Frühstück.

Das ist nicht _____ Schwester, das ist _____ Schwester.

Das ist nicht _____ Fahrkarte, das ist _____ Fahrkarte.

Das ist nicht _____ Auto, das ist _____ Auto.

Das ist nicht _____ Uhr, das ist _____ Uhr.

Das ist nicht _____ Problem, das ist _____ Problem.

13 *Put the sentences in the right order and write the text.*

Niki heißt Bat mit Familiennamen.
Aber er möchte die Sprache gern lernen.
Die Eltern sind 1960 nach Deutschland gekommen. Jetzt haben sie ein chinesisches Restaurant.
Das ist das Restaurant in der Hafenstraße. Das Essen dort ist sehr gut, sagt man.
Er wohnt und arbeitet in Berlin und ist auch hier geboren.
Deshalb ist nur der Familienname Chinesisch, nicht der Vorname. Er spricht auch kein Chinesisch.

14 *Revision*

Likes and dislikes

(Kaffee/…) mag ich nicht.	*I don't like … (coffee/…).*
Ich mag keine/-n … (Milch/Kaffee …).	*I don't like (any) … (milk/coffee …).*
Ich trinke … (keinen Kaffee).	*I don't drink … (coffee/…).*
Ich mag lieber … (Tee/…).	*I prefer … (tea/…).*
Ich esse … (keinen Salat).	*I don't eat … (any) (salad).*
Ich mag … (Birgit/…) sehr.	*I like … (Birgit/…) a lot.*
Ich mag … (Lisa/…) nicht so sehr.	*I don't like … (Lisa/…) much.*
Ich finde … (Claudia/Robert/Frau Klein)	*I (don't) think/(don't) find …*
sympathisch/nicht so sympathisch.	*(Claudia/Robert/Frau Klein) (is) (so) nice.*

a and ä

ä is the umlaut belonging to the vowel *a*. Some verbs have *ä* in the *du* and *er/sie* form *(fahren - du fährst, er/sie fährt; einladen – du lädst ein, er/sie lädt ein)*; *ä* is also used in the plural of some nouns *(Vater – Väter)*.

15 *Listen and repeat. Try to imitate the speaker's pronunciation as closely as possible.*

fahren	–	Claudia fährt	der Hafen	–	die Häfen
schlafen	–	Robert schläft schon.	der Kanal	–	die Kanäle
das Bad	–	zwei Bäder	das Land	–	die Länder
mein Vater	–	die Väter	der Vorschlag	–	die Vorschläge

u und ü

u has the umlaut *ü*. This *ü* can be short or long. We're going to practise it now.

16 *Listen and repeat.*
Try to imitate the speaker's pronunciation as closely as possible.

Mutter und Mütter	viel früher
Bruder und Brüder	übrigens
das Frühstück	er fliegt zurück
vier Brüder	eine Viertelstunde früher
viel Glück	Das ist gemütlich.

Cultural info – Jumbled words (Textbook page 56)

If there's a word you don't know, look it up in the wordlist.
Find the words. There are 7 generic terms. Note down the article too.

der Vater (= Papa), die Väter	der Cousin, die Cousins
die Mutter (= Mama), die Mütter	die Cousine, die Cousinen
der Mann, die Männer	der Onkel, die Onkel
die Frau, die Frauen	die Tante, die Tanten
das Kind, die Kinder	der Enkel, die Enkel
das Baby, die Babys	die Enkelin, die Enkelinnen
die Eltern (Plural)	der Schwiegersohn, die Schwiegersöhne
der Sohn, die Söhne	die Schwiegertochter, die Schwiegertöchter
die Tochter, die Töchter	der Schwiegervater, die Schwiegerväter
der Bruder, die Brüder	die Schwiegermutter, die Schwiegermütter
die Schwester, die Schwestern	
der Großvater (= Opa), die Großväter	
die Großmutter (= Oma), die Großmütter	

Vocabulary

1. *Here are some important expressions that you'll want to use often. Match the right translation.*

1. Christian ist schon weg.
☐ Christian has already arrived.
☐ Christian is here now.
☐ Christian has already left.

3. Jan geht noch zur Schule.
☐ Jan is going to school.
☐ Jan doesn't go to school.
☐ Jan is still in school.

5. Übrigens …
☐ Actually …
☐ By the way …
☐ Over …

2. Sag mal … hast du Hunger?
☐ Say again … are you hungry.
☐ Tell me … what is hunger?
☐ Tell me … are you hungry?

4. Was meinst du?
☐ What does she mean?
☐ What do you think?
☐ Was that right?

6. Wirklich?
☐ Ready?
☐ Really?
☐ Why?

2. *Fill in the appropriate word.*

1. Mutter und _____

2. Bruder und _____

3. Oma und _____

4. Tochter und _____

5. Onkel und _____

6. Schwiegervater und _____

7. Mann und _____

Grammar

3. *There is some trouble here about what belongs to whom. Fill in the correct form. The possessive article is missing.*

1. Das ist mein Handy, nicht _____ Handy.

2. Das ist mein Auto, nicht _____ Auto.

3. Das ist mein Problem, nicht _____ Problem.

4. Das ist mein Lieblingsessen, nicht _____ Lieblingsessen.

5. Das ist meine Wohnung, nicht _____ Wohnung.

6. Das sind meine Geschwister, nicht _____ Geschwister.

4. *Fill in* mögen *or* möchten.

1. _____ du Brot oder Brötchen?

2. Ich _____ lieber Brötchen.

3. Ich _____ keinen Tee.

4. _____ du Kaffee? – Ja, gern.

5. _____ du deine Schwester Kerstin?

6. Ich _____ Kerstin sehr.

Check your answers in the key at the back of the book and then add up your points.

Total:
1 – 13 Before you carry on, you really should do this unit again.
14 – 21 Quite good, but not perfect yet. Please go over the dialogue and the grammar again.
22 – 25 Very good. You can carry straight on.

14

Wir besuchen meine Familie – We're visiting my family

This lesson is all about the family. People meet and talk. You'll learn the names of countries and languages. The past forms of *sein* and *haben* open up new ways for you to express yourself.

1 *Listen to what Claudia has to say.*
Claudia and Robert set off straight after breakfast and visit her parents during the morning. Robert is looking forward to meeting Claudia's brother and sister.
On the way to her parents, Claudia talks about her family. Listen to what she says and write the names on the sketch.

2|19

2 The family
→ *Now listen to the family greeting each other and hear what they have to say. Listen to the conversation at least twice.*

2|20

Mama is the familiar form of *Mutter*. *Papa* the familiar form of *Vater*.

→ *If you want to have a closer look at the words and sentences, here they are:*

Wir besuchen meine Familie	*We're visiting my family.*
lange nicht gesehen = Ich habe dich lange nicht gesehen.	*long time no see = I haven't seen you for a long time.*
Du bist sicher Robert.	*You must be Robert.*
sicher	*certain(ly)*
Claudia hat schon viel von dir erzählt.	*Claudia has told us a lot about you.*
Wirklich?	*Really?*
Mama = Mutter (die), die Mütter	*mum(my) = mother*
Papa = Vater (der), die Väter	*dad(dy) = father*
Wie gefällt Ihnen Berlin?	*How do you like Berlin?*
gefallen – er/sie/es gefällt, hat gefallen	*like*
Das war in einer Sprachenschule in England.	*That was in a language school in England.*
Sprachenschule (die), die Sprachenschulen (die Sprache + die Schule)	*language school*
ich hatte Semesterferien	*I was on vacation*
Semesterferien (die Plural) (das Semester + die Ferien)	*vacation*
Da bin ich nach England gefahren und habe Englisch gelernt.	*I went to England and learned English.*
Englisch	*English*
lernen – er/sie lernt, hat gelernt	*learn*
Und da waren auch Claudia und Niki.	*And Claudia and Niki were there too.*
Und jetzt sprechen Sie die Sprache perfekt, nicht wahr?	*And now you speak the language perfectly, don't you?*

perfekt	*perfect(ly)*
Kinder, ihr habt bestimmt Hunger.	*Children, I'm sure you're hungry.*
Ich habe dein Lieblingsessen gekocht.	*I've cooked your favourite meal.*
Lieblingsessen (das)	*favourite meal*
Das siehst du gleich.	*You'll see in a minute.*

3 *What is the correct order?*
Put the conversations in the right order. The greeting comes first of course.

4 *Please complete.*
war *and* hatte *occur in the dialogue. They are the past tense forms of* sein *and* haben. *Do this short gap-fill exercise.*

5 *What is right?*
Mark the right sentences with a cross.

6 *Here are all the five people in the conversation. Who said what?*
Please match.

7 *Speaking exercise.*
First read the example and the prompts. Then listen to the question and reply.

8 *Jumbled letters*
Claudia's favourite meal is hidden in this letter matrix. There are three words: a vegetable that is eaten in the spring up till June, and what is eaten with it.
If you can't find it, here's a tip: look at the word Legraps. This is an anagram of the main ingredient.

Find Claudia's favourite food.

Past of *sein* and *haben* / Präteritum von *sein* und *haben*: *war* und *hatte*

		sein	**haben**
Singular	ich	war	hatte
	du	warst	hattest
	er / sie / es	war	hatte
Plural	wir	waren	hatten
	ihr	wart	hattet
	sie / Sie	waren	hatten

Once you've learned *war* and *hatte* and some perfect forms, you can talk about things that happened in the past.

9 *Fill in the missing verbs.*
Here you can report something in the past.

Wir _____ (sein) gestern zu Hause bei Guido. Guidos Brüder _____ (sein)

auch da. Guidos Schwester _____ (haben) aber keine Zeit. Sie _____ (sein)

bei Christine. Das ist eine Freundin. Die Eltern _____ (sein) in der Stadt.

Ich _____ (haben) meine CDs mit. Es _____ (sein) sehr gemütlich.

Personal pronouns in the accusative/Personalpronomen: Akkusativ: *Ich habe dich lange nicht gesehen.*

Singular	ich	Verstehst du	**mich**	?
	du	Ich habe	**dich**	lange nicht gesehen.
	er / sie / es		**ihn/sie/es**	
Plural	wir	Verstehst du	**uns**	?
	ihr	Ich habe	**euch**	lange nicht gesehen.
	sie / Sie		**sie/Sie**	

- Most verbs take the accusative. *Ich finde **deinen Bruder** sehr sympathisch.*
- An article + noun can be replaced by a pronoun: *Ich finde **ihn** sehr sympathisch.*
  A pronoun is used when you want to avoid repeating a noun.

10 *Replace the noun with a pronoun.*

Wie finden Sie das Essen?   – Ich finde _____ gut.

Bitte rufen Sie Herrn Schneider an.   – Ich habe _____ schon angerufen. Er ist nicht da.

Wie findest du Evas Schwester?   – Ich finde _____ interessant.

Hast du die Adresse?   – Ja, ich habe _____.

Brauchen Sie den Wagen?   – Ja, ich brauche _____ heute.

Kennen Sie die Leute?   – Nein, ich kenne _____ auch nicht.

11 *Noun + noun*
The word Lieblingsessen *occurred in the text. You can also use* Lieblings- *with other words.*
Try it. You'll see from the meaning of the words which ones it can be used with.

| stadt | bruder | dienstag | schwester | brot | film |

| hotel | anmeldung | regisseur | zimmer |

Lieblings_____   Lieblings_____   Lieblings_____   Lieblings_____

Lieblings_____   Lieblings_____   Lieblings_____

12 *Countries and Nationalities*
Here's a table with names of countries and nationalities. Complete the table with the
missing words. All the adjectives end in -isch.

Land	Nationalität	Land	Nationalität
	Tschechisch		Chinesisch
Polen			Koreanisch
Russland		Österreich	
Türkei			Schweizerisch
Japan			Mexikanisch
	Spanisch	Ungarn	
	Italienisch		Griechisch

The names of languages are written with a capital letter, as in English:
Das ist Französisch.
Wie heißt das auf Französisch?

13 *Revision*

Asking someone to say something

Sag mal, … (wo wohnst du eigentlich)?	*Tell me, … (where in fact do you live)?*
Was meinst du?	*What do you think?*
Wie gefällt dir/Ihnen … (die Stadt)?	*How do you like … (the city)?*
Woher kennst du/kennen Sie …?	*How do you know …?*
Ich habe noch eine Frage.	*I have a/another question.*
Eine Frage, …	*A question, …*
Sprichst du/Sprechen Sie … (Deutsch)?	*Do you speak … (German)?*
– Ja natürlich./Ja, aber nicht gut./	*– Yes, of course./Yes, but not well./*
Nur wenig.	*Only a little.*
Sprechen Sie perfekt … (Deutsch)? –	*Do you speak perfect … (German)?*
– Nicht perfekt, aber gut.	*– Not perfect, but good.*

Endung -(i)sch

14 *Listen closely and repeat.*

Französisch	Sprechen Sie Französisch?	Chinesisch	Ist das Chinesisch?
Englisch	Sprechen Sie Englisch?	Australisch	Ist das Australisch?
Deutsch	Sprechen Sie Deutsch?	Irisch	Ist das Irisch?
Italienisch	Sprechen Sie Italienisch?	Griechisch	Ist das Griechisch?
Spanisch	Sprechen Sie Spanisch?	Polnisch	Ist das Polnisch?
Japanisch	Sprechen Sie Japanisch?	Tschechisch	Ist das Tschechisch?

15 a. *Now listen to the conversation between the two friends. The stessed syllables are underlined. Listen closely.*

Melanie:	Sag mal, hast du eigentlich Geschwister?
Lisa:	Klar.
Melanie:	Und wie viele?
Lisa:	Drei. Zwei Schwestern und einen Bruder.
Melanie:	Toll! Ich habe leider keine Geschwister.
Lisa:	Macht doch nichts. Du hast ja deine Freunde.
	Sag mal, was machst du heute Abend?
	Wir machen eine Party. Zu Hause.
Melanie:	Ja, prima, und wann?
Lisa:	Na so gegen acht.
Melanie:	Ich komme. Wo wohnst du?
Lisa:	In der Baumstr. 10.
Melanie:	Ah, da kommt mein Bus. Also dann bis heute Abend. Tschüs.
Lisa.	Tschüs!

15 b. *Now listen and speak at the same time.*

Cultural info (Textbook page 6o)

c) Bavaria is well-known for its beer. Not many people know that more beer is brewed in northern Germany than in Bavaria. Dortmund beer is famous.
f) This of course is Hamburg.

Here are six drawings. Match the six texts to the right drawings.

Vocabulary

1. Supply the language: for example England – Englisch.

1. Frankreich _____

2. Polen _____

3. Österreich _____

4. Türkei _____

5. Australien _____

6. China _____

7. Slowenien _____

8. Italien _____

Grammar

2. Fill in the correct form. It's the verb that's missing.

1. Gestern _____ ich frei.

2. Meine Schwester _____ auch Zeit.

3. Wir _____ in der Stadt.

4. Meine Schwester _____ das Auto.

5. Das _____ prima.

6. Um acht _____ wir wieder zu Hause.

3. Fill in the correct form. The personal pronoun is missing.

1. Wo ist mein Handy? – Ich habe _____ nicht gesehen.

2. Wie findest du die CD? – Ich finde _____ klasse.

3. Ich habe ein Problem. – So? Was ist _____ denn?

4. Wie findest du meine Eltern? – Ich finde _____ sehr sympathisch

5. Wie findest du meine Wohnung? – Ich finde _____ nicht schlecht.

6. Besuchst du heute deine Geschwister? – Nein, ich habe _____ gestern besucht.

Check your answers in the key at the back of the book and then add up your points.

Total: | 1 – 10 It would be a good idea to do this unit again straightaway.
| 11 – 17 Pretty good. But it wouldn't hurt to go over the dialogues and the grammar again.
| 18 – 20 Excellent. If you like, you could go over the vocabulary again, otherwise you can carry straight on.

Eine Mail von Robert – A mail from Robert

When Robert, Claudia and Niki are all back home in the evening, Robert writes an e-mail to his friend Jonas.

This lesson is all about jobs and professions. You'll also learn how to write letters and mails.

1 *Please match the professions.*
What do the people do for a living?

2   Robert writes an e-mail to his friend Jonas

Read the text. If you don't understand everything, don't worry. The main thing is that you find out what each of them does for a living.

→   *Listen and read.*

→   *Learn the vocabulary.*

herzliche Grüße	*best wishes*
Ich bin ein paar Tage bei Freunden.	*I'm staying with friends for a few days.*
Freund (der), die Freunde	*friend*
Ich glaube, du kennst sie.	*I think you know them.*
Heute haben wir die Familie von Claudia besucht.	*Today we visited Claudia's family.*
Claudias Vater ist Ingenieur.	*Claudia's father is an engineer.*
Er arbeitet als Controller.	*He works as a controller.*
Controller (der), die Controller	*controller*
Claudias Mutter ist Malerin.	*Claudia's mother is a painter.*
Malerin (die), die Malerinnen	*(woman) painter*
Sie arbeitet aber auch als Übersetzerin.	*But she also works as a translator.*
Übersetzerin (die), die Übersetzerinnen	*(woman) translator*
Claudias Bruder geht noch zur Schule.	*Claudia's brother is still at school.*
Er ist bald fertig.	*He'll soon be finished.*
bald	*soon*
fertig	*finished*
Regisseurin (die), die Regisseurinnen	*(female) director, producer*
Sie hat einen Film in Australien gemacht.	*She made a film in Australia.*
Film (der), die Filme	*film*
Australien	*Australia*
Für das Fernsehen.	*For television.*
Fernsehen (das)	*television*
Toll, was?	*Great, isn't it?*
toll	*great*
Was gibt's in München?	*What's on in Munich?*
Alles klar?	*Everything OK?*

3 *Answer the questions.*
Create your answers by putting the bits of the sentence into the right order.

In speech you can leave out the person and the verb if they have already occurred in the question. Then you get the following answers: *Bei Claudias Eltern. / Ingenieur. / Malerin. / Er geht noch zur Schule. / Katrin. / Interessant.*

4 *Claudia's family*
You'll find out more about the genitive in the grammar section.

5 *Robert is talking. Underline the correct form.*
You've already come across war *and* hatte. *In this text they occur again.*
Fill in the forms of sein. *Pay close attention to which sentence is in the past, and which is in the present.*

6 *Speaking exercise – First read the prompts.*
Listen to the question and answer as in the example. Then you'll hear the answer on the CD.

Someone would like to know what you do for a living. Use the suggestions we give you and choose the feminine or the masculine form. When you get to the fifth question, you can say what your real job is.

7 *Speaking exercise*
Answer as in the example. Then you'll hear the answer on the CD.

Again you're going to be asked about your job. This time your answer is more precise. Again you have to choose the feminine or masculine form.

8 *I write a mail.*
Write a mail home. Put the mail together from the text blocks that are given.

The genitive with proper nouns – Der Genitiv bei Eigennamen

Claudias Vater ist Controller. (= der Vater von Claudia)
Claudias Mutter ist Malerin. (= die Mutter von Claudia)

The genitive of proper nouns is formed as in English with *s*, but there is no apostrophe.
In speech people also use *von* + name: *die Mutter von Claudia.*

9 *How else can you say it?*
Imagine you're looking at some photos. You'll need these expressions. Transform the phrase
with von *into one with the genitive.*

Das ist die Mutter von Ralf.   – Das ist _____ _____ .
Das sind die Eltern von Maxi.   – Das sind _____ _____ .
Das ist der Bruder von Marie.   – Das ist _____ _____ .
Das ist die Tochter von Frau Lehmann.   – Das ist Frau _____ _____ .
Das ist der Sohn von Herrn Müller.   – Das ist Herrn _____ _____ .
Das ist das Auto von Birgit.   – Das ist _____ _____ .

10 *Match the right job names.*
We've selected a few jobs for you that didn't occur in the dialogues.

a. die Lehrerin

b. die Hausfrau

c. der Maurer

d. der Maler

e. der Frisör

f. die Verkäuferin

g. der Taxifahrer

_____   _____   _____

_____   _____   _____

Feminine job names – Feminine Berufsbezeichnungen

der Politiker, die Politiker	die Politiker**in**, die Politiker**innen**
der Student, die Studenten	die Student**in**, die Student**innen**
der Geschäftsmann, die Geschäftsleute	die Geschäfts**frau**, die Geschäfts**frauen**

The feminine form has the ending *-in*, plural *-innen*.
Careful: sometimes the vowel is changed into an
umlaut: *der Arzt, die Ärztin.*

11 *Fill in the missing forms.*
A lot of job titles for women end in -in (plural -innen). In the following table, either the male term or the female term is missing.

der	die	der	die
Regisseur		Informatiker	
	Malerin		Technikerin
Student		Lehrer	
Übersetzer			Schülerin
	Ingenieurin		Ärztin
	Frisörin		Taxifahrerin
Medien-Designer		Verkäufer	
Schornsteinfeger			Köchin
!!!	Hausfrau		Rechtsanwältin
Handwerker		Kfz-Mechaniker	
	Kellnerin		Redakteurin
Notarzt		Busfahrer	

12 *Revision*

Writing a personal mail

Hallo, … (+ Vorname)	*Hello/Hi …, (+ first name)*
Lieber / Liebe … (+ Vorname)	*Dear … (+ first name)*
Herzliche Grüße aus … (+ Stadt / Land)	*Best wishes from … (+ city/country)*
Bussi	*Kisses*

Jobs

arbeiten bei (Volkswagen) in (Wolfsburg) – er / sie arbeitet	*work for (Volkswagen) in (Wolfsburg)*
die Arbeit	*work*
das Büro, die Büros	*office*
das Gehalt, die Gehälter	*salary*
das Geschäft, die Geschäfte	*business, shop*
der Beruf, die Berufe	*job, profession*
der Job, die Jobs	*job*
der Stellenmarkt	*job market/situations vacant*
die Firma, die Firmen	*firm, company*
die Karriere, die Karrieren	*career*
die Stelle, die Stellen	*job/position*
verdienen – er / sie verdient, hat verdient	*earn*

13 *Listen carefully and repeat.*

Taxifahrer	Ich bin Taxifahrer	Ich bin Taxifahrerin.
Student	Ich bin Student.	Ich bin Studentin.
Schornsteinfeger	Ich bin Schornsteinfeger.	Ich bin Schornsteinfegerin.
Maurer	Ich bin Maurer.	
Verkäufer	Ich bin Verkäufer.	Ich bin Verkäuferin.
Übersetzer	Ich bin Übersetzer.	Ich bin Übersetzerin.

die Designerin	der Software-Entwickler
die Ärztin	der Informatiker
die Journalistin	der EDV-Kaufmann
die Stewardess	der Kfz-Mechaniker
die Architektin	der Ingenieur
die Sozialarbeiterin	der Maschinenbaumechaniker
die Bürokauffrau	der Polizist
die Bankkauffrau	der Elektroinstallateur
die Lehrerin	der Jounalist
die Rechtsanwältin	der Architekt

Cultural info (Textbook page 64)

Here are some job titles. You know all the terms already.
Careful: two jobs have only one form.

What's the job? Note down the masculine or feminine form too.

Statistics of dream jobs
The figures show the percentage of students interested in the following jobs:
You can listen to all the job titles in exercise 13 and repeat them.

Vocabulary

1. Write the sentence.

1. | Franz | | sein | | Übersetzerin / Übersetzer | _____

2. | Ulrike | | sein | | Arzt / Ärztin | _____

3. | Tommy | | sein | | Taxifahrerin / Taxifahrer | _____

4. | Steffi | | sein | | Schüler / Schülerin | _____

5. | Frau Sommer | | sein | | Maler / Malerin | _____

6. | Herr Gruber | | sein | | Verkäufer / Verkäuferin | _____

2. Write the masculine or feminine form of the job title.

1. der Politiker _____   4. die Verkäuferin _____

2. die Geschäftsfrau _____   5. der Student _____

3. der Arzt _____   6. der Ingenieur _____

Grammar

3. Write the genitive: Eva – Freund: Evas Freund.

1. | Stefan | | Vater | _____   4. | Anna | | Tante | _____

2. | Filip | | Schwester | _____   5. | Ulrike | | Freundin | _____

3. | Frau Meier | | Tochter | _____   6. | Katharina | | Familie | _____

4. Write the plural.

1. die Studentin _____   4. die Pilotin _____

2. die Ärztin _____   5. die Übersetzerin _____

3. die Freundin _____   6. die Politikerin _____

Listening Comprehension

(2|29)

5. First listen to the dialogue. Then listen again and mark with a cross.

1. Christine M. und Julia S.
☐ sind im Hotel.
☐ sind in der Firma.
☐ sind zu Hause.

3. Sie frühstücken
☐ um acht Uhr.
☐ um halb acht.
☐ um acht Uhr fünfzehn.

5. Sie haben einen Termin
☐ um neun Uhr.
☐ um halb neun.
☐ um zehn.

2. Es ist
☐ noch früh.
☐ Mittag.
☐ Abend.

4. Sie fahren
☐ eine halbe Stunde.
☐ eine dreiviertel Stunde.
☐ eine Stunde.

Check your answers in the key at the back of the book and then add up your points.

Total: | 1 – 15 Oh dear, that's a pity. Please do this unit again.
16 – 25 Not so bad. But even so, it would be a good idea to go over the dialogue and the grammar again.
26 – 29 Excellent. There's nothing to stop you carrying on.

In der Kantine – In the Canteen

The three business partners just have a quick lunch. They want to get back to work.
And anyway, they're going out to dinner together in the evening.
Over lunch they talk about new employees. You will learn expressions that you can use
to give and exchange information.
First of all have a look at the jobs you need to understand the text.

1 *Which jobs do you think are connected to the internet or intranet?*
Fill in ein *or* kein.

2 Conversation in the canteen

→ *First listen to the conversation between Frau Bruckner and Herr Kühne. They exchange*
information about their two companies. Listen to the conversation at least twice.

→ *If you need help, you can look in the vocabulary list of course.*

Kommen Sie.	*This way.*
Unser Tisch ist dahinten.	*Our table is over there.*
unser, unsere	*our*
Tisch (der), die Tische	*table*
dahinten	*over there*
Bitte nehmen Sie Platz.	*Have a seat, please.*
Wer bekommt den Fisch?	*Who is having the fish?*
bekommen – er/sie bekommt, hat bekommen	*get, receive*
Fisch (der), die Fische	*fish*
Gemüseteller (der), die Gemüseteller	*vegetable dish*
Sie haben den Fisch bestellt, nicht wahr?	*You ordered the fish, didn't you?*
bestellen – er/sie bestellt, hat bestellt	*order*
Wie viele Mitarbeiter haben Sie hier?	*How many employees do you have here?*
Wie viele?	*How many?*
Mitarbeiter (der), die Mitarbeiter	*employee*
im Moment	*at the moment*
Hier im Haus und im Lager zusammen.	*Here in this building and in the warehouse together.*
zusammen	*together*
Sie wissen ja, unsere Firma ist klein.	*You know our firm is small.*
wissen – du weißt, er/sie weiß, hat gewusst	*know*
Firma (die), die Firmen	*firm, company*
klein	*small, little*
Wir sind sechs Leute.	*There are six of us.*
Leute (die Plural)	*people*
Wir geben viel nach außen.	*We give a lot out (have a lot done outside).*

geben – du gibst, er / sie gibt, hat gegeben	*give*
nach außen	*outside*
Das tun wir auch.	*We do that too.*
tun – er / sie tut, hat getan	*do*
Wir suchen aber trotzdem Leute.	*We are looking for people nevertheless.*
trotzdem	*nevertheless*
Unsere Internet-Abteilung wächst.	*Our Internet department is growing.*
Internet-Abteilung (die), die -Abteilungen	*Internet department*
wachsen – er / sie wächst, ist gewachsen	*grow*
Unsere Homepage ist neu.	*Our homepage is new.*
Homepage (die), die Homepages	*homepage*
Seit Februar haben wir zwei	*Since February we have two female*
Internet-Redakteurinnen.	*Internet editors.*
seit	*since*
Februar (der)	*February*
Internet-Redakteurin (die),	*Internet editor*
die Internet-Redakteurinnen	
Service-Techniker (der), die Service-Techniker	*service technician*
informativ	*informative*
aktuell	*up to date*
Das ist auch wichtig.	*That's important too.*
Qualität (die)	*quality*
Schnelligkeit (die)	*speed*
Unterschied (der), die Unterschiede	*difference*
Preis (der), die Preise	*price*

3 *What's right? Mark with a cross.*
Sometimes there's more than one sentence that's right.

4 *Who says what?*
First read the sentences. Then listen and mark with a cross.

5 *There are some words missing here. Please complete.*
There are some important job words missing in the text.

6 *Speaking exercise*
A manager introduces his company. It's a big company, but you work in a small one.
Listen to what the manager says. Then talk about your company, using the prompts given.
Your sentences will give a profile of your firm.

7 *Chris Bruckner's notes*

Possessive articles – Possessivartikel *unser/Ihr*

		masculine	feminine	neuter
personal pronoun		er	sie	es
definite article	*nom. sing.*	der Tisch	die Firma	das Haus
indefinite article		ein Tisch	eine	ein
negative article		kein	keine	kein
possessive article		mein	meine	mein
		unser	unsere	unser
		Ihr	Ihre	Ihr
indefinite article	*acc. sing.*	einen Tisch	eine Firma	ein Haus
negative article		keinen	keine	kein
possessive article		meinen	meine	mein
		unseren	unsere	unser
		Ihren	Ihre	Ihr

You've seen this table before. We've just added the *unser-* and *Ihr-* forms.

The plural is quite easy. Plural = feminine singular:
die Tische – kein**e** Tische, mein**e**/dein**e**/unser**e**/Ihr**e** Tische

8 *Fill in the possessive article* unser-.
A young couple are talking. There seems to be some trouble here.

- Das ist mein Computer. ▶ Stimmt nicht, das ist _____ Computer.
- Das ist mein Auto. ▶ Stimmt nicht, das ist _____ Auto.
- Das ist meine Küche. ▶ Stimmt nicht, das ist _____ Küche.
- Das ist meine Wohnung. ▶ Was? Das ist _____ Wohnung.
- Das ist mein Erfolg. ▶ Was? Das ist _____ Erfolg.
- Das ist mein Handy. ▶ Was? Das ist _____ Handy.

9 *Put in the correct forms of* kein-.
Here's somebody who is not in need of anything, someone quite happy with their lot.

- Brauchst du ein Haus? ▶ Eigentlich nicht, ich brauche _____ Haus.
- Brauchst du ein Handy? ▶ Eigentlich nicht, ich brauche _____ Handy.
- Brauchst du eine Uhr? ▶ Eigentlich nicht, ich brauche _____ Uhr.
- Brauchst du ein Auto? ▶ Eigentlich nicht, ich brauche _____ Auto.
- Brauchst du einen Beruf? ▶ Eigentlich nicht, ich brauche _____ Beruf.
- Brauchst du Geld? ▶ Eigentlich nicht, ich brauche _____ Geld.

How much? / How many? – Wie viel? / Wie viele?

Wie viel Zeit	brauchen wir?
Wie viele Mitarbeiter	hat die Firma?

- *Wie viel* (= how much) is used, as in English, before collective terms like *Geld, Obst, Käse* etc, and in front of things that we can't count *(Milch, Zucker)*.
- *Wie viele* (= how many) is used in front of things that can be counted *(Leute, Äpfel)*.

10 *Put the nouns in the right group:*

Platz	Leute	Tisch	Mitarbeiter	Monat	Gemüseteller	Techniker

Firma	Haus	Lager	Zeit	Käse	Arbeit	Teller	Obst	Gast	Frage

Wie viel …   Geld   _____ _____ _____ _____ _____

Wie viele …   Reisen   _____ _____ _____ _____ _____ _____

_____ _____ _____ _____ _____ _____

11 *Fill in the missing forms.*

wissen

Singular	ich	_____	Plural	wir	wissen
	du	_____		ihr	wisst
	er / sie	_____		Sie / Sie	wissen

12 *Revision*

Exchanging information

Ich habe eine Frage./	*I have a question./*
Ich möchte Sie (et)was fragen.	*I'd like to ask you something.*
Wie viele … (Mitarbeiter haben Sie)?	*How many … (employees do you have)?*
Wir sind … (Mitarbeiter). Und Sie?	*We are … (employees). And you?*
Sie wissen ja, …	*As you know, …*
Wie viel … (Platz, Zeit, Geld)?	*How much … (room, time, money)?*
Wer …?	*Who …?*
Was kostet …?	*What does … cost?*
Wie groß ist … (die Firma)?	*How big is … (the company)?*
Wo ist … (die Kantine)?	*Where is … (the canteen)?*

Months

der Januar	*January*	der Juli	*July*
der Februar	*February*	der August	*August*
der März	*March*	der September	*September*
der April	*April*	der Oktober	*October*
der Mai	*May*	der November	*November*
der Juni	*June*	der Dezember	*December*

A diphthong consists of two letters spoken as one.

ei = e + i   ich weiß
au = a + u   das Auto
eu = e + u   der Euro
äu = ä + u   der Verkäufer

13 *First fill in the correct diphthong.*
Then listen and check, and repeat out loud.

das h____ßt	____er	P____se
ich w____ß	____n	R____se
nach ____ßen	H____ser	R____m
gl____ch	gl____ben	Schornst____nfeger
____tomat	H____s(frau)	St____
____stralien	Kl____nstadt	w____t
____fzug	m____nen	zu H____se
D____tschland		

Cultural info (Textbook page 68)

Würste – Sausages
People eat sausage in Germany at any time of the day, for breakfast, for lunch or supper.
It's eaten hot or cold.
What's special about sausage is that it tastes quite different in different parts of the
country, in northern or southern Germany, in east or west Germany. It's also worth men-
tioning that each region is especially proud of its local sausage specialities and won't
have anything said against them.

Match the names to the photos.
Now write down the city or federal state that is part of the name.

Federal states:
There are 16 federal states. The cities of Berlin, Hamburg and Bremen are states as well.

Vocabulary

1. Mark the right translation with a cross.

1. der Mitarbeiter
☐ employer
☐ employee
☐ boss

2. die Leute
☐ men
☐ editors
☐ people

3. Sie wissen ja …
☐ This way …
☐ It is growing.
☐ You know …

4. Bitte nehmen Sie Platz.
☐ Have a seat, please.
☐ We do that, too.
☐ Please have this place.

5. Das gefällt mir gut.
☐ That looks good to me.
☐ I like that.
☐ We do that too.

6. seit Februar
☐ during February
☐ since February
☐ for February

Grammar

2. Fill in the ending. (m = masculine, f = feminine, n = neuter)

1. Unser____ Firma (f) ist nicht groß.

2. Haben Sie unser____ Homepage (f) schon gesehen?

3. Wir besichtigen jetzt unser____ Haus (n).

4. Wie finden Sie mein____ Kaffee (m)?

5. Das ist unser____ Internet-Abteilung (f).

6. Mögen Sie Ihr____ Beruf (m)?

3. Fill in wissen *or* kennen.

1. Du _____ ja, Onkel Franz kommt.

2. _____ du Martin schon?

3. _____ Sie, wie es Frau Neubert geht?

4. Frau Neubert _____ ich nicht.

5. _____ du, wo Neuschwanstein liegt?

6. Das _____ ich nicht.

4. Fill in Wie viel? *or* Wie viele?

1. _____ Großstädte gibt es in Deutschland?

2. _____ Studenten studieren in Köln?

3. _____ Geld brauche ich pro Semester?

4. _____ Stunden dauert die Stadtrundfahrt?

5. _____ kostet das?

6. _____ Fahrkarten brauchen wir?

Check your answers in the key at the back of the book and then add up your points.

Total:	1 – 13	Before you carry on, you really should do this unit again.
	14 – 20	Quite good, but not perfect yet. Please go over the dialogue and the grammar again.
	21 – 24	Very good. You can carry straight on.

Im Supermarkt – At the Supermarket

The visit to Claudia's parents didn't last that long. There's still enough time to do something else. Claudia and Robert first go shopping. Then they want to go into town. You'll learn some important shopping expressions, and weights and measures.

1 *Here's a selection of drinks. What are the drinks called? Please match.*
Then listen and repeat.

Wein (der), die Weine	*wine*
Bier (das), die Biere	*beer*
Mineralwasser (das)	*mineral water*
Sekt (der)	*champagne, sparkling wine*
Milch (die)	*milk*
Orangensaft (der) (die Orange + der Saft)	*orange juice*
Apfelsaft (der) (der Apfel + der Saft)	*apple juice*

2 Claudia and Robert in the supermarkt
→ *Now listen to the dialogue. Claudia and Robert are working out what they need.*
   Listen to the dialogue at least twice.
→ *If you need some support, you can look up the vocabulary again.*

Supermarkt (der), die Supermärkte	*supermarket*
Nimm einen Wagen.	*Take a trolley.*
Wagen (der), die Wagen	*trolley*
Wir kaufen zuerst die Getränke.	*We'll buy the drinks first.*
kaufen – er / sie kauft, hat gekauft	*buy*
zuerst	*first (of all)*
Getränk (das), die Getränke	*drink*
Saft (der), die Säfte	*juice*
Drei Flaschen Mineralwasser.	*Three bottles of mineral water.*
Flasche (die), die Flaschen	*bottle*
Schorle (die), die Schorlen	*mixed drink with mineral water*
Apfelschorle (die), die Apfelschorlen	*apple juice mixed with mineral water*
Nicht so viel. Der bleibt nur übrig.	*Not so much. It only gets left over.*
übrig bleiben – er / sie bleibt übrig, ist übrig geblieben	*be/get left (over)*
Wie teuer ist der Wein?	*How expensive is the wine?*
teuer	*expensive*
Das ist Wein aus Franken.	*That's wine from Franconia.*
Der ist aber gut. Da bin ich Spezialist.	*It's a good one. I'm a specialist.*
Spezialist (der), die Spezialisten	*specialist*
Wie viel Wurst brauchen wir?	*How much sausage do we need?*
Nimm 200 Gramm.	*Take 200 grammes.*

Gramm (das) (= g)	*gramme*
Das ist genug.	*That's enough.*
Weintraube (die), die Weintrauben	*grape*
Kirsche (die), die Kirschen	*cherry*
Was ist los?	*What's the matter?*
Warum bleibst du stehen?	*Why are you stopping?*
Warum?	*Why?*
stehen bleiben – er/sie bleibt stehen, ist stehen geblieben	*stop, stand still*
Ich habe was vergessen.	*I've forgotten something.*
vergessen – du vergisst, er/sie vergisst, hat vergessen	*forget*
Zwiebel (die), die Zwiebeln	*onion*
Bleib hier!	*Stay here!*
bleiben – er/sie bleibt, ist geblieben	*stay, remain*
Kilo(gramm) (das) (= kg)	*kilo(gramme)*
Pfund (das) (= Pf.)	*pound*
genau	*exact(ly), right*

3 *Please complete.*
When you go shopping, you say of course how much of something you want. For that you need a few important expressions of quantity.

Did you notice? Expressions of quantity have no plural: 3 Kilo, 5 Pfund, 100 Gramm.

4 *Was wächst in Deutschland?*
We're at the market. Have a look at the fruit. What fruit comes from Germany, what from abroad? Note down what grows in Germany.
Markets are popular because the produce farmers sell is always fresh.

5 *What belongs where? Please sort.*

das Obst	*fruit*
die Südfrüchte (Pl)	*tropical fruit*
das Gemüse	*vegetables*
das Getränk, die Getränke	*drink(s)*

6 *What do the guests reply?*
There are always lots of people at a party. The hosts of course try to satisfy their guests' wishes so that they feel happy and enjoy themselves. Mark the answer that fits. Then listen to the question and answer.

7 *In the supermarket – Please reply.*
You're in a supermarket with a friend. Tell him or her what you need. Put the bits of the sentence in the right order.

Imperative / Imperativ

	du	ihr	Sie
kommen	Komm!	Kommt!	Kommen Sie!
kaufen	Kauf!	Kauft!	Kaufen Sie!
nehmen	Nimm!	Nehmt!	Nehmen Sie!
geben	Gib!	Gebt!	Geben Sie!
sehen	Sieh!	Seht!	Sehen Sie!

The formation of the imperative is quite easy. You just derive the forms from the present tense:

du kommst ẛt→ Komm!   ihr nehmt → Nehmt!   Sie kommen → Kommen Sie!
du nimmst ẛt→ Nimm!   ihr kommt → Kommt!   Sie nehmen → Nehmen Sie!

Note that with the *Sie*-form you need the personal pronoun as well.

8 *Put in the imperative form.*

Peter, _____ (nehmen) mal den Wagen.

Peter und Alex, _____ (kommen) jetzt!

Peter, _____ (geben) mir mal die Milch, bitte.

Peter und Alex, _____ (vergessen) die Fahrkarten nicht.

Peter, _____ (sehen) mal, gefällt dir meine Homepage?

Peter, _____ (kommen) mal schnell.

Peter und Alex, _____ (kaufen) nicht so viel.

Peter und Alex, _____ (nehmen) die Taschen.

9 *Fill in what mustn't be forgotten.*

Vergiss _____ nicht! (Tasche)   _____ nicht! (Flaschen)

_____ nicht! (Geld)   _____ nicht! (Käse)

_____ nicht! (Mineralwasser)   _____ nicht! (Handy)

_____ nicht! (Weintrauben)   _____ nicht! (Nummer)

_____ nicht! (Tüte)

Questions with *Welcher / Welche / Welches*? – Fragen mit *Welcher / Welche / Welches*?

	masculine	feminine	neuter
	der Wein	**die** Wurst	**das** Bier
nom. sing	Welch**er** Wein	Welche Wurst	Welch**es** Bier
acc. sing	Welch**en** Wein	Welche Wurst	Welch**es** Bier

When you are shopping, there is always a selection of things to buy. You have to decide whether to buy red or white wine, which sort of sausage or beer. You ask a question with the question word *Welch-*. The ending is determined by the following noun and its case.

- **Welcher** Wein kommt aus Franken?
- **Welchen** Wein nehmen wir? Den Rotwein oder den Weißwein?

10 *Supply the right form of* Welch-... .

Nimm doch ein paar Flaschen Wein!   –   _____ Wein?

Kauf doch die Weintrauben!   –   _____ Weintrauben?

Nimm doch den Käse!   –   _____ Käse?

Kauf doch etwas Wurst!   –   _____ Wurst?

Nimm doch ein paar Stück Kuchen!   –   _____ Kuchen?

Kauf doch Kartoffeln!   –   _____ Kartoffeln?

11 *Revision*

Going shopping

einkaufen gehen	*going shopping*
Wie viel Geld haben wir?	*How much money do we have?*
Was brauchen wir?	*What do we need?*
Nimm … / Nimm doch …	*Take …*
Kauf …	*Buy …*
Gib mir mal eine Tüte.	*Give me a bag, will you?*
Das ist genug.	*That's enough.*
Was ist mit … (Weintrauben …)?	*What about … (grapes …)?*
Haben wir genug …?	*Do we have enough …?*
Das reicht. / Das ist alles.	*That's enough. / That's all.*
Ich habe (et)was vergessen.	*I've forgotten something.*

Currency, weights and measures

der Euro	*euro*	Stück (das)	*piece*
(= 100 Cent)	*(= 100 cents)*	(1 Stück Kuchen)	*(1 piece of cake)*
der Cent	*cent*	die Tüte, die Tüten	*bag*
m = der Meter	*metre*	die Packung,	*packet*
km = der Kilometer	*kilometre*	die Packungen	
m² = der Quadratmeter	*square metre*	die Flasche,	*bottle*
kg = das Kilo(gramm)	*kilogramme*	die Flaschen	
g = das Gramm	*gramme*	der Becher,	*carton*
Pf. = das Pfund	*pound*	die Becher	
l = der Liter	*litre*	(ein Becher Jogurt)	

12 *Listen and repeat.*

Hol doch den Wagen.
Nimm auch Orangensaft.
Nimm zwei Flaschen.
Bleib hier.

Bleib stehen.
Kauf doch den Wein.
Iss mehr Obst.

13 sch, sp *and* st.
Listen and underline the sound that is pronounced sch.

Example: Stunde, Flasche

spät	Spanisch	Englisch	Stadt
Stück	falsch	Unterschied	Straße
August	Stelle	Supermarkt	Spezialist
Spanien	Gespräch	Schule	schnell

Cultural info (Textbook page 72)

These short conversations are all about food. Listen closely and note down the correct picture.

And now read this info on an important food item:

The potato is Europe's top food and goes from strength to strength. Worldwide, rice is the most important food, but in Europe it's second, after the potato. Even though it's not so very long ago that the potato was introduced into Europe – in about 1500 when the conquistador Francisco Pizarro brought the knobbly plant back from South America.

For about 200 years it led a fairly secluded life in the pleasure gardens of princes and was regarded as an exotic ornamental plant. Till Frederick II of Prussia, Frederick the Great that is, discovered it and then propagated it, resorting to a cunning ruse.
In the beginning the potato was only used as a food for soldiers, and little known. But then the King gave the order to plant fields of potatoes and have them closely guarded. That of course awakened the peasants' curiosity. They started wondering what it was that was so valuable that it had to be guarded like this. They procured the forbidden fruit by the sackful and planted their own fields with it too. Then the townsfolk had to be won over, too. Frederick went about it in a crafty way. He had potatoes served up when he was visiting small towns, and so gradually people began to develop a taste for them. Potatoes are also called „Erdäpfel" (earth apples), because the edible part of the plant is at the end of the roots hidden away in the earth. And they are harvested from the soil. The word „Kartoffel" is derived from Tartuffo, meaning truffle, because it is similar to the truffle in appearance. Of course this is a bit of a fraud really, a case of mistaken identity.

Cookery books have pages and pages of potato recipes. There are three main ways of preparing them.

Vocabulary

1. *Mark the right translation with a cross.*

1. Was brauchen wir denn?
- ☐ How much do we need?
- ☐ What do we need?
- ☐ What about drinks?

2. Bleib hier!
- ☐ Buy this.
- ☐ Stay here.
- ☐ Take this here.

3. Das ist genug.
- ☐ That's good.
- ☐ That's exactly right.
- ☐ That's enough.

4. Was ist los?
- ☐ What's loose?
- ☐ What did you order?
- ☐ What's the matter?

5. Warte hier.
- ☐ This way.
- ☐ Wait here.
- ☐ How much is this here?

6. Ich habe was vergessen.
- ☐ I've forgotten something.
- ☐ I have bought something.
- ☐ I'll tell you what.

2. *Singular and / or plural? Mark with a cross.*
Example: das Geld (= Singular); die Tüten (= Plural);
der Becher, die Becher (= Singular + Plural)

	1. Zwiebeln	2. Wurst	3. Getränke	4. Käse	5. Wagen	6. Wein	7. Saft	8. Kirschen	9. Brötchen	10. Flaschen
Singular	☐	☐	☐	☐	☐	☐	☐	☐	☐	☐
Plural	☐	☐	☐	☐	☐	☐	☐	☐	☐	☐
Singular + Plural	☐	☐	☐	☐	☐	☐	☐	☐	☐	☐

Grammar

3. *Fill in the imperative singular – the* du-*form in sentences 1–4, and the polite form in sentences 5–10.*

1. _____ (vergessen) nichts!
2. _____ (kommen) schnell!
3. _____ (machen) Platz!
4. _____ (sehen) mal, da ist ein Platz frei!
5. _____ (vergessen) Sie nichts!
6. _____ (kommen) Sie schnell.
7. _____ (nehmen) Sie bitte Platz.
8. _____ (sprechen) Sie bitte.
9. _____ (hören) Sie den Text.
10. _____ (warten) Sie hier.

4. *Fill in* Welcher / Welche / Welches.

Was haben Sie gesagt?
1. _____ Text?
2. _____ Straße?
3. _____ S-Bahn?
4. _____ Auto?
5. _____ Wort?
6. _____ Beruf?
7. _____ Schule?
8. _____ Firma?

Check your answers in the key at the back of the book and then add up your points.

Total:
- 1 – 17   It would be a good idea to do this unit again straightaway.
- 18 – 29   Pretty good. But it wouldn't hurt to go over the dialogue and the grammar again.
- 30 – 34   Excellent. If you like, you could go over the vocabulary again, otherwise you can carry straight on.

Was ist mit Eis? – What about ice-cream?

There are plastic bags at the check-out for packing your shopping in. There are usually sweets and ice-cream on offer here too. And then Robert has an important question …
You'll learn what to say when you are for or against something, and when you want somebody to do something.

1 *Mix a drink. Here are the ingredients.*

There are no end of ways to mix a drink. When you're thirsty it's nice to drink a spritzer, a drink made by mixing something with mineral water.
Shandy (= Radler) is a speciality in southern Germany. There they mix beer and lemonade. That's a real thirst-quencher.
If you fancy something special, order an iced coffee – coffee served cold with ice cream.

2 Robert, Claudia and Katrin
→ *Listen to the conversation at least twice.*
→ *If you need help, here's the vocabulary list.*

2|41

Eis (das)	ice(-cream)
Sieh mal die Schlange!	Just look at the queue.
Nicht so schlimm!	Never mind.
Das geht schnell.	It won't take long.
Gib mal zwei Tüten.	Give me two plastic bags.
Kauf drei Packungen.	Buy three packets.
Becher (der), die Becher	carton
Packung (die), die Packungen	packet
Oder magst du lieber Kuchen?	Or do you prefer cake?
Kuchen (der), die Kuchen	cake
Der Kuchen im Supermarkt schmeckt nicht.	Supermarket cake doesn't taste very good.
schmecken – er / sie schmeckt, hat geschmeckt	taste
So, und jetzt fahren wir schnell nach Hause und dann in die Stadt.	Right, we'll quickly go home and then into town.
Hast du was dagegen?	Do you mind?
dagegen – dafür	contra – pro
Was heißt das?	What do you mean?
Ich rufe sie jetzt an …	I'll phone her …
… dann treffen wir sie zu Hause …	… then we'll meet her at home …
treffen – du triffst, er / sie trifft, hat getroffen	meet
Na gut, dann ruf gleich an.	Go on then, phone.
Nimm mal die Tüten, die sind so schwer.	Take the bags, they're so heavy.
schwer	heavy

107

3 *There's some information missing here. Please complete.*
Then listen to the text again and compare.

 4 *Who is who? First listen to the dialogues.*
Who is speaking in dialogue 1, who in dialogue 2? What do the people look like? Mark with a cross.

5 *2 words or 1 word – Present or perfect*

6 *Phone! Write the imperatives.*
Imperatives always sound much more friendly with bitte.
Imperatives have more force if you use doch *in your request.*

 7 *Speaking exercise*
Listen and answer using the prompts.

8 *My brother Alex*
Tell a story. There are some prompts to help you. 5 or 6 sentences are enough.
There's a model answer in the key.

9 lieber *and* besser *are comparatives. You can compare two things with* als.
am liebsten / am besten *are superlatives.*

The comparative has the ending *-er: schön**er**, lieb**er**, bess**er***.
The superlative is made up of *am* + the ending *-sten*.

Ich esse **gern** Kuchen.   I like eating cake.
Ich esse Eis **lieber als** Kuchen.   I prefer eating ice cream to cake.
Ich esse **am liebsten** Eis.   I like eating ice cream best.

Fill in the appropriate words.

gern gut	Was trinkst du _____ ?	Margit trinkt _____ Saft.	Geht's dir wieder _____ ?
lieber (als) besser (als)	Möchtest du _____ Bier?	Magst du Wein _____ _____ Schorle? _____ Schorle.	Ja, _____ _____ gestern.
am liebsten am besten	Alex trinkt Bier _____ _____ .	_____ _____ trinke ich Weinschorle.	_____ _____ geht's mir morgens.

108

Demonstrative pronouns – Demonstrativpronomen: *der/die/das*

personal pronoun		er	sie	es
definite articles		**Der/Dieser Wein,**	**Die/Diese Schorle,**	**Das/Dieses Eis,**
demonstrative pronoun	*nom.*	**der** ist gut.	**die** schmeckt nicht.	**das** schmeckt.
	acc.	**den** mag ich nicht.	**die** mag ich nicht.	**das** mag ich.

- The demonstrative pronouns *der, die, das* are used instead of a definite article plus noun. The demonstrative pronoun is used when the noun has already been mentioned. In English we use a personal pronoun (e.g. *it*).
- The demonstrative pronouns *dieser, diese, dieses* are used to indicate somebody or something more precisely. They have the same ending as *der, die, das*:
  Dieser *Weißwein ist gut.*   **This** *white wine is good.*
  Diese *Frau hat Ideen.*   **This** *woman has good ideas.*

10 *The demonstrative pronouns are missing here. Look at the nouns, and complete.*

Da ist Obst.   _____ brauchen wir. (das Obst)

Dahinten sind Kartoffeln.   _____ brauchen wir. (die Kartoffeln)

Wo ist Gemüse?   _____ ist dahinten rechts. (das Gemüse)

Hast du schon Eis?   _____ nehmen wir. (das Eis)

Da ist Wein.   _____ ist aus Franken. (der Wein)

Trinkst du Schorle?   _____ mag ich nicht. (die Schorle)

Separable Verbs – Trennbare Verben: *an/rufen*

an/rufen					
Singular	ich	rufe … an	Plural	wir	rufen … an
	du	rufst … an		ihr	ruft … an
	er/sie	ruft … an		sie/Sie	rufen … an

- German has verbs with a prefix. From now on we're going to make a special note of all verbs that have a separable prefix. In previous units we had *zurück/fliegen – er/sie fliegt zurück*. The prefix is separated from the rest of the verb and put at the end of the sentence:

  an/rufen   *Ich* **rufe** *morgen* **an.** (= Präsens)
                         Ruf *bitte* **an!** (= Imperativ)
  zurück/fliegen   *Wann* **fliegen** *Sie* **zurück?**
  ein/laden   *Wen* **ladet** *ihr* **ein?**

- The prefix is not separated off in the perfect:
  Rufst du Petra an?
  Ich habe sie schon **angerufen**.

11 *You ask the questions.*

| morgen | zurückfliegen | Sie |

Fliegen Sie morgen zurück?

| Frau Fritz | zu Hause | anrufen | Sie |

_____ ?

| einladen | du | auch Familie Wegner |

_____ ?

| haben | einladen | du | Patrick |

_____ ?

Word order II – Satzstellung II

I	II	I	II		
Ich	fahre	jetzt nach Hause.	Jetzt	fahre	ich nach Hause.
Ich	fahre	morgen in die Stadt.	In die Stadt	fahre	ich morgen.

Often an element other than the subject is placed at the beginning of the sentence. It depends on what element is important in the sentence and in the text.

But note: the verb is *always* in second position.

12 *Finish the sentence.*

Ich rufe Karsten morgen an.   – Morgen _____

Ich habe heute Abend Zeit.   – Heute Abend _____

Wir machen jetzt eine Firmenbesichtigung.   – Jetzt _____

Das Informationszentrum ist da links.   – Da links _____

Wir gehen dann ins Konferenzzimmer.   – Dann _____

Wir essen um zwölf.   – Um zwölf _____

13 *Say the opposite, and contradict.*

Ich bin dafür.   ↔ Ich bin _____   Das stimmt.   ↔ _____

Das ist richtig.   ↔ _____   Ich gehe nach Hause. ↔ _____

Da haben Sie recht. ↔ _____   Ich rufe Peter an. ↔ _____

14 *Revision*

Confirming / contradicting something

Hast du was dagegen?	*Do you mind?*
Ich bin dagegen / dafür.	*I'm against / for it.*
Was heißt das?	*What does that mean?*
Das ist richtig / nicht richtig / falsch.	*That's right / not right / wrong.*
Das stimmt / stimmt nicht.	*That's right / not right.*
Nein. – Doch. – Natürlich.	*No. – Yes. – Of course.*
Du hast recht / nicht recht.	*You're right / not right.*
Ja, warum nicht?	*Yes, why not?*

ß (Eszett)

All learners are puzzled by this letter. If it's any consolation, computers all over the world have trouble with it, too – because it's a letter that only exists in German.

The rule is this:
After a short vowel we write ss: *Wasser, essen, wissen*
After a long vowel or a diphthong we write ß: *zu Fuß, ich weiß*

15 *Fill in ss or ß.*
Here are some words and sentences where we've left out ß and ss. Listen carefully to how the words are spoken and complete the words.

wi_____en   das Wa_____er   zu Fu_____

Das wei_____ ich nicht.   die Gro_____stadt   die Stra_____e

Wir wi_____en nichts.   die Gro_____mutter   Ru_____land

Was i_____t du?   kla_____e   Sie vergi_____t viel.

Wir e_____en nur Obst.   der Gro_____vater   Ich habe was verge_____en.

das E_____en   der Spa_____

In Switzerland they only use ss, so they make no distinction between ss and ß.

16 *ß, ss, s or z?*

Wie i_____t der Prei_____?

Da_____wei_____ ich nicht.

Wir wi_____en nicht_____.

Wa_____ i_____t lo_____?

Hast du wa_____ verge_____en?

_____aft und Wa_____er, Wur_____t und _____wiebeln.

Ob_____t und Gemü_____e.

Cultural info (Textbook page 76)

People in Germany talk a lot about healthy eating and the fact that fruit and vegetables should be top of the menu.
Italian cuisine is also recommended as being very good for you.

Listen to and read the two dialogues. Which do you like better?

Then repeat your text.

111

Vocabulary

1. *Match the right translations. There are again some important expressions, and short sentences in the texts, phrases that will always come in useful.*

1. (d) Was ist mit Obst?   a That tastes good.
2. ( ) Sieh mal …   b Would you prefer ice cream?
3. ( ) Magst du lieber Eis?   c OK.
4. ( ) Am liebsten Kuchen.   d What about fruit?
5. ( ) Der schmeckt gut.   e What does that mean?
6. ( ) Nicht so schlimm!   f Never mind.
7. ( ) Na gut.   g I'd prefer cake.
8. ( ) Hast du was dagegen?   h Just look …
9. ( ) Was heißt das?   i Do you mind?

2. *Write the opposite.*

1. gut _____   4. richtig _____
2. links _____   5. billig _____
3. dafür _____   6. klein _____

Grammar

3. *The articles and pronouns are missing here.*

1. ____ Kuchen   – ____ ist gut.   4. ____ Reise   – ____ machen wir.
2. ____ Obst   – ____ ist heute teuer.   5. ____ Termin   – ____ haben wir.
3. ____ Weißwein – ____ kaufen wir.

4. *What is the sentence?*

1. | Martin | anrufen | Alexander | _____
2. | Petra | Familie Müller | einladen | _____
3. | Herr Wagner | nach Brüssel | zurückfliegen | _____
4. | Herr Schade | anrufen | die Schule | _____

Listening Comprehension

(2|51)

5. *Two tourists are touring a city. They've got heavy backpacks. They stop outside a supermarket. Mark the sentences that are correct statements.*

1. ☐ Frank und Walter sind im Supermarkt.   4. ☐ Er möchte drei Flaschen Bier holen.
2. ☐ Walter hat Durst.   5. ☐ Frank mag kein Bier.
3. ☐ Es ist sehr warm.   6. ☐ Walter holt 2 Flaschen Limo.

Check your answers in the key at the back of the book and then add up your points.

Total: | 1 – 16 | Oh dear, that's a pity. Please do this unit again.
            | 17 – 26 | Not so bad. But even so, it would be a good idea to go over the dialogues and the grammar again.
            | 27 – 31 | Excellent. There's nothing to stop you carrying on.

Wo bist du denn? – Where are you?

Robert finds Katrin, Claudia's sister, very attractive. He'd like to see her again. In fact, when he phones her, he is actually a bit nervous.

But before we listen to the dialogue, let's have a look at some vocabulary that you'll find useful in this lesson. You'll be learning how to ask the way and find out about places.

1 *Please match.*

am Fluss entlang	*along the river*
über die Brücke	*over the bridge*
zur Bank	*to the bank*
zum Bahnhof	*to the station*
am Sportplatz vorbei	*past the sports ground*
an der Ampel	*at the traffic lights*

2 Robert phones Katrin

→ *Now listen to how Robert and Katrin arrange to meet. Listen to the conversation at least twice.*

→ *You can find support, if you need it, as always in the vocabulary list.*

Kommst du mit?	*Are you coming (with us)?*
mit / kommen – er / sie kommt mit, ist mitgekommen	*come (with somebody)*
Na, bei Claudia zu Hause.	*At Claudia's place.*
Ich war noch nicht bei ihr.	*I've not been to her place.*
bei + Dativ	*at + dative*
Ich erkläre dir den Weg.	*I'll explain / tell you the way.*
erklären – er / sie erklärt, hat erklärt	*Explain, tell*
Das ist ganz einfach …	*It's quite easy / simple …*
einfach	*easy, simple*
Ich komme mit dem Auto.	*I'm coming by ("with the") car.*
mit + Dativ	*with + dative*
Schieß los!	*Go ahead.*
Du fährst in Richtung Stadt.	*You drive towards / in the direction of town.*
Richtung (die), die Richtungen	*direction*
Circa fünf Kilometer.	*About five kilometres.*
Dann kommt eine Kreuzung mit Ampel.	*Then there's a junction with traffic lights.*
Kreuzung (die), die Kreuzungen	*junction, crossroads*
Ampel (die), die Ampeln	*(set of) traffic lights*
Da fährst du nach rechts.	*There you turn right.*
Was hast du gesagt?	*What did you say?*
Nach links in die Oranienburger Straße?	*Left into Oranienburger Street?*

Du fährst um den Platz herum und geradeaus weiter.	*You drive round the square and straight on.*
um … herum	*round*
Dann fährst du die dritte Straße nach links.	*Then you take the third street on the left.*
gleich rechts	*immediately on the right*
Wir sind hier im dritten Stock.	*We're here on the third floor.*
Stock (der)	*floor, storey*
Ich habe alles notiert.	*I've noted all that.*
Ich fahre sofort los.	*I'll set off straightaway.*
los / fahren – du fährst los, er / sie fährt los, ist losgefahren	*set off, drive off, leave*

3 *Now read the following summary.*
Which sentences are incorrect? Mark what is not right with a cross.

4 *Find 7 words (exercise 4).*
The words are places and destinations in town. First read the directions:

an (der Ampel, Kreuzung) /	*at (the traffic lights, crossroads) /*
am … (Bahnhof)	*at the … (station)*
zum / zur … (Museum / Kirche)	*to the … (museum / church)*
um … (den Platz) herum	*around … (the square)*
an / am … (Fluss / der Straße) entlang	*along the … (river / road)*
Sie kommen direkt zum …(Schloss) / zur … (Schule)	*That'll take you straight to the … (castle / school)*

5 *Note down the seven letters from the puzzle in exercise 4.*
What is the word they make?

6 *Listen.*
Two colleagues at work are talking about a weekend trip to a small town. Follow the route.

7 *Speaking exercise*
The people ask you the way. You know where the places are. Listen to the question. Read the prompts and use them in your answer.

8 *Put the sentences in the right order and write the text.*

9 *Robert's diary*
Mark the forms in the perfect.

Personal pronouns: dative – Personalpronomen: Dativ

Singular	ich	Du erklärst	**mir**	den Weg.
	du	Ich erkläre	**dir**	
	er / sie		**ihm / ihr**	
Plural	wir	Du erklärst	**uns**	den Weg.
	ihr	Ich erkläre	**euch**	
	sie / Sie		**ihnen / Ihnen**	

- Some verbs take the dative:

  gehen: *Wie geht's dir/euch/Ihnen?*   **geben:** *Gib mir mal die Karte.*
  gefallen: *Wie gefällt Ihnen das Restaurant?*   **sagen:** *Sag mir die Adresse.*
  schmecken: *Wie schmeckt Ihnen das Essen?*   **nehmen:** *Nimm dir das Geld.*

- A number of verbs have both a dative and an accusative object. The dative object comes first, then the accusative object:
  *Du erklärst **mir den Weg.***

- The dative is often a person: *mir*, the accusative a thing: *den Weg*.

- Most verbs take the accusative. There are only a few that also take the dative. It's easy to remember them.

10 *Fill in the personal pronoun in the right case.*

Ich erkläre _____ (du) den Weg.

Schmeckt _____ (Sie) der Kuchen?

Geben Sie _____ (ich) bitte die Karte?

Du hast _____ (wir) nichts gesagt.

Wie geht es _____ (sie – Sg.)?

_____ (ihr) gefällt die Wohnung sehr, nicht wahr?

Prepositions – Präpositionen: *am / an der – im / in der – zum / zur*

	masculine	feminine	neuter
Wo bist du?	**am**	**an der**	**am**
	Bahnhof	Bank	Hotel
	Kindergarten	Schule	Museum
	Supermarkt	Kirche	Restaurant
Wo bist du?	**im**	**in der**	**im**
	Bahnhof	Bank	Hotel
	Kindergarten	Schule	Museum
	Supermarkt	Kirche	Restaurant

	masculine	feminine	neuter
Wohin gehst / fährst du?	**zum**	**zur**	**zum**
	Bahnhof	Bank	Hotel
	Kindergarten	Schule	Museum
	Supermarkt	Kirche	Restaurant
	Sportplatz	Haltestelle	

- *an* and *in* take the dative with expressions of fixed place in answers to the question *Wo?* (am = an dem; im = in dem)
- *zu* always takes the dative. (zum = zu dem; zur = zu der)

11 *This exercise is about using the right case. Use the preposition in the bracket and put in the preposition + article.*

Wo bist du? – ____ ____ Post. (an)   Wo bist du? – ____ Restaurant. (in)
Wo bist du? – ____ ____ Bank. (in)   Wo bist du? – ____ ____ Schule. (in)
Wo bist du? – ____ Hotel. (an)   Wo bist du? – ____ Bahnhof. (an)

12 *Now you are not at a particular place, but you are going there. Fill in zu + article.*

Wohin gehst du? – _____ Bahnhof.   Wohin gehst du? – _____ Schule.
Wohin fährst du? – _____ Bank.   Wohin fährst du? – _____ Museum.
Wohin fährst du? – _____ Supermarkt.   Wohin gehst du? – _____ Post.

Ordinal numbers – Ordinalzahlen

1	eins	→	der / die **erste**	die erste Straße
2	zwei	→	der / die **zweite**	die zweite Straße
3	drei	→	der / die **dritte**	die dritte Straße

Ordinal numbers are used, as in English, with the definite article. The definite article is declined.

13 *Revision*

Asking the way and giving directions

Entschuldigung, wie komme ich zum / zur … (Bahnhof / Post)?	*Excuse me, how do I get to the …* *(station / post office)?*
Fahren Sie (mit dem Bus / mit der Bahn bis … (Friedrichstraße).	*Take (the bus / train) as far as …* *(Friedrichstraße)*
Gehen Sie hier nach rechts.	*Turn right here.*
nach (links / Erlangen)	*(to the) left*
dann geradeaus	*then straight on*
bis zum (Marktplatz) / zur (Ampel)	*as far as the (marketplace / traffic lights)*
ungefähr / circa … (einen Kilometer, 300 Meter)	*about … (a kilometre, 300 metres)*

14 *Listen and repeat.*

der Bahnhof	zum Bahnhof
links	nach links
die Ampel	an der Ampel
die Kirche	zur Kirche
das Museum	zum Museum
der Platz	um den Platz herum
die Brücke	über die Brücke
der Fluss	am Fluss entlang
der Supermarkt	am Supermarkt vorbei
die Straße	die zweite Straße
ungefähr	ungefähr einen Kilometer
circa	circa 500 Meter

15 *Listen and repeat.*

zur Post	Entschuldigung, wie komme ich zur Post?
nach rechts	Fahren Sie hier nach rechts.
an der Kreuzung	Dann an der Kreuzung nach links.
zum Marktplatz	Fahren Sie bis zum Marktplatz.
nach links	Am Marktplatz nach links.
über die Brücke	Dann kommen Sie über eine Brücke.
am Fluss entlang	Fahren Sie links am Fluss entlang.
am Supermarkt vorbei	Fahren Sie am Supermarkt vorbei.
an einen Platz	Dann kommen Sie an einen Platz.
Da ist die Post.	

Cultural info (Textbook page 80)

People taking a taxi on their own like to sit on the passenger seat in the front. That makes it easier to give directions or talk to the taxi driver.

Now you're a taxi driver and have a passenger in your car. You're driving and he's telling you the way.
Listen and follow the route on the map.
Read the text to check.

Vocabulary

1. Mark the correct translation with a cross.

1. ganz einfach
□ immediately on the right
□ quite easy
□ go ahead

2. um den Platz herum
□ over the crossroads
□ round the square
□ straight on

3. die dritte Straße rechts
□ the second street on the right
□ the second street on the left
□ the third street on the right

4. am Hotel vorbei
□ at the hotel
□ as far as the hotel
□ past the hotel

5. bis zur Kirche
□ as far as the church
□ by the church
□ towards the church

6. geradeaus zum Supermarkt
□ left at the supermarket
□ left to the supermarket
□ straight on to the supermarket

2. Here are some important expressions. Match the translations.

1. Kommst du mit?
2. Wo bist du denn?
3. In Richtung Stadt.
4. Wo finde ich hier Stadtpläne?
5. Wie komme ich zum Bahnhof?
6. Wo fährt hier der Bus nach Erlangen?

a. Where do I find city maps here?
b. Where are you?
c. Where does the bus to Erlangen go from?
d. Are you coming?
e. How do I get to the station?
f. Towards town.

Grammar

3. This exercise is about giving directions. Fill in the prepositions.

1. Fahren Sie _____ Erlangen?

2. Nehmen Sie den Bus Nummer 3 _____ Bahnhof.

3. Wir möchten _____ Museum.

4. Dann gehen Sie _____ der Kirche vorbei geradeaus.

5. Wo geht's hier _____ Fluss?

6. Gehen Sie zuerst _____ rechts, dann geradeaus _____ Hotel vorbei.

4. Write out in full.

1. das 3. Wort von links _____

2. der 10. Buchstabe _____

3. im 15. Stock _____

4. im 8. Stock _____

5. der 9. Buchstabe _____

6. die 1. Straße _____

Check your answers in the key at the back of the book and then add up your points.

Total:	1 – 12	Before you carry on, you really should do this unit again.
	13 – 20	Quite good, but not perfect yet. Please go over the dialogue and the grammar again.
	21 – 24	Very good. You can carry straight on.

Im Restaurant, Teil 1 – In the restaurant Part 1

On the way to the restaurant, the three business partners did a quick tour of the city. Now they're sitting comfortably in a nice little open-air restaurant right on the banks of the Spree.
A good opportunity to learn all the expressions that you need in a restaurant.

1 *Picture dictionary*
Picture plus word. Tidy things up and match the items.

Kaufhaus, das, Pl. ⸚er	*department store*
Stadtplan, der; Pl. ⸚e	*city map*
Pullover, der; Pl. –	*pullover*
Tasche, die; Pl. -n	*bag*
Postkarte, die; Pl. -n	*postcard*
Schirm, der; Pl. -e	*umbrella*
Sandwich, das; Pl. -es	*sandwich*

2 **In a restaurant right on the Spree**
First listen to what the three of them order. Listen to the conversation at least twice. If you need help, here is the vocabulary list.

Direkt an der Spree.	*Right on the Spree.*
Karte (die), die Karten	*menu*
Was möchten Sie trinken?	*What would you like to drink?*
Ich nehme zuerst ein Bier.	*I'll have a beer first.*
Möchten Sie jetzt bestellen?	*Would you like to order now?*
Gemüsepfanne (die) (das Gemüse + die Pfanne)	*(mixed) vegetable dish*
Zander (der) (= ein Fisch)	*zander (= a fish)*
Tomatensuppe (die), die Tomatensuppen (die Tomate + die Suppe)	*tomato soup*
Tomate (die), die Tomaten	*tomato*
Suppe (die), die Suppen	*soup*
Rindsroulade (die), die Rindsrouladen	*beef roulade*
Rind (das), die Rinder	*cow/bull, cattle*
Wie schmeckt Ihnen das Bier?	*How do you like the beer? How does the beer taste?*
Es ist nicht sehr stark.	*It isn't very strong.*
stark	*strong*
Zu Hause trinken wir gern ein Glas Wein.	*At home we like to drink a glass of wine.*
Glas Wein (das)	*glass of wine*
Glas (das), die Gläser	*glass*

Keine Maß Bier?	No litre mug of beer?
Maß (die)	litre mug
Doch, die trinken wir im Sommer	Yes, we drink that in the beer
im Biergarten.	garden in the summer.
Sommer (der)	summer
Biergarten (der), die Biergärten	beer garden
Am liebsten abends nach der Arbeit.	I like it best in the evening after work.
am liebsten (gern – lieber – am liebsten)	preferably, (I like it) best
Ja ja, die Münchner Biergärten sind	Yes yes, the Munich beer gardens
berühmt.	are famous.
berühmt	famous, well-known

In a good restaurant you book a table. Elsewhere you just sit down at a free table, without asking.
Usually the waiter brings the menu automatically, so to say *Die Karte, bitte!* is then a bit impolite.

3 *Some important words are missing here. Please complete.*
Then listen to the text again. Careful: the text is spoken at normal speed.

Seasons

die Jahreszeit, die Jahreszeiten	season
der Frühling (März bis Mai)	spring (March to May)
der Sommer (Juni bis August)	summer (June to August)
der Herbst (September bis November)	autumn/fall (September to November)
der Winter (Dezember bis Februar)	winter (December to February)

4 *Match the right article and fill in the missing plural forms.*

5 *The department store*
Here is a department store with a basement, ground floor and four upper storeys. Listen to the dialogues and place the objects on the right floor.

6 *You work in a department store and answer lots of questions every day.*
Listen to the questions and reply as in the example. It would be best to cover up the questions first with a piece of paper.

7 *Write the answer with* doch. *First read the example.*

Question and answer – Frage und Antwort: *Ja – Nein – Doch*

Trinken Sie gern Wein?	–	**Ja**, ich trinke gern Wein aus Frankreich.
Trinken Sie gern Wein?	–	**Nein**, ich trinke lieber Bier.
Trinken Sie **keinen** Wein?	–	**Doch**, ich trinke gerne Wein.

If there is a negative (*kein* or *nicht*) in a question, you answer with *doch*, not with *ja*.

8 *Answer with a positive (+) or negative (–) statement.*

Trinkst du kein Bier? (+)   Doch, natürlich trinke ich Bier.

Trinkst du kein Bier? (–)   Nein, Bier trinke ich nicht.

Kommst du nicht mit? (+)   _____

Hast du kein Auto? (–)   _____

Essen Sie kein Fleisch? (+)   _____

Mögen Sie keinen Fisch? (–)   _____

Hast du keine Kamera? (+)   _____

Machen wir keinen Ausflug? (+)   _____

Time expressions: *when?* and *where?* – Zeitangaben: *Wann?* und *Wo?*

	Verb	**Zeit**	**Ort**
Katrin	kommt	um 12 Uhr	zu Claudia.

gestern → heute → morgen → übermorgen

am	**um**	**im**	**im**
Donnerstag	drei Uhr	Frühling	Januar

The verb is in second position in a sentence. Other information follows: when and where (to). The time expression comes first:
*Wir fahren **um 12 in die Stadt**. Wir essen **heute im Restaurant**.*

9 *It's your choice. Decide on the suitable expression or word. Careful: there are more words than gaps to be filled.*

im   am   übermorgen   um   mit   um   am

1. _____ ist Sonnabend. Habt ihr da Zeit?

2. Nein, _____ Sonnabend sind wir nicht da.

3. Und was ist _____ Sonntag?

4. Sonntag geht, aber erst _____ Abend.

5. Was heißt Abend? _____ sechs Uhr?

6. Nein, später. Am liebsten _____ acht.

7. Gut, _____ Sommer ist das kein Problem.

möchten + infinitve – möchten + Infinitiv

	Position II (= modal verb)		End of the sentence (= infinitive)
Was	**möchtest**	du	**trinken?**
Was	**möchtest**	du	**essen?**
Was	**möchten**	Sie	**bestellen?**

The modal verb is in position II, the infinitive is at the end of the sentence. The "verbal bracket" is a typical feature of German (see also the section on separable verbs in lesson 18).

The infinitive is often omitted after *möchte*, as after "would like" in English: *Ich möchte eine Suppe.* It is clear that the infinitive *essen* is meant, for example.

10 *Imagine you have a group of people in front of you. You ask what they want and get six different answers. The words are in jumbled order.*
First read the question. Then put the words in the right place in the sentence. You will end up with six answers.

Was möchten Sie?

essen	Wir	möchten	um 12	_____
Ich	möchte	machen	eine Pause	_____
einen Tisch	Wir	bestellen	möchten	_____
besichtigen	die Stadt	möchten	Wir	_____
sehen	das Museum	möchte	Ich	_____
nach Hause	Ich	fahren	möchte	um sechs	_____

11 *Revision.*

In a department store

Kaufhaus (das), die Kaufhäuser	*department store*
einkaufen gehen – er / sie geht einkaufen	*go shopping*
Wann / Wo gehen wir einkaufen?	*When / Where are we going shopping?*
Supermarkt (der), die Supermärkte	*supermarket*
Kiosk (der), die Kioske (am Kiosk)	*kiosk*
Fahrstuhl (der), die Fahrstühle (mit dem Fahrstuhl)	*lift*
im ersten / zweiten / dritten … Stock	*on the first / second / third … floor*
im Untergeschoss	*in the basement*
Wo finde ich … (Schirme)?	*Where will I find … (umbrellas)?*
Wo gibt es / Haben Sie … (Postkarten)?	*Where are there / Do you have … (postcards)?*

Statements and wh-questions – Aussagen und W-Fragen

At the end of a sentence the speaker's voice goes either up or down. In statements and wh-questions it goes down. In all other questions and with *Wie bitte?* it goes up.

12 *We're going to read out some questions. Listen closely and mark whether the voice goes up or down.*

↑ ↓
☐ ☐ Wie geht es Ihnen?
☐ ☐ Danke, gut. Und Ihnen?
☐ ☐ Es geht.
☐ ☐ Das Wetter ist so schlecht.
☐ ☐ Wie bitte?

↑ ↓
☐ ☐ Es regnet seit zwei Tagen.
☐ ☐ Wir möchten die Stadt besichtigen.
☐ ☐ Gehen Sie doch ins Museum!
☐ ☐ Kommen Sie mit?
☐ ☐ Warum nicht?

Questions and commands – Fragesätze und Imperativsätze

In a yes/no-question the speaker's voice goes up at the end, in a command it goes down.

13 *Listen closely to the sentences that are going to be read to you. Mark whether the voice goes up or down. Then listen to the sentences again and repeat.*

↑ ↓
☐ ☐ Kommen Sie mit?
☐ ☐ Kommen Sie doch mit!
☐ ☐ Erklären Sie mir den Weg?
☐ ☐ Erklären Sie mir bitte den Weg!
☐ ☐ Fahren Sie zum Bahnhof?

↑ ↓
☐ ☐ Fahren Sie bitte zum Bahnhof!
☐ ☐ Fahren Sie geradeaus?
☐ ☐ Fahren Sie bitte geradeaus!
☐ ☐ Fahren Sie sofort los?
☐ ☐ Fahren Sie sofort los!

Cultural info (Textbook page 84)

What do people like eating in northern Germany, in southern Germany, in Austria and Switzerland? Match the country or region and the speciality.

Each country and region has its own specialities. We've selected four typical dishes:
- Plaice is a flat fish with creamy white flesh. This fish is eaten with melted butter and thickly sliced fried potatoes. This dish tastes especially good in little restaurants right on the Baltic or North Sea coast.
- Roast pork and potato dumplings is a good solid meal that's a speciality in the south. It tastes good washed down with a glass of beer. *Knödl* are called *Klöße* in the north.
- Dumplings are also eaten in Austria. If they're filled with *Marillen*, the Austrian word for apricots, they're considered a real speciality.
- *Zürcher Geschnetzeltes* is a famous dish made of thinly sliced veal served with *Rösti*. *Rösti* are small fried potato patties.

123

Vocabulary

1. *Note down all the items you can buy in a department store. Write the plural forms.*

| der Winter | der Koffer | der Schirm | der Weg | der Stadtplan | der Sportplatz |

| der Kuss | der März | die Bonbons | der Kuchen | der Tisch | der Appetit |

| der Durst | die Apotheke | die CDs | der Erfolg |

1. _____   5. _____

2. _____   6. _____

3. _____   7. _____

4. _____

2. *Match the expressions and translations.*

1. direkt am Wasser   a. a glass of wine

2. das schmeckt gut   b. after work

3. ein Glas Wein   c. that tastes good

4. das Bier ist stark   d. I'll order now

5. nach der Arbeit   e. right by the water

6. ich bestelle jetzt   f. the beer is strong

Grammar

3. *Some people are talking on mobile phones. Mark the the right word.*

1. Sind Sie schon zu Hause?   – (Ja / Doch), ich bin jetzt zu Hause.
2. Sind Sie schon im Hotel?   – (Ja / Nein), ich bin noch im Taxi.
3. Kommen Sie nicht zur Party?   – (Ja / Doch), ich komme bestimmt.
4. Haben Sie kein Auto?   – (Ja / Doch), ich habe ein Auto.
5. Kommen Sie mit dem Auto?   – (Nein / Doch), meine Schwester hat den Wagen.
6. Nehmen Sie ein Taxi?   – (Ja / Nein), ich nehme die Bahn.

4. *Fill in am, im or um.*

1. _____ Freitag Abend   4. _____ Sommer

2. _____ vier Uhr   5. _____ Wochenende

3. _____ Restaurant   6. _____ Biergarten

Check your answers in the key at the back of the book and then add up your points.

Total:	1 – 13	It would be a good idea to do this unit again straightaway.
	14 – 21	Pretty good. But it wouldn't hurt to go over the dialogue and the grammar again.
	22 – 25	Excellent. If you like, you could go over the vocabulary again, otherwise you can carry straight on.

Die Speisekarte – The Menu

There are restaurants or bistros on the trains of the German railways, too. So in the ICE trains running between the major cities you can sit comfortably, have something to eat and of course gaze out of the window.

This is an opportunity for you to have a closer look at a German menu and puzzle it out.

1 *Potato dishes*
What do you think? What is it? Note down the right letters.
Potatoes are a staple on the menu, appearing in many different variations. There are fat cookbooks full of tasty potato dishes.

Kartoffelsuppe	*potato soup*
Salzkartoffeln	*boiled potatoes*
Pellkartoffeln	*potatoes boiled in their jackets*

2 Eating on the train
Here is a small selection of things you can get on trains.
The menu contains some typical German dishes. You're bound to recognise them when you see a real German menu. At any rate you'll be able to understand the menu better and maybe order on your own, without having to ask for help.

It is common and is also considered polite to wish people „Guten Appetit" at the beginning of a meal.

Here is the translated menu.

Blumenkohlsuppe	*Cauliflower cream soup*
Brot oder Brötchen	*bread or bread roll*
Kartoffelsuppeneintopf	*Thick potato soup*
mit Eisbeinfleisch	*with knuckle of pork*
Brot oder Brötchen	*bread or bread roll*
Verschiedene frische Blattsalate	*Selection of fresh green salads*
mit Tomate, Gurke und	*with tomato, cucumber and*
Streifen von der Hühnchenbrust	*strips of chicken breast*
Frischer gemischter Salat	*Fresh mixed salad*
mit Thunfisch und	*with tuna fish and*
Zwiebelringen	*onion rings*
Snacks & Speisen	*Snacks & Meals*
Räucherlachs	*Smoked salmon*
mit Rührei	*with scrambled eggs*
und Salatbouquet	*and salad garnish,*
Butter, Brot oder Brötchen	*served with bread or roll and butter*

Gebackene Kartoffel	*Baked potato*
mit Sauerrahm	*with sour cream*
und Salatgarnitur	*and salad garnish*
Penne	*Pasta quills*
mit Tomatensoße	*with tomato sauce*
Asiatische Reispfanne	*Asian stir-fried rice*
mit Gemüse und Schweinefleisch	*with vegetables and pork*
Kuchen	*Cakes*
Auf Wunsch mit Sahne	*optionally with whipped cream*

3 *Listen and note down the prices.*
Two people are sitting in a dining car. There's only one menu.
Did you understand the short conversation?
Here's the text.

Er: Gibt es hier eine Speisekarte?
Sie: Ich glaube ja.
Er: Dann lies doch mal vor.
Sie: Auch die Preise?
Er: Ja, klar.
Sie: Also: Blumenkohlsuppe 3 € 50 …

4 *What is eaten cold? Please mark.*

5 *Speaking exercise*
Reply as in the example.

6 *This is your menu. What goes together? Write the words.*

7 *Speaking exercise*
The waitress asks and you give your order now. Listen and use the prompts for your answer.

8 *Noun + Noun*
What goes together? Write the words.
In German there are nouns that are made up of two or more words.

9 *Note down both nouns with their article.*

Word order: separable verbs – Satzstellung: Trennbare Verben

		Position II (= Verb)		End of the sentence (= prefix)
mit / kommen	Ich	**komme**	morgen	**mit.**
zurück / fahren	Er	**fährt**	mit dem Zug	**zurück.**
los / fahren	Sie	**fährt**	gleich	**los.**
ein / laden	Er	**lädt**	mich	**ein.**

- There are a lot of separable verbs in German. They are made up of two parts, the prefix and the actual verb. A verb can have various different prefixes: *losfahren, zurückfahren*. There's also *wegfahren, abfahren, hinfahren* and others too.
- The prefixes have their own meaning: *zurück* (back), *los* (off), *weg* (away), *hin* (to, there), *ab* (off, away, down) etc.
- The verb is placed in position II, and the prefix goes to the end of the sentence.

In the units to come you'll recognise the separable verbs by the hyphen after the separable prefix.

10 *Put in the infinitive and the third person singular.*

	Infinitiv	**3. Person Präsens**
Kommst du mit?	_____	er / sie _____ _____
Fährst du heute zurück?	_____	er / sie _____ _____
Wann fährt Katrin los?	_____	er / sie _____ _____
Peter lädt seine Freunde zur Party ein.	_____	er / sie _____ _____

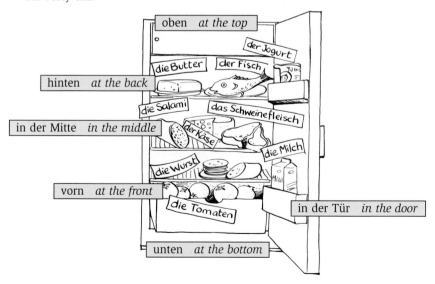

oben   *at the top*

der Jogurt

die Butter   der Fisch

hinten   *at the back*

die Salami   das Schweinefleisch

in der Mitte   *in the middle*   der Käse

die Milch

die Wurst

vorn   *at the front*

die Tomaten   in der Tür   *in the door*

unten   *at the bottom*

127

11 *You know where everything is. Tell someone.*

Wo ist denn das Schweinefleisch?   Wo ist denn der Jogurt?

Wo ist denn die Wurst?   Wo ist denn die Butter?

Wo sind denn die Tomaten?   Wo ist denn die Milch?

Wo ist denn die Salami?   Wo ist denn der Käse?

Wo ist denn der Fisch?

> **Wann fährt** der Zug?
> Weißt du, **wann** der Zug **fährt**?
> Der Zug **fährt** um acht.

12 *Write the question.*

Weißt du, _____? – Die Wurst ist im Kühlschrank

Weißt du, _____? – Christian kommt um sechs.

Weißt du, _____? – Das Restaurant heißt „Zur Kartoffel".

Weißt du, _____? – Es gibt heute Zander.

Weißt du, _____? – Zander ist Fisch.

13 *Have a good look at the drawing and note where the numbers are. There are six buildings or places. Then cover the drawing up with a piece of paper and complete the sentences without looking at the drawing. This is a good way to test whether you have a good visual memory.*

1. Das ist die _____

2. Das ist die _____

3. Das ist das _____

4. Das ist die _____

5. Das ist die _____

6. Das ist der _____

14 *Revision*

In a restaurant

Was (möchten Sie trinken / trinken Sie)?	*What would you like to drink?*
Bitte zahlen. / Die Rechnung, bitte.	*The bill, please.*
Zusammen. / Getrennt.	*Together. / Separate.*

15 *Listen and repeat.*

Ein Bier bitte.	Bitte ein Bier.	Ich trinke ein Bier.
Eine Tomatensuppe.	Die Tomatensuppe bitte.	Ich nehme die Tomatensuppe.
Den Fisch.	Den Fisch bitte.	Ich esse den Fisch.
Bitte zahlen	Zahlen bitte.	Ich möchte zahlen.
Bitte die Rechnung.	Die Rechnung bitte.	
Zusammen.	Bitte zusammen.	Bitte getrennt.

Cultural info (Textbook page 88)

Who says what? Mark the answer. Check with the key.

Kunde (der)/Kundin (die)   *customer*

Read the following text. It tells you about a place where both locals and visitors feel very much at home.

What is a beer garden?

A visit to a beer garden in the summer is the ultimate experience. Beer gardens are a special attraction in the south. Their origins date back to the days when breweries planted shady chestnut trees on top of their cellars to keep the beer cool. Then they set up tables and benches to sell the beer direct to the public. That of course incurred the wrath of the publicans, who saw the brewers as their suppliers, but not as their competitors. So, almost two hundred years ago, the King of Bavaria decreed that the brewers should be allowed to sell beer, but not food. This is how it came about that visitors to beer gardens brought their picnics with them. A custom that has survived to the present day. In a genuine beer garden you're allowed to bring your own food. Of course there are things to buy as well, just in case your fridge at home was empty or there wasn't enough time to go shopping. You're not allowed to bring your own drinks.

Beer garden customers are a motley, classless mixture of friends, families, business people, visitors, young and old, the stolid and the freaky. Under the chestnut trees all are equals … and if you listen to what's going on around you, you notice that topics of conversation cover everything under the sun.

There are many beer-drinking rituals, but you can't learn them, just experience them live. When you clink glasses, for example, it's important that you look the person in the eyes. Don't forget, or this could have terrible effects for the next seven years!

Prost! or Zum Wohl!

Vocabulary

1. Mark the right translation with a cross.

1. Guten Appetit!
☐ Enjoy your meal.
☐ Separate, please.
☐ The bill, please.

2. Was ist Rösti, bitte?
☐ Where is the Rösti?
☐ Who is the Rösti for?
☐ What is Rösti?

2. You are the cook. Decide what goes together. Match.

| Sahne | Rösti | Kartoffeln | Thunfisch | Brot oder Brötchen | Rührei |

1. Tomatensuppe mit _____

2. Lachs mit _____

3. Kuchen mit _____

4. Zürcher Geschnetzeltes mit _____

5. Gemischter Salat mit _____

6. Spargel mit _____

Grammar

3. Write the infinitive.

1. Sie fährt gern Auto. _____

2. Er fährt morgen los. _____

3. Sie fährt übermorgen zurück. _____

4. Wir laden Erich ein. _____

5. Komm doch mit ! _____

4. Complete the question.

Können Sie mir sagen, wo

1. Wo ist das Restaurant? _____

2. Wann fährt der Zug? _____

3. Wie komme ich zum Bahnhof? _____

4. Wie heißt der Platz hier? _____

5. Wie weit ist es zum Schloss? _____

6. Wo finde ich Reiseführer ? _____

Listening Comprehension

(3|5)

5. Two friends are shopping. Listen to what they are discussing. Listen to the dialogue twice and then complete the sentences.

1. Zuerst kaufen Beate und Anne _____ _____, _____ _____ und _____ _____. (ein Schirm, ein Pullover, eine Tasche)

2. Beate braucht noch _____ _____. (ein Reiseführer)

3. Den Reiseführer kauft sie _____ _____. (Bahnhof)

Check your answers in the key at the back of the book and then add up your points.

Total:	1 – 11	Oh dear, that's a pity. Please do this unit again.
	12 – 19	Not so bad. But even so, it would be a good idea to go over the dialogue and the grammar again.
	20 – 22	Excellent. There's nothing to stop you carrying on.

Was habt ihr heute gemacht? –
What have you done today?

When Claudia, Katrin and Robert get back in the evening, Niki of course wants to know what they've been doing. He's keen to find out if he's been missing out on something. In this lesson you're going to learn how to tell a story and give a report. The perfect of course plays an important part in this, and prepositions do too.

1 *This is the centre of Berlin. You can see four major sights.*
Complete the sentences.

The Brandenburg Gate is the emblem of Berlin.
The Federal Chancellor lives and works in the Chancellory.
The President of the Republic resides in Bellevue Castle.
Potsdamer Platz is the finest and most modern square in Berlin.

2 Claudia and Robert report
Now listen to what Claudia and Robert have to report. Listen to the conversation at least twice. Here is our vocabulary list again.

Erzählt mal. Was habt ihr heute gemacht?	*Tell me what you've been up to.*
Ihr habt mich gar nicht angerufen.	*You didn't phone me at all.*
gar nicht	*not at all*
Entschuldige …	*Sorry, …*
Am Brandenburger Tor haben wir geparkt und sind dann gelaufen.	*We parked at the Brandenburg Gate and then walked.*
Zuerst zum Reichstag.	*First to the Reichstag.*
Die Kuppel ist großartig.	*The dome is magnificent.*
Kuppel (die), die Kuppeln	*dome*
großartig	*magnificent, splendid, wonderful*
Die hat mir sehr gefallen.	*I liked it.*
Im Westen sieht man das Kanzleramt und dahinter das Schloss Bellevue	*In the west you can see the Chancellery and, behind that, Bellevue Castle.*
Das Gebäude ist alt, aber die Kuppel ist ganz modern.	*The building is old, but the dome is very modern.*
Gebäude (das), die Gebäude	*building*
Kanzleramt (das)	*Chancellery*
dahinter	*behind/beyond it*
Bundespräsident (der)	*President of the Republic*
Dann sind wir durch den Tiergarten gelaufen.	*Then we walked through the Tiergarten.*
durch + Akk.	*through*
Und von da zum Potsdamer Platz.	*And from there to Potsdamer Platz.*
Die Restaurants waren sehr voll.	*The restaurants were very full.*

131

Aber unter dem Dach sitzt man sehr schön.	*But there's nice seating under the roof.*
Dach (das), die Dächer	*roof*
Wir haben da einen Aperitif getrunken.	*We drank an aperitif there.*
Dann waren wir Unter den Linden und sind zur Humboldt-Universität gelaufen.	*Then we went along Unter den Linden to the Humboldt University.*
Auf der Straße stehen im Augenblick Bären-Plastiken.	*There are bear sculptures in the street at the moment.*
Bär (der), die Bären	*bear*
Bestimmt zwanzig Bären.	*At least twenty bears.*
Die Bären sind ganz bunt.	*The bears are all (brightly) coloured.*
bunt/rot/blau/grün	*(brightly) coloured/red/blue/green*
Das sieht lustig aus.	*It looks funny.*
Ein Bär steht sogar auf dem Kopf.	*One bear is even standing on its head.*

- The bear is Berlin's emblem. The bear sculptures are donations and they were painted all different colours by schoolchildren and students.
- The Tiergarten is a park between the Reichstag and the Brandenburg Gate. The avenue in front of the Brandenburg Gate is called Unter den Linden.
- The Humboldt University is named after the brothers Alexander and Wilhelm von Humboldt, famous natural scientists, global travellers and scholars in the 18th century.

3 *Some important verbs are missing here. Please complete.*

4 *You're in Berlin for the first time and want to do some sightseeing. These sentences will come in very useful. Please complete.*

5 *You read the word* rot. *What do you see?*
Write the words under the colour.

Schnee (der)	Papier (das)	Gewitter (das)	Baum (der), ¨e	Ärger (der)

Wald (der), ¨er	Himmel (der)	Angst (die)	Feuer (das)

gelb	grau	rosa	braun	schwarz	lila
___	___	___	___	___	___
___	___	___	___	___	___

6 *National colours – Please complete*
Kreuz (das), -e   *cross*

7 *Finer and better. – What goes together?*
Please listen and fill in.

8 *Tidy things up. Write the sentences as they should be.*

Perfect with *sein* and *haben* – Perfekt mit *sein* und *haben*

			machen	stehen	trinken	anrufen
Singular	ich	habe	gemacht	gestanden	getrunken	angerufen
	du	hast				
	er / sie	hat				
Plural	wir	haben				
	ihr	habt				
	sie / Sie	haben				

			fahren	gehen	laufen
Singular	ich	bin	gefahren	gegangen	gelaufen
	du	bist			
	er / sie	ist			
Plural	wir	sind			
	ihr	seid			
	sie / Sie	sind			

- Separable verbs have -*ge*- between the prefix and the stem: hat … an*ge*rufen, ist … zurück*ge*kommen, ist … los*ge*fahren.
- There is often a vowel change in the stem: g*e*hen - g*e*gangen, st*e*hen - gest*a*nden, tr*i*nken - getr*u*nken.
- The perfect of verbs of motion is formed with *sein*, not with *haben*. Verbs of motion are strong verbs, so their past participle always has the ending -*en*.

9 *Please don't guess. Look closely. We give you the perfect form, you note down the infinitive.*

Example:

Wir sind nach Hause gelaufen.   laufen

1. Ich habe gut geschlafen.   _____
2. Was haben Sie heute gemacht?   _____
3. Wir sind in die Stadt gefahren.   _____
4. Wo haben Sie geparkt?   _____
5. Was haben Sie gesehen?   _____
6. Was haben Sie besichtigt?   _____
7. Haben Sie ein Taxi genommen?   _____
8. Haben Sie die Uni gleich gefunden?   _____
9. Sie haben nicht angerufen.   _____
10. Wann sind Sie zurückgefahren?   _____

Word order: Perfect – Satzstellung: Perfekt

		Position II (= auxiliary verb)		End of sentence (= past participle)
machen	Was	**habt**	ihr	**gemacht?**
fahren	Wir	**sind**	ins Zentrum	**gefahren.**
parken	Wir	**haben**	am Brandenburger Tor	**geparkt.**
laufen	Wir	**sind**	durch den Tiergarten	**gelaufen.**
trinken	Wir	**haben**	einen Aperitif	**getrunken.**
anrufen	Wir	**haben**	dich gleich	**angerufen.**

The verbal bracket, which you are familiar with from separable verbs and modal verbs, also occurs with the perfect. The auxiliary verb *haben* or *sein* is in position II in the sentence. The past participle goes to the end of the sentence. Other information is placed in between.

10 *Combine the sentences. Use* letzte Woche, zuerst, und, dann, zuletzt, am Schluss, dort. *There are various possibilities.*

Wir haben einen Ausflug nach Oberdorf gemacht.
Wir haben das Auto auf dem Parkplatz geparkt.
Wir sind über die große Brücke ins Zentrum gelaufen.
Wir sind einkaufen gegangen.
Wir waren zwei Stunden im Kaufhaus.
Wir haben Würstchen mit Kartoffelsalat gegessen.
Wir haben noch einen Kaffee getrunken.
Wir haben Markus getroffen.
Wir sind nach Hause gefahren.

11 *Revision*

Reporting experiences

Zuerst sind wir … (ins Zentrum) gefahren.	*First we went … (into the centre).*
Dann sind wir … (zum Reichstag) gelaufen.	*Then we walked … (to the Reichstag).*
Von da sind wir …	*From there we went …*
(zum Potsdamer Platz) gefahren.	*(to Potsdamer Platz).*
Der hat mir sehr gefallen.	*I liked that very much.*
Dann waren wir … (in der Universität).	*Then we were … (in the university).*
Dort haben wir …	*We … there.*
Endlich sind wir …	*We … finally/at last …*
Zuletzt haben wir …	*We … last./We last …*
Zum Schluss …	*At the end …*

12 *Listen and repeat.*

Zuerst sind wir in die Stadt gefahren.
Dann sind wir zum Potsdamer Platz gelaufen.
Der hat mir sehr gefallen.
Dann sind wir zur Universität gelaufen.
Zuletzt waren wir im Reichstag.
Zum Schluss haben wir etwas gegessen.

13 *You're going to hear a telephone conversation. Take the part of the caller and talk about the weekend. Listen sentence by sentence, and repeat.*

Das Fitness-Center ist wirklich prima. Ich war am Wochenende da. Das gefällt dir be-stimmt. Was es da gibt? Alles: Jazz Dance, Gymnastik, Squash, Sauna, Aerobic, Tennis, Inline Skating … Und dann geht man ins Bistro. Das ist nicht schlecht. Fahr doch mal hin und sieh es dir an. Es ist in Haar draußen. Du fährst die Kirchberger Landstraße immer geradeaus. Dann siehst du das Center auf der rechten Seite. Das Center heißt Fitness-Park Kirchberg. Oder ruf zuerst an! Telefon: 04498–5543.

Cultural info (Textbook page 92)
Claudia and Robert went into town by car. Here is some important car vocabulary.

Benzin (das)	*petrol/gas*
Diesel (der)	*diesel*
tanken – er/sie tankt – hat getankt	*fill up*
Tankstelle (die), die Tankstellen	*petrol/gas station*
der Scheinwerfer	*headlight*
der Motor	*engine*
das Lenkrad	*steering wheel*
das Rad	*wheel*
die Kupplung	*clutch*
die Bremse	*brake*
das Gaspedal	*accelerator pedal*
die Tür	*door*
der Sitz	*seat*
der Schalthebel	*gear-shift*
das Dach	*roof*
der Kofferraum	*boot/trunk*

Vocabulary

1. *Please complete.*

1. kommen   Tommy _____ .

2. parken   Er _____ sein Auto.

3. aussehen   Wie _____ das neue Auto _____?

4. stehen   Da _____ es.

5. gefallen   _____ es dir?

6. fahren   Tommy _____ gern Auto.

7. laufen   Er _____ nicht gern.

8. gehen   Er _____ nicht gern zu Fuß.

2. *What are the colours? Give the answers.*

1. Der 1. Buchstabe ist r. _____   4. Der 1. Buchstabe ist s. _____

2. Der 1. Buchstabe is b. _____   5. Der 1. Buchstabe ist w. _____

3. Der 1. Buchstabe ist g. _____   6. Viele Farben: Das ist _____

Grammar

3. *Write the infinitive.*

1. Conny hat in Bremen gewohnt.   _____

2. Dann hat sie Arbeit in Nürnberg gefunden. _____

3. Sie hat an der Universität gearbeitet.   _____

4. Dann ist sie ins Ausland gegangen.   _____

5. Sie ist nach Südamerika geflogen.   _____

6. Sie hat Spanisch gelernt.   _____

7. Sie hat viel gesehen.   _____

8. Gestern hat sie mich angerufen.   _____

4. *Put the words in order and write the sentences.*

1. | geparkt | | haben | | im Zentrum | | wir | _____

2. | Madeleine und Thomas | | getroffen | | wir | | haben | _____

3. | einkaufen | | gegangen | | dann | | sind | | wir | _____

4. | Thomas | | ein Eis | | gekauft | | hat | _____

5. | hat | | prima | | geschmeckt | | das | _____

6. | Madeleine | | lieber | | hat | | gegessen | | Kuchen | _____

Check your answers in the key at the back of the book and then add up your points.

Total: 1 – 14   Before you carry on, you really should do this unit again.

        15 – 24   Quite good, but not perfect yet. Please go over the dialogue and the grammar again.

        25 – 28   Very good. You can carry straight on.

Im Restaurant, Teil 2 – In the restaurant, part 2

The three business partners have taken their time in the restaurant. At the end of the meal they've got on to an important private topic of conversation, holidays. Each of them has their own particular ideas and preferences.

You'll learn a lot about sport and leisure activities.

1 *Do you have holiday plans too? Here's our questionnaire.*

2 Small talk in the restaurant   3|10

→ *Now listen to what the three of them have to say to each other. Listen to the conversation at least twice.*

→ *If you want to have a closer look at the words and sentences, here's the vocabulary list.*

Was macht der Urlaub?	*What are your holiday plans?*
Wir gehen immer im August in Urlaub.	*We always go on holiday in August.*
in Urlaub gehen – er / sie geht in Urlaub, ist in Urlaub gegangen	*go on holiday*
Da ist das Geschäft sehr ruhig.	*Business is very quiet then.*
ruhig	*quiet, calm*
Haben Sie schon ein Ziel?	*Do you know where you're going? (Literally: Do you already have a destination?)*
Wir bleiben zu Hause.	*We're staying at home.*
Wir fahren zwei Tage an den Bodensee, dann ein Wochenende nach Dresden und ein paar Tage an die Ostsee.	*We're going to Lake Constance for two days, then to Dresden for a weekend and to the Baltic for a few days.*
Bodensee (der)	*Lake Constance*
Ostsee (die)	*the Baltic Sea*
Im August ist das Wetter meistens schön.	*The weather is usually nice in August.*
In Dresden war ich zum Beispiel noch nie.	*I have never been to Dresden, for example.*
zum Beispiel	*for example*
Beispiel (das), die Beispiele	*Example*
noch nie	*never (before)*
Dort gibt es so viel zu besichtigen.	*There's so much to see there.*
Wir machen immer im Winter Urlaub.	*We always go on holiday/have our holiday in the winter.*
Da hat man zwei Möglichkeiten.	*Then you have two possibilities.*
Möglichkeit (die), die Möglichkeiten	*possibility*
Entweder wir fahren in die Berge	*Either we go to the mountains*
oder wir fahren weit weg.	*or we go far away.*
entweder – oder	*either – or*
Berg (der), die Berge	*mountain*
weg / fahren – du fährst weg, er / sie fährt weg, ist weggefahren	*go away*

137

Ich treibe viel Sport …	*I do a lot of sport.*
Sport treiben – er / sie treibt Sport, hat Sport getrieben	*do sport*
Ski fahren – du fährst Ski, er / sie fährt Ski, ist Ski gefahren	*ski*
Rad fahren – du fährst Rad, er / sie fährt Rad, ist Rad gefahren	*cycle*
Mountainbike (das), die Mountainbikes	*mountainbike*
Fußball spielen – er / sie spielt Fußball, hat Fußball gespielt	*play football*
schwimmen – er / sie schwimmt, ist geschwommen	*swim*
Motorrad fahren – du fährst Motorrad, er / sie fährt Motorrad, ist Motorrad gefahren	*ride a motorbike*
Das finde ich zu gefährlich.	*I find that too dangerous.*
gefährlich	*dangerous*
Da gehe ich lieber spazieren.	*I prefer to go walking.*
spazieren gehen – er / sie geht spazieren, ist spazieren gegangen	*go walking, go for a walk*
Sport ist ungesund.	*Sport is not good for you.*
Sport (der)	*sport*
ungesund (↔ gesund)	*Not good for you, unhealthy (↔ good for you, healthy)*
Am liebsten lese ich oder ich faulenze.	*I like reading and lazing around best.*
faulenzen – er / sie faulenzt, hat gefaulenzt	*laze (around)*
Da kommt unser Espresso.	*There's our espresso.*

faulenzen is a very vivid, colloquial word, a wonderful way to express the idea of being lazy. If you like, but only if you want to, you can learn it and commit it to memory.

 3 *Listen to the text again. Note down the correct order.*

4 *There's so much you can do at the weekend. Fill in the appropriate verbs.*

 5 *Tell your friends what you prefer to do. First listen. Then reply, using the prompts.*

 6 *We'd like to know your opinion. But unfortunately you don't like anything! First listen to the question. Then reply, using the prompt and zu.*

sehr kalt	*very cold*
so kalt	*so cold*
zu kalt	*too cold*

7 *An email. Put the parts in the right order and write the text. South Tyrol is in northern Italy. It is a popular hiking and skiing area.*

Prepositions of direction: *Wohin*? – Präpositionen nach *Wohin*?

Wohin fahren/gehen/fliegen Sie …?

	Singular			Plural
	masculine	feminine	neuter	
in	in den Harz	in die Stadt	ins Ausland	in die Berge
	in den Norden	in die Wüste	ins Gebirge	in die Tropen
	in den Süden		ins Mittelgebirge	in die Alpen
an	an den Bodensee	an die Ostsee	ans Mittelmeer	an die Osterseen
	an den Atlantik	an die Nordsee	ans Schwarze Meer	
	an den Rhein	an die Donau		
auf	auf den Berg	auf die Zugspitze	aufs Schiff	auf die Malediven
	auf den Fernsehturm	auf die Insel Sylt	aufs Land	
in/ nach	in den Iran	in die Schweiz	nach Italien	in die Niederlande
	in den Libanon	in die Türkei	nach Dresden	in die USA
	in den Irak	in die Slowakei	nach Berlin	
			nach Asien, Europa	

8   *There are many different holiday destinations throughout the year. Fill in the article.*

Im Januar fahren wir in _____ Süden.

Im Februar fahren unsere Freunde in _____ Schweiz.

Im März fahren meine Eltern a_____ Schwarze Meer.

Im April fährt Ulli an _____ Rhein.

Im Mai fährt meine Schwester in _____Türkei.

Im Juni fährt unser Bruder an _____ Atlantik.

Im Juli fährt meine Mutter an _____ Bodensee.

Im August sind Ferien. Da fahren wir a_____ Mittelmeer.

The accusative singular – Der Akkusativ Singular

Singular		masculine	feminine	neuter
Personal pronoun	*nom.*	er	sie	es
Definite article		der Bruder	die Schwester	das Kind
Indefinite article		ein Bruder	eine Schwester	ein Kind
Possessive article		mein Bruder	meine Schwester	mein Kind
Personal pronoun	*acc.*	ihn	sie	es
Definite article		d**en** Bruder	die Schwester	das Kind
Indefinite article		ein**en** Bruder	eine Schwester	ein Kind
Possessive article		mein**en** Bruder	meine Schwester	mein Kind

The accusative plural – Der Akkusativ Plural

Plural				
Personal pronoun	*nom.*	sie		
Definite article	+ *acc*	die Eltern		
Indefinite article		–		
Possessive article		meine Eltern		

- All the other forms are the same in the nominative and the accusative.
- The indefinite article has no plural:
  *Hast du **ein Fahrrad**?*
  *Habt ihr **Fahrräder**?*

9 *Articles are missing here. Fill the gaps.*

1. Was macht _____ Urlaub?

2. Haben Sie schon _____ Ziel?

3. Im August ist _____ Wetter meistens schön.

4. Wir kennen _____ Hotel am Meer.

5. Usedom ist _____ Insel.

6. Wir mögen _____ Meer.

10 *Complete with the missing noun.*

| Gäste | Mitarbeiter | Hotels | Fahrräder | Kleinstädte | Inseln |

Hier steht ein Fahrrad.   – Hier stehen _____ .

Das ist ein Hotel.   – Das sind _____ .

Usedom ist eine Insel.   – Usedom und Sylt sind _____ .

Rosenheim ist eine Kleinstadt.   – Rosenheim und Wasserburg sind _____ .

Wir haben einen Gast.   – Wir haben _____ .

Das ist ein Mitarbeiter von uns. – Das sind _____ von uns.

11 *Revision*

Expressing a judgment

Das finde ich … (gut/sehr gut/prima …).	*I think that's … (good/very good/great …).*
Das finde ich nicht … (gut/schlecht …).	*I don't think that's … (good/bad …).*
Das ist mir zu … (gefährlich/ungesund …).	*That's too … (dangerous/unhealthy …) for me.*
Ich mag Sport/keinen Sport.	*I like/don't like sport.*
… (Radfahren) gefällt mir / gefällt mir nicht/gut/sehr gut.	*I like/don't like … (cycling)/a lot.*
Das mag ich/mag ich nicht.	*I like/don't like that.*
Das geht/geht nicht.	*That's OK/not OK.*

Urlaub zu Hause?

12 *A magazine journalist is interviewing two people about their holiday plans. They each have different ideas of what they want to do. Listen to both interviews, paying attention to the differing views expressed.*

Dialogue A

Interviewer:	Entschuldigung, ich komme von der Zeitschrift *Eltern heute*. Ich möchte Sie etwas fragen.
Christine F.:	Ja, bitte? Ich habe es aber sehr eilig.
Interviewer:	Nein, nein, es dauert nicht lange. Wir möchten Sie fragen: Bleiben Sie in den Ferien zu Hause oder fahren Sie weg?
Christine F.:	Wir haben zwei Kinder. Die sind jetzt drei und fünf Jahre alt. Wir bleiben in den Ferien zu Hause.
Interviewer:	Und was machen Sie dann alles?
Christine F.:	Sehr viel.
Interviewer:	Erzählen Sie mal!
Christine F.:	Unsere Freunde haben auch Kinder. Die Kinder spielen dann zusammen im Garten.
Interviewer:	Und was machen Sie noch?
Christine F.:	Am liebsten fahren wir an einen See. Mein Sohn lernt gerade schwimmen.
Interviewer:	Ja, und Sie schwimmen bestimmt auch gern.
Christine F.:	Ja, wir haben auch ein Boot. Das macht viel Spaß.
Interviewer:	Danke schön. Das reicht. Vielen Dank auch.

Now listen to Dialogue B. You should be able to understand almost everything. But if you want to read the text, you'll find it in the key.

Now you decide. Take over the role of either Christine F. or Armin H. Speak the part out loud as you listen.

Cultural info (Textbook page 96)

You want to find out which sport your friends and the children do or are learning. Listen. Then match to the correct drawing.
What's your favourite sport?
If you can't find the word here, please look it up in a dictionary.

Sport is also subject to fashion. It's often a question of how well-known the top sports stars are. World-famous footballers and tennis players, for example, made football and tennis very popular. Excitement about ski-jumpers, tobogganers, sailors and Formula I drivers, however, is largely restricted to TV reporting.

New trendy sports are discovered almost yearly: hang gliding, inline skating, skydiving, kayaking on the sea, beach volleyball etc. Walking, snowboarding, climbing, mountainbiking have become almost everyday sports. And the list is being added to all the time.

Vocabulary

1. Mark the correct translation with a cross.

1. in Urlaub gehen
☐ go on an adventure holiday
☐ go on holiday
☐ go to the seaside

2. zu Hause bleiben
☐ go away
☐ laze around at home
☐ stay at home

3. zum Beispiel
☐ at the moment
☐ for example
☐ together

4. Sport treiben
☐ do sport
☐ ride a bike
☐ watch sport

5. weit wegfahren
☐ go far away
☐ go on holiday
☐ have a few days off

6. spazieren gehen
☐ go sightseeing
☐ go for a walk
☐ stay at home

7. Das ist mir lieber.
☐ I like that best.
☐ I prefer that.
☐ That is not good for me.

8. Was ist dir am liebsten?
☐ What are your holiday plans?
☐ What do you like best?
☐ What do you think?

9. Bitte zahlen.
☐ Please wait.
☐ The bill, please.
☐ The menu, please.

Grammar

2. Fill in the preposition.

1. Fahr doch _____ die Ostsee.
2. Geht doch _____ die Berge.
3. Fliegt doch _____ die Malediven.
4. Fahrt doch _____ den Fernsehturm.
5. Flieg doch _____ die USA.
6. Fahren Sie doch _____ Südamerika.

3. You are given the nominative form in brackets. Write the accusative form.

1. Kennst du _____ (ich) noch?
2. Kennst du _____ (sie = Singular)?
3. Kennst du _____ (sie = Plural)?
4. Kennst du _____ (wir) noch?
5. Kennst du _____ (Herr Mai)?
6. Ich kenne _____ (er) schon zehn Jahre.

4. Personal pronouns are used in place of nouns. Try it; replace the nouns with pronouns.

1. Kennen Sie meinen Bruder? – Kennen Sie _____?
2. Haben Sie meine Schwester gesehen? – Haben Sie _____ gesehen?
3. Möchten Sie das Schloss besichtigen? – Möchten Sie _____ besichtigen?
4. Brauchen Sie die Bücher? – Brauchen Sie _____?
5. Haben Sie das Geld erhalten? – Haben Sie _____ erhalten?
6. Haben Sie die Karte gelesen? – Haben Sie _____ gelesen?
7. Hat Christian die Kamera gekauft? – Hat er _____ gekauft?
8. Wann triffst du deine Eltern? – Wann triffst du _____?

Check your answers in the key at the back of the book and then add up your points.

Total:
1 – 15 It would be a good idea to do this unit again straightaway.
16 – 25 Pretty good. But it wouldn't hurt to go over the dialogues and the grammar again.
26 – 29 Excellent. If you like, you could go over the vocabulary again, otherwise you can carry straight on.

Der Reiseprospekt – The travel brochure

Two colleagues are sitting in the canteen. One of them has a grammar problem: what term is used for the inhabitants of various countries? That quickly leads on to another topic, holidays.

1 *First read a few adverts in a travel brochure. You'll find you understand quite a lot.*

Reisemarkt (der) (die Reise + der Markt)	*travel market*
Malediven vom Spezialisten	*Maldives from the specialist*
Flug (der), die Flüge	*flight*
Täglich über 2,5 Mio. Top-Angebote.	*Over 2.5 million top offers daily.*
Angebot (das), die Angebote	*offer*
Reisen per Rad	*travel by bike, cycling holidays*
Europas Nummer Eins in der Radtouristik.	*Number 1 in Europe for cycling tourism.*
Bestellen Sie den neuen Katalog von Schweiz Tourismus.	*Order the new catalogue from Swiss Tourism.*
Katalog (der), die Kataloge	*catalogue*
Tourismus (der)	*tourism*
Die ersten Besteller erhalten eine Flasche Schweizer Wein.	*The first to order will receive a bottle of Swiss wine.*
6-tägige Rundreise	*6-day tour*
Rundreise (die), die Rundreisen	*tour*
Reisetermin (der), die Reisetermine	*date of travel*
Doppelzimmer (das), die Doppelzimmer	*double room*
Abenteuer pur	*adventure pure*
Abenteuer (das), die Abenteuer	*adventure*
segeln – er/sie segelt, ist gesegelt	*sail*
Karibik (die)	*Caribbean*
mit/fahren – du fährst mit, er/sie fährt mit, ist mitgefahren	*go / come along, go / come with somebody*
Erholung auf der Sonneninsel	*relaxation on the sunny island*
Erholung (die)	*relaxation*
Schwarzwald (der)	*Black Forest*
Auf 720 m Höhe	*720m up, at an altitude of 720m*
Höhe (die)	*height, altitude*
Hallen- und Freibad	*indoor and outdoor swimming pool*
Wanderweg (der), die Wanderwege	*hiking trail*
Fahrradverleih (der)	*bicycle hire*
Vollpension (die)	*full board*

2 Do you have holiday plans?

Now listen to what the two colleagues are talking about. The travel brochure is also mentioned. Listen to the text at least twice. Here is our vocabulary list.

Wie heißen die Einwohner von Spanien?	*What are the inhabitants of Spain called?*
Einwohner (der), die Einwohner	*inhabitant*
Spanier (der), die Spanier	*Spaniard*
Schweizer (der), die Schweizer	*Swiss (person)*
Österreicher (der), die Österreicher	*Austrian (person)*
Genauso wie die Einwohner von Städten.	*Just like the inhabitants of cities.*
Aber was ist mit den Bayern und Franken?	*But what about Bavarians and Franconians?*
Franzose (der), die Franzosen	*Frenchman*
Schwede (der), die Schweden	*Swede*
Finne (der), die Finnen	*Finn*
Wohin geht's denn?	*Where are you off to then?*
Ich weiß noch nicht.	*I don't know yet.*
Das ist ja mein Problem.	*That's my problem.*
Haben Sie eine Idee?	*Do you have an idea?*
Idee (die), die Ideen	*idea*
Reiseprospekt (der), die Reiseprospekte	*travel brochure*
(die Reise + der Prospekt)	
Prospekt (der), die Prospekte	*brochure, prospectus*

3 *Six words are hidden here. Find them and note them down with their article. Careful: the words are compound nouns.*
There is one element that occurs three times.

4 *Holiday preferences*
Your colleagues have lots of different preferences for their next holiday. Make suggestions to them.
→ *First read our travel brochure.*
→ *Then read the first request and find an appropriate destination. Match the rquest and destination.*
→ *Then read the next request etc. Careful: There's one person who doesn't need either a suggestion or a brochure.*

5 *Four photos and four seasons.*
Note down the seasons.

6 *Which sport is it? You'll see some pictograms. Match the text that goes with each one.*

7 *The names of the months are missing in this calendar. Put them in the right order.*

Compound nouns – Zusammengesetzte Nomen

der Reiseprospekt	die Reise	+	der Prospekt	Nomen + Nomen
die Urlaubspläne	der Urlaub	+	die Pläne	Nomen + s + Nomen
die Rundreise	rund	+	die Reise	Adjektiv + Nomen

The article always relates to the last part of the compound: *Auto* is **das** *Auto*, but **die** *Autonummer* because it's **die** *Nummer*.
The first part can also be an adjective.

8 *You see the first part of a compound word. Find the second part and note down the compound nouns.*

| platz | essen | zimmer | kalender | nummer | hafen | reise | prospekt |

1. der Termin_____

2. der Reise_____

3. der Sport_____

4. das Doppel_____

5. das Abend_____

6. die Auto_____

7. die Rund_____

8. der Flug_____

9 *There are a number of words that are almost always used only in the singular. Mark which words exist as a singular and plural, and which are only used in the singular.*

	Mai	Wurst	Zug	Wolke	Wasser	Frühstück
Singular und Plural	☐	☐	☐	☐	☐	☐
Nur Singular	☐	☐	☐	☐	☐	☐

	Urlaub	Osten	Glück	Jahr	Hunger	Sport
Singular und Plural	☐	☐	☐	☐	☐	☐
Nur Singular	☐	☐	☐	☐	☐	☐

10 *Certain words are used in the plural more often than in the singular. Write the plural form.*

1. der Plan   – die _____

2. die Kartoffel – die _____

3. das Getränk – die _____

4. die Kirsche   – die _____

5. der Kilometer   – die _____

6. die Weintraube – die _____

11 *On the other hand, some words are used more in the singular. Fill in the singular form, with the article.*

1. die Auskünfte   – die _____

2. die Besuche   – ___ _____

3. die Marmeladen – ___ _____

4. die Mieten   – ___ _____

5. die Säfte   – ___ _____

6. die Mittage   – ___ _____

145

12 *Supply the appropriate verb.*

1. Rad _____
2. Sport _____
3. Fußball _____
4. Motorrad _____
5. Ski _____
6. spazieren _____

13 *Here's an extended list of countries and languages. The words for the inhabitants of the countries are also included, both the male and female forms (see also page 144).*
Please read through the questions below and then look at the table. Then it'll be no problem to complete the rules we've formulated.

Land	Sprache	Bewohner (er)	Bewohner (sie)
Bulgarien	Bulgarisch	Bulgare, -n	Bulgarin, -nen
China	Chinesisch	Chinese, -n	Chinesin, -nen
Deutschland	Deutsch	Deutsche, -n	Deutsche, -n
England	Englisch	Engländer, –	Engländerin, -nen
Griechenland	Griechisch	Grieche, -n	Griechin, -nen
Italien	Italienisch	Italiener, –	Italienerin, -nen
Japan	Japanisch	Japaner, –	Japanerin, -nen
Kroatien	Kroatisch	Kroate, -n	Kroatin, -nen
Mexiko	Mexikanisch	Mexikaner, –	Mexikanerin, -nen
Österreich	Österreichisch	Österreicher, –	Österreicherin, -nen
Polen	Polnisch	Pole, -n	Polin, -nen
Russland	Russisch	Russe, -n	Russin, -nen
Schweiz	Schweizerisch	Schweizer, –	Schweizerin, -nen
Slowakei	Slowakisch	Slowake, -n	Slowakin, -nen
Slowenien	Slowenisch	Slowene, -n	Slowenin, -nen
Spanien	Spanisch	Spanier, –	Spanierin, -nen
Tschechien	Tschechisch	Tscheche, -n	Tschechin, -nen
Türkei	Türkisch	Türke, -n	Türkin, -nen
Ungarn	Ungarisch	Ungar, -n	Ungarin, -nen

• Languages have the ending _____ .
• The male inhabitants of countries have the ending _____ or _____ .
• The female form ends in the singular in _____ and in the plural in _____ .

14 *Revision*

In the hotel

das Einzelzimmer, die Einzelzimmer	*single room*
das Doppelzimmer, die Doppelzimmer	*double room*
mit Bad / mit Dusche	*with bath (en suite) / with shower (en suite)*
das Frühstück(sbuffet)	*breakfast (buffet)*
die Kreditkarte, die Kreditkarten	*credit card*

Separation in and between words

15 *Separate the words and syllables when speaking, even if they start with a vowel or a diphthong.*
Listen closely. Repeat what you hear, imitating the speaker's pronunciation as closely as you can.

der Urlaub	–	in Urlaub gehen
der August	–	im August
das Ende	–	das Wochenende
Europa und Asien	–	in Europa und in Asien
einfach	–	ganz einfach
der Abend	–	morgen Abend
das Auto	–	mit dem Auto
der Mitarbeiter	–	unsere Mitarbeiter
arbeiten	–	er hat gearbeitet

16 *How many syllables has the word got? First read the words and mark the number of syllables. Then listen to the words and check your answers. Repeat out loud.*

② ③ ④ Silben

Wochenende	besichtigen	Geburtsort	Beruf	gegenüber
② ③ ④	② ③ ④	② ③ ④	② ③ ④	② ③ ④

geradeaus	natürlich	besuchen	studieren	Autonummer
② ③ ④	② ③ ④	② ③ ④	② ③ ④	② ③ ④

Cultural info (Textbook page 100)

A. *In German there are a lot of compounds. First answer our questions.*

B. *Note down the second element of the word. Supply the article. Careful: nouns are written with a capital letter.*

C. *The solution consists of three words. You can use this expression when you don't think something is at all good or when you've had bad luck.*
Extract the letters now from the words you've written (without the article).

The large number of compound nouns in German is a distinctive feature of the language. But don't try making up compounds of your own if you're not quite sure about them. That can easily lead to mistakes. Always check in the dictionary to see if the compound really exists.

Vocabulary

1. *What are the inhabitants called?*

1. Dänemark die _____

2. Holland   die _____

3. Japan   die _____

4. England   die _____

5. Korea   die _____

6. Italien   die _____

7. Frankreich   die _____

8. Griechenland die _____

9. Australien   die _____

10. China   die _____

Grammar

2. *Which words are only used in the singular? Mark them with a cross.*

Only singular
1. ☐ der Urlaub
2. ☐ der Plan
3. ☐ die Wurst
4. ☐ das Getränk

Only singular
5. ☐ der Süden
6. ☐ der Kilometer
7. ☐ der Hunger
8. ☐ das Jahr

3. *Note down the plural of the remaining words.*

1. _____

2. _____

3. _____

4. _____

5. _____

Listening Comprehension

3|22

4. *Two colleagues are chatting in the corridor during a short break. Listen once. Then mark all the statements that are not correct.*

Frau Ulrich:
1. ☐ Sie hat zwei Kinder.
2. ☐ Sie geht im August in Urlaub.
3. ☐ Die Kinder studieren.
4. ☐ Die Familie fährt an die Ostsee.
5. ☐ Sie fahren auf die Insel Usedom.
6. ☐ Sie bleiben dort fünf Wochen.
7. ☐ Das Wetter ist meistens gut.

Frau Mandl:
8. ☐ Ihr Mann möchte weit weg fahren.
9. ☐ Sie möchte zu Hause bleiben.
10. ☐ Er fährt gern Ski.
11. ☐ Sie fährt nicht gern Ski.
12. ☐ Sie möchte im Sommer ans Meer.
13. ☐ Sie schwimmt gern.
14. ☐ Er mag das Wasser.

Check your answers in the key at the back of the book and then add up your points.

Total:		
	1 – 19	Oh dear, that's a pity. Please do this unit again straightaway.
	20 – 31	Not so bad. But even so, it would be a good idea to go over the dialogue and the grammar again.
	32 – 37	Excellent. There's nothing to stop you carrying on.

Mein Computer spinnt – My computer's playing up

Claudia seems to be having problems with her computer. Robert is giving some "good advice". Claudia discovers that she has received a mail. Her friend in Argentina has written.

Having encountered modal verbs, we're now going to learn *können, müssen* and *dürfen* systematically.

1 *Here are some questions to prepare you for the text. Answer as fast as you can.*

Alt. / Nicht so alt.	*Old. / Not so old.*
Neu. / Ganz neu.	*New. / Brand new.*
PC-Fortbildung (die)	*PC course*
Haben Sie allein gelernt?	*Did you study on your own?*
Hat Ihnen ein Freund / eine Freundin geholfen?	*Did a friend help you?*

If you answered yes to more than three of the questions, you're well prepared for this lesson.

2 Can you help me?
Now listen to Claudia and Robert talking. Listen to the conversation at least twice. Here again is the vocabulary list.

3|23

Kannst du mir helfen?	*Can you help me?*
helfen – du hilfst, er / sie hilft, hat geholfen	*help*
Computer (der), die Computer	*computer*
spinnen (umg.) – er / sie spinnt, hat gesponnen	*play up, go crazy*
du bist nur nervös	*you're just nervous*
nervös	*nervous*
Jetzt gib deine PIN ein.	*Now key in your PIN.*
PIN (die), die PINs	*PIN*
ein / geben – du gibst ein, er / sie gibt ein, hat eingegeben	*key in*
Ich muss unbedingt eine PC-Fortbildung machen.	*I really must do a PC course.*
müssen – er/sie muss	*must*
PC (der), die PCs	*PC*
unbedingt	*absolutely, really*
Du bist doch schon fit.	*But you're already pretty nimble.*
Außerdem kann dir Niki alles erklären.	*Besides, Niki can explain everything to you.*
außerdem	*besides*
Da braucht man keinen Kurs.	*You don't need a course.*
Kurs (der), die Kurse	*course*
Das kannst du allein lernen.	*You can learn that on your own.*

Ich möchte das systematisch lernen.	*I want to learn it systematically.*
systematisch	*systematic(ally)*
Niki ist abends müde.	*Niki is tired in the evenings.*
müde	*tired*
Und gut erklären kann er auch nicht.	*And he's not much good at explaining either.*
Das darf er aber nicht hören.	*He mustn't hear that.*
dürfen – er / sie darf	*be allowed to*
nicht dürfen	*must not*
E-Mail (die), die E-Mails	*e-mail*
ab / holen – er / sie holt ab, hat abgeholt	*collect, pick up*
Eine Mail von Laura aus Argentinien.	*A mail from Laura in Argentina.*
Das ist eine Freundin von mir.	*That's a friend of mine.*
Ich bin nächsten Monat in Deutschland.	*I'm in Germany next month.*
Ich habe ein Stipendium bekommen.	*I have got a scholarship.*
Stipendium (das), die Stipendien	*scholarship*
Bitte antwortet mir schnell!	*Please reply quickly!*

 If you're faced with a text you don't know, try and understand the title or heading first. It will give you important clues.

3 *There are some important words missing in this text. Please complete.*

4 *Reconstruct the mail.*

5 *You are writing to friends and to business partners. What is formal business style, what is personal? First read exercise 12 here in the book.*

 6 *Speaking exercise.*

7 *Robert's diary*
Fill in kann *or* können.

Modal verbs – Modalverben: *können, müssen, dürfen*

			können	müssen	dürfen
Singular	1. Person	ich	**kann**	**muss**	**darf**
	2. Person	du	**kannst**	**musst**	**darfst**
	3. Person	er/sie	**kann**	**muss**	**darf**
Plural	1. Person	wir	können	müssen	dürfen
	2. Person	ihr	könnt	müsst	dürft
	3. Person	sie/Sie	können	müssen	dürfen

The modal verbs *können, müssen, dürfen* have special forms in the singular.

No perfect is given for modal verbs, because it is not generally used.

8 *Practise the forms.*

Ich kann segeln. Und du? _____ du auch segeln?

_____ Daniela schon schwimmen?

_____ Ulrike mir mal helfen?

_____ Sie am Montag kommen?

_____ du schon nach Hause?

Patrick _____ heute lernen.

Er _____ nicht zum Fußballspielen gehen. (dürfen)

Word order: modal verbs + infinitive – Satzstellung: Modalverben + Infinitiv

		Position II (= modal verb)		End of sentence (= infinitive)
können	Du	**kannst**	mir	**helfen.**
	Sie	**können**	jetzt	**kommen.**
müssen	Ich	**muss**	zu Hause	**bleiben.**
	Wir	**müssen**	heute	**arbeiten.**
dürfen	Peter	**darf**	nicht Motorrad	**fahren.**
	Er	**darf**	aber	**klettern.**

- The famous verbal bracket, so typical of German, is used again with modal verbs. But note:

  Perfect: *Ich habe heute lange **gearbeitet**.*   (= **Partizip II**)
  Modal verb: *Ich muss heute lange **arbeiten**.*   (= **Infinitiv**)

- And this is what the modal verbs mean:

segeln:	*Das **kann** ich nicht.*	= I haven't learnt it.
helfen:	***Kannst** du mir helfen?*	= I'm asking politely.
arbeiten:	*Das **muss** ich jetzt nicht.*	= Nothing is forcing me.
klettern:	*Das **darf** ich nicht.*	= Somebody has forbidden it.

151

- So *müssen* means "must", but *nicht müssen* means "don't have to". *nicht dürfen* is the equivalent of "mustn't":

  Du musst es nicht machen. = You don't have to do it. *(It's not necessary, not essential.)*
  Du darfst es nicht machen. = You mustn't do it. *(It's forbidden.)*

- If the infinitive is self-explanatory, it can be omitted:

  Ich muss nach Hause. = Ich muss nach Hause fahren / gehen.
  Ich kann das nicht. = Ich kann das nicht machen.
  Das darfst du nicht. = Das darfst du nicht tun.

9 *Wir fragen, Sie antworten. Write the answers.*

1. Machst du eine Fortbildung? – ⬚ eine Fortbildung ⬚ muss ⬚ machen ⬚ Ich ⬚

_____

2. Hilfst du mir? – ⬚ Ich ⬚ kann ⬚ helfen ⬚ dir ⬚

_____

3. Erklärt er gut? – ⬚ gut ⬚ Er ⬚ kann ⬚ erklären ⬚

_____

4. Wie lernst du? ⬚ systematisch ⬚ Ich ⬚ will ⬚ lernen ⬚

_____

5. Was machst du jetzt? ⬚ fahren ⬚ muss ⬚ Ich ⬚ nach ⬚ Hause ⬚

_____

10 *Revision*

Salutation: Business letter – Anrede: Geschäftsbrief

Sehr geehrter Herr … (+ Nachname),	*Dear Mr … (+ surname),*
Sehr geehrte Frau … (+ Nachname),	*Dear Mrs … (+ surname),*
Sehr geehrte Damen und Herren,	*Dear Sirs / Dear Sir or Madam,*

Salutation: Personal letter – Anrede: Persönlicher Brief

Liebe … (Frau Meyer/Familie Kraus/Marion)	*Dear … (Frau Meyer/Family Kraus/Marion)*
Lieber … (Herr Stolz/Helmut)	*Dear … (Herr Stolz/Helmut)*
Hallo … (+ Vorname)	*Hello/Hi … (+ first name)*

Complimentary close: Business letter – Schlussformel: Geschäftsbrief

Mit freundlichen Grüßen	*Yours sincerely / faithfully*
Mit den besten Grüßen	*With best wishes*

Complimentary close: Personal letter – Schluss: Persönlicher Brief

Herzliche Grüße / Liebe Grüße	*Warmest / Best wishes / Love*
Viele Grüße	*All good wishes*
euer … (Fritz) / eure … (Laura)	*Yours … (Fritz) / Yours … (Laura)*

Fragen und Bitten – Questions and requests

11 *There are questions and requests that you need time and time again. We're going to describe a situation to you. You say your question or request in German.*

1. Imagine your suitcase is too heavy. Ask someone for help.

Bitte, können _____ _____ *helfen?*

2. Ask for the information desk.

Bitte, wo _____ _____ _____?

3. Ask for the airport bus.

Bitte, wo _____ _____ _____-*Bus?*

4. Ask how you get to the city.

Bitte, wie _____ _____ _____ _____ _____?

5. There's something you haven't understood. Ask the person to repeat it.

Bitte, können _____ _____ *wiederholen?*

6. Say that you haven't understood the other person. Ask him or her not to speak so quickly.

_____ *verstehe* _____ _____. *Bitte sprechen* _____ _____ _____ _____.

7. Say that you haven't understood the word. Ask the person to spell it.

Ich habe _____ _____ _____ *verstanden. Bitte* _____ _____ *es.*

8. Ask somebody to spell their name.

Bitte, buchstabieren _____ *Ihren* _____.

Now listen to the correct answers and correct your own answers if necessary.

Cultural info (Textbook page 104)

Here's a short overview of how people spend their free time.
Guess who is talking. Who do you think it is?

Vocabulary

1. Mark the right translation.

1. Können Sie mir helfen?
☐ Can you help me?
☐ Do you need help?
☐ I hope you're well?

2. Du musst einen Kurs machen.
☐ She must do a course.
☐ You must do a course.
☐ You must do it of course.

3. Er kann nicht erklären.
☐ He's pretty nimble.
☐ He can't explain.
☐ It's playing up.

4. Das kann ich allein lernen.
☐ I want to learn it systematically.
☐ I really must do a course.
☐ I can learn that on my own.

5. Bitte antwortet schnell!
☐ Please answer by snail mail.
☐ Please send an answer.
☐ Please reply quickly.

6. Sehr geehrte Damen und Herren,
☐ Dear Everybody
☐ Dear Friends
☐ Dear Sirs

7. Mit freundlichen Grüßen
☐ Dear …
☐ Love …
☐ Yours sincerely

8. Herzliche Grüße
☐ Very best wishes
☐ Yours faithfully
☐ Yours sincerely

Grammar

2. Write the modal verb.

1. können   Peter _____ uns helfen.

2. möchten   _____ du eine Fortbildung machen?

3. müssen   Ich _____ eine Fortbildung machen.

4. dürfen   Hier _____ ihr nicht parken.

5. können   Karla _____ Motorrad fahren.

3. Fill in the correct modal verb. You have the choice between können, müssen, dürfen *and* möchten.

1. Die Kinder _____ zur Schule gehen.

2. Ulli _____ keinen Kaffee trinken.

3. Herr Meyer _____ gut Ski fahren.

4. _____ Sie mir helfen?

5. Frank _____ Japanisch lernen.

6. Conny _____ sparen.

Check your answers in the key at the back of the book and then add up your points.

Total:	1 – 10	Before you carry on, you really should do this unit again.
	11 – 16	Quite good, but not perfect yet. Please go over the dialogue and the grammar again. It'll be worth it.
	17 – 19	Very good. You can carry straight on.

Postkarte oder SMS? – Postcard or SMS text message?

Robert has written a postcard to his parents and is talking to Claudia about whether writing postcards is still up-to-date.
In this lesson we've drawn together some important prepositions used to answer the question *Wo?*

1 *Here are some words and pictures to do with writing. First read the words. Then find the matching picture.*
You'll find the words and translations in section 12.

If you talk about a *Karte*, it is not clear without a context what is meant. *Karte* can be: 1. *eine Postkarte*, 2. *eine Landkarte*, 3. *eine Speisekarte*.

2 Very best wishes from the capital
→ *Now listen to what Claudia and Robert have to say to each other. Listen to the conversation at least twice.*
→ *If you want to have a look at the words and sentences, here is the vocabulary list.*

Hauptstadt (die), die Hauptstädte	*capital (city)*
Das war ein Erlebnis.	*It has been an experience.*
Ich habe eine Postkarte an meine Eltern geschrieben.	*I've written a postcard to my parents.*
Hast du eine Briefmarke?	*Do you have a stamp?*
Briefmarke (die), die Briefmarken	*stamp*
extra für dich	*special(ly) for you*
Sind Postkarten eigentlich altmodisch?	*Are postcards old-fashioned really?*
altmodisch	*old-fashioned, out of date*
überhaupt nicht	*not at all*
alle freuen sich	*everybody is pleased*
sich freuen – er/sie freut sich, hat sich gefreut	*be pleased*
SMS (das)	*SMS*
nur der Inhalt ist so langweilig.	*only the contents are so boring.*
Inhalt (der)	*contents [singular in German]*
langweilig	*boring*
Heute Abend gibt's eine Überraschung für dich.	*There's a surprise for you this evening.*
Hör auf, Robert!	*Stop it, Robert.*
auf/hören – er/sie hört auf, hat aufgehört	*stop*
Ich habe jetzt keine Zeit mehr.	*I haven't got any more time now.*
kein/keine/nicht … mehr	*no more, no longer*
(Das) finde ich aber spannend.	*But I think it's exciting.*
spannend	*exciting*

Laura kann auch bei meinen Eltern schlafen.	*Laura can sleep at my parents' (place).*
Das ist nett von dir.	*That's nice of you.*
Aber ich muss ja wieder nach Hause.	*But I have to get back home.*
Mal sehen.	*I'll see.*

3 *What is correct? Please mark with a cross.*

4 *Something's happened to Robert's postcard. Rearrange the parts and put them back in the correct order.*

5 *Speaking exercise*
Lisa is phoning friends. What does she ask first? Hallo, wo bist du denn? *of course.*
Listen to the question. Then read the prompt and reply.

6 *Speaking exercise*
Parents are always dissatisfied and ask: Warum habt ihr nicht angerufen?
You reply. Use the prompts given.

7 *What is the opposite? Please match.*

8 *There's something wrong with the postcard here. Timo is in Italy and is writing his parents a very special card. Write the card correctly. Pay attention to capital and small letters and to the spacing between words.*

Prepositions after *Wo?* – Präpositionen nach *Wo?*

Wo sind Sie denn jetzt?

	Singular			Plural
	masculine	**feminine**	**neuter**	
an	am Bodensee	an der Ostsee	am Mittelmeer	an den Osterseen
	am Atlantik	an der Nordsee	am Schwarzen Meer	
	am Rhein	an der Donau		
auf	auf dem Berg	auf der Zugspitze	auf dem Schiff	auf den Malediven
	auf dem Fernsehturm	auf der Kuppel	auf dem Land	
in	im Reichstag	in der Stadt	im Ausland	in den Bergen
	im Norden	in der Wüste	im Gebirge	in den Tropen
	im Süden			
		im Mittelgebirge	in den Alpen	
	im/in Iran	in der Schweiz	in Italien	in den Niederlanden
	im/in Irak	in der Türkei	in Japan	in den USA
	im Libanon	in der Slowakei	in China	

9 *You are ringing up because you want to speak to a friend. First, of course, you ask where he is.*

Wo bist du denn?

1. _____ Reichstag.
2. _____ Supermarkt.
3. _____ Fluss.
4. _____ d_____ Fernsehturm.
5. _____ d_____ Kirche.
6. _____ d_____ Tankstelle.

7. _____ Hotel.
8. _____ d_____Firma.
9. _____ Büro.
10. _____ d_____Bergen.
11. _____ Spanien.
12. _____ d_____ Zugspitze.

***aus / mit / bei / zu / von* + dative – Dativ**

Ich komme	**aus** dem Ausland.	Ich fahre	**zum** Bahnhof.
	aus der Stadt.	Ich fahre	**zur** Schule.
Ich fahre	**mit** dir.	Ich wohne	**bei** dir.
	mit meinem Bruder.	Ich arbeite	**bei** der Firma Techno. / bei Techno.
	mit meinen Eltern.	Ich bin	**beim** Arzt / bei meinen Eltern.
	mit der Bahn.	Ich komme	**vom** Arzt.
	mit dem Bus.	Ich komme	**von** meiner Schwester.
	mit dem Auto.	Ich komme	**von** meinen Eltern.
Ich komme	**zu** dir.		
Ich fahre	**zu** meinem Bruder.		
Ich fahre	**zu** meinen Eltern.		

157

The preposition *mit* has occurred a lot of times already in previous lessons.
mit is one of the most frequent prepositions. It doesn't change its form, just like *aus*.
zu without an article is used with people, *zum/zur* with things.

10 *The preposition is missing here. You can choose from* zu, zum / zur, von *and* bei.

Fahren Sie _____ dem Bus Nummer 7.

Dann kommen Sie _____ Bahnhof.

Karla kann _____ uns wohnen.

Ich fahre _____ den Eltern.

Der Brief ist _____ meinem Onkel.

Michael fährt _____ seinem Freund.

Reflexive verbs: *sich freuen* – **Reflexive Verben:** *sich freuen*

Singular	1. Person	ich	freue	mich	(= personal pronoun)
	2. Person	du	freust	dich	(= personal pronoun
	3. Person	er / sie	freut	**sich**	
Plural	1. Person	wir	freuen	uns	(= personal pronoun)
	2. Person	ihr	freut	euch	(= personalpronoun)
	3. Person	sie / Sie	freuen	**sich**	

Reflexive verbs have a reflexive pronoun that is identical to the accusative personal pronoun. Exception: the 3rd person = *sich*. More verbs in Lesson 30.

11 *Fill in the forms of* sich freuen.

Tante Beate kommt. _____ du _____?

Warum _____ er _____ nicht?

Hat _____ Tommy gefreut?

Wir sehen uns also heute Abend. Ich _____ _____.

Christoph bekommt eine Mail von Caroline. Er _____ _____ sehr.

Bald machen wir Urlaub. Wir _____ _____ schon.

12 *Revision*

Mail or letter

die Mail, die Mails / das Fax, die Faxe	*mail / fax*
die Postkarte, die Postkarten (= die Karte, die Karten)	*postcard*
der Brief, die Briefe	*letter*
die Briefmarke, die Briefmarken	*stamp*
schicken – er / sie schickt, hat geschickt	*send*
senden – er / sie sendet, hat gesendet	*send*

13 *Listen closely and repeat the exclamations. Imitate the intonation as closely as you can.*

Das ist klasse!	Das finde ich spannend!
Das ist super!	Das ist nett von dir!
Hör auf!	Das macht Spaß!

Cultural info (Textbook page 108)

Greeting cards

There's a real boom in postcards at the moment. The shelves are overflowing with post-cards, everywhere where they are on sale, especially in stationery shops. There's a card with a snappy message to lighten someone's heart for every conceivable situation and experience.

Postcards can be divided into various different categories. There are

1. the quite conventional ones. *Herzlichen Glückwunsch zum Geburtstag* for example, or sometimes, in English, "Happy Birthday". Decorated with a flower, and that's it. Other occasions are weddings, so-called "round" birthdays (at 30, 40, 50, 75, 80, 90, and even a 100th birthday is no longer quite so rare as it once was). Christmas and New Year cards are part of the annual ritual, too, of course.

2. elegant cards: they are tastefully designed, often with a picture of a famous painting on the front. Suitable for all occasions.

3. fun cards: the texts are sometimes quite long, well-meant wishes or funny ideas that have something to do with the people they are intended for.

4. and first and foremost holiday postcards: these of course are usually photos intended to create the impression of an absolutely wonderful holiday.

The culture of letter-writing, the extensive correspondence by letter of centuries gone by, that seems to have died with the electronic age of rapid information exchange. What remain, however, are the personal gestures, greetings and good wishes sent to friends and relatives. They are expressed on colourful cards on which the imagination knows no bounds.

Which card are you going to send? Select the appropriate one:
birthday / wedding / exam / birth of a baby
What are you going to write? Select the appropriate greeting:
Happy birthday and all the best.
Congratulations on your marriage. We wish you much happiness.
Congratulations on the birth of ... and all good wishes.
Congratulations on passing your exam and all the best for the future.

Vocabulary

1. Supply the article.

1. _____ Fax   4. _____ Postkarte

2. _____ Mail   5. _____ Notiz

3. _____ Brief   6. _____ SMS

2. Write the plural.

1. der PC   _____   4. die Postkarte _____

2. die Mail   _____   5. die Notiz   _____

3. der Brief _____   6. der Gruß   _____

Grammar

3. Which prepositions fit?

1. Am Wochenende war ich _____ meinen Geschwistern.

2. Wann warst du zuletzt _____ Hause?

3. Ich fahre _____ meinem Bruder in Urlaub.

4. Wir fahren _____ dem Auto.

5. Hast du die Mail-Adresse _____ deiner Schwester?

6. Bringst du mich _____ Bahnhof?

4. The preposition and the article are both missing here.

1. Grüße _____ _____ Urlaub.

2. Wir sind _____ Reichstag _____ _____ Kuppel.

3. Wir sind _____ _____ Zugspitze.

4. Wir sind _____ Atlantik.

5. Wir sind _____ _____ Alpen.

6. Wir sind _____ _____ Nordsee.

7. Wir sind _____ _____ Donau.

Check your answers in the key at the back of the book and then add up your points.

Total:	1 – 13	It would be a good idea to do this unit again straightaway.
	14 – 21	Pretty good. But it wouldn't hurt to gov over the dialogue and the grammar again.
	22 – 25	Excellent. If you like, you could go over the vocabulary again, otherwise you can carry straight on.

Ich antworte gleich – I'll reply straightaway

Claudia writes straight back to Laura. She's looking forward to her visit. Laura is Argentinian. She has been to Germany before, but Claudia has never been to Argentina. In this lesson you'll find all the important forms that have to do with the dative.

1 *When was that? When is that? When will that be?*
Put the time expressions in the right order.
- For the past, use the perfect or the preterite.
- For the future, use an adverb + the present tense: *Morgen schreibe ich.*
- When you want to express an intention to do something, use *werden* + the infinitive: *Wir **werden** dir **schreiben.***

in zwei Jahren/vor zwei Jahren	*in two years (time)/two years ago*
nächste Woche/letzte Woche	*next week/last week*
letzten Monat/nächsten Monat	*last month/next month*
vorgestern/gestern/heute/ morgen/übermorgen	*the day before yesterday/yesterday/today/ tomorrow/the day after tomorrow*

2 Claudia writes a mail
Now listen to Robert and Claudia talking about Laura. Listen to the conversation at least twice. Here's the vocabulary list.

… und schreibe Laura eine Mail.	*… and write Laura a mail.*
Wem gehören eigentlich die Zettel hier und das Buch?	*Who do these pieces of paper and the book belong to?*
Wem?	*Who to? To whom?*
gehören – es/das gehört, hat gehört	*belong*
Zettel (der), die Zettel	*piece of paper*
Das habe ich mir gedacht.	*That's what I thought.*
denken (sich) – er/sie denkt, hat gedacht	*think*
Mach doch mal ein bisschen Ordnung.	*Come on, tidy up a bit. (Literally: Make a bit of order.)*
Ordnung (die)	*order*
Das ist ja schrecklich!	*This is (really) awful.*
schrecklich	*awful, terrible*
Bleib ganz ruhig.	*Don't get worked up. (Literally: Stay quite calm.)*
Das dauert nur eine Sekunde.	*It will only take a second.*
Sekunde (die), die Sekunden	*second*
Wann warst du das letzte Mal da?	*When were you here the last time?*
letzte Mal (das)	*last time*
War das vor zwei Jahren?	*Was it two years ago?*
vor + Dativ (– zwei Jahren)	*ago*

Nächsten Monat sind wir zu Hause.	*We're at home next month.*
Dann können wir weiter planen.	*Then we can plan further.*
planen – er / sie plant, hat geplant	*plan*
Genau weiß ich es nicht.	*I don't know [it] exactly.*
Warst du schon mal da?	*Have you been there before?*
Nein, noch nicht.	*No, not yet.*
Aber ich möchte gern mal hinfahren.	*But I'd like to go (there).*
hin / fahren – du fährst hin, er/sie fährt hin, ist hingefahren	*go (there)*

The word *schrecklich* is often used in colloquial speech instead of sehr: *Das ist schrecklich teuer/alt/schwer.*

3 *Who said it, Claudia or Robert?*
Mark the right answer.

4 *We're going to ask you some questions now.*
Which answers do you think are correct? Mark them.

5 *The verb is missing here. Please complete.*
This exercise is about the imperative 2nd person singular. You'll find the grammar explanation in the manual before exercise 10.

6 *Please complete. You learned the names of countries, languages and nationalities in Lesson 24. Look them up there and revise them. Pay special attention to the endings.*

7 *Speaking exercise – Repeat the sentences with* ja.
First listen to the example.
The particle ja *is also used to express surprise and also involvment.*

8 *Speaking exercise – Repeat the sentences with* mal.
First listen to the example.
The particle mal *is used frequently in colloquial speech. One of its uses is to make a command much more friendly.*

9 *An email – Fill in* ja, mal *or* denn.
Emails are always written in a much more casual style than letters or postcards. Have a go at putting in the right fillers.

The dative – Der Dativ

Singular		masculine	feminine	neuter
Personal pronouns	*Nom.*	er	sie	es
Definite article		der Bruder	die Schwester	das Kind
Indefinite article		ein Bruder	eine Schwester	ein Kind
Possessive article		mein Bruder	meine Schwester	mein Kind
Personal pronoun	*Akk.*	ih**n**	sie	es
Definite article		de**n** Bruder	die Schwester	das Kind
Indefinite article		ein**en** Bruder	eine Schwester	ein Kind
Possessive article		mein**en** Bruder	meine Schwester	mein Kind
Personal pronoun	*Dativ*	ih**m**	ih**r**	ih**m**
Definite article		de**m** Bruder	de**r** Schwester	de**m** Kind
Indefinite article		ein**em** Bruder	ein**er** Schwester	ein**em** Kind
Possessive article		mein**em** Bruder	mein**er** Schwester	mein**em** Kind

Plural		masculine + feminine + neuter		
Personal pronoun	*Nom.*	sie/Sie		
Definite article	*+ Akk.*	die Eltern		
Indefinite article		–		
Possessive article		meine Eltern		
Personal pronoun	*Dativ*	**ihnen/Ihnen**		
Definite article		**de**n Eltern		
Indefinite article		–		
Possessive article		mein**en** Eltern		

- You learnt the following expression in the very first lesson. Now you can see that it's a dative:
  *Wie geht es **dir/Ihnen/ihnen**?*
- In the dative plural there is also an *-n* added to the noun:
  *Wie geht es de**n** Geschwister**n**?* (Nom: die *Geschwister*)
- *Wem?* is used to ask about a person in the dative:
  ***Wem** hast du geschrieben? – **Der** Tante.*

10 *Nobody has tidied up. Ask who the things belong to.*

Example: Wem gehört die Uhr?   (ich)   – *Mir.*

1. Wem gehört die Tasche?   (meine Freundin) – _____

2. Wem gehört die Kamera?   (mein Freund)   – _____

3. Wem gehört die Tasse?   (die Oma)   – _____

4. Wem gehört das Buch?   (unser Vater)   – _____

5. Wem gehört der Einkaufszettel? (unsere Mutter) – _____

6. Wem gehören die Flaschen?   (der Opa)   – _____

163

11 *Someone is writing a letter. The opening phrase* Ich hoffe ... *is typical. You can continue of course by asking after other people. Put in the dative.*

1. Ich hoffe, es geht _____ (ihr) gut.

2. Ich hoffe, es geht _____ (Sie) gut.

3. Ich hoffe, es geht _____ (du) gut.

4. Ich hoffe, es geht _____ _____ (dein Bruder) gut.

5. Ich hoffe, es geht _____ _____ (deine Schwester) gut.

6. Ich hoffe, es geht _____ _____ (deine Eltern) gut.

Imperative 2nd person singular – Imperativ 2. Person Singular

Here is a special feature of the imperative. Forms which are difficult to pronounce have an -e at the end.

antworten – Antworte doch!
klettern   – Klettere nicht so hoch!
segeln   – Segle nicht so weit!

If you'd like to revise the other imperative forms, have a look back at Lesson 17.

12 *Write the imperative.*

_____ doch mal! (schreiben)

_____ uns doch! (helfen)

_____ doch ruhig! (bleiben)

_____ doch _____! (hinfahren)

_____ doch _____! (aufhören)

_____ doch mal! (antworten)

13 *Revision and summary*

Expressing possession

Wem gehört das?	*Who does that belong to?*
Wem gehört ... (das Buch) hier?	*Who does ... (this book) belong to?*
Das gehört ... (mir / dir / ihm).	*That belongs to ... (me / you / him).*
gehören – er / sie / es gehört	*belong to*
Das ist mein / dein ... (Buch).	*That is my / your ... (book).*
Ich habe ein / kein ... (Auto).	*I have / don't have a ... (car).*
Das ist ... (das Auto) von ... (Peter).	*That is ... (Peter's) (car).*

164

Consonants

14 *In German you often get several consonants one after another in a word. It makes a difference whether the consonants are all part of one syllable or are spread over two syllables. Within one syllable say them one after another with no pauses in between: for example **du kommst**. If there are two separate syllables you speak the syllables separately: for example die Sprach-schule. Try it.*
Listen closely, and repeat.

du da**rfst**	wir **antw**orten (ant-wor-ten)
du ka**nnst**	in **Ordn**ung (Ord-nung)
abe**nds**	mein Spra**chk**urs (Sprach-kurs)
die **Str**aße	ein bi**ssch**en (biss-chen)
die **Spr**ache	die Hau**ptst**adt (Haupt-stadt)
die Ge**schw**ister	eine Po**stk**arte (Post-karte)

15 *Listen and add the missing consonants.*

1. die Blume wä _ _ _ _
2. der Gebu _ _ _ ort
3. he _ _ _ iche Grüße
4. Wo wa _ _ _ du?
5. Was habt ihr gema _ _ _ ?
6. am lie _ _ _ en
7. ich bu _ _ _ _ abiere
8. du _ _ _ i _ _ _ _
9. _ _ _ _ ell
10. die Ta _ _ _ _ elle
11. der fü _ _ _ e April
12. der e _ _ _ e Mai

Cultural info (Textbook page 112)

Have a guess and complete the explanation.

Result:

If you had half or more right:	You're a wizard on culture and geography. Congratulations!
If you were able to solve the task with the help of an atlas:	Very good. You have learned a lot of new things.
If you looked at the answers first:	Well, that's wasn't so good, was it? But if you've remembered everything, the learning goal has been achieved.

Karneval (der)	Carnival
Million (die), die Millionen	million
EU (die)	EU

Vocabulary

1. What is the right translation?

1. in zehn Jahren _____

2. vor 50 Jahren _____

3. letztes Jahr _____

4. nächste Woche _____

5. vorgestern _____

6. übermorgen _____

Grammar

2. The dative is missing here.

1. Das habe ich _____ gedacht.

2. Schreib _____ (wir) mal, ja?

3. Warum antwortest du _____ (ich) nicht?

4. Sag _____ (dein) Bruder viele Grüße.

5. Anja hat Geburtstag. Wann gratulierst du _____?

6. Hast du mit _____ _____ (deine Geschwister) telefoniert?

Listening Comprehension

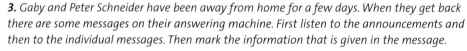

3|35

3. Gaby and Peter Schneider have been away from home for a few days. When they get back there are some messages on their answering machine. First listen to the announcements and then to the individual messages. Then mark the information that is given in the message.

1. a. Gaby und Peter sind nicht zu Hause.
   b. Sie möchten den Namen und die Telefonnummer.

2. a. Ein Freund hat angerufen.
   b. Er heißt Schneider.
   c. Er lädt Gaby und Peter zum Geburtstag ein.
   d. Der Geburtstag ist morgen.

3. a. Sascha hat angerufen.
   b. Er möchte Gaby sprechen.
   c. Er hat Probleme mit dem Computer.
   d. Peter soll ihm helfen.

4. a. Die Eltern von Peter haben angerufen.
   b. Peter soll anrufen.
   c. Sie wollen verreisen.

5. a. Die Firma Technocom hat angerufen.
   b. Der Drucker ist noch nicht fertig.

6. a. Oliver hat angerufen.
   b. Der Anruf ist für Gaby.
   c. Oliver möchte Tennis spielen.

Check your answers in the key at the back of the book and then add up your points.

Total:		
	1 – 9	Oh dear, that's a pity. Please do this unit again straightaway.
	10 – 15	Not so bad. But even so, it would be a good idea to go over the dialogue and the grammar again.
	16 – 18	Excellent. There's nothing to stop you carrying on.

Fast perfekt – Almost perfect

The Lernfabrik company visit is drawing to a close. Everybody is pretty sure that this meeting will be the beginning of an ongoing cooperation. Before they say goodbye to their visitor, Herr Kühne and Herr Heinrich have an opportunity to have a brief exchange of their impressions. These turn out to be very positive.

This lesson gives you an opportunity to learn how to express an opinion and a judgement.

1　*Wie finden Sie die / den / das ...?*

(zu) alt – jung	*(too) old – young*
(zu) groß – klein	*(too) big – small*
(zu) dick – dünn	*(too) thick, fat – thin*
freundlich – unfreundlich	*friendly – unfriendly*
nett – nicht besonders nett	*nice – not particularly nice*
hübsch – hässlich	*pretty – ugly*
sympathisch – unsympathisch	*nice, pleasant – not nice, unpleasant*

un- is always the negative opposite.
You can also add *sehr* or *zu: sehr nett, zu dick*.

You know this of course: people say that talking about other people is something that's not done. But sometimes you have to. In formal conversations judgments are usually balanced and tend to be positive. In private conversations people are more direct.

2　**What is your impression?**
→　*Now listen to what the two of them have to say. Listen to the conversation at least twice.*　
→　*Here again is our vocabulary list for you.*

Eindruck (der), die Eindrücke	*impression*
Die Firma ist klein, aber sie arbeitet gut.	*The firm is small, but it works well.*
Sie soll pünktlich und zuverlässig sein.	*It is said to be punctual and reliable.*
pünktlich	*punctual*
zuverlässig	*reliable*
Aber nicht besonders schnell, oder?	*But not particulary fast, right?*
die Qualität stimmt	*the quality is good (literally: is correct)*
Die Software ist fast perfekt.	*The software is almost perfect.*
Was heißt hier „fast"?	*What does "almost" mean here?*
Sie muss absolut perfekt sein.	*It must be absolutely perfect.*
Sie wissen doch.	*You know.*
Es gibt keine Software ohne Fehler.	*There is no software without defects.*
ohne + Akk.	*without*
Fehler (der), die Fehler	*mistake, error, defect*
Schon gut.	*OK.*
Und wie gefällt Ihnen Frau Bruckner?	*And what do you think of Frau Bruckner?*

Ich finde sie sehr kompetent.	*I find her very competent.*
kompetent	*competent*
Und Humor hat sie auch.	*And she has a sense of humour too.*
Humor (der)	*(sense of) humour*
Die Zusammenarbeit mit ihr ist sehr angenehm.	*Working with her is very pleasant.*
Zusammenarbeit (die)	*working (together); cooperation*
angenehm	*pleasant*
Ja, ich finde sie auch sehr sympathisch.	*Yes, I find her very likeable too.*
Was ist mit der Konkurrenz?	*What about the competition?*
Konkurrenz (die)	*competition*
Sie haben doch mit der Konkurrenz gesprochen.	*You've spoken to the competition, haven't you?*
Die ist zu teuer.	*They are too expensive.*
Außerdem sind die Konkurrenzfirmen zu weit entfernt.	*Besides the competitors are too far away.*
Konkurrenzfirma (die), die Konkurrenzfirmen (die Konkurrenz + die Firma)	*competitor*
weit entfernt	*far away*
Entfernungen spielen heute keine Rolle.	*Distances don't matter today.*
Entfernung (die), die Entfernungen	*distance*
Rolle (die): eine Rolle spielen	*role: play a role, matter, be of importance*
Aber persönliche Kontakte, die müssen sein.	*But personal contacts, you can't do without them.*
persönlich	*personal*
Kontakt (der), die Kontakte	*contact*
Das haben wir jetzt erlebt.	*We've seen (literally: experienced) that now.*
erleben – er/sie erlebt, hat erlebt	*experience*

3 *Mark what's right.*

4 *Some important information is missing here. Reconstruct the text.*

 5 *You want to make a video film and are doing the casting, in other words you're selecting your actors. You are looking at photos together with colleagues. Match the texts and photos.*

6 *The forms of* müssen *are missing here.*

7 *Nobody knows much about the company. – Put in* sollen.

 8 *Speaking exercise*
You don't really know. Answer with sollen.

Modal verb – Modalverb *sollen*

		sollen
Singular	ich	**soll**
	du	sollst
	er/sie	**soll**
Plural	wir	sollen
	ihr	sollt
	sie/Sie	sollen

- Note the difference between *wollen* and *sollen*:
  Ich *will* nichts kaufen. (= That is my wish.)
  Ich *soll* Herrn … anrufen. (= That's what my colleague tells me to do.)
  Die Firma *soll* zuverlässig sein. (= That's what people say about the company.)
- *sollen* has two meanings:
  1. "should" or "be to": A gives instructions that B is to carry out: *Er soll …*
  2. "be said to" There is hearsay about someone / something: *Die Firma soll zuverlässig sein.*

9 *Supply the first and third person singular. Then you'll see which verbs have special forms in the singular.*

1. mögen – ich / er / sie _____
2. können – ich / er / sie _____
3. dürfen – ich / er / sie _____
4. sollen   – ich / er / sie _____
5. wissen – ich / er / sie _____
6. müssen – ich / er / sie _____

10 *How many verbs with special forms in the singular did you count?*

Das sind _____ Verben: die Modalverben und das Verb _____ .

Interrogative pronouns – Fragepronomen: *Wer?, Was?, Wen?, Wem?*

Personen	Sachen	
Nominativ	**Wer?**	**Was?**
Akkusativ	**Wen?**	**Was?**
Dativ	**Wem?**	–

Wer ist der Mann?	Das ist Herr Binder.
Wen treffen Sie heute?	Herrn Binder.
Wem geben Sie die Arbeit?	Frau Karlow.

Was ist das?	Ein Brief von Ingo.
Was machst du?	Ich arbeite.

mit can also be placed in front of *Wem?*: **Mit wem** hast du gesprochen?

11 *You're at a conference. Ask a checking question. You can choose between* Wer? Wen? Wem? *and* Was?

Example: Das ist Christine Meyer.   Wer? Christine Meyer? Aha.

1. Wie finden Sie Herrn Müller heute?   _____? Herrn Müller? Super!

2. Spricht Herr Hirmer mit Herrn Fischer?   Mit _____? Nein, das ist doch Helmut Ost.

3. Ich sehe heute Herrn Matthes nicht.   _____? Herrn Matthes? Da steht er doch.

4. Das Handy gehört Marlene.   _____? Nein, mir.

5. Da steht Frau Krechel.   _____? Frau Krechel?

6. Wie finden Sie die Ergebnisse?   _____? Welche Ergebnisse?

und, oder, aber

und	Sie ist schnell. Sie ist zuverlässig.	Sie ist **schnell und zuverlässig**.
	Die Qualität ist perfekt. Der Preis stimmt.	**Die Qualität** ist perfekt **und der Preis** stimmt.
oder	Sie telefoniert. Sie schreibt eine Mail.	Sie **telefoniert oder schreibt** eine Mail.
aber	Er ist sympathisch. Er ist nicht kompetent.	Er ist **sympathisch, aber nicht kompetent.**

You can join two whole sentences or parts of sentences with *und, oder* and *aber*. Careful: *Sie telefoniert oder (sie) schreibt eine Mail.* The second noun or pronoun is omitted when it is identical.

12 *Combine the sentences with* und *or* aber.

1. Die Firma ist klein. Die Mitarbeiter sind zuverlässig.
2. Die Software ist ohne Fehler. Die Qualität stimmt.
3. Herr Lüders ist sehr kompetent. Er hat keinen Humor.
4. Die Konkurrenz ist nicht schlecht. Sie ist zu teuer.
5. Wir haben einen guten Eindruck. Wir möchten Sie gerne einladen.
6. Die Entfernungen sind groß. Persönliche Kontakte müssen sein.

13 *Revision*

Talking about someone / something

Wie ist Ihr / dein Eindruck?	*What's your impression?*
Wie finden Sie / findest du … (die Firma)?	*What do you think of … (the company)?*
Mein Eindruck ist … (gut / sehr gut …).	*My impression is … (good / very good).*
Frau … / Herr … ist … (sehr nett / nicht sehr sympathisch / etwas unsympathisch).	*Mrs … / Mr … is … (very nice / not very nice / not quite nice).*
Frau … / Herr … soll … (zuverlässig …) sein.	*Mrs … / Mr … is said to be … (reliable …).*
Die Firma ist klein, aber sie arbeitet gut.	*The company is small, but it works well.*

Stress in a word group

In a word group it is always the most important information that is stressed. This information can be contained in a noun, verb, adjective or adverb *(da, heute, sehr)*. Articles,
auxiliary verbs *(sein, haben)* and modal verbs are not stressed.

14 *Listen closely. Mark the word that carries the stress.*

1. 2. 3. 4.	Wort	1. 2. 3. 4.	Wort
☐ ☐	die Firma	☐ ☐	zu teuer
☐ ☐ ☐	mit der Konkurrenz	☐ ☐	sehr sympathisch
☐ ☐ ☐	Sie wissen doch	☐ ☐	fast perfekt
☐ ☐ ☐ ☐	die Zusammenarbeit mit ihr	☐ ☐ ☐ ☐	keine Software ohne Fehler

Now listen to the word groups again and compare your solutions. Then repeat the phrases.

15 *Word groups are often complete short sentences. The stress is usually at the end of the
sentence.*
Try it out. Listen closely and mark which word is stressed.

1. 2. 3. 4.	Wort	1. 2. 3. 4.	Wort
☐ ☐ ☐ ☐	Das ist meine Firma.	☐ ☐ ☐	Die Qualität stimmt.
☐ ☐	Guten Tag.	☐ ☐ ☐ ☐	Sie ist sehr kompetent.
☐ ☐ ☐ ☐	Die Firma ist klein.	☐ ☐ ☐ ☐	Vielen Dank für alles.
☐ ☐ ☐	Sie arbeitet gut.	☐ ☐ ☐ ☐	Ich komme nächste Woche.
☐ ☐ ☐	Das ist perfekt.	☐ ☐ ☐ ☐	Das können wir organisieren.

Cultural info (Textbook page 116)

A game

You can also play this game on your own. You just need a coin and a dice.
Every time you've finished a square, check with the key. But don't cheat please. Don't
whatever you do look at the next answer. Cover the answers up with a piece of paper so
that you always see just the one answer.
This is how you play:
Right answer: move forward 1 square.
Wrong answer: move back one square.
If you manage to do it in under 10 minutes, you've done very well.

Vocabulary

1. What's missing? Do you remember?

1. Wie ist Ihr Ei_ _ _ _ _ ?

2. Die Qu_ _ _ _ _ stimmt.

3. Sie w_ _ _ _ _ doch, es gibt keine Software ohne F_ _ _ _ _ .

4. Ich f_ _ _ _ sie auch sehr sympathisch.

5. Die Konkurrenz ist zu t_ _ _ _ .

6. Au_ _ _ _ _ _ sind die Firmen zu weit entfernt.

2. Insert the word in brackets into the sentence.

1. Das ist weit. (zu) _____

2. Die Firma ist gut. (sehr) _____

3. Sie ist schnell. (besonders) _____

Grammar

3. Fill in the interrogative pronoun.

1. Mit _____ hast du gesprochen?   4. _____ machst du heute noch?

2. _____ war das?   5. _____ ist das?

3. _____ hast du angerufen?   6. _____ hast du geholfen?

4. Insert the modal verb.

1. Er hat Geld. (sollen) _____

2. Er macht Urlaub. (können) _____

3. Er fährt nach Italien. (möchten) _____

4. Er fliegt nicht. (mögen) _____

5. Er fährt mit dem Zug. (müssen) _____

6. Er ist in vierzehn Tagen zurück. (müssen) _____

5. Join the sentences with oder, und *or* aber.

1. Sie schreibt eine Mail. Sie schreibt ein(e) SMS. (oder)

_____

2. Die Qualität stimmt. Die Software ist perfekt. (und)

_____

3. Herr Schröder arbeitet zuverlässig, Er ist nicht besonders schnell. (aber)

_____

Check your answers in the key at the back of the book and then add up your points.

Total:		
	1 – 12	Before you carry on, you really should do this unit again.
	13 – 20	Quite good, but not perfect yet. Please go over the dialogue and the grammar again. It'll be worth it.
	21 – 24	Very good. You can carry straight on.

Ich studiere hier – I'm studying here

Robert has been in Berlin for several days now. He has to return home, as he has already told us. But he hasn't disclosed yet what plans he has after that. That's what we're going to hear now.

Claudia is prepared to reorganise the flat for him. We learn a lot about prepositions and the verbs *stehen* and *stellen*.

1 *Which word fits?*
Here you're looking for words that have to do with studying. You've heard them all before.

Fach (das), die Fächer	*subject*

2 Are you leaving or staying a bit longer?
→ *Now listen to Robert's news. Listen to the conversation at least twice.*
→ *Here again is our vocabulary list.*

Hör mal!	*Now listen!*
Sag mal, willst du nun fahren oder bleibst du noch?	*Tell me now, do you want to leave or are you staying?*
wollen – du willst, er / sie will	*want*
Ich muss das jetzt unbedingt wissen.	*I really have to know that now.*
unbedingt	*really, absolutely*
Das habe ich mir fast gedacht.	*That's what I thought / expected.*
Nächstes Semester studiere ich hier.	*I'm studying here next semester.*
Semester (das), die Semester	*semester, term*
Was sagst du dazu?	*What do you say to that?*
… und meine Schwester hat bestimmt auch nichts dagegen.	*… and I bet my sister won't mind either.*
Willst du an die TU?	*Do you want to go to the TU?*
TU (die) = Technische Universität	*TU = Technical University*
Die ist sehr gut in meinem Fach.	*It's very good for my subject.*
Nächste Woche fahre ich nach Hause und komme dann in drei Wochen wieder.	*I'm going home next week and then I'm coming back in three weeks (time).*
in drei Wochen	*in three weeks (time)*
Zu Semesterbeginn.	*For the beginning of term.*
Semesterbeginn (der)	*beginning of term / the semester*
Deine Sachen kannst du hier lassen.	*You can leave your things here.*
Sachen (die Plural)	*things*
lassen – er / sie lässt, hat gelassen	*leave*
Au ja, prima.	*Oh great.*
Ich muss mir bald ein Zimmer oder eine Wohnung suchen.	*I shall have to look for a room or a flat soon.*

Aber zuerst kommst du zu uns.	*But first you'll come to us.*
Da räumen wir ein bisschen um.	*We'll move things round a bit.*
umräumen – er / sie räumt um, hat umgeräumt	*rearrange things, move things round*
Wir haben eine Liege.	*We have a sofa-bed.*
Liege (die), die Liegen	*sofa-bed, folding bed*
Die stellen wir ins Wohnzimmer.	*We'll put it in the living-room.*
stellen – er / sie stellt, hat gestellt	*put*
Dann bleibt Laura auch hier.	*Then Laura will stay here too.*
Und was sagt Niki dazu?	*And what will Niki say?*

3   *Read what Claudia has to say. Then find Robert's answer.*

4   umräumen *is a separable verb. We want to practise it now. Complete the sentences.*

5   *You're sitting at home in your living room. Do you know what the pieces of furniture are called in German? We want to practise that now. Which picture goes with which word? Look up any unknown words in the glossary.*

6   *Now listen to what Claudia says. She's reorganising things, and you're helping here. Note on the sketch which piece of furniture goes where.*

7   *Speaking exercise – A few questions for a student*
Answer using the prompts.

Prepositions after Wo? and Wohin? – Präpositionen nach Wo? und Wohin?

Akkusativ

Ich fahre/gehe …

nach Griechenland.
in die Türkei.
ins Ausland.
an den Rhein.
auf den Fernsehturm.

Dativ

Morgen bin ich …

in Griechenland.
in der Türkei.
im Ausland.
am Rhein.
auf dem Fernsehturm.

In answer to the question **Wohin?** – *Ich gehe/stelle etwas* …

an up to the edge of something: *an den Fluss, an den Schreibtisch, an die Wand*

auf 1. onto something that is higher: *auf den Tisch, auf den Berg*
2. onto something that is flat and open: *auf die Straße/den Platz/den Sportplatz, auf die Insel, auf den Teller*
3. Note: we say *ins Gebirge, in die Berge, in die Alpen*

in 1. into an enclosed space: *ins Zimmer, ins Haus, in die Küche/Schule*
2. into something enclosed that surrounds you: *ins Wasser, in den Garten*
3. to countries that have an article: *in die Schweiz/Türkei/Slowakei/in den Norden*

nach 1. countries, continents that have no article, and points of the compass: *nach Spanien, nach Asien, nach Norden*; cities: *nach Warschau/Peking*

In answer to the question **Wo?** – *Ich stehe/bin* …

an on the edge of something: *am Fluss, am Schreibtisch, an der Wand*

auf 1. up on something that is higher: *auf dem Tisch, auf dem Berg*
2. on something that is flat and open: *auf der Straße/dem Platz/dem Sportplatz, auf der Insel, auf dem Teller*
3.Note: we say *im Gebirge, in den Bergen, in den Alpen*

in 1. in an enclosed space: *im Zimmer, im Haus, in der Küche/der Schule*
2. in something that surrounds you: *im Wasser, im Garten*
3. in countries with an article and places to the north/south/east/west: *in der Schweiz/Türkei/Slowakei, im Norden*
4. in countries, continents without an article, in cities: *in Spanien/Asien/Rom*

stehen and *stellen*

Stell den Stuhl **in die Küche**, bitte.	(= Akkusativ)
Der **steht** schon **in der Küche**.	(= Dativ)

stellen (= put) means that something is moved. So *stellen* takes the accusative.
stehen (= stand, be) does not of course indicate any movement, hence the dative.

175

8 *Fill in the article in the accusative or the dative. Have a close look at the verb each time. Then you'll know whether there is movement involved (= accusative) or not (= dative).*

Fahren Sie an den Bodensee?   – Nein, ich war im April _____ Bodensee.

Fahren Sie _____ _____ Schweiz?   – Nein, ich war im Mai in der Schweiz

Fahren Sie an die Ostsee?   – Nein, ich war im Sommer _____ _____ Ostsee.

Fahren Sie _____ _____ Rhein?   – Nein, ich war schon so oft am Rhein.

Fahren Sie auf den Fernsehturm?   – Nein, ich war gestern _____ _____ Fernsehturm.

Gehen Sie _____ Museum?   – Nein, ich war schon im Museum.

9 *First locate the verb and then decide whether the accusative or the dative should follow. Fill in the article.*

Bitte, stell das Obst auf _____ Tisch. (der Tisch)

Wo ist der Orangensaft? Der steht schon auf _____ Tisch.

Stell bitte den Koffer in _____ Flur. (der Flur)

Wo stehen die Getränke? In _____ Küche. (die Küche)

Stell die Stühle i_____ Wohnzimmer. (das Wohnzimmer)

Wohin soll ich das Fahrrad stellen? – In _____ Keller. (der Keller)

10 *You have lots of plans. Fill in* wollen *or* werden.

Nächstes Semester _____ ich nach Berlin gehen. (wollen)

Ich _____ da ein Semester studieren. (werden)

Ich _____ ein Appartment mieten. (werden)

Das _____ bestimmt teuer werden. (werden)

*ich werde
du wirst
er / sie wird*

11 *Revision and summary*

Telephoning 2

As preparation for the pronunciation exercise please read the following words.

Ich rufe jetzt … (Marius) an.	*I'm going to call … (Marius) now.*
Auskunft (die)	*directory enquiries*
auflegen – er / sie legt auf, hat aufgelegt	*hang up*
zurückrufen – er / sie ruft zurück, hat zurückgerufen	*call back*
auf Band sprechen – er / sie spricht, hat gesprochen	*leave a message (on the answering machine)*
Anrufbeantworter (der)	*answering machine*
Pfeifton (der) (nach dem Pfeifton)	*beep*
Leider keiner da.	*I'm afraid there's nobody here / there.*

12 *You're no doubt familiar with this situation: the answerphone is running at the other end of the line and you're struggling to find the right words ... This is what the following conversation between two young people is about.*

→ *Listen to the conversation.*
→ *Then read the text.*

Leider keiner da

Stephanie:	Ich rufe jetzt Eva und Frank an. Hast du die Nummer?
Norbert:	Augenblick ... 789 28 40.
Stephanie:	Da ist ein Fax dran.
Norbert:	Dann probier mal die Nummer 789 28 41.
Stephanie:	Jetzt klingelt es ... Anrufbeantworter!
Norbert:	Warum legst du denn auf?
Stephanie:	Ich weiß nicht ... Was soll ich sagen?
Norbert:	Was? So ein Unsinn! Sag einfach: Hier Stephanie. Ruft bitte zurück. Danke.
Stephanie:	Das ist zu kurz. Das ist ja unhöflich.
Norbert:	Dann schreib ein Fax.
Stephanie:	Nein, nein, ich spreche jetzt aufs Band. Also noch einmal: 789 ..
Band:	*Leider keiner da. Bitte sprechen Sie nach dem Pfeifton. Sagen Sie Ihren Namen und Ihre Telefonnummer. Wir rufen sofort zurück. Danke.*
Stephanie:	Hallo! Hier Stephanie. Was macht ihr am Wochenende? Wir planen einen Ausflug. Kommt ihr mit? Ruft bitte an! Tschüs! Anrufbeantworter sind schrecklich!

13 *Listen to the text again and repeat the sentences.*

14 *Now take over Stephanie's role.*

- Say that you're calling Eva and Frank now. Ask for their number.
- Say that a fax is on at the other end.
- Say that it's now ringing and that it's an answerphone.
- Say I don't know and ask her what you should say.
- Say that it is too short and that it is impolite.
- Say no and that you'll speak on the tape. Call again.
- Now leave a message: Say hello and say who you are. Then ask what your friends are doing at the weekend. Say that you're planning an excursion. Ask if your friends are coming with you. Say they should phone you. Say goodbye.

Cultural info (Textbook page 120)

My room

1. Find the furniture. Write each piece down with its article and plural or singular form.

2. What does your study look like at home? Write a description. The key offers a model answer.

Vocabulary

1. Read the word and find the second word that goes with it.

Example: der Süden – der Norden

| das Wochenende | die Studenten | der Bahnhof |

| der Einkaufszettel | der Schirm | das Flugzeug | der See |

1. die Woche   – _____
2. der Zug   – _____
3. der Flughafen   – _____
4. die Universität – _____

5. schwimmen – _____
6. regnen   – _____
7. einkaufen – _____

2. Note down the words that are directly related to studying. Add the articles and verb forms.

| Semester | Prüfung | Sachen | umräumen | Fach | Wörter | Semesterbeginn |

| helfen | studieren | Wohnzimmer | stellen | Studium | Student | Studentin |

| Möbel | Geld | Semesterferien | Universität | wollen | denken |

1. _____
2. _____
3. _____
4. _____
5. _____

6. _____
7. _____
8. _____
9. _____
10. _____

Grammar

3. Fill in the preposition.

Wir gehen / fliegen

1. _____s Ausland.
2. _____ den See.

3. _____ Süden.
4. _____ den Sportplatz.

5. _____ Bahnhof.
6. _____ links.

4. Fill in the preposition.

Wir stehen / sind

1. _____ dem Sportplatz.
2. _____ der Tankstelle.

3. _____ der Kirche.
4. _____ der Straße.

5. _____ Schloss.
6. _____ dem Turm.

Check your answers in the key at the back of the book and then add up your points.

Total:		
	1 – 13	It would be a good idea to do this unit again straightaway.
	14 – 25	Pretty good. But it wouldn't hurt to gov over the dialogue and the grammar again.
	26 – 29	Excellent. If you like, you could go over the vocabulary again, otherwise you can carry straight on.

Bis bald – See you soon

Frau Bruckner has now dealt with everything. She says goodbye and then goes to the station.
We learn all the important phrases that you need when you say goodbye, and new words on the topic of travel.

1 *There is one key word in this text. Everything revolves around it. What is it? Put the syllables together in the right order.*

2 Goodbye
Now listen to the three business partners saying goodbye. Listen to the conversation at least twice. If you need help, you can look up the vocabulary list.

So, mein Taxi ist da.	*Right, my taxi is here.*
Hatten Sie einen Mantel?	*Did you have a coat?*
Nein, eine Jacke.	*No, a jacket.*
Und einen Schal.	*And a scarf.*
Schal (der), die Schals	*scarf*
In einer Stunde.	*In an hour('s time).*
Da habe ich genug Zeit.	*I have enough time.*
Und noch einmal vielen Dank für alles.	*And thank you very much again for everything.*
Sie hören sofort von mir.	*You'll hear from me straightaway.*
Ich schicke Ihnen das Angebot spätestens in einer Woche.	*I'll send you the offer in a week at the latest.*
in einer Woche	*in a week('s time)*
Wir freuen uns auf die Zusammenarbeit.	*We're looking forward to working together.*
Und danke für die Einladung gestern.	*And thank you for the invitation yesterday.*
Einladung (die), die Einladungen	*invitation*
Man isst dort sehr gut.	*The food there is very good.*
Vielleicht zum Vertragsabschluss.	*Maybe when we complete the contract.*
Vertragsabschluss (der), die Vertragsabschlüsse	*completion/conclusion of a contract*
Sie wissen ja, da ist die Küche auch nicht schlecht.	*You know the food's not bad there either.*
Bis bald.	*See you/Hear from you soon.*

At business meetings in Germany people tend to get to the point pretty quickly. People are polite, but soon show how strong their interest is.

3 *There are some important sentences missing in this text.*
People say them when they say goodbye. Listen to the text again and put the missing sentences back in.

4 Auf Wiedersehen *or* Tschüs?
What do you say in a private and/or business situation? Sort the expressions.

5 *I'm packing my suitcase.*
What do I have to remember to pack?

6 *Speaking exercise*
Here various people are saying goodbye to you. Listen to what they say. Then reply using the prompts given.

7 *Chris Bruckner's notes*

Time adverbials – Zeitangaben

Wann kommen Sie?

Nächst**en** Monat./Nächst**en** Donnerstag.	(der Monat, der Donnerstag)
Nächst**e** Woche.	(die Woche)
Nächst**es** Jahr./Nächst**es** Wochenende.	(das Jahr, das Wochenende)

In vierzehn Tagen.	(der Tag)
In einer Woche.	(die Woche)
In einem Jahr.	(das Jahr)

Nächsten Monat, nächstes Jahr are accusative forms (ending *-en*).
In einer Woche, in einem Jahr are datives (endings *-er* and *-em*).

Ich komme nächsten Monat. (= sometime during the course of the month)
Ich komme in einem Monat. (= I'm coming in four weeks time.)

Note that, in German, time adverbials come before place adverbials, and not the other way round.
Ich fahre (time:) *nächsten Monat* (place:) *nach Berlin.*

8 *Put* nächst- *with the appropriate ending in front of each word.*

Ich komme …

1. das Jahr _____ Jahr
2. der Monat _____ Monat
3. die Woche _____ Woche
4. der Dienstag _____ Dienstag
5. das Wochenende _____ Wochenende
6. das Semester _____ Semester

Reflexive verbs – Reflexive Verben / Reciprocal verbs – Reziproke Verben

sich freuen		
ich	freue	mich
du	freust	dich
er/sie	freut	**sich**
wir	freuen	uns
ihr	freut	euch
sie/Sie	freuen	**sich**

sich sehen			
wir	sehen	uns	bald
ihr	seht	euch	
sie/Sie	sehen	**sich**	

- Reciprocal means that two parties are involved in the same way. So there are only plural forms.
- There's more on reflexive verbs in Lesson 26. The following verbs are also reflexive.

sich anziehen	*get dressed*	sich beschweren	*complain*
sich ausruhen	*have a rest*	sich duschen	*have a shower*
sich ausziehen	*get undressed*	sich verletzen	*hurt oneself*
sich beeilen	*hurry*	sich waschen	*wash (oneself)*

9 *This is how reflexive verbs often occur. Please complete.*

Hast du _____ verletzt?

Duschst du _____ noch?

Ich habe _____ schon ausgezogen und liege im Bett.

Beeil _____ doch!

Willst du _____ beschweren?

Ruh _____ doch ein bisschen aus.

Ich habe _____ schon ausgezogen und gewaschen.

10 *Time expressions*

Gestern bin ich gekommen.	*I came yesterday.*
Heute habe ich viel Arbeit.	*I have a lot of work today.*
Morgen mache ich frei.	*Tomorrow I'll have a day off.*
morgens	*in the morning(s)*
mittags	*at lunchtime*
abends	*in the evening(s)*
nachmittags	*in the afternoon(s)*
nachts	*at night*

nächsten Monat (der Monat)	*next month*
nächste Woche (die Woche)	*next week*
nächstes Jahr (das Jahr)	*next year*
in einem Monat / drei Monaten	*in a month / in three months (time)*
in einer Woche / drei Wochen	*in a week / in three weeks (time)*
in einem Jahr / drei Jahren	*in a year / three years (time)*

11 *Revision*

Leave-taking phrases

Wir freuen uns / Ich freue mich auf die Zusammenarbeit.	*We are / I am looking forward to our cooperation / to working together.*
Vielen Dank für die Einladung.	*Thank you very much for the invitation.*
Vielen Dank für das Gespräch.	*Thank you for the meeting.*
Vielen Dank für alles.	*Thank you very much for everything.*
Bis bald.	*See / Hear from you soon.*
Auf Wiedersehen.	*Goodbye.*

12 *Listen closely and repeat. In the second person singular you often find several consonants occurring together.*

Duschst du dich? Suchst du mich?
Wäschst du dich jetzt? Buchst du die Reise?
Beschwerst du dich? Brauchst du das Buch?
Tankst du bald?

Cultural info (Textbook page 124)

Every city has something typical. Paris, for example, has the Eiffel Tower, Rome the Colosseum. Here's a selection of nine sights. Guess which city it is.

Here are the cities and a brief description of the sights.

Lucerne (Switzerland)
The city's landmark is the old bridge, built in about 1300.

Hamburg (Germany)
The harbour and port are among the largest in the world. A boat trip round them is a special attraction.

Munich (Germany)
The Munich Oktoberfest draws about 7 million tourists from all over the world every year. They drink five million steins of beer, and consume 700,000 *Hendl* (roast chickens).

Potsdam (Germany)
Sanssouci (= French sans souci = without a care) is a rococo castle dating from the 18th century. It was the favourite residence of the Prussian ruler Frederick the Great.

Weimar (Germany)
The summer house was a present from the Duke to Johann Wolfgang von Goethe. His finest lyrical work was written there. Today it is a popular museum.

Berlin (Germany)
The Reichstag, seat of the German Parliament, was built between 1884 and 1894. It was completely destroyed at the end of the Second World War.

Dresden (Germany)
The Frauenkirche, the city's landmark, was completely destroyed in the war. It was rebuilt – partly with the aid of donations – according to old plans.

Vienna (Austria)
The Cathedral of St. Stephan, an 800-year-old church in the middle of the city, is the emblem of Austria.

Salzburg (Austria)
The city and its festival are a big tourist attraction. The world-famous composer Wolfgang Amadeus Mozart was born here in 1756.

183

Vocabulary

1. Mark the right translation.

1. in drei Stunden
☐ in three hours
☐ in three weeks
☐ in three months

2. spätestens in einer Woche
☐ in at least a week
☐ in a week at the latest
☐ in a week's time

3. wirklich sehr schön
☐ next week
☐ very soon indeed
☐ really very nice

4. schicken
☐ leave
☐ send
☐ think

5. Was planen Sie?
☐ What are you planning?
☐ Where are you planning to go?
☐ What plane are you taking?

6. Wir kommen gern.
☐ We look forward to that.
☐ We'll be glad to come.
☐ We'll complete the contract.

7. Sie wissen ja …
☐ You know …
☐ You'll see …
☐ You'll hear …

8. Die Küche ist auch nicht schlecht.
☐ The kitchen is not small.
☐ The food is not bad either.
☐ The coat's with the scarf.

Grammar

2. Add the ending.

1. nächst_____ Jahr

2. nächst_____ Monat

3. nächst_____ Woche

4. in ein_____ Woche

5. in ein_____ Jahr

6. nächst_____ Freitag

3. What's the pronoun?

1. Wir duschen _____ jetzt.

2. Wäschst du _____ nicht?

3. Warum beschweren Sie _____ nicht?

4. Freust du _____ ?

5. Beeil _____ doch!

6. Wir ruhen _____ jetzt aus.

Listening Comprehension

3|51

4. Listen and guess where I am.

Wo bin ich? – Ich bin am _____.

Check your answers in the key at the back of the book and then add up your points.

Total:		
	1 – 11	Oh dear, that's a pity. Please do this unit again straightaway.
	12 – 18	Not so bad. But even so, it would be a good idea to go over the dialogue and the grammar again.
	19 – 21	Excellent. There's nothing to stop you carrying on.

Some study tips:

1. Do the first lesson and time how long you need. The lessons are all roughly the same length, so this will tell you how much time you should plan for each lesson.
2. Try and set aside half an hour a day for studying. That is more effective than, for example, doing two or three hours at the weekend.
3. Make a point of listening to the texts and speaking exercises on the CDs over and over again (pictograms in the Workbook). This is a sure way of getting your ear accustomed to the sound of the language and the sentences. Repeat the pronunciation exercises as often as you can.
4. Buy a German newspaper or magazine from time to time. You'll soon discover words that you've learned and now know.
5. And most important of all: if you suddenly have the feeling that you're not making any progress, don't give up! As the proverb says, you can't expect to get everything right first time.

And now we've reached the end of the course. You've learned a lot of useful everyday language that you can use right away. And something about the German-speaking countries too. If you have time, come and visit us at: www.hueber.de. You'll find some information and tips on our homepage, and we'd like you to keep up your German and include it in your daily programme of study. Cheerio and see you soon!

Glossar – Glossary   German – English

Numbers refer to lessons

A

ab sofort	9	*immediately, with immediate effect*
Ab wann?	29	*Starting when? From when?*
Abend (der), -e	1	*evening*
Abendessen (das)	14	*supper, dinner*
abends	10	*in the evening(s)*
Abenteuer (das), -	24	*adventure*
aber	2	*but*
Abschied (der)	30	*farewell, leave-taking*
absolut	28	*absolute(ly)*
Abteilung (die), -en	16, 22	*department*
Ach was!	8	*not at all, no*
achten auf – er/sie achtet, hat geachtet	9	*pay attention to*
Achtung!	24	*Careful!*
Adieu	1	*(good)bye*
Adjektiv (das), -e	4	*adjective*
Adresse (die), -n	3	*address*
Aerobic (das)	22	*aerobics*
Akkusativ (der), -e	9	*accusative*
aktuell	16	*up-to-date, present*
Alkohol (der)	17	*alcohol*
alle	4	*all, everybody, everyone*
Allee (die), -n	22	*boulevard, avenue*
allein	25	*alone, on your own, yourself*
alles	8	*everything*
Alles bestens.	8	*Everything's fine. Just great.*
alles Gute	26	*all the best*
Alles klar?	15	*Everything OK?*
Alpen (die Pl)	23, 26	*Alps*
als (weiter als)	10	*than*
also	6	*right, so*
alt	5	*old*
altmodisch	26	*old-fashioned, out-of-date*
am besten (gut – besser – am besten)	22, 24	*best (good – better – best)*
am liebsten (gern – lieber – am liebsten)	20, 22	*like best (like – like better – like best)*
Amerika (das)	14	*America*
Ampel (die), -n	19	*traffic light(s)*
an + Dat./Akk.	19, 23, 29	*at, to*
an/am ... entlang	19	*along ...*
an/am ... vorbei	19	*past ...*
Ananas (die)	17	*pineapple*
anbieten – er/sie bietet an, hat angeboten	7	*offer*
andere	27	*other, different*
Angebot (das), -e	3, 24	*offer*

angenehm	28	*pleasant*
Angst (die), ⸚e	22	*fear*
Anmeldung (die), -en	12	*booking, reception*
Anrede (die), -n	25	*salutation*
Anruf (der), -e	27	*phone call*
Anrufbeantworter (der), -	29	*answerphone, answering machine*
anrufen – er/sie ruft an, hat angerufen	10, 18	*phone, call*
ansehen – du siehst an, er/sie sieht an, hat angesehen	22	*look at*
Antwort (die), -en	2, 3	*answer*
antworten – er/sie antwortet, hat geantwortet	2	*answer*
anwenden – er/sie wendet an, hat angewendet	9	*use*
Anzeige (die), -n	9	*ad, advert*
anziehen sich – er/sie zieht sich an, hat sich angezogen	30	*get dressed*
Anzug (der), ⸚e	30	*suit*
Aperitif (der)	22	*aperitif*
Apfel (der), ⸚e	8	*apple*
Apfelsaft (der), ⸚e	17	*apple juice*
Apfelschorle (die), -n	17	*apple juice mixed with mineral water*
Apotheke (die), -n	20	*chemist, pharmacy*
Appartement (das), -s: 1-Zimmer-Appartement	9	*flat, apartment: one-room flat/ apartment*
Appetit (der)	21	*appetite*
Aprikose (die), -n	20	*apricot*
April (der)	24	*April*
Arbeit (die), -en	6	*work, job*
arbeiten (als ...) – er/sie arbeitet, hat gearbeitet	5, 15	*work (as ...)*
Arbeitszimmer (das), -	29	*study*
Architekt (der), -en/Architektin (die), -nen	13	*architect*
Archiv (das), -e	11	*filing room, storeroom*
Argentinien (das)	3	*Argentina*
Argentinier (der), -/Argentinierin (die), -nen	27	*Argentinian (man/woman)*
Ärger (der)	22	*trouble*
Arm (der), -e	12	*arm*
Armbanduhr (die), -en	10	*watch*
Artikel (der), -	3	*article*
Arzt (der), ⸚e / Ärztin (die), -nen	6	*doctor*
asiatisch	21	*Asian*
Asien (das)	13	*Asia*
Atlantik (der)	23	*Atlantic*
Au ja	29	*oh yes*
auch	1	*too, also*
auf Deutsch	3	*in German*
Auf Wiederhören	7	*Goodbye [on the pone]*
Auf Wiedersehen/Auf Wiederschaun	1	*Goodbye*
aufhören – er/sie hört auf, hat aufgehört	26	*stop*
auffordern – er/sie fordert auf, hat aufgefordert	14	*ask*
auflegen – er/sie legt auf, hat aufgelegt	29	*hang up*
aufrufen – er/sie ruft auf, hat aufgerufen	25	*call up*
aufschreiben – er/sie schreibt auf, hat aufgeschrieben	29	*write down*

Aufzug (der), ⸚e	11	*lift*
Auge (das), -n	12, 22	*eye*
Augenblick (der), -e: im Augenblick	22	*moment, instant: at the moment*
August (der)	23, 24	*August*
aus + Dativ	1, 2	*from, out of*
Ausdruck (der), ⸚e	24	*expression*
Ausflug (der), ⸚e	11	*trip, excursion*
ausfüllen – er/sie füllt aus, hat ausgefüllt	3	*fill in*
Auskunft, ⸚e	24, 29	*enquiry*
Ausland (das)	17, 28	*abroad*
Ausländer (der), -/Ausländerin (die), -nen	3, 27	*foreigner*
ausruhen sich – er/sie ruht sich aus, hat sich ausgeruht	30	*have a rest, relax*
aussehen – du siehst aus, er/sie sieht aus, hat ausgesehen	22	*look*
außen: nach außen geben	16	*outside: give out*
außerdem	25	*besides*
aussuchen – er/sie sucht aus, hat ausgesucht	30	*select, find*
Australien (das)	3	*Australia*
Australier (der), -/Australierin (die), -nen	24	*Australian (man/woman)*
australisch	14	*Australian*
Ausweis-Nummer (die), -n	3	*identity card number*
ausziehen sich – er/sie zieht sich aus, hat sich ausgezogen	30	*get undressed*
Auto (das), -s: Auto fahren	2, 11	*car: to go by car*
Autobahn (die), -en	19	*highway, motorway*
Automat (der), -en	5	*machine*
Autonummer (die), -n	24	*car number*

B

Baby (das), -s	13	*baby*
Baby-Wäsche (die)	21	*baby clothes*
backen – er/sie backt, hat gebacken	21	*bake*
Bad (das), ⸚er	9	*bath(room)*
Bademode (die), -n	21	*swimwear*
baden – er/sie badet, hat gebadet	9	*(have a) bath; go swimming*
Baden (das)	25	*swimming*
Bahn (die), -en	6	*railway, train*
Bahnfahrt (die), -en	25	*railway/train journey*
Bahnhof (der), ⸚e	11	*station*
Bahnhofsuhr (die), -en	10	*station clock*
bald	15	*soon*
Balkon, -e	9	*balcony*
Banane (die), -n	17	*banana*
Band (das): auf Band sprechen	29	*tape: leave a message on an answering machine*
Bank (die), -en	12	*bank*
Bankkaufmann (der), -leute/Bankkauffrau (die), -en	13	*bank clerk*
Bär (der), -en	22	*bear*
Bauch (der), ⸚e	12	*stomach*

Baum (der), ⸚e	22	*tree*
Bayer (der), -n / Bayerin (die), -nen	24	*Bavarian (man/woman)*
bayerisch	16	*Bavarian*
Bayern (das)	1	*Bavaria*
beantworten – er / sie beantwortet, hat beantwortet	6	*answer*
Becher (der), -	17	*carton*
bedeuten – es / das bedeutet, hat bedeutet	3	*mean*
beeilen sich – er / sie beeilt sich, hat sich beeilt	30	*hurry (up)*
begrüßen – er / sie begrüßt, hat begrüßt	12	*greet*
bei + Dat.	6, 19	*for, at*
beide	3, 18	*both*
Bein (das), -e	12	*leg*
Beispiel (das), -e	6, 23	*example: for example*
bekommen – er / sie bekommt, hat bekommen	16	*get, receive*
Belgien (das)	3	*Belgium*
Benzin (das)	22	*petrol/gas*
Berg (der), -e	23	*mountain*
Bergsteigen (das)	24	*mountain climbing*
Berliner (der), - / Berlinerin (die), -nen	24, 27	*Berliner*
Beruf (der), -e	6	*job, profession*
Berufsbezeichnung (die), -en	15	*job title*
berühmt	20, 29	*famous*
beschweren sich – er / sie beschwert sich, hat sich beschwert	30	*complain*
besichtigen – er / sie besichtigt, hat besichtigt	11	*look around, see*
Besichtigung (die), -en	11	*guided tour*
besonders	6	*especially*
besser (als) (gut – besser – am besten)	22	*better (good – better – best)*
bestehen – er / sie besteht, hat bestanden	26	*pass*
bestellen – er / sie bestellt, hat bestellt	2, 16	*order*
Besteller (der), -	24	*person ordering*
bestimmt	7	*definite(ly), certainly*
Besuch (der)	9	*visit*
besuchen – er / sie besucht, hat besucht	13	*visit*
betont	14	*stressed*
betreiben – er / sie betreibt, hat betrieben	23	*do*
Bett (das), -en : ins Bett gehen	29	*bed: go to bed*
Bettwaren (die Pl)	21	*bedding*
Bettwäsche (die)	21	*bed-linen*
Bewohner (der), -	24	*inhabitant*
bezahlen – er / sie bezahlt, hat bezahlt	25	*pay*
Bier (das), -e	14	*beer*
Biergarten (der), ⸚	20, 21	*beer garden*
Bierglas (das), ⸚er	22	*beer glass*
Bild (das), -er	6, 17	*picture*
Bildwörterbuch (der), ⸚er (das Bild + das Wörterbuch)	20	*picture dictionary*
billig	11	*cheap*
bis (Mittag / morgen / ...)	7	*till (noon/tomorrow/...)*
Bis bald!	30	*See you soon!*
Bis gleich.	10	*See you soon/later.*

Bis zum nächsten Mal.	30	*Till next time.*
Bistro (das), -s	22	*bistro*
bitte	3	*please*
bitte (Danke – Bitte.)	5	*You're welcome*
Bitte sehr.	7	*Here you are.*
Bitte (die), -n	25	*request*
Bitte?	5	*Sorry?*
Blattsalat (der), -e	21	*green salad*
(das Blatt, Blätter)		*(leaf, sheet)*
blau	22	*blue*
bleiben – er/sie bleibt, ist geblieben	9	*stay, remain*
Blume (die), -n	18, 29	*flower*
Blumenkohlsuppe (die), -n	21	*cauliflower soup*
Bluse (die), -n	30	*blouse*
Bodensee (der)	23	*Lake Constance*
Bonbon (das), -s	20	*sweet*
Boot (das), -e: Boot fahren	23	*boat: go in a boat, by boat*
Boutique (die), -n	12	*boutique*
Brandenburg (das)	16, 22	*Brandenburg*
Brasilien (das)	3	*Brazil*
Bratkartoffeln (die Pl)	20	*fried potatos*
Bratwurst (die), ⸚e	16	*sausage (fried/for frying)*
brauchen – er/sie braucht, hat gebraucht	10	*need*
braun	22	*brown*
Braune (der) (= Kaffeesorte)	7	*brown coffee (type of coffee)*
Bremse (die), -n	22	*brake*
Brief (der), -e	26	*letter*
Briefkasten (der), ⸚	19	*letterbox*
Briefmarke (die), -n	26	*stamp*
Brille (die), -n	30	*(pair of) glasses*
bringen – er/sie bringt, hat gebracht	9	*bring; take*
Brot (das), -e	13	*bread; sandwich*
Brötchen (das), -	13	*roll*
Brücke (die), -n	19	*bridge*
Bruder (der), ⸚	13	*brother*
Brust (die)	21	*breast*
Buch (das), ⸚er	21, 23	*book*
Buchhaltung (die)	12	*accounts (department)*
Buchstabe (der), -n	7	*letter*
Buchstaben-Labyrinth (das), -e	11	*puzzle, maze*
Buchstabensalat (der), -e	8	*jumbled letters*
buchstabieren -er/sie buchstabiert, hat buchstabiert	3	*spell*
Bulgare (der), -n/Bulgarin (die), -nen	24	*Bulgarian (man/woman)*
Bulgarien (das)	3	*Bulgaria*
bulgarisch	24	*Bulgarian*
Bundeskanzler (der)	22	*Federal Chancellor*
Bundesland (das), ⸚er	5	*federal state*
Bundespräsident (der), -en	22	*President of the Republic*
bunt	22	*(brightly) coloured*
Büro (das), -s	4	*office*

Bürokaufmann (der), ⸚er, -leute / Bürokauffrau (die), -en	13	*office clerk / administrator*
Bus (der), -se	7	*bus*
Bussi	15	*kiss*
Butter (die)	13	*butter*
bzw. (= beziehungsweise)	15	*or*

C

Café (das), -s	7	*café*
Campari (der)	18	*campari*
Camping (das)	21	*camping*
Cappuccino (der) (= Kaffeesorte)	7	*cappuccino*
Casino (das), -s	12	*canteen*
Casting (das)	28	*casting*
CD (die), -s	14	*CD*
Cent (der), -s	18, 28	*cent*
Center (das), -	22	*centre*
Chef (der), -s / Chefin (die), -nen	7	*boss*
Chilene (der), -n / Chilenin (die), -nen	27	*Chilean (man / woman)*
Chinese (der), -n / Chinesin (die), -nen	24	*Chinese (man / woman)*
chinesisch	13, 19	*Chinese*
Ciao	1	*cheerio*
circa	12	*about*
Co. (= Company)	21	*co.*
Cola (die)	22	*cola*
Computer (der), -	25	*computer*
Controller (der), - / Controllerin, -nen	15	*controller*
Controlling (das)	12	*controlling (department)*
Couch (die), -s	29	*couch, sofa*
Cousin (der), -s / Cousine (die), -n	13	*(male) cousin; (female) cousin*

D

da	2	*here*
da sein – du bist da, er / sie ist da, ist da gewesen	18	*be here*
dabei	29	*at the same time*
Dach (das), ⸚er	22	*roof*
Dachwohnung (die), -en (das Dach + die Wohnung)	9	*penthouse*
dafür (sein)	18	*pro*
dagegen (sein)	18	*contra*
dagegen haben (etwas ...)	18	*mind, be against*
dahinten	16	*over there*
dahinter	22	*behind / beyond it*
Dame (die), -n	25	*lady*
Damenbekleidung (die)	21	*ladies' fashions*
Damenwäsche (die)	21	*lingerie*
Däne (der), -n / Dänin (die), -nen	24	*Dane, Danish (man / woman)*
Dänemark (das)	5	*Denmark*
dänisch	24	*Danish*

Dank (der)	3, 21	*thanks*
danke	1	*thank you*
Danke schön / sehr.	5, 23	*Thank you very much.*
danken – er / sie dankt, hat gedankt: Nichts zu danken.	21	*thank: You're welcome.*
dann	4	*then*
Das: Das bin / sind …	1	*That: That is …*
dass	12	*that*
Dativ (der), -e	19	*dative*
Datum (das)	3	*date*
dauern – es dauert, hat gedauert	11	*last; take [time]*
dazu	9	*to it*
dein, deine	13	*your*
Demonstrativpronomen (das), -	18	*demonstrative pronoun*
denken sich – er / sie denkt sich, hat sich gedacht	27, 29	*think*
denn (Wie ist es denn in München?)	4	*then*
Der Apfel fällt nicht weit vom Stamm.	8	*It's in the blood.*
Der Ton macht die Musik.	8	*It's the tone that makes the music.*
der, die, das	3	*the*
deshalb	12	*hence, thus, so*
Designer (der), - / Designerin (die), -nen	6	*designer*
deutsch	3	*German*
Deutsche (der / die), -n	24	*German (man / woman)*
Deutschland (das)	1	*Germany*
Dezember (der)	16, 24	*December*
Dialog (der), -e	3	*dialogue*
dick	28	*fat, thick*
Dienstag (der)	7	*Tuesday*
Diesel (der)	22	*diesel*
dieser, diese, dieses	18	*this, that*
Digitaluhr (die), -en	10	*digital watch*
direkt	4	*direct(ly)*
doch	12	*in fact*
Donau (die)	23	*Danube*
Donnerstag (der)	11	*Thursday*
Doppelmokka (der) (= Kaffeesorte)	7	*double mocca*
Doppelzimmer (das), -	24	*double room*
dort	2	*there*
dran sein – er / sie ist dran, ist dran gewesen	8	*be someone's turn*
draußen	22	*outside*
drehen – er / sie dreht, hat gedreht	28	*make (a film)*
Dreiviertelstunde (die)	10	*three quarters of an hour*
Drucker (der), -	27	*printer*
du	1	*you*
dumm	28	*silly, stupid*
dünn	28	*thin*
durch (geteilt …)	9	*by (divided …)*
durch + Akk.	22	*through*
dürfen – er / sie darf	3, 25	*be allowed to*
Durst (der): Durst haben	7	*thirst: be thirsty*

Dusche (die), -n	24	*shower*
duschen sich – er/sie duscht sich, hat sich geduscht	30	*have a shower*

E

Ecke (die), -n	29	*corner*
EDV-Fachmann (der), ⸚er, -leute / EDV-Fachfrau (die), -en	13	*EDP-specialist*
Ei (das), -er	13	*egg*
Eiffelturm (der)	30	*Eiffel Tower*
Eigenname (der), -n	15	*proper noun*
eigentlich	13	*actually, in fact, really*
eilig	10	*in a hurry*
ein/eine	3	*a*
ein bisschen	1	*a bit*
ein paar	5	*a few*
eingeben – du gibst ein, er/sie gibt ein, hat eingegeben	25	*key in*
Eindruck (der), ⸚e	12	*impression*
einfach	19	*easy, simple*
Einfamilienhaus (das), ⸚er	9	*(semi-)detached house (for one family)*
Eingang (der), ⸚e	11	*entrance*
einhalb	11	*and a half*
einige	9	*some, a few*
einkaufen – er/sie kauft ein, hat eingekauft: einkaufen gehen	22, 29	*shop: go shopping*
Einkaufszettel (der), -	27	*shopping list*
einladen – du lädst ein, er/sie lädt ein, hat eingeladen: zum Essen einladen	11	*invite: invite (s.o.) to dinner/lunch*
Einladung (die), -en	30	*invitation*
einordnen – er/sie ordnet ein, hat eingeordnet	3, 17	*sort*
einsetzen – er/sie setzt ein, hat eingesetzt	28	*fill/put in*
Eintopf (der), ⸚e	21	*soup, stew*
Eintrittskarte (die), -n	6	*ticket*
einverstanden	7	*OK, fine*
Einwohner (der), -	24	*inhabitant*
Einzelzimmer (das), -	24	*single room*
Eisbein (das)	21	*knuckle of pork*
Eisbeinfleisch (das)	21	*pork (from the knuckle)*
Eis (das)	18	*ice-cream*
Eiskaffee (der)	18	*iced coffee*
elegant	12	*elegant*
Elektrogerät (das), -e	21	*electrical appliance*
Elektroinstallateur (der), -e / Elektroinstallateurin (die), -nen	13	*electrician*
Eltern (die Pl)	13	*parents*
E-Mail (die), -s	3	*e-mail*
Empfang (der)	12	*reception*
Ende (das)	24	*end*
Ende gut, alles gut!	30	*All's well that ends well.*

endlich	13	*at last, finally*
Endung (die), -en	9	*ending*
England (das)	2	*England*
Engländer (der), –/Engländerin (die), -nen	24	*Englishman/woman, English (man/woman)*
englisch	14	*English*
Enkel (der), –/Enkelin (die), -nen	13	*grandson/granddaughter*
entfernt	28	*(far) away*
Entfernung (die), -en	28	*distance*
entlang	19	*along*
entscheiden – er/sie entscheidet, hat entschieden	25	*decide*
entschuldigen sich – er/sie entschuldigt sich, hat sich entschuldigt	12	*apologize*
Entschuldigen Sie ...	3	*Sorry ...*
Entschuldigung (die) ...	3	*Sorry ...*
entweder ... oder	23	*either ... or*
er	1	*he*
Erdgeschoss (das), -e	12	*ground floor*
Erfahrung (die), -en	30	*experience*
Erfolg (der), -e	16	*success*
ergänzen – er/sie ergänzt, hat ergänzt	1	*complete*
ergeben sich – es/das ergibt sich, hat sich ergeben	11	*make (up)*
Ergebnis (das), -se	27	*result*
erhalten – du erhältst, er/sie erhält, hat erhalten	24	*receive*
Erholung (die)	24	*relaxation*
erkennen – er/sie erkennt, hat erkannt	4	*recognise*
erklären – er/sie erklärt, hat erklärt	19, 25	*explain*
Erklärung (die), -en	27	*explanation*
erleben – er/sie erlebt, hat erlebt	28	*experience*
erste (der)	22, 24	*first (the)*
erzählen – er/sie erzählt, hat erzählt	12	*tell*
es (Personalpronomen)	3	*It*
es eilig haben – er/sie hat es eilig, hat es eilig gehabt	10	*be in a hurry*
es gibt (→ geben)	7	*there is, there are*
Es ist ... (1 Uhr)	10	*it is ... (1 o'clock)*
es: Wie geht es ...?	1	*How are/is ...?*
Espresso (der) (= Kaffeesorte)	7	*espresso (type of coffee)*
Essen (das), -	11	*meal, food, dinner*
essen – du isst, er/sie isst, hat gegessen	8	*eat*
essen gehen – er/sie geht essen, ist essen gegangen	8	*go out for a meal*
etwas	7	*something*
euer, eure	15	*your*
Euro (der), -s	5	*Euro*
Europa (das)	13	*Europe*
Europäische Union (die) (= EU)	27	*European Union*
extra	8	*on purpose, specially*

F

Fach (das), ¨er	29	*subject*
fahren – du fährst, er/sie fährt, ist gefahren	5	*go, drive*

Fahrer (der), - / Fahrerin (die), -nen	21	*driver*
Fahrkarte (die), -n	5	*ticket*
Fahrrad (das), ¨er: Fahrrad fahren	21, 23	*bicycle: to cycle*
Fahrradverleih (der)	24	*bicycle hire*
Fahrstuhl (der), ¨e	20	*lift, elevator*
Fahrt (die), -en	12	*trip, journey*
fallen – du fällst, er / sie fällt, ist gefallen	8	*fall*
falsch	4	*wrong*
falsch gehen (Uhr)	10	*be wrong (watch)*
Familie (die), -n	13	*family*
Familienname (der), -n	3	*surname, family name*
Familienstand (der)	3	*family status*
Farbe (die), -n	22	*colour*
fast	10	*almost, nearly*
faulenzen – er / sie faulenzt, hat gefaulenzt	23	*laze (around)*
Fax (das), -e	3	*fax*
Fax-Nummer (die), -n	11	*fax number*
Februar (der)	16, 24	*February*
fehlen – es / das fehlt, hat gefehlt	6	*be missing*
Fehler (der), -	28	*mistake, error, defect*
feminin	7	*feminine*
Ferien (die Pl)	23	*holidays*
Fernsehen (das)	15	*television*
Fernsehturm (der), ¨e	26	*television tower*
fertig	15	*finished; ready*
Fest (das), -e	12	*special occasion, festival*
Festspielhaus, ¨er	30	*festival hall*
Feuer (das)	22	*fire, light*
Fiaker (der) (= Kaffeesorte)	7	*Fiaker (= sort of coffee)*
Film (der), -e	14	*film*
finden – er / sie findet, hat gefunden: eine Lösung finden	5, 9	*find; think: find a solution*
Finne (der), -n/Finnin (die), -nen	24	*Finn, Finnish (man/woman)*
Firma (die), -en	6	*firm, company*
Firmenbesichtigung (die), -en	11	*(guided) tour of a company*
Firmenname (der), -n	6	*company name*
Fisch (der), -e	16	*fish*
fit	25	*nimble, fit*
Fitness-Center (das), -	22	*fitness center*
Fitness-Park (der), -s	22	*fitness park*
Flasche (die), -n	17	*bottle*
Fleisch (das)	17	*meat*
fliegen – er / sie fliegt, ist geflogen	10	*fly*
Fliegenpilz (der), -e (die Fliege + der Pilz)	9	*fly agaric*
Flug (der), ¨e	24	*flight*
Flughafen (der), ¨	10	*airport*
Flugzeug (das), -e	11	*plane*
Flur (der), -e	9	*hall(way)*
Fluss (der), ¨e	19	*river*
Form (die), -en	12	*form, shape*
formell-geschäftlich	25	*formal business style*

förmlich	12	*formal*
Formular (das), -e	3	*form*
Fortbildung (die), -en	25	*(further) (training) course*
Foto (das), -s	10	*photo*
Frage (die), -n	2, 3	*question*
Fragebogen (der), ⸚	23	*questionnaire*
fragen – er/sie fragt, hat gefragt	2	*ask*
Fragepronomen (das), -	28	*interrogative pronoun*
Fragesatz (der), ⸚e	20	*question, interrogative*
Fragewort (das), ⸚er	2	*question word*
Franke (der), -n/Fränkin (die), -nen	24	*Franconian (man/woman)*
Franken	17	*Franconia*
Frankfurter Würste (die Pl)	16	*Frankfurter sausages*
Frankreich (das)	2	*France*
Franzose (der), -n/Französin (die), -nen	24	*Frenchman/Frenchwoman*
französisch	14	*French*
Frau (die), -en	1	*Mrs.; wife; woman*
Frauenkirche (die)	30	*Church of Our Lady*
frei	9	*free; available*
frei haben – er/sie hat frei, hat frei gehabt	14	*have [time] off*
frei machen – er/sie macht frei, hat frei gemacht	11	*have (a day) off*
Freibad (das), ⸚er	24	*outdoor swimming pool*
Freitag (der)	11	*Friday*
freuen sich - er/sie freut sich, hat sich gefreut	26	*be pleased*
Freund, -e/Freundin, -nen	12, 14	*friend, girlfriend*
freundlich	14	*friendly*
Friedrich der Große	30	*Frederick the Great*
frisch	21	*fresh*
Frisör (= Friseur), -e/die Frisörin (= Friseurin), -nen	12, 15	*hairdresser*
früh	8	*early*
früher	8	*earlier, once*
Frühling (der)	13	*spring*
Frühstück (das)	13	*breakfast*
frühstücken – er/sie frühstückt, hat gefrühstückt	13	*have breakfast*
für + Akk.	9	*for*
furchtbar (... viel)	5	*terrible/terribly (a ... lot)*
Fuß (der), ⸚e	11	*foot*
Fußball (der), ⸚e	6	*football*
Fußball spielen – er/sie spielt Fußball, hat Fußball gespielt	23	*play football*

G

Gabel (die), -n	13	*fork*
ganz	5	*quite; very*
gar nicht	22, 24	*not at all*
Garage (die), -n	9	*garage*
Garten (der), ⸚	9	*garden*
Gartenhaus (das), ⸚er	30	*summerhouse*
Gartenrestaurant (das), -s	21	*garden restaurant*
Gaspedal (das), -e	22	*accelerator pedal*

Gast (der), ⁼e	12	*visitor, guest*
Gäste-Casino (das)	12	*visitors' canteen*
gebacken: gebackene Kartoffel	21	*baked: baked potato*
Gebäude (das), -	22	*building*
geben – es gibt, hat gegeben	7, 17	*there is, there are*
Gebirge (das), -	23	*mountains, mountain range*
geboren sein (in)	3	*be born (in)*
Geburt (die), -en	26	*birth*
Geburtsdatum (das), -daten	3	*date of birth*
Geburtsjahr (das), -e	3	*year of birth*
Geburtsland (das), ⁼er	3	*country of birth*
Geburtsname (der), -n	3	*maiden name*
Geburtsort (der), -e	3	*place of birth*
Geburtstag (der), -e	12	*birthday*
gefährlich	23	*dangerous*
gefallen – du gefällst, er/sie gefällt, hat gefallen	14	*like*
Geflügel (das)	21	*poultry*
gegen	14	*about*
Gegenteil (das)	8	*opposite*
gegenüber	12	*opposite*
Gehalt (das), ⁼er	9	*salary*
gehen – er/sie geht, ist gegangen	7	*go*
gehen – Wie geht's?	1	*How are you?*
gelb	22	*yellow*
Geld (das), -er	9	*money*
Gelegenheit (die), -en	9	*opportunity, occasion*
gemischt-: der gemischte Salat	21	*mixed: mixed salad*
Gemüse (das)	16, 21	*vegetable(s)*
Gemüsepfanne (die) (das Gemüse + die Pfanne)	20	*(mixed) vegetable dish*
Gemüseteller (der), -	16	*vegetable dish*
gemütlich	9	*cosy; comfortable*
genau	17, 27	*exact(ly), right*
genauso	24	*just like*
Genitiv (der)	15	*genitive*
genug	3, 17	*enough*
genügen – es/das genügt, hat genügt	19	*be enough*
geöffnet (von ... bis ...)	12	*open (from ... to ...)*
gerade	23	*just*
geradeaus	11	*straight ahead/on*
gern, gerne	2	*gladly; I'd like that.*
Geschäft (das), -e	1	*business; shop*
Geschäftsbrief (der), -e	25	*business letter*
Geschäftsleitung (die)	11	*management*
Geschäftsmann (der), ⁼er, Geschäftsleute/ Geschäftsfrau (die), -en	6, 15	*businessman, businessmen/ businesswoman*
Geschäftspartner (der), -	12	*business partner*
Geschenk (das), -e	6	*present*
Geschichte (die)	6	*history*
geschieden	3	*divorced*
Geschlecht (das), -er	3	*gender*

geschlossen (Montag ...)	12	*shut, closed (Monday ...)*
Geschwister (die Pl)	13	*brothers and sisters*
Gespräch (das), -e	6	*conversation*
gestern	8	*yesterday*
gesund	12	*healthy, good for you*
Gesundheit (die)	12	*health*
Getränk (das), -e	17	*drink*
getrennt	21, 26	*separate*
Gewitter (das)	22	*thunderstorm*
Glas (das), ¨er	20	*glass*
Glaube (der)	12	*belief, religion*
glauben – er/sie glaubt, hat geglaubt	12	*believe, think*
gleich	9	*in a minute, straightaway*
Glossar (das), -e	1	*glossary*
Glück (das): Glück bringen	1, 9	*luck*
Glückwunsch (der), ¨e	26	*congratulations*
GmbH (die), -s	3	*Ltd, PLC*
Gramm (das) (= g)	17	*gramme*
Grammatik (die)	1	*grammar*
Grammatik-Problem (das), -e	24	*grammar problem*
grammatisch	24	*grammatical*
gratulieren – er/sie gratuliert, hat gratuliert	27	*congratulate*
Grieche (der), -n/Griechin (die), -nen	24	*Greek (man/woman)*
Griechenland (das)	10	*Greece*
griechisch	14	*Greek*
groß	5	*big, large, tall*
großartig	22	*magnificent, splendid, wonderful*
Großbritannien (das)	3	*Great Britain*
große Braune (der) (= Kaffeesorte)	7	*large brown (= sort of coffee)*
Großeltern (die Pl)	13	*grandparents*
Großmutter (die), ¨ / Großvater (der), ¨	13	*grandmother/grandfather*
Großstadt (die), ¨e	5	*city*
grün	22	*green*
Grünkohl (der) mit Pinkel	16	*curly kale with sausage*
Gruß (der), ¨e	12	*greeting*
Grüß Gott/Grüezi/Griaß di	1	*Hello*
Gurke (die), -n	21	*cucumber*
gut	1	*good*
Gute Besserung!	30	*Get well soon!*
Gute Nacht	1	*Good night*
Gute Reise!	30	*Have a good journey!*
Guten Abend	1	*Good evening*
Guten Appetit!	21	*Enjoy your meal!*
Guten Morgen	1	*Good morning*
Guten Tag	1	*Hello: Good morning/afternoon*
Gymnastik (die)	22	*gymnastics*

H

Haar (das), -e	12	*hair*
haben – er/sie hat, hat gehabt	3	*have*

Hafen (der), ⸚	10	*docks, harbor, port*
Hafenrundfahrt (die), -en	30	*trip round the harbour*
Hähnchen (das), -	21	*chicken*
halb (... drei)	10	*half*
halbe Stunde (die): eine halbe (1/2) Stunde	10	*half an hour*
Hallo	1	*hello; hi*
Hals (der), ⸚e	12	*neck*
Haltestelle (die), -n	13	*stop*
Hamburger (der), - / Hamburgerin (die), -nen	27	*person from Hamburg*
Hand (die), ⸚e: sich die Hand / Hände schütteln	12	*hand: shake hands*
Handschuhe (die Pl)	21	*gloves*
Handwerker (der), - / Handwerkerin, -nen	15	*tradesman, craftsman / tradeswoman, craftswoman*
Handy (das), -s	7	*mobile (phone)*
Handy-Nummer (die), -n	6	*mobile number*
Harz (der)	23	*Harz*
hässlich	12	*ugly*
Hauptstadt (die), ⸚e	10	*capital (city)*
Haus (das), ⸚er	9	*house, building*
Hausfrau (die), -en / Hausmann (der), ⸚er	13	*housewife; house husband*
Hausnummer (die), -n	11	*house number*
heißen – er / sie heißt	1	*to be called*
heißen: das heißt	11	*that is, actually*
helfen – du hilfst, er / sie hilft, hat geholfen	7	*help*
Hemd (das), -en	30	*shirt*
Herbst (der)	24	*autumn*
Herr (der), -en (Sehr geehrte Damen und...)	1, 25	*Mr*
Herrenbekleidung (die)	21	*menswear*
Herrenwäsche (die)	21	*men's underwear*
Herstellung (die)	12	*production (department)*
herum	19	*round*
herzlich	1	*warm; hearty*
Herzlich willkommen	1	*welcome*
herzliche Grüße (aus)	15	*best wishes (from)*
Herzlichen Glückwunsch	26	*Congratulations*
heute	5	*today*
heute Abend / Mittag	10, 11	*this evening*
hier	3	*here*
Hilfe (die), -n: Hilfe!	12	*help: Help!*
Himmel (der)	22	*heaven, sky*
hinfahren – du fährst hin, er / sie fährt hin, ist hingefahren	23, 26	*go (there)*
hinten	17	*at the back*
Hobby (das), -s	6	*hobby*
hoch	27	*high, up*
Hochzeit (die), -n	26, 28	*wedding*
hoffen – er / sie hofft, hat gehofft	12	*hope*
höflich	7	*polite*
Höhe (die)	24	*hight, altitude*
holen – er / sie holt, hat geholt	17	*get, fetch, collect*
Holland (das)	14	*Holland*

Holländer (der), –/Holländerin (die), -nen	24, 27	*Dutchman/Dutchwoman*
holländisch	14	*Dutch*
Holzbrücke (die), -n	30	*wooden bridge*
Homepage (die), -s	16	*homepage*
hören – er/sie hört, hat gehört	1	*hear; listen to*
Hotel (das), -s	3	*hotel*
Hotelanmeldung (die), -en	3	*hotel registration (form)*
Hotelzimmer (das), -	7	*hotel room*
hübsch	28	*pretty*
Hufeisen (das), -	9	*horseshoe*
Hühnchen (das), -	21	*chicken*
Hühnchenbrust (die)	21	*breast of chicken*
Humor (der)	28	*(sense of) humor*
Hunger (der): Hunger haben	7	*hunger: be hungry*

I

ich	1	*I*
Idee (die), -n	24	*idea*
ihr	2	*you (plural)*
ihr, ihre	6	*her, your*
im Norden/Süden von …	6	*to the north/south of …*
immer	6	*always*
Imperativ (der), -e	17, 18	*imperative*
Imperativsatz (der), ⁔e	20	*command*
in + Dat./Akk.	2, 23, 29	*in*
„in" sein	12	*be "in"*
in der Nähe	13	*nearby*
in einer Woche	30	*in a week('s time)*
in Urlaub gehen – er/sie geht in Urlaub, ist in Urlaub gegangen	23	*go on holiday*
Indien (das)	3	*India*
Indonesien (das)	3	*Indonesia*
Infinitiv (der), -e	20	*infinitive*
Informatik (die)	6	*computer science*
Information (die), -en	11	*information*
Informationszentrum (das), -zentren	12	*information centre*
informativ	16	*informative*
informell	10	*informal*
Ingenieur (der), -e/Ingenieurin (die), -nen	6, 15	*engineer*
Inhalt (der), -e	1, 26	*contents*
Inlineskaten (das)	22, 25	*inline skating*
Insel (die), -n	23	*island*
intelligent	28	*intelligent*
interessant	6	*interesting*
Interkulturelle Studien	29	*intercultural studies*
Internet-Abteilung (die), -en	16	*internet department*
Internet-Beruf (der), -e	16	*internet job*
Internet-Redakteur (der), -e/Internet-Redakteurin (die), -nen	16	*internet editor*

Interview (das), -s	4	*interview*
Interviewer (der), - /Interviewerin (die), -nen	23	*interviewer*
Irak (der/-)	3	*Iraq*
Iran (der/-)	3	*Iran*
irisch	14	*Irish*
IT-Abteilung (die), -en	12	*IT department*
Italien (das)	2	*Italy*
Italiener (der), – /Italienerin (die), -nen	24, 27	*Italian (man/woman)*
italienisch	14	*Italian*

J

ja	17	*yes*
Ja/Nein-Frage (die), -n	4	*yes/no-question*
ja: Sie sind ja ...	4	*yes, indeed, in fact; In fact you are ...*
Jacke (die), -n	30	*jacket*
Jahr (das), -e	2	*year*
Jahreszeit (die), -en	13, 24	*season*
Januar (der)	16, 24	*January*
Japan (das)	3	*Japan*
Japaner (der), – /Japanerin (die), -nen	24	*Japanese (man/woman)*
japanisch	14	*Japanese*
Jazz Dance (der)	22	*jazz dancing*
jeder, jede, jedes	30	*each, every*
jemand	8, 11	*somebody*
Jemen (der)	14	*Yemen*
jetzt	3	*now*
Job (der), -s	3	*job*
Jogurt (der)	6	*yoghurt*
Journalist (der), -en /Journalistin (die), -nen	15	*journalist*
Juli (der)	13	*July*
jung	16	*young*
Junge (der), -n	13, 28	*boy*
Juni (der)	13	*June*

K

Kaffee (der), -s	7	*coffee*
Kaffeepause (die), -n	7	*coffee break*
Kalender (der), -	12, 24	*calendar*
kalt	12	*cold*
Kamera (die), -s	4	*camera*
Kanal (der), ⁼e	10, 13	*canal, channel*
Kantine (die), -n	7	*canteen*
Kantinenessen (das)	7	*canteen food/meal*
Kantinenleitung (die)	12, 21	*canteen management*
Kanzleramt (das)	12	*chancellery*
kaputt	11, 22	*broken*
Kapuziner (der), (= Kaffeesorte)	11	*Kapuziner (= sort of coffee)*
Karibik (die)	7	*Caribbean*
Karriere (die), -n	6, 24	*career*

Karte (die), -n	6	*map*
Kartengruß (der), ⸚e	7	*greeting on a card*
Kartoffel (die), -n	26	*potato*
Kartoffeleintopf (der), ⸚e	14	*thick potato soup*
Kartoffelgericht (das), -e	21	*potato dish*
Kartoffelkloß, ⸚e	21	*potato dumpling*
Kartoffelknödel (der), -	21	*potato dumpling*
Kartoffelsalat (der), -e	22	*potato salad*
Kartoffelsuppe (die), -n	21	*potato soup*
Kartoffelsuppeneintopf (der)	21	*potato soup/stew*
Käse (der)	13, 17	*cheese*
Kasse (die), -n	13	*checkout*
Katalog (der), -e	24	*catalogue*
kaufen – er/sie kauft, hat gekauft	17, 18	*buy*
Kaufhaus (das), ⸚er	17	*(department) store*
kein, keine	16	*no*
Keller (der), -	11	*cellar, basement*
kennen – er/sie kennt, hat gekannt	11	*know*
kennen lernen – er/sie lernt kennen, hat kennen gelernt	2	*get to know*
Kfz-Mechaniker (der), -/Kfz-Mechanikerin (die), -nen (Kfz = Kraftfahrzeug)	15	*mechanic*
kg (= Kilogramm)	13	*kilogramme*
Kilo(gramm) (= kg) (das)	17	*kilogramme*
Kilometer (= km) (der), -	16, 19	*kilometre*
Kind (das), -er	10, 28	*child*
Kindergarten (der), ⸚	7	*kindergarten*
Kinderkonfektion (die), -en	21	*children's wear*
Kiosk (der), -e	20	*kiosk*
Kirche (die), -n	19	*church*
Kirsche (die), -n	19	*cherry*
klar	17, 21	*of course [lit: clear]*
klasse	2	*great*
Kleeblatt (das), ⸚er	8	*cloverleaf*
Kleid (das), -er	9	*dress*
klein	16, 28	*small, little*
kleine Braune (der) (= Kaffeesorte)	5	*small brown (= sort of coffee)*
Kleinstadt (die), ⸚e	7	*small town*
klettern – er/sie klettert, ist geklettert	5	*climb, go climbing*
klingeln – er/sie klingelt, hat geklingelt	29	*ring (phone)*
km (= Kilometer)	10	*kilometre*
Koch (der), ⸚e/Köchin (die), -nen	15	*cook*
kochen – er/sie kocht, hat gekocht	17, 25	*cook*
Koffer (der), -	8	*suitcase*
Koffer packen – er/sie packt Koffer, hat Koffer gepackt	30	*pack a suitcase*
Kofferraum (der), ⸚e	30	*boot/trunk*
Kollege (der), -n/Kollegin (die), -nen	12, 22	*colleague*
Kolosseum (das)	12	*Collosseum*
kommen – er/sie kommt, ist gekommen	11	*come*
Kommt Zeit, kommt Rat.	2	*Take your time and you'll find an answer.*

kompetent	8	*competent, able*
Konferenz (die), -en	21	*conference*
Konferenzraum (der), ¨e	21	*conference room*
Konferenzzimmer (das), -	12	*conference room*
Konkurrenz (die)	3, 28	*competition*
Konkurrenzfirma (die), -en	28	*competitor*
können – er/sie kann	25	*can, be able to*
Kontakt (der), -e	7	*contact*
Kontrolle (die), -n: zur Kontrolle	13	*checkpoint, control: for checking purposes*
Kopf (der), ¨e	12, 22	*head*
kopieren – er/sie kopiert, hat kopiert	12	*copy*
Korea (das)	22	*Korea*
Koreaner (der), –/Koreanerin (die), -nen	4, 24	*Korean (man/woman)*
koreanisch	24	*Korean*
korrigieren – er/sie korrigiert, hat korrigiert	14	*correct*
Kosmetik (die)	8	*cosmetics*
kosten – es/das kostet, hat gekostet	5, 17	*cost*
krank	5	*ill*
Krankenzimmer (das), -	12	*sickbay*
Krankheit (die), -en	11, 12	*illness, disease*
Kreditkarte (die), -n	12	*credit card*
Kreuz (das), -e	22	*cross*
Kreuzung (die), -en	19	*junction, crossroads*
Krimi (der), -s	7	*thriller*
Kroate (der), -n/Kroatin (die), -nen	24	*Croatian (man/woman)*
Kroatien (das)	24	*Croatia*
kroatisch	3	*Croatian*
Küche (die), -n	24	*kitchen; cuisine*
Kuchen (der), -	9	*cake*
Küchenuhr (die), -en	10	*kitchen clock*
Kuckucksuhr (die), -en	10	*cuckoo clock*
Kugelschreiber (der), -	10	*ballpoint pen*
Kühlschrank (der), ¨e	21	*fridge*
Kunde (der), -n/Kundin (die), -nen	21	*customer*
Kuppel (die), -n	22	*dome*
Kupplung (die), -en	22	*clutch*
Kurs (der), -e	22	*course*
kurz: der kurze Vokal	5, 10, 23	*short: short vowel*
Kuss (der), ¨e	5, 10	*kiss*

L

l (= Liter)	17	*litre*
Lachs (der), -e	21	*salmon*
Lager (das), -	16	*warehouse, stockroom*
Lampe (die), -n	12	*lamp*
Land (das), ¨er	20	*country*
Ländername (der), -n	3	*name of a country*
Landesfarbe, n (die)	3	*national colour*

Landkarte (die), -n	26	*map*
Landstraße (die), -n	5	*(main) road*
lang, lange	22	*for a long time*
lang: der lange Vokal	2	*long: long vowel*
langsam	10	*slow(ly)*
langweilig	3	*boring*
lassen – du lässt, er/sie lässt, hat gelassen	29	*let*
last Minute	24	*last minute*
laufen – du läufst, er/sie läuft, ist gelaufen	3, 22	*walk, run*
leben – er/sie lebt, hat gelebt	18, 27	*live*
Lebensmittel (die Pl)	2	*food*
Lederwaren (die Pl)	21	*leather goods*
ledig	3, 28	*single*
Lehrer (der), -/Lehrerin (die), -nen	3	*teacher*
leicht	13, 15	*easy, light*
leid tun: es tut mir leid	7, 12	*be sorry*
leider	7	*unfortunately, I'm afraid*
Leiter (der), -	4	*head*
Leitfaden (der), ⸚	19, 21	*booklet, guide*
Leitung (die), -en	12	*management*
Lektion (die), -en	11	*lesson*
Lenkrad (das), ⸚er	1	*steering wheel*
lernen – er/sie lernt, hat gelernt	22	*learn*
lesen – du liest, er/sie liest, hat gelesen	13	*read*
Lettland (das)	4	*Latvia*
letzte Mal (das)	7	*last time*
Leute (die Pl)	16, 17	*people*
Libanon (der)	14	*Lebanon*
Liebe Grüße	3	*love (from)*
lieber (als) (gern – lieber – am liebsten)	15, 22	*like more (than) (like – like more – like most)*
Lieber .../Liebe ...	13, 25	*Dear ...*
Lieblings(essen/bruder/film/hotel ...)	14	*favourite (meal ...)*
Lieblingsfarbe (die), -n	13, 14	*favourite color*
Lieblingssport (der)	23	*favourite sport*
Liege (die), -n	29	*sofa-bed, folding bed*
liegen – es/das liegt	6, 18	*lie, be situated, located*
Likör (der)	6	*liqueur*
Limo (die), -s = Limonade (die), -n	8, 18	*lemonade*
links	12, 17	*(on the) left*
Liter (= l) (der)	10	*litre*
Löffel (der), -	13	*spoon*
los sein (etwas ist los)	13	*be the matter*
losfahren – du fährst los, er/sie fährt los, ist losgefahren	19	*set off, drive off, leave*
Lösung (die), -en	9, 16	*solution, answer*
Lösungswort (das), -e	1	*solution word*
lustig	22, 28	*funny*
Luxemburg (das)	5	*Luxembourg*

M

m (= Meter)	5	*metre*
m² (der) (Quadratmeter), -	9, 17	*square meter*
Mach's gut. Macht's gut.	17	*Take care.*
machen – er/sie macht, hat gemacht	30	*make, do*
machen: Das macht nichts.	4	*That OK/alright./That doesn't matter.*
macht nichts (= Das ...)	10	*that's OK/alright*
Mädchen (das), -	7	*girl*
Mahlzeit (die)	12, 13	*hello (greeting among colleagues in the middle of the day)*
Mai (der)	24	*May*
Mail (die), -s	15	*email*
Mail-Adresse (die), -n	26	*email address*
Mal sehen.	26	*I'll see.*
mal: Sag mal ...	9, 13	*Tell me ...*
Malediven (die Pl)	24	*Maledives*
Maler (der), -/Malerin (die), -nen	13, 15	*painter*
Mama (die)	13	*mum(my)*
man	8	*one; you; people*
Manager (der), -/Managerin (die), -nen	16	*manager*
manchmal	12	*sometimes*
Mann (der), ⸚er	3	*man; husband*
männlich	3	*male*
Mantel (der), ⸚	30	*coat*
Marienkäfer (der), - (der Käfer)	9	*ladybird (beetle)*
Marillenknödel (der), -	20	*apricot [sweet] dumpling*
Marketing (das)	12	*marketing*
Marketing-Abteilung (die), -en	12	*marketing (department)*
Marketing-Chef (der)	7	*head of marketing*
markieren – er/sie markiert, hat markiert	1	*mark*
Markt (der), ⸚e	12, 17	*market*
Marktplatz (der), ⸚e	19	*marketplace, market square*
Marmelade (die), -n	13	*jam*
März (der)	24	*March*
Maschinenbaumechaniker (der), -	13	*mechanic, engineer*
maskulin	7	*masculine*
Maß (die), -	20	*litre mug*
Maurer (der), – / Maurerin (die), -nen	13, 15	*bricklayer*
Medien-Design	6	*media design*
Medien-Designer (der), –/Medien-Designerin (die), -nen	6	*media designer*
Medienkunde (die)	29	*media studies*
Meer (das), -e	13, 24	*sea*
mehr	24, 26	*more*
mehrere	30	*several*
mein, meine	1, 13	*my*
meinen – er/sie meint, hat gemeint	13	*think*
Meinung (die), -en	23	*opinion*
meistens	12	*usually, mostly*
Melange (die) (= Kaffeesorte)	7	*Melange (= sort of coffee)*

Menu (das), -s	21	*menu*
Messer (das), -	13	*knife*
Meter (der / das), -	9, 17	*metre*
Mexikaner (der), –/Mexikanerin (die), -nen	24	*Mexican (man/woman)*
mexikanisch	14	*Mexican*
Mexiko	14	*Mexico*
Miete (die), -n	9	*rent*
mieten – er/sie mietet, hat gemietet	11	*rent*
Milch (die)	7	*milk*
Milchkaffee (der), -s	7	*milky coffee, coffee with milk*
Million (die), -en (siehe Mio.)	27	*million*
minus	9	*minus*
Minute (die), -n	5	*minute*
Mio. (Abkürzung Million)	24	*m. (abbreviation for million)*
Mit (den) besten Grüßen (der Gruß, Grüße)	25	*Best wishes (greeting)*
mit + Dat.	2	*with*
Mit freundlichen Grüßen	25	*Yours sincerely/faithfully*
Mit wem?	28	*who to?*
mit/fahren – du fährst mit, er/sie fährt mit, ist mitgefahren	24	*go/come along, go/come with someone*
Mitarbeiter (der), -/Mitarbeiterin (die), -nen	16, 28	*employee*
mitkommen – er/sie kommt mit, ist mitgekommen	13	*come along, come with someone*
Mittag (der), -e	7	*lunchtime, midday*
Mittagessen (das), -	14	*lunch*
mittags	10	*at lunchtime*
Mitte (die): in der Mitte	21, 28	*middle: in the middle*
Mittelgebirge (das), -	24	*highlands, low mountain range*
Mittelmeer (das)	23	*Mediterranean*
Mittwoch (der)	11, 12	*Wednesday*
mixen – er/sie mixt, hat gemixt	18	*mix*
Möbel (die Pl.)	29	*furniture*
Möbelstück (das), -e	29	*piece of furniture*
möchten – er/sie möchte	7	*would like*
Modalverb (das), -en	25	*modal verb*
Modellantwort (die), -n	14	*model answer*
modern	6	*modern*
mögen – er/sie mag, hat gemocht	12	*like*
Möglichkeit (die), -en	23	*possibility*
Mokka (der), (= Kaffeesorte)	7	*mocca (= sort of coffee)*
Moldawien (das)	3	*Moldavia*
Moment (der), -e: Einen Moment ...; im Moment	11, 16	*moment: Just a moment ...; at the moment*
Monat (der), -e	3	*month*
monatlich	9	*monthly*
monatlich kalt / warm	9	*basic (rent without heating)/ including heating*
Monatsname (der), -n	24	*name of the month*
Montag (der)	12	*Monday*
morgen	4	*tomorrow*
Morgen (der), -	1	*morning*
morgens	10	*in the morning*

Motor (der), -en	22	*engine*
Motorboot (das), -e	23	*motor boat*
Motorrad (das), ¨er: Motorrad fahren – du fährst Motorrad, er/sie fährt Motorrad, ist Motorrad gefahren	23	*motorbike: ride a motorbike*
Mountainbike (das), -s	23	*mountainbike*
müde	25	*tired*
Multimedia	21	*multimedia*
Münchner (der), -/Münchnerin (die), -nen	24	*person from Munich*
Mund (der), ¨er	12	*mouth*
mündlich	10	*oral(ly)*
Museum (das), -en	19	*museum*
Musik (die)	6	*music*
Müsli (das)	13	*muesli*
müssen – er/sie muss	25	*must, have to*
Mustertext (der), -e	29	*model text*
Mutter (die), ¨	13	*mother*

N

na bitte	25	*there you are*
na gut	18	*OK*
na ja	2	*well*
na klar	8	*of course*
nach	5, 23	*to*
nach Hause	5	*home*
nach: nach rechts	12	*to: to the right*
Nachbarland (das), ¨er	5	*neighbouring country*
nachgehen: die Uhr geht nach, ist nachgegangen	10	*lose: the watch is slow*
Nachmittag (der), -e	22	*afternoon*
nachmittags	10	*in the afternoon(s)*
Nachname (der), -n	1	*last name, surname*
nachschlagen – du schlägst nach, er/sie schlägt nach, hat nachgeschlagen	27	*look up*
nachsprechen – du sprichst nach, er/sie spricht nach, hat nachgesprochen	13	*repeat*
nächst-	24, 29	*next*
Nacht (die), ¨e: Gute Nacht	1	*night: Good night*
nachts	11	*in the night*
Nähe (die)	13	*proximity*
Name (der), -n	1	*name*
nämlich	8	*namely, in fact*
Nationalität (die), -en	3	*nationality*
natürlich	7	*of course*
negativ	4	*negative*
nehmen – du nimmst, er/sie nimmt, hat genommen	5	*take*
Nein	2	*No*
nervös	25, 27	*nervous*
nett	5	*nice*
neu	1	*new*
Neuseeland (das)	4	*New Zealand*

neutral	7	*neuter*
nicht	2	*not*
nicht wahr?	14	*don't you?*
nichts	7	*nothing*
nie	12	*never*
Niederlande (die Pl)	3	*Netherlands*
niemand	8	*nobody*
noch	5	*still*
noch einmal	5	*once again*
noch nie	19, 23	*never (up till now)*
Nomen (das), -	3	*noun*
Nominativ (der), -e	9	*nominative*
Norddeutschland (das)	1	*Northern Germany*
Norden (der)	6	*north*
Nordeuropa (das)	7	*Northern Europe*
nördlich (von)	6	*north (of)*
Nordsee (die)	23	*North Sea*
Norwegen (das)	10	*Norway*
Notarzt (der), ¨e/Notärztin (die), -nen	12	*emergency doctor*
notieren – er/sie notiert, hat notiert	5	*note (down)*
Notiz (die), -en: Notizen machen	7, 26	*note*
November (der)	24	*November*
null (= 0)	3	*zero*
nur	7	*only*
Nürnberger (der), -/Nürnbergerin, -nen	24	*person from Nuremberg*

O

oben	28	*at the top, above, up*
Ober (der), -	20	*waiter*
Oberbegriff (der), -e	13	*generic term*
Obst (das)	13	*fruit*
Obstbaum (der), ¨e	19	*fruit tree*
oder	1	*or*
offiziell	10	*official(ly)*
öffnen – er/sie öffnet, hat geöffnet	12	*open*
Öffnungszeiten (die Pl)	12	*opening times/hours*
oft	12	*often*
ohne + Akk.	2	*without*
Oktober (der)	24	*October*
Oktoberfest (das)	30	*Oktoberfest*
Oma (die), -s	13	*grandma*
Onkel (der), -s	13	*uncle*
Opa (der), -s	13	*grandpa*
Orange (die), -n	17	*orange*
Ordinalzahl (die), -en	19	*ordinal number*
organisieren – er/sie organisiert, hat organisiert	28	*organize*
Original ... (... Frankfurter Würste)	16	*original ... (... Frankfurter sausages)*
Ort (der), -e	3	*place*
Osten (der)	6	*east*
Österreich (das)	1	*Austria*

Österreicher (der), –/Österreicherin (die), -nen	24	*Austrian (man/woman)*
österreichisch	14	*Austrian*
Osterseen (die Pl)	23	*Easter Lakes (place name)*
östlich (von)	6	*east (of)*
Ostsee (die)	23	*Baltic Sea*

P

packen	30	*pack*
Packung (die), -en	18	*packet*
Papa (der), -s	13	*daddy*
Papier (das)	22	*paper*
Paprika (die)	17	*paprika, pepper*
parken – er/sie parkt, hat geparkt	22	*park*
Parkplatz (der), ¨e	22	*car park*
Partei (die), -en.	30	*party*
Partner (der), -/Partnerin (die), -nen	30	*partner*
Party (die), -s	6	*party*
Pass (der), ¨e	3	*passport*
passen - es passt, hat gepasst	1	*fit*
passend	2	*suitable, fitting*
passieren – es/das passiert, ist passiert	12	*happen*
Pass-Nummer (die), -n	3	*passport number*
Pause (die), -n	7	*break, pause*
PC (der), -s	25	*PC*
PC-Fortbildung (die)	25	*PC course*
Pellkartoffeln (die Pl)	21	*potatoes boiled in their jackets*
Penne (die Pl)	21	*penne [Italian pasta variety]*
Pension (die), -en	11	*boarding house*
per (Rad)	24	*by*
perfekt	14	*perfect(ly)*
Perfekt (das)	8	*perfect tense*
Perfektform (die), -en	19	*perfect form*
Person (die), -en	1	*person*
Personalpronomen (das), -	19	*personal pronoun*
Pf. (= Pfund) (das)	17	*pound*
Pfanne (die), -n	20	*dish, frying pan*
Pfeifton (der): nach dem Pfeifton	29	*beep, tone*
Pfirsich (der), -e	17	*peach*
Pfiat di	1	*cheers*
Pfund (= Pf.) (das)	17	*pound*
Piktogramm (das), -e	24	*pictogram*
Pilot (der), -en/Pilotin (die), -nen	15	*pilot*
PIN (die), -s	25	*PIN*
Plakat (das), -e	12	*poster*
Plan (der), ¨e	24	*plan*
planen – er/sie plant, hat geplant	27	*plan*
Plastik (die), -en	22	*sculpture; plastic*
Platz (der), ¨e: viel/wenig Platz; Platz nehmen; Platz machen	3, 9, 16, 17	*place: a lot of/little space; sit down, take a seat; make room*
plötzlich	12	*sudden(ly)*

Plural (der), -e	1	*plural*
Pluralform (die), -en	29	*plural form*
plus	9	*plus*
Pole (der), -n / Polin (die), -nen	24	*Pole*
Polen (das)	2	*Poland*
Politiker (der), - / Politikerin (die), -nen	15	*politician*
Polizei (die)	19	*police*
Polizist (der), -en / Polizistin (die), -nen	13	*police officer*
polnisch	14	*Polish*
Portemonnaie (das)	30	*purse, wallet*
Portugal (das)	10	*Portugal*
positiv	4	*positive*
Possessivartikel (der), -	13	*possessive article*
Post (die)	19	*post (office)*
Postkarte (die), -n	20, 26	*postcard*
Postleitzahl (= PLZ) (die), -en	3	*postcode, zipcode*
praktisch	4	*practical, handy*
Präposition (die), -en	19	*preposition*
Präsens (das)	2	*present*
Präteritum (das)	14	*past*
Praxis (die), -en	12	*practice, surgery*
Preis (der), -e	16	*price*
prima	4	*great, fantastic*
privat	30	*private*
pro	9, 24	*per*
probieren – er / sie probiert, hat probiert	8	*try (out)*
Probieren geht über studieren.	8	*The proof of the pudding is in the eating.*
Problem (das), -e; Kein Problem.	10	*problem; No problem.*
Produktion (die)	12	*production (department)*
Produktion (die), -en	12	*production (department)*
Prosecco (der)	17	*prosecco*
Prospekt (der), -e	24	*brochure, prospectus*
Prüfung (die), -en	26	*exam*
Pullover (der), -	3, 20	*pullover*
pünktlich	28	*punctual(ly)*
Pünktlichkeit (die)	12	*punctuality*
pur	24	*pure*

Q

Quadratmeter (der), - (qm = m^2)	9, 17	*square metre*
Qualität (die)	16, 28	*quality*
Quittung (die), -en	10	*receipt*
Quiz (das)	2	*quiz*

R

Rad (das), ¨er	22, 24	*wheel*
Rad fahren – du fährst Rad, er / sie fährt Rad, ist Rad gefahren	23	*cycle*

Radler (die) (Getränk)	18	*shandy (beer + lemonade)*
Radtouristik (die)	24	*cycling tours/tourism*
raten – du rätst, er/sie rät, hat geraten	25, 27	*guess*
Ratespiel (das)	24	*guessing game*
Rätsel (das), -	9	*puzzle*
Räucherlachs (der), -e	21	*smoked salmon*
Raum (der), ˝e	11	*room, space*
rechnen – er/sie rechnet, hat gerechnet	9	*do sums, calculate*
Rechnung (die), -en	21	*bill*
recht haben – er/sie hat recht, hat recht gehabt	8	*be right*
rechts	12	*(on the) right*
Rechtsanwalt (der), ˝ e/ Rechtsanwältin (die), -nen	13	*lawyer, attorney*
Redaktion (die), -en	12	*editorial (department)*
reflexiv	3, 26	*reflexive*
Region (die), -en	20	*region*
Regisseur (der), -e/Regisseurin (die), -nen	13	*director, producer*
regnen – es regnet, hat geregnet	4	*rain*
reichen – es/das reicht, hat gereicht	9	*be enough*
Reihenfolge (die), -n	1	*order*
Reis (der)	21	*rice*
Reise (die), -n	4	*journey, trip, travel*
Reisebüro (das), -s	21	*travel agency*
Reiseführer (der), -	21	*travel guide*
Reisekompetenz (die)	24	*travel expertise*
Reisemarkt (der), ˝e	24	*travel market*
reisen – er/sie reist, ist gereist	23, 25	*travel*
Reiseprospekt (der), -e	24	*travel brochure*
Reisetermin (der), -e	24	*date of travel*
Reisewunsch (der), ˝e	24	*desired destination*
Reiseziel (das), -e	10	*destination*
Reispfanne (die), -n	21	*stir-fried rice*
rekonstruieren – er/sie rekonstruiert, hat rekonstruiert	25	*reconstruct*
Reporter (der), -	3	*reporter*
reservieren – er/sie reserviert, hat reserviert	23	*reserve, book*
Restaurant (das), -s	12	*restaurant*
reziprok	30	*reciprocal*
Rhein (der)	23, 25	*Rhine*
richtig	2	*correct*
richtig gehen: die Uhr geht richtig, ist richtig gegangen	10	*be right: the watch/clock is right*
Richtung (die), -en; in Richtung auf	19	*direction. towards, in the direction of*
Rind (das), -er	20	*cow/bull, cattle*
Rindsroulade (die), -en	20	*beef roulade*
Rock (der), ˝e	30	*skirt*
Rolle (die), -n: eine Rolle spielen	28	*role: play a role*
rosa	22	*pink*
Rösti (das)	20	*fried potato slices*
rot	22	*red*
Rotwein (der), -e	17	*red wine*

rufen – er/sie ruft, hat gerufen	12	*call*
ruhig	23, 27	*quiet, calm*
Rührei (das)	21	*scrambled egg*
Rumänien (das)	3	*Romania*
rund um(s) ...(Auto)	22	*to do with the ... (car)*
Rundreise (die), -n	24	*tour*
Russe (der), -n/Russin (die), -innen	24	*Russian (man/woman)*
russisch	14	*Russian*
Russland (das)	3	*Russia*

S

Sachen (die Pl.)	29	*things*
Saft (der), ⁼e	17, 18	*juice*
sagen – er/sie sagt, hat gesagt: sagt man	2, 8	*say, tell: people say*
Sahne (die)	21	*cream*
Salami (die)	21	*salami*
Salat (der), -e	8	*salad*
Salatbouquet (das)	21	*salad garnish*
Salatgarnitur (die), -en	21	*salad garnish*
Salut	1	*bye*
Salzkartoffeln (die Pl)	21	*boiled potatoes*
Sandwich (das), -es	20	*sandwich*
Satz (der), ⁼e	3	*sentence*
Satzstellung (die), -en	12	*word order*
Satzteil (der), -e	17	*part of a sentence*
Sauerrahm (der)	21	*sour cream*
Sauna (die), Saunen	24	*sauna*
S-Bahn (die) (S = schnell), -en	5	*S-Bahn; city and suburban railway*
schade	8	*pity*
Schal (der), -s	30	*scarf*
Schale (die), -n (= Kaffeetasse)	7	*bowl (= coffee cup)*
Schalthebel (der), -	22	*gear-shift*
Schauspieler (der), -	28	*actor*
scheinen – er/sie scheint, hat geschienen	4	*shine; seem*
Scheinwerfer (der), -	22	*headlight*
schicken – er/sie schickt, hat geschickt	30	*send*
Schieß los!	19	*Go ahead.*
Schiff (das), -e	24, 25	*ship; boat*
Schirm (der), -e	20	*umbrella*
schlafen – du schläfst, er/sie schläft, hat geschlafen	9	*sleep*
Schlafzimmer (das), -	9	*bedroom*
Schlange (die), -n	18	*queue; snake*
schlecht	4	*bad(ly)*
schlimm	5	*bad(ly)*
Schloss (das), ⁼er	6	*castle*
Schloss Bellevue (das)	22	*Bellevue Castle*
Schluss (der): zum Schluss	14	*end: at the end*
Schlüssel (der), -	30	*key*
Schlüsselwort (das), ⁼er	30	*key word*
Schlussformel (die), -n	25	*complimentary close*

schmecken – es schneckt, hat geschmeckt	17	*taste*
Schmerzen (die Pl)	12	*pain. ache*
Schmuck (der)	21	*jewellery*
Schnee (der)	22	*snow*
schneien – es schneit, hat geschneit	4	*snow*
schnell	3	*quick(ly), fast*
Schnelligkeit (die)	16	*speed*
Schnellrestaurant (das), -s	19	*snackbar*
Schokolade (die)	22	*chocolate*
Scholle (die), -n	20	*Dover sole*
schon	2	*already*
schön	1	*nice, pretty, beautiful*
Schorle (die), -n	17	*mixed drink with mineral water*
Schornsteinfeger (der), - / Schornsteinfegerin (die), -nen	9, 15	*chimney sweep*
Schrank (der), ⸚e	29	*cupboard*
schrecklich	10	*awful(ly), terrible/terribly*
schreiben – er/sie schreibt, hat geschrieben	1	*write*
Schreibtisch (der), -e	29	*desk*
Schreibwaren (die Pl)	21	*stationery*
Schuh (der), -e	21	*shoe*
Schule (die), -n	13	*school*
Schüler (der), - /Schülerin (die), -nen	6, 15	*schoolboy/-girl*
schütteln sich die Hand – er/sie schüttelt, hat geschüttelt: sich die Hand schütteln	12	*shake hands*
schwarz	22	*black*
Schwarze (der), (= Kaffeesorte)	7	*black (= sort of coffee)*
Schwarze Meer (das)	23	*Black Sea*
Schwarzwald (der)	24	*Black Forest*
Schwede (der), -n/Schwedin, (die), -nen	24	*Swede, Swedish (man/woman)*
Schweden (das)	10	*Sweden*
Schwein (das), -e	21	*pig; pork*
Schweinebraten (der), -	20	*roast pork*
Schweinefleisch (das)	21	*pork*
Schweiz (die)	1	*Switzerland*
Schweizer (der), - /Schweizerin (die), -nen	24	*Swiss (man/woman)*
schweizerisch	14	*Swiss*
schwer	6	*difficult; heavy*
Schwester (die), -n	13	*sister*
Schwiegersohn (der), ⸚e /Schwiegertochter (die), ⸚	13	*son-in-law/daughter-in-law*
Schwiegervater (der), ⸚/Schwiegermutter (die), ⸚	13	*father-in-law/mother-in-law*
schwimmen – er/sie schwimmt, ist geschwommen	23	*swim*
See (der), -n	23	*lake*
segeln – er/sie segelt, ist gesegelt: segeln gehen	24	*sail: go sailing*
sehen – du siehst, er/sie sieht, hat gesehen	9	*see*
sich sehen – sie sehen sich, haben sich gesehen	3, 27	*see each other*
Sehenswürdigkeit (die), -en	22	*sight*
sehr	2	*very (much)*
Sehr geehrte/r	25	*Dear*
sein – er/sie ist, ist gewesen	1	*be*
sein, seine	6	*his, its*

seit	16	*since; for*
Seite (die), -n	9	*side; page*
Sekretariat (das), -e	11	*secretaries' office*
Sekt (der)	17	*sparkling wine*
Sekunde (die), -n	27	*second*
Selbstbedienung (die)	12	*self-service*
Semester (das), -	29	*semester, term*
Semesterbeginn (der)	29	*start of term/the semester*
Semesterferien (die Pl)	13	*(university) vacation*
senden – er / sie sendet, hat gesendet	26	*send*
senkrecht	7	*vertical(ly); down (in crossword)*
September (der)	24	*September*
serbisch	27	*Serbian*
Service-Techniker (der), -/Service-Technikerin (die), -nen	16	*service technician*
Serviette (die), -n	7	*serviette, napkin*
Servus	1	*bye*
Sessel (der), -	29	*chair*
sich anziehen – er / sie zieht sich an, hat sich angezogen	30	*get dressed*
sich ausruhen – er / sie ruht sich aus, hat sich ausgeruht	30	*have a rest*
sich ausziehen – er / sie zieht sich aus, hat sich ausgezogen	30	*get undressed*
sich beeilen – er / sie beeilt sich, hat sich beeilt	30	*hurry (up)*
sich beschweren – er / sie beschwert sich, hat sich beschwert	30	*complain*
sich denken – er / sie denkt sich, hat sich gedacht	27	*think (to oneself)*
sich die Hand schütteln – sie schütteln sich die Hand, haben sich die Hand geschüttelt	12	*shake hands*
sich duschen – er / sie duscht sich, hat sich geduscht	30	*have a shower*
sich entschuldigen – er / sie entschuldigt sich, hat sich entschuldigt	12	*apologise*
sich freuen – er / sie freut sich, hat sich gefreut	30	*be pleased*
sich unterhalten – du unterhältst dich, er / sie unterhält sich, hat sich unterhalten	24	*talk*
sicher	14	*certain(ly), definite(ly)*
sie (Pl)	1	*they*
sie (Sg)	1	*she*
Sie (Sg/Pl)	1	*you (formal)*
Silbe (die), -n	11	*syllable*
Singular (der)	1	*singular*
Singularform (die), -en	29	*singular form*
Sitz (der), -e	22	*seat*
sitzen – er / sie sitzt, hat gesessen	12	*sit*
Skandinavien	25	*Scandinavia*
Skifahren – du fährst Ski, er / sie fährt Ski, ist skigefahren	6	*ski, go skiing*
Skizze (die), -n	12	*sketch*
Slowake(der), -n/Slowakin (die), -nen	24	*Slovakian (man/woman)*
Slowakei (die)	23	*Slovakia*

slowakisch	24	*Slovakian*
Slowene (der), -n/Slowenin (die), -nen	24	*Slovenian (man/woman)*
Slowenien (das)	3	*Slovenia*
slowenisch	24	*Slovenian*
SMS (die) (= Short Message System)	26	*SMS*
Snack (der), -s	21	*snack*
so	2	*so*
so gegen ...	14	*about ...*
sofort	9	*at once, immediately*
Software (die)	28	*software*
Software-Entwickler (der), -/ Software-Entwicklerin (die), -nen	13	*software developer*
sogar	9	*even*
Sohn (der), ⁻e	13	*son*
sollen – er/sie soll	28	*shall*
Sommer (der)	13	*summer*
Sonnabend/Samstag (der), -e	11	*Saturday*
Sonne (die)	4	*sun*
Sonneninsel (die), -n	24	*sunny island*
Sonntag (der), -e	11, 12	*Sunday*
sonst	25	*otherwise, else*
Sorgen (die Pl)	8	*worries*
Sozialarbeiter (der), -/Sozialarbeiterin (die), -nen	13	*social worker*
Spaghetti (die Pl)	8	*spaghetti*
Spanien (das)	3	*Spain*
Spanier (der), -/Spanierin (die), -nen	24	*Spaniard, Spanish (man/woman)*
spanisch	14	*Spanish*
spannend	26	*exciting*
sparen – er/sie spart, hat gespart	9	*save*
Spargel (der), -	14	*asparagus*
Spaß (der): Spaß machen	8	*fun: be fun*
spät	5	*late*
später	8	*later*
spätestens	30	*at the latest*
spazieren gehen – er/sie geht spazieren, ist spazieren gegangen	23	*go for a walk*
Speisekarte (die), -n	20, 21	*menu*
Speisen (die Pl)	21	*food, dish*
Spezialist (der), -n/Spezialistin (die), -nen	17, 24	*specialist*
Spezialität (die), -en	20	*speciality*
Spiel (das), -e	28	*game, match*
spielen – er/sie spielt, hat gespielt	23	*play*
Spielwaren (die Pl)	21	*toys*
spinnen (umg.) – er/sie spinnt, hat gesponnen	25	*play up, go crazy (coll.)*
Spitzbergen (das)	25	*Spitzbergen*
Sport (der)	23	*sport*
Sportbekleidung (die)	21	*sportswear*
Sportgerät (das), -e	21	*(piece of) sports equipment*
Sportplatz (der), ⁻e	19	*sports field/ground*
Sprache (die), -n	6	*language*
Sprachenschule (die), -n	14	*language school*

Sprachkurs (der), -e	27	language course
sprechen – du sprichst, er/sie spricht, hat gesprochen	3	speak
Sprechstunde (die), -n	12	surgery
Sprechübung (die), -en	10	speaking exercise
Spree (die) (Fluss)	20	Spree (river)
Sprichwort (das), ¨er	8	proverb
Squash (das)	22	squash
Stadt (die), ¨e	2	town, city
Stadtautobahn (die), -en	10	urban motorway/freeway
Städtename (der), -n	2	name of a town/city
Stadtführer (der), -	20	town/city guide
Stadtplan (der), ¨e	12	town/city map
Stadtrundfahrt (die), -en	4	town/city tour
stark	20	strong
Start (der), -s	3	start
starten – er/sie startet, ist gestartet	11	start, set off, take off
Stau (der), -s	10	traffic jam, tailback
stehen – er/sie steht, hat gestanden	22, 29	stand; be
stehen bleiben – er/sie bleibt stehen, ist stehen geblieben	17	stop, stay
steigen – er/sie steigt, ist gestiegen	23	climb, rise
Stelle (die), -n	15	job
stellen – er/sie stellt, hat gestellt: Fragen stellen	29	put: ask questions
Stellenmarkt (der), ¨e	15	job market; situations vacant
Stephansdom (der)	30	St. Stephan's Cathedral
Steward (der), -s/Stewardess (die), -en	6, 13	steward/stewardess
Stichwort (das), ¨er	13	note, entry, headword, keyword
stimmen – es/das stimmt, hat gestimmt	5	be right
Stipendium (das), -en	25	scholarship
Stock (der), Stockwerke	19	floor, storey
Straße (die), -n	3	street; road
Streifen (der), -	21	strip
Strumpf (der), ¨e	21	stocking, sock
Stück (das), -e	17	piece
Student (der), -en/Studentin (die), -nen	6	student
Studien (die Pl.)	29	studies
studieren – er/sie studiert, hat studiert	6	study
Studium (das), Studien	29	studying, studies
Stuhl (der), ¨e	29	chair
Stunde (die), -n	5, 10	hour
suchen – er/sie sucht, hat gesucht	2	look for
Südamerika (das)	24	South America
Sudan (der)	3	Sudan
Süddeutschland (das)	20	Southern Germany
Süden (der)	6	south
Südfrucht (die), ¨e (der Süden + die Frucht)	17	(sub)tropical fruits
südlich (von)	6	south (of)
Südtirol (das)	21	South Tyrol
super	2	super
Supermarkt (der), ¨e	12, 17	supermarket
Suppe (die), -n	20	soup

surfen – er/sie surft, hat gesurft	25	*surf*
süß	23	*sweet*
Symbol (das), -e	9	*symbol*
sympathisch	6	*nice*
systematisch	25	*systematic*

T

Tabak (der)	21	*tobacco*
Tag (der), -e	1	*day*
Tagebuch (das). –"er	8	*diary*
tägig (6-)	24	*day (6-...)*
täglich	12	*daily*
tanken – er/sie tankt – hat getankt	22	*fill up with petrol/gas*
Tankstelle (die), -n	19	*filling station*
Tante (die), -n	13	*aunt*
Tasche (die), -n	3, 20	*pocket*
Taschenuhr (die), -en	10	*pocket watch*
Tasse (die), -n	7	*cup*
Taxi (das), -s	10, 11	*taxi*
Taxifahrer (der), -/Taxifahrerin (die), -nen	10, 15	*taxi driver*
Techniker (der), -/Technikerin (die), -nen	15	*technician*
Tee (der), -s	7	*tea*
Teil (der), -e	11	*part*
Teilwort (das), ¨er	24	*part of a word*
Tel./Telefon (das)	3, 24	*(tele)phone*
telefonieren – er/sie telefoniert, hat telefoniert	7, 28	*(tele)phone, make a phone call*
Telefonnummer (die), -n	6	*(tele)phone number*
Teller (der), -	13	*plate*
Tennis (das)	6	*tennis*
Teppich (der), -e	21	*carpet*
Termin (der), -e	10	*appointment*
Terminkalender (der), -	24	*diary*
Terrasse (die), -n	9	*terrace, patio*
Tessin (das)	24	*Ticino*
Test (der), -s	13	*test*
teuer	11	*expensive*
Text (der), -e	5	*text*
Textbaustein (der), -e	15	*text block*
Textbuch (das), "er	1	*textbook*
Thunfisch (der), -e	21	*tuna fish*
Thüringen (das)	16	*Thuringia*
Thüringer (der), -/Thüringerin (die), -nen	16	*Thuringian (man/woman)*
Thüringer Bratwurst (die), ¨e	16	*Thuringian sausage*
Ticket (das), -s	6	*ticket*
Tiergarten (der)	22	*zoo*
Tipp (der), -s	12	*tip*
Tisch (der), -e	16, 29	*table*
Tochter (die), ¨	13	*daughter*
Toilette (die), -n	9	*toilet*
toll	14	*great*

Tomate (die), -n	17	*tomato*
Tomatensauce/soße (die), -n	21	*tomato sauce*
Tomatensuppe (die), -n	20	*tomato soup*
Ton (der), ¨e	8	*tone*
Top-Angebot (das), -e	24	*top offer*
Tourismus (der)	24	*tourism*
Tourist (der), -en	12	*tourist*
Traumberuf (der), -e	15	*dream job*
träumen – er/sie träumt, hat geträumt	10	*dream*
traurig	28	*sad(ly)*
treffen – du triffst, er/sie trifft, hat getroffen	18	*meet*
treiben (Sport ...) – er/sie treibt Sport, hat Sport getrieben	23	*do sport*
trennbare Verb (das), -en	18	*separable verb*
Treppe (die), -n	11	*stairs, staircase*
trinken – er/sie trinkt, hat getrunken	7	*drink*
Tropen (die Pl)	23	*tropics*
trotzdem	16	*nevertheless*
Tscheche (der), -n/Tschechin (die), -nen	24	*Czech (man/woman)*
Tschechien (das)	5	*Czech Republic*
tschechisch	14	*Czech*
Tschüs	1	*bye; cheerio*
TU (die) = Technische Universität, -en	29	*technical University*
tun – er/sie tut, hat getan	12	*do; put*
Tür (die), -en	9, 21	*door*
Türke (der) –n/Türkin (die), -nen	24	*Turk, Turkish (man/woman)*
Türkei (die)	3	*Turkey*
türkisch	14	*Turkish*
Turm (der), ¨e	29	*tower*
Tut mir leid.	7	*I'm sorry.*
Tüte (die), -n	18	*bag*
typisch	30	*typical*

U

üben – er/sie übt, hat geübt	11	*practise*
über + Akk./Dat.	19	*over*
überhaupt	23	*at all*
übermorgen	15, 27	*the day after tomorrow*
Überraschung (die), -en	8	*surprise*
übersetzen – er/sie übersetzt, hat übersetzt	15	*translate*
Übersetzung (die), -en	9	*translation*
übrig bleiben – er/sie bleibt übrig, ist übrig geblieben	17	*be/get left (over)*
übrigens	13	*by the way*
Übung (die), -en	1	*exercise*
Uf Widerluege	1	*goodbye*
Uhr (die), -en: Es ist 6 Uhr.	10	*clock, o'clock: It's 6 o'clock*
Uhrzeit (die), -en	10	*time*
um (...6 Uhr)	9	*at (... 6 o'clock)*
um ... herum	19	*round ...*
um/räumen – er/sie räumt um, hat umgeräumt	29	*rearrange things, move things around*

Umgangssprache (die)	8	*colloquial language/speech*
unbedingt	25	*absolutely, really*
unbestimmt	7	*indefinite*
und	1	*and*
unfreundlich	28	*unfriendly*
Ungar (der), -n/Ungarin (die), -nen	24	*Hungarian (man/woman)*
ungarisch	24	*Hungarian*
Ungarn	24	*Hungary*
ungefähr	10	*about, roughly*
ungesund	23	*unhealthy*
unhöflich	29	*impolite*
Uni (= Universität) (die), -s	12	*uni (= university)*
Universität (die), -en	7	*university*
Universitätsstadt (die), ¨e	24	*university town/city*
unpünktlich	12	*unpunctual*
unser, unsere	16	*our*
Unsinn (der)	29	*nonsense*
unsympathisch	28	*not nice, unpleasant*
unten	21	*below, at the bottom*
unter + Akk./Dat.	22	*under, below*
Unter den Linden (Allee in Berlin)	22	*Unter den Linden (boulevard in Berlin)*
Untergeschoss (das), -e	20	*basement*
unterhalten sich – du unterhältst dich, er/sie unterhält sich, hat sich unterhalten	24	*talk*
Unterschied (der), -e	16	*difference*
Unterschrift (die), -en	3	*signature*
unterstreichen – er/sie unterstreicht, hat unterstrichen	1	*underline*
unzufrieden	26	*dissatisfied*
Urlaub (der): in Urlaub fahren; Urlaub machen	13, 26	*holiday: go on holiday*
Urlaubsland (das), ¨er	24	*country people go to for their holidays*
Urlaubsplan (der), ¨e	23	*holiday plans*
USA (die Vereinigten Staaten von Amerika)	3	*USA*
usw. (= und so weiter)	3	*etc*

V

Vater (der), ¨	13	*father*
verabschieden sich - er/sie verabschiedet sich, hat sich verabschiedet	30	*take one's leave*
Verb (das), -en	2	*verb*
verboten	6	*forbidden*
verdienen – er/sie verdient, hat verdient	15	*earn, deserve*
vergessen – du vergisst, er/sie vergisst, hat vergessen	17	*forget*
vergleichen – er/sie vergleicht, hat verglichen	1	*compare*
verheiratet	3	*married*
Verkäufer (der) -/die Verkäuferin, -nen	15	*(shop) assistant*
Verkehr (der)	10	*traffic*
verletzen sich - er/sie verletzt sich, hat sich verletzt	30	*hurt oneself*
verlieren – er/sie verliert, hat verloren	30	*lose*

Verneinung (die)	4	*negation*
verreisen – er/sie verreist, ist verreist gewesen	27	*go away (on holiday)*
Versand (der)	12	*despatch (department)*
verschicken – er/sie verschickt, hat verschickt	26	*send*
verschieden	21	*different*
verstecken – er/sie versteckt, hat versteckt	24	*hide*
verstehen – er/sie versteht, hat verstanden	5	*understand*
Vertrag (der), ¨e	30	*contract*
Vertragsabschluss (der), ¨e	30	*completion/conclusion of a contract*
Vertrieb (der)	11	*sales (department)*
Videofilm (der), -e	28	*video film*
Viel Glück!	9	*Good luck!*
Viel Spaß!	11	*Have a good time!/Enjoy yourself/yourselves!*
viel, viele	5	*much, many*
viele Grüße (aus ...)	15	*best wishes (from ...)*
Vielen Dank	5	*Thank you very much*
vielleicht	4	*perhaps, maybe*
Viertel (vor/nach ...)	10	*a quarter (to/past ...)*
Viertelstunde (die)	10	*quarter of an hour*
Visitenkarte (die), -n	3	*business card*
Visum (das), Visa	3	*visa*
Vokabel (die), -n	19, 22	*word, vocabulary item*
Vokal (der), -e	8	*vowel*
Vokalwechsel (der), -	8	*vowel change*
Volkswagen (der), -	15	*Volkswagen*
voll	22	*full*
Vollpension (die)	24	*full board*
von ... bis	12	*from ... till*
von + Dat.	3	*of, from*
von Beruf (sein)	6	*by profession, work as a ...*
Von nichts kommt nichts. (Sprichwort)	8	*You don't get anything without effort. (Proverb)*
vor (... 6 Uhr)	10	*to (... 6)*
vor/nach (Minuten)	10	*to/past (minutes)*
vorbei	19	*past*
vorgehen: die Uhr geht vor, ist vorgegangen	10	*be fast: the clock is fast*
vorgestern	27	*day before yesterday*
Vorhang (der), ¨e	29	*curtain*
vorkommen – es kommt vor, ist vorgekommen	24	*happen, occur*
vorlesen – du liest vor, er/sie liest vor, hat vorgelesen	21	*read out (loud), read to someone*
Vormittag (der)	12	*morning*
vormittags	10	*in the morning(s)*
vorn	21	*at the front*
Vorname (der), -n	1	*first name*
Vorschlag (der), ¨e	11	*suggestion*
Vorwahlnummer (die), -n	11	*dialling code, area code*
Vorwort (das)	1	*foreword, introduction*

W

waagerecht	7	*horizontal; across (in crossword)*
Wachau (die)	24	*Wachau*
wachsen – er/sie wächst, ist gewachsen	16	*grow*
Wagen (der), -	14	*car*
Wahrzeichen (das), -	22	*emblem*
Wald (der), ¨er	22	*forest, wood(s)*
Wand (die), ¨e	29	*wall*
wandern – er/sie wandert, ist gewandert	24	*go walking/hiking, hike*
Wanderweg (der), -e	24	*hiking trail*
Wann?	5	*When?*
warm	4	*warm*
warten – er/sie wartet, hat gewartet	11	*wait*
Warum?	11	*Why?*
was = etwas	8	*something*
Was?	3	*What?*
waschen sich – er/sie wäscht sich, hat sich gewaschen	30	*wash, get washed*
Wasser (das)	10	*water*
WC (das), -s	9	*WC*
Weg (der), -e	11, 12	*way, path*
weg sein – er/sie ist weg, ist weg gewesen	11	*be away, be gone*
wegfahren – du fährst weg, er/sie fährt weg, ist weggefahren	23	*go (away)*
Wegbeschreibung (die), -en	19	*directions, route description*
wehtun – es/das tut weh, hat weh getan	12	*hurt*
weiblich	3	*female*
Wein (der), -e	2, 17	*wine*
Weinschorle (die), -n	18	*wine mixed with mineral water*
Weintraube (die), -n (der Wein + die Traube)	17, 18	*grape*
weiß	22	*white*
Weißwein (der), -e	17	*white wine*
Weißwurst (die), ¨e: Bayerische Weißwurst	16	*white sausage: Bavarian white sausage*
weit	4	*far, a long way*
Welcher?/Welche?/Welches?	5, 17	*What? Which?*
Wem?	27	*To whom?*
Wen?	28	*Who(m)?*
wenig, wenige	5	*little, few*
wenn	12	*when*
Wer Sorgen hat, hat auch Likör.	8	*He who has wories also has liqueur.*
Wer?	5	*Who?*
werden – du wirst, er/sie wird, ist geworden	12, 29	*become*
Westen (der)	6	*west*
westlich (von)	6	*west (of)*
Wetter (das)	4	*weather*
W-Frage (die), -n	6	*wh-questions*
wichtig	12	*important*
widersprechen – du widersprichst, er/sie widerspricht, hat widersprochen	18	*contradict*

wie (A wie Anton)	6	*as (A for/as in Anton)*
Wie alt?	6	*How old?*
Wie bitte?	5	*Sorry?*
Wie lange?	5	*How long?*
Wie spät (ist es)?	10	*What's the time?*
Wie viel?/Wie viele?	16, 17	*How much?/How many?*
Wie weit?	10	*How far?*
Wie?	1	*How? What?*
wieder	5	*again*
wiederholen – er/sie wiederholt, hat wiederholt	3	*repeat*
wiederkommen – er/sie kommt wieder, ist wieder gekommen	29	*come back*
Wiener Melange (die) (= Kaffeesorte)	7	*Viennese Melange (= sort of coffee)*
willkommen	1	*welcome*
windig	4	*windy*
Winter (der)	23	*winter*
wir	1	*we*
wirklich	13	*really*
wissen – du weißt, er/sie weiß, hat gewusst	16	*know*
Wo?	2	*Where?*
Woche (die), -n	13	*week*
Wochenendausflug (der), ⸚e	19	*weekend trip/excursion*
Wochenende (das), -n	13	*weekend*
Wochentag (der), -e	12	*day of the week*
Woher?	2	*Where from?*
Wohin?	8	*Where to?*
wohl	18	*probably, perhaps*
wohnen – er/sie wohnt, hat gewohnt	2	*live*
Wohnung (die), -en	9	*flat*
Wohnzimmer (das), -	9	*living room*
Wolke (die), -n	24	*cloud*
wollen – er/sie will	29	*want (to)*
Wort (das), ⸚er	1	*word*
Wörtersalat (der)	13	*jumbled words*
Wortteil (der), -e	24	*part of a word*
Wunsch (der), ⸚e: auf Wunsch	7, 21	*wish: optionally*
wünschen – er/sie wünscht, hat gewünscht	26	*wish*
Wurst (die), ⸚e	16	*sausage*
Würstchen (das), -	22	*sausage*
Wüste (die)	23, 26	*desert*

Z

Zahl (die), -en	3	*number*
zahlen- er/sie zahlt, hat gezahlt	21	*pay*
Zahn (der), ⸚e	12	*tooth*
Zahnschmerzen (die Pl)	12	*toothache*
Zander (der), - (Fisch)	20	*zander [type of fish]*
Zauberflöte Die	30	*Magic Flute*
zeichnen – er/sie zeichnet, hat gezeichnet	12	*draw*
Zeichnung (die), -en	23	*drawing*

zeigen – er/sie zeigt, hat gezeigt	24	*show, point*
Zeit (die). -en	4	*time*
Zeit (die): Zeit haben	6	*time: have time*
Zeit ist Geld!	30	*Time is money.*
Zeitangabe (die), -n	11	*time expression*
Zeitschrift (die), -en	12, 21	*magazine*
Zeitung (die), -en	21	*newspaper*
Zentrum (das), Zentren	4	*centre*
Zettel (der), -	27	*piece of paper*
Ziel (das), -e	3	*destination; goal, target*
ziemlich	15	*fairly, quite*
Zimmer (das), -	9	*room*
zu (viel/wenig/kalt/warm ...)	8, 23	*too (much/little/cold/warm ...)*
zu + Dat.	6	*to*
zu Fuß (gehen)	11	*on foot (walk)*
zu Hause	5	*at home*
zu spät: zu spät kommen	12	*too late: be late*
Zucker (der)	7	*sugar*
zuerst	4	*(at) first*
zufrieden – er/sie ist zufrieden, ist zufrieden gewesen	28	*satisfied*
Zug (der), ̈e	11	*train*
Zugrestaurant (das), -s	21	*dining car*
Zugspitze (die)	27	*Zugspitze*
zuhören – er/sie hört zu, hat zugehört	3	*listen*
Zukunft (die)	26	*future*
zuletzt	29	*last, the last time*
zum /zur: zur Schule gehen	10, 13	*to the: go to school*
zum Glück	12	*luckily, fortunately*
zum Schluss	14	*at the end, finally*
Zuname (der), -n	6	*surname*
zuordnen – er/sie ordnet zu, hat zugeordnet	1	*match*
Zürcher Geschnetzelte (das)	20	*veal in cream sauce*
zurückfahren – er/sie fährt zurück, ist zurückgefahren	12	*drive/go back*
zurückfliegen – er/sie fliegt zurück, ist zurückgeflogen	11	*fly back*
zurückgehen – er/sie geht zurück, ist zurückgegangen	12	*go back*
zurückkommen – er/sie kommt zurück, ist zurückgekommen	22	*come back*
zurückrufen – er/sie ruft zurück, hat zurückgerufen	29	*call back*
zusammen	16	*together*
Zusammenarbeit (die)	28	*cooperation*
zusammengehören – es/das gehört zusammen, hat zusammengehört	3	*belong together*
zusammenkommen – sie kommen zusammen, sind zusammengekommen	17	*come together*
zusammenpassen – das passt zusammen, hat zusammengepasst	1	*go together, fit*

zusammensetzen – er/sie setzt zusammen, hat zusammengesetzt	15	*put together*
zusammensuchen – er/sie sucht zusammen, hat zusammengesucht	24	*look for, find*
zustimmen – er/sie stimmt zu, hat zugestimmt	8	*agree*
Zutaten (die Pl)	18	*ingredients*
zuverlässig	28	*reliable*
Zwiebel (die), -n	17	*onion*
Zwiebelring (der), -e	21	*onion ring*
zwischen + Dat.	14	*between*

Lösungen / Key to the exercises

Lesson 1

1 a3, b4, c1, d2, e5

3 Guten Tag. Sind Sie Herr Heinrich? / Ja, das bin ich. / Mein Name ist Bruckner, Chris Bruckner. / Guten Tag, Frau Bruckner. Herzlich willkommen. Hallo, Rob. / Hallo, Claudia. / Wie geht's dir? / Danke, gut.

4 Hallo, Rob. – Hallo, Claudia.
Wie geht es Ihnen? – Danke, gut. Und Ihnen?
Guten Tag, ich bin Chris Bruckner. – Guten Tag, Frau Bruckner. Herzlich willkommen.
Wie geht's dir? – Gut, danke.
Sind Sie Herr Heinrich? – Ja, das bin ich.

5 **Sie:** Sie, Guten Tag, Frau; **du:** Hallo, Hallo

6 **Sie:** Sind, bin, ist
du: Bist, bin, bin, bin

7 1. Guten Tag, 2. Danke, gut, 3. Hallo, 4. Ich bin Felix.

8 1a, 2c, 3a

9 Das sind Sie. Das sind wir. Das seid ihr. Das ist sie (*Sing.*). Das bin ich. Das ist er. Das sind sie (*Pl.*).

10 Ich bin, Sind Sie, Bist du, Herr Heinrich ist, Wir sind, Seid ihr, Sind Sie

11 Grüß Gott. – Grüß Gott.; Hallo, ..., wie geht's? – Gut, und dir?; Grüezi. – Grüezi, Nina.

Workbook page 9 / Textbook page 8:
Guten Tag, Servus, Grüezi

1 (Norddeutschland:) Guten Tag. Hallo. Auf Wiedersehen. Tschüs.

2 (Bayern:) Grüß Gott. Griaß di. Auf Wiederschaun. Pfiat di.

3 (Österreich:) Grüß Gott. Servus. Baba.

4 (Schweiz:) Grüezi. Uf Widerluege. Salut.

Test

1. 1. Hello, Good morning, Good afternoon, 2. Good morning, 3. Hello, Hi, 4. How are you?, 5. Fine, thanks. 6 Goodbye.

2. 1. Nacht, 2. Wiedersehen, 3. Guten, 4. Guten, 5. Guten, 6. Tschüs

3. 1. bin, 2. bist, 3. ist, 4. ist, 5. ist, 6. Sind, 7. Sind, 8. Sind

4. 1. bin, 2. Bist, 3. Sind, 4. bin, 5. ist, 6. ist

Lesson 2

2   Sind Sie aus Berlin, Herr Heinrich?
Ja, klar. Und Sie, woher kommen Sie?
Aus Österreich, ich bin aus Wien. Aber ich lebe in München. Schon lange.
Sind Sie gern in München?
Ja, sehr gern. Ich wohne schon fünf Jahre dort.
Kennen Sie Berlin?
Ja, aber nicht gut.

3   1. Sind, 2. kommen, 3. bin, 4. lebe, 5. Sind, 6. wohne

4   aus Berlin, in Berlin, aus Österreich, in München, fünf Jahre dort, Berlin nicht gut

5   1. Nein, ich bin aus Wien. 2. Ja, schon lange. 3. Ja, aber nicht gut.

6   1. Nein, aus München. 2. Ja, klar. 3. Ja, das bin ich.

8   lebt, wohnt, wohnen, kommt, kommen, kennt, Kennen
Lebt Pierre in Paris? – Ja, er lebt in Paris. / Er ist aus Paris.
Kennen Sie Paris? – Ja, aber nicht gut. / Ich kenne London gut.

9   sein, wohnen, heißen, kennen

10 kennst, kennt, leben, wohnst, wohnt, wohnen, heiße, heißen

11 Ich heiße ... (your name), Wie heißt ..., Er heißt ..., Wie heißen ..., Wir heißen ...,
Wie heißt ..., Karla und Fritz heißen ...

12 kommt Andrea – Sie kommt; Lebt Pierre – Pierre lebt; kommen Graziella und Paolo
– sie kommen; Wohnt Juan – Juan wohnt; Kennen Sie – ich kenne; Wohnt Elsbeta –
sie wohnt

Workbook page 15 / Textbook page 12:
Städte-Quiz

Hamburg, Köln, Leipzig, Augsburg, Bern, Zürich, Salzburg, Graz
D ist Deutschland. A ist Österreich. CH ist die Schweiz.

Test

1.   1. How are you? 2. Yes, of course. 3. Yes, I am.

2.   1. kommen, 2. leben / wohnen, 3. heißen, 4. sein, 5. kennen

3.   1. aus, 2. Kommen, 3. wohne, 4. Sie, 5. Kennen, 6. Kommen

4.   1. Woher kommen Sie? 2. Sind Sie aus Hamburg? 3. Wohnen Sie in München?
4. Kennen Sie Berlin? 5. Sind Sie Herr Müller? 6. Wie geht es Ihnen?

Lesson 3

1 a. Groß, b. Julian, c. Stuttgart, d. Berlin, e. 10543, f. Neue Straße 10, g. Deutschland, h. *Julian Groß*

der Name – name, der Vorname – first name, der Geburtsort – place of birth, die Adresse – address, der Ort – place, die Postleitzahl – postcode / zipcode, die Straße – street / road, das Land – country, die Unterschrift – signature

4 a1, b1, c2, d8 oder 3, e8 oder 3, f4, g5, h7, i6

5 der Ort, der Name, die Postleitzahl, der Vorname, die Straße, die Adresse, das Land

6 Adresse

8 der Pass – das Visum, der Name – der Vorname, der Ort – die Postleitzahl, männlich – weiblich, ledig – verheiratet, das Hotel – die Adresse, der Geburtsort – das Geburtsjahr, Datum – Unterschrift

10 in, in, aus, in

11 Argentinien, Australien, Belgien, Brasilien, Bulgarien, Großbritannien, Indien, Indonesien, Italien, Kroatien, Moldawien, Rumänien, Slowenien

12 Aus Russland, Aus Frankreich, Aus den USA, Aus Deutschland, Aus der Schweiz, Aus Japan

13 null, eins, zwei, drei, vier, fünf, sechs, sieben, acht, neun, zehn

14 70190, 80805, 76137, 60313, 69118, 20143

18 fünf, zwei, vier, neun

Workbook page 21 / Textbook page 16:
Ausländer in Deutschland

Entschuldigen Sie, woher sind Sie?
Aus Deutschland.
Aus Deutschland?
Ja, klar. Ich bin aus Berlin. Ich wohne hier.
Und wie heißen Sie?
Özcan Saglem.
Aha.

Test

1. 1. What's your name? 2. Where were you born? 3. Please spell it. 4. I'm divorced, 5. Where … from? 6. Your passport number, please.

2. 1. das, 2. die, 3. die, 4. der, 5. der, 6. das

3. 1. verheiratet, 2. wohnen Sie, 3. Ihre Adresse, 4. kommen Sie, 5. die Pass-Nummer, 6. aus Österreich

4. 1. Müller, 2. Janssen, 3. Hamburg

Lesson 4

1 Wie geht's? – 1, 2, 4
Wie ist das Wetter? – 2, 3
Wie ist das Hotel? – 1, 2, 3
Wie war die Reise? – 1, 2, 4

2 Das Wetter ist auch prima.
Ja, es ist schön und sehr warm. Wie ist es denn in München?
Leider schlecht. Es regnet schon zwei Tage.
Da haben Sie hier Glück. Kennen Sie die Stadt?
Nicht sehr gut.
Dann machen wir eine Stadtrundfahrt. Vielleicht morgen?
Ja, gerne.

3 **Bruckner:** b, e, f, h; **Kühne:** a, c, d, g, i, j

4 a. gut, b. direkt im Zentrum, c. praktisch, d. nicht schlecht, e. in München,
f. nicht sehr gut.

6 **Richtig:** Frau A. wohnt im Hotel Amsterdam. – Frau A. wohnt im Amsterdam.
– Das Hotel ist sehr praktisch.

8 gut, gut, weit, praktisch, prima, schön, warm, schlecht, gut

9 Tag, Frau, Reise, Herr, Hotel, Zentrum, Wetter, München, Glück, Stadt,
Stadtrundfahrt

10 die Reise, das Zentrum, die Adresse, das Land, der Name, der Tag, die Stadt,
das Hotel, das Wetter, die Stadtrundfahrt, das Glück

11 Geschäft – es, Tag – er, Stadt – sie, Euro – er, Reise – sie, Haus – es, Auto – es,
Zeit – sie, Adresse – sie

12 gut, herzlich, prima, schön, warm, schlecht, geschieden, ledig, neu, richtig, langsam,
männlich, schnell, weiblich, falsch, kalt, negativ, praktisch, weit

13 Nein, das Wetter ist nicht schön. Nein, es regnet nicht. Nein, das Zentrum ist nicht
weit. Nein, das Hotel ist nicht praktisch. Nein, die Reise ist nicht prima.

17 der Name, das Land, der Familienstand, die Adresse, das Geburtsland, die Nationalität

Workbook page 27 / Textbook page 20:
Ländernamen

Neuseeland, England, Türkei, Russland, Deutschland, Österreich, China, Korea, Italien,
Brasilien
4 Korea, 9 Österreich, 7 China, 5 Deutschland, 8 Brasilien, 6 England, 10 Russland,
1 Neuseeland, 3 Türkei, 2 Italien, 11 Frankreich

Test

1. 1. How are you? 2. Very well. 3. Bad, I'm afraid.

2. 3 Es ist sehr warm. 1 Es ist windig. 5 Es ist kalt. 4 Die Sonne scheint. 6 Es regnet.
2 Es schneit.

3. 1. der, 2. die, 3. das, 4. die, 5. das, 6. das

4. 1., 3., 4., 5., 8.

5. 1. Nein, das ist nicht weit. 2. Nein, das ist nicht schön. 3. Nein, es ist nicht kalt.
4. Nein, es ist nicht windig. 5. Nein, es regnet nicht. 6. Nein, es schneit nicht.

Lesson 5

1 a2, b5, c1, d4, e3

3 Was, Wo, Wie lange, Wie, Wann,

4 Die Fahrkarte kostet zwei Euro. – Robert und Claudia sind in Berlin. – Rosenheim ist
eine Kleinstadt. – Berlin ist eine Großstadt. – Niki arbeitet furchtbar viel / sehr viel.
– Robert arbeitet furchtbar wenig / sehr wenig / nicht viel.

5 heiße, ist, sind, ist, heißt

6 Zwei Euro. – Eine Stunde. – Super. – Mit der S-Bahn. – Spät. – Nein, furchtbar
wenig.

7 Eine Stunde, die Fahrkarte, eine Frage, ein Hotel, eine Großstadt, ein Bundesland?

8 du: hast, arbeitest, fährst; er/sie/es: hat; arbeitet, fährt; ihr: arbeitet

9 die Minute, die Fahrkarte, die Großstadt, der Euro, die Kleinstadt, die Stunde,
die S-Bahn, das Auto

10 1 Fahrkarten, 2 Minuten, 3 Stunden, 4 Namen, 5 Länder, 6 Wörter

11 eine – Minuten, eine – Stunden, eine – Städte, eine – Großstädte, eine – Kleinstädte,
ein – Geschäfte, eine – S-Bahnen, ein – Autos

13 Stadt – Städte, Land – Länder, Wort – Wörter, Satz – Sätze, Pass – Pässe

14 in Bremen, schon ein Jahr dort, kennt

Workbook page 33 / Textbook page 24:
Nachbarländer

Dänemark, Polen, Tschechien, Österreich, die Schweiz, Frankreich, Luxemburg, Belgien,
die Niederlande

Test

1. 1. Thank you. 2. How much is it? 3. home, 4. little time, 5. terribly hard, 6. Sorry?

2. 1. die Stadt, 2. eine Minute, 3. eine Stunde, 4. die Fahrkarte, 5. das Wort, 6. ein Land

3. 1. Arbeitest, 2. Hast, 3. arbeiten, 4. Fahrt, 5. fahren, 6. kostet

4. 1. die, 2. die, 3. die, 4. der, 5. die, 6. das

5. 1. Stadt, 2. Wörter, 3. Sätze, 4. Land, 5. Pass, 6. Pässe

Lesson 6

1   a4, b5, c3, d1, e2, f7, g6

3   Berlin: wohnen, Rosenheim: wohnt, München: studiert

4   Wer, geboren, Jahre, Beruf, bei, Hobbys; Wer, aus, München, Student, Zeit, findet

5   Sie ist in Berlin geboren. – Sie ist 23 Jahre alt. – Sie ist Medien-Designerin von Beruf. – Sie arbeitet bei Art & Design. – Ihre Hobbys sind Reisen und Sprachen. – Robert kommt aus Rosenheim.

6   a2, b1, c5, d6, e3, f4

8   *Example:* Ich finde Claudia sympathisch.

9   1c, 2e, 3f, 4g, 5d, 6a, 7b

10 (ein)hundertfünfzig, fünfundzwanzig, dreiundsiebzig, fünfzehn, fünf, neunundneunzig

11 1. 089 – 46 37 49, 2. 040 – 77 88 90, 3. 030 – 307 26 50, 4. 069 – 32 56 80

Workbook page 39 / Textbook page 28:
Ein Schloss in Bayern

1. Im Süden von München, 2. 150 Kilometer, 3. 8 Euro

Test

1. 1. Kleinstadt, 2. vielen Dank, 3. Telefonnummer, 4. nach Hause, 5. Hobby, 6. interessant

2. 1. Er studiert. 2. Sie studiert in Hamburg. 3. Er ist in Deutschland geboren. 4. Er ist drei Jahre alt. 5. Wo arbeiten Sie? 6. Was sind Sie von Beruf?

3. 1. arbeitest, 2. studiert, 3. fahre, 4. kommst, 5. hast

4. 1. Wo, 2. Was, 3. Wo, 4. Wie, 5. Wie lange, 6. Was

5. 1. ist nicht in Deutschland geboren, 2. arbeitet, 3. schon fünf Jahre da

Lesson 7

1   Kaffee / Tee, Milch und Zucker, Milch / Zucker.

3   2, 4, 3, 1

4   1b, 2d, 3a, 4g, 5c, 6e, 7f

5   leid, Mittag, gern, Kantine, Tee; DANKE

6   a. Ja, gerne. b. Tee, bitte. c. Ja, danke. d. Ja, bitte. e. Nur Milch, bitte. f. Ja, gerne.

7   a. Fahrkarte, b. Hobby, c. Sprache, d. Buchstabe, e. sympathisch, f. Informatik

8   liegt, gut, fünf Jahre, Herr, Chef, alt, Beruf

9   eine Kleinstadt, eine Handy-Nummer, ein Vorname, ein Land, eine Postleitzahl, ein Wort

10 ich: möchte, kann; du: nimmst, möchtest, kannst; er / sie: nimmt, kann; ihr: möchtet; sie / Sie: können

11 Möchten Sie, Kann ich, Kann ich, Möchten Sie, Kann ich, Möchten Sie, Können Sie, Können Sie

12 wo das Hotel, wann der Bus, wie der Herr, was die Fahrkarte, woher Herr Bünzli, wer Herr Heinrich

14 kurz: hat, dann, Stadt, schlecht, kommt, sind, Stunde; **lang:** haben, da, Jahr, Tee, schon, Sie, nur

15 Who is that please? ... – Wer ist dort bitte? ... / Is that Meier? ... – Ist dort Meier? ... / Is that Meier? ... Goodbye. – Ist dort Meier? ... Auf Wiederhören.

Workbook page 45 / Textbook page 32:
Kaffee trinken

In Deutschland, In Österreich, In der Schweiz

Test

1. 1. Tee, 2. Zitrone, 3. nichts, 4. Frau, 5. Beruf, 6. Süden
2. 1. That's OK. 2. Can I please ...? 3. I'd like ..., 4. OK? 5. I'm sorry. 6. Yes, of course.
3. 1. Möchten Sie, 2. Ich möchte, 3. Ich nehme, 4. Wir arbeiten, 5. Wer geht, 6. Machen Sie, 7. Können wir, 8. kann
4. 1. eine, 2. ein, 3. eine, 4. eine, 5. eine, 6. ein, 7. eine, 8. ein

Lesson 8

1 arbeiten, kochen, trinken, essen, sprechen, fahren
3 zu Hause, prima, Spaß, Pause, recht, Hunger, Überraschung, Salat
4 Hunger und Durst
5 a. zu Hause, b. früher gegangen, c. viel, d. recht, e. Hunger, f. Spaghetti und Salat
6 Er ist, Er ist, Er hat, Die Arbeit hat, Er hat, Wir haben, Wir haben
7 a. Klasse! *oder* Prima! b. Na klar. c. Na klar. d. Na ja. *oder* Bestens. e. Na ja. f. Ach was. *oder* Na klar. g. Schade. *oder* Macht nichts.
8 Hause, gegangen, arbeitet, recht, und, gemacht, fahren, fährt
9 **G** = Fahrt ihr in die Stadt? Was heißt das? Hast du Hunger? Du hast recht. Wohin fährt die Bahn?
V = Was hast du heute gemacht? Wo bist du geboren? Ich habe schon gegessen. Hast du gearbeitet? Ich bin früh nach Hause gegangen.
10 *lesen* – du liest, er/sie liest
essen – du isst, er/sie isst
haben – du hast, er/sie hat
geben – du gibst, er/sie gibt
fahren – du fährst, er/sie fährt
nehmen – du nimmst, er/sie nimmt
sprechen – du sprichst, er/sie spricht
11 Ich habe heute etwas gekocht. Da ist niemand. Nein, ich arbeite zu viel. Ich bin extra früher gegangen.

15 Hallo.

Wer ist dort bitte?

Hier Meyer.

Ist dort Meyer, Telefon 46 88 11?

Nein, hier Meyer, Telefon 46 77 11.

Oh, Entschuldigung.

Bitte sehr.

Workbook page 51 / Textbook page 36: Sprichwörter

Kommt Zeit, kommt Rat. Der Apfel fällt nicht weit vom Stamm. Probieren geht über Studieren. Der Ton macht die Musik. Wer Sorgen hat, hat auch Likör.

Test

1. 1. recht, 2. dran, 3. Hunger, 4. Spaß, 5. nichts, 6. was

2. 1. Er ist extra früher gegangen. 2. Er arbeitet viel. 3. Sie hat recht. 4. Das ist eine Überraschung. 5. Wer hat gekocht? 6. Er hat Spaghetti gekocht.

3. 1. hast, 2. Ist, 3. Seid, 4. haben, 5. hat, 6. hast

4. 1. fährt, 2. isst, 3. nimmt, 4. gibt, 5. ist, 6. spricht

Lesson 9

1

das Wohnzimmer	der Balkon
	die Küche
der Flur	
	die Toilette
das Schlafzimmer	das Bad

3 1. im Zentrum, 2. zwei Zimmer mit Bad, 3. Dachwohnung, 4. im Wohnzimmer, 5. 550 Euro warm, 6. im Norden

4 haben wir, Ich habe, haben wir, Ich habe

5 a2, b4, c1, d3, e6, f5

6 1. 12 (zwölf), 2. 5 (fünf), 3. 45 (fünfundvierzig), 4. 10 (zehn) Euro; 1.050 ((ein)tausend(und)fünfzig) Euro

7 baden, kochen, schlafen, wohnen, arbeiten, fahren

8 Ich finde die Wohnung super. Ich finde das Bad praktisch. Ich finde den Balkon schön. Ich finde den Kaffee gut. Ich finde das Hotel schlecht.

9 Das praktische Bad. Der nette Markus. Das schlechte Hotel. Die sympathische Daniela. Die richtige Lösung.

10 1b, 2a, 3d, 4c, 5e, 6f

11 1. eine Kantine, 2. ein Bad, 3. ein Wohnzimmer, 4. ein Balkon, 5. eine Küche, 6. ein Schlafzimmer

12 Die Kantine, Das Bad, Das Wohnzimmer, Der Balkon, Die Küche, Das Schlafzimmer
13 die Kantine, das Bad, das Wohnzimmer, den Balkon, die Küche, das Schlafzimmer
14 eine Wohnung, eine Anzeige, eine Lösung, einen Salat, ein Büro
17 5 Euro, 99 Euro, 550 Euro, 2.500 Euro, 450 Euro, 250 Euro

Workbook page 57 / Textbook page 40:
Rätsel

A	= eins	K	= elf	U	= einundzwanzig
B	= zwei	L	= zwölf	V	= zweiundzwanzig
C	= drei	M	= dreizehn	W	= dreiundzwanzig
D	= vier	N	= vierzehn	X	= vierundzwanzig
E	= fünf	O	= fünfzehn	Y	= fünfundzwanzig
F	= sechs	P	= sechzehn	Z	= sechsundzwanzig
G	= sieben	Q	= siebzehn	Ä	= siebenundzwanzig
H	= acht	R	= achtzehn	Ö	= achtundzwanzig
I	= neun	S	= neunzehn	Ü	= neunundzwanzig
J	= zehn	T	= zwanzig	ß	= dreißig

Answer: Viel Glück!

Test

1. 1. flat, 2. advert, 3. garage, 4. 500 euros … basic rent, 5. available immediately, 6. The flat is cosy.
2. 1. ein, ein, 2. einen, eine, ein, 3. keine, 4. einen, 5. Das, 6. Die
3. 1. gefunden, 2. gesagt, 3. gespart, gewohnt, 4. gelesen, 5. gemietet
4. 2 Zimmer, 35 qm, 600 Euro kalt, 0911 - 62424

Lesson 10

1 a2, b6, c5, d3, e1, f4
3 Frau Bruckner: a, c, d, f, Taxifahrer: b, e
4 Straße, Verkehr, Termin, Minuten, Wasser, Viertelstunde, Stau, Nummer, Euro, Quittung
5 a3, b4, c2, d1
8 **Singular:** 2. (Frage), 4.(Auto), 7. (Quittung), 8. (Anzeige)
  Plural: 1. (Kinder), 3. (Städte), 5. (Uhren), 6. (Nummern)
9 das Hobby, die Adressen, das Kind, die Hotels, der Name, die Tage, die Autos, die Nummern, die Stunde, das Land, die Fragen
10 Es ist halb zwölf. Es ist Viertel nach vier. Es ist Viertel vor elf. Es ist ein Uhr. (= Es ist eins.) Es ist zehn nach neun. Es ist zwanzig vor zehn.
12 **lang:** viel, abends, Problem, Kanal; **kurz:** links, fast, schrecklich, morgens

Workbook page 63 / Textbook page 44:
Wie weit ist das von Frankfurt?

1 Oslo 1.099 km, 2 Stockholm 1.188 km, 3 Moskau 2.023 km, 4 Warschau 892 km,
5 Brüssel 316 km, 6 Bern 363 km, 7 Wien 598 km, 8 Lissabon 1.892 km,
9 Madrid 1.447 km, 10 Athen 1.803 km

Nach Moskau ist es weiter als nach Madrid. Nach Madrid ist es weiter als nach Oslo.
Nach Athen ist es weiter als nach Bern.

Test

1. 1. sind, 2. möchten, 3. Nach, 4. lange, 5. Stunde, 6. Quittung.
2. 1. The clock is wrong. 2. The clock is fast. 3. The clock is slow. 4. About 20 minutes.
5. Quarter past three. 6. Quarter to seven.
3. 1. fünfzehn Uhr zehn, 2. sechzehn Uhr fünfundfünfzig, 3. achtzehn Uhr fünfzehn,
4. neunzehn Uhr fünfundvierzig, 5. neun Uhr siebenunddreißig, 6. elf Uhr fünfundfünfzig
4. 1. die Städte, 2. die Taxis, 3. die Quittungen, 4. die Termine, 5. die Büros, 6. die
Anzeigen, 7. die Häuser, 8. die Nummern

Lesson 11

1 *Examples:* Fahren Sie gern mit dem Zug? – Ja, sehr gern. Zug fahren ist sehr gemütlich. / Fliegen Sie gern? – Nein, nicht so gern. Fliegen ist teuer. / Fahren Sie gern mit
dem Bus? Nein, nicht gern. Bus fahren dauert sehr lange.
3 11 Uhr, um 12 Uhr, um 12, heute Abend, sieben Uhr, halb acht, um halb acht,
Morgen
4 1. Herr Heinrich, Frau Bruckner und Herr Kühne, 2. Herr Kühne, 3. Wir möchten Sie
zum Essen einladen. 4. Um halb acht. 5. Sie fährt mit dem Zug. 6. Sechseinhalb
Stunden.
5 Nein, ich habe ... keine Firma. / keinen Aufzug. / keinen Keller. / kein Archiv. /
kein Sekretariat.
6 *nehmen:* den Vertrieb, *möchten:* einen Tag, *haben:* einen Bahnhof, *kennen:* die
Stunde, *mieten:* eine Straße
8 Uhr, mit, wenig, Mittags, Essen, halb
9 den Bus – der, die Bahn – die, den Zug – der, das Flugzeug – das, das Auto – das
10 eine Kantine – die, einen Aufzug – der, eine Pause – die, ein Hotel – das, eine
Dachwohnung – die
11 einen Termin, den Bus und die Bahn, einen Kaffee, den Hafen, den Reichstag, einen
Ausflug
12 kein Tee, keine Pension – ein Hotel, keine Telefonnummer – eine Fax-Nummer, kein
Vorname – ein Nachname, kein Land – ein Erdteil, keine Vorwahlnummer – eine
Postleitzahl

13 kein Auto, fliege nicht, nicht gern, nicht mit dem Auto, keine Zeit, komme nicht, keine Frage

15 **1. Silbe (1st syllable):** Straße, Quittung, Nummer, morgens, Reise, machen, Handy, Zimmer, Mittag, München, Norden, gestern, Frage, Vorschlag

2. Silbe (2nd syllable): Verkehr, Termin, Beruf, Geschäft, Besuch, Berlin

16 **1. Silbe (1st syllable):** Stadtrundfahrt, Anzeige, Telefon, arbeiten, Fahrkarte

2. Silbe (2nd syllable): Adresse, sympathisch, Kantine, Geburtsort, Grammatik

3. Silbe (3rd syllable): –

17 **1. Silbe (1st syllable):** –

2. Silbe (2nd syllable): besichtigen, Entschuldigung

3. Silbe (3rd syllable): buchstabieren, Informatik;

4. Silbe: interessant, Information, geradeaus

Workbook page 69 / Textbook page 48:
Buchstaben-Labyrinth

Wann haben Sie Zeit? Ich moechte (= möchte) Sie zum Essen einladen.

Test

1. 1. invitation, 2. by train, 3. It's fun. 4. invite someone to dinner, 5. this evening, 6. suggestion

2. 1. haben, 2. einladen, 3. nehmen, 4. fahren, 5. gehen, 6. haben/machen

3. 1. ein – kein, 2. einen – keinen, 3. eine – keine, 4. einen – keinen, 5. eine – keine, 6. einen – keinen

4. 1. den Hafen, 2. den Bus, 3. den Stau, 4. den Zug, 5. den Aufzug, 6. die Kantine, 7. den Raum, 8. die Arbeit

Lesson 12

1 2 der Empfang, 7 die IT-Abteilung, 1 die Buchhaltung, 8 die Redaktion, 5 das Lager, 3 das Informationszentrum, 4 die Kantine, 6 der Konferenzraum
Words that come from English: Controlling, IT, Produktion, Marketing

3 A (Informationszentrum), E (Empfang und Redaktionen), D (Buchhaltung), F (IT-Abteilung), B (Controlling), C (Kantine)

5 Wir haben, Dann haben wir, Wir sind, Dann habe ich, Das Lager habe ich, Um 12 sind

6 1f, 2c, 3e, 4a, 5b, 6d

8 4 Montag, 5 Dienstag, 6 Mittwoch, 7 Donnerstag, 8 Freitag, 9 Samstag / Sonnabend, 10 Sonntag

9 Wir arbeiten bis elf Uhr. Dann machen wir eine Pause. Um 11 Uhr 15 machen wir eine Firmenbesichtigung. Die Firmenbesichtigung dauert bis 12. Um 12 gehen wir in die Kantine. Wir essen bis eins. Dann arbeiten wir bis 3. Um 3 machen wir eine Stadtrundfahrt. Um 7 sind wir im Hotel zurück.

10 Jetzt machen wir eine Firmenbesichtigung. Um 12 Uhr komme ich in die Kantine. Heute Abend habe ich Zeit. Morgen fahre ich zurück nach München. Vielleicht nehme ich den Zug. Dann rufe ich an.

13 **1. Silbe (1st syllable):** Erdgeschoss, Firmenbesichtigung
2. Silbe (2nd syllable): Empfang
3. Silbe (3rd syllable): Redaktion, gegenüber, Konferenzräume
4. Silbe (4th syllable): geradeaus, Informationszentrum

Workbook page 75 / Textbook page 52:
Kleine Tipps

Richtig: 1. Man schüttelt sich die Hand bei Geburtstagen und Festen. Geschäftspartner schütteln sich die Hand.
2. *Mahlzeit* sagt man nur mittags bei der Arbeit. Der Gruß ist hässlich, sagen viele.
3. Pünktlichkeit ist in Deutschland wichtig. Man sagt: *Tut mir leid, dass ich zu spät komme. / Ich komme leider ein paar Minuten zu spät.*

Test

1. 1. Konferenzraum, 2. Kantine, 3. Einladung, 4. Lager, 5. Informationszentrum, 6. Redaktion
2. 1. Hier ist kein Platz. 2. Ich glaube nicht. 3. Da geradeaus. 4. Das macht Spaß. 5. Ich verstehe.
3. 1. Heute besichtigen wir den Hafen. 2. Um eins nehmen wir den Bus. 3. Morgen haben wir Raum 3. 4. Bis 18 Uhr ist das Casino geöffnet. 5. Am Vormittag besichtigen wir die Firma. 6. Mittwoch fahre ich wieder zurück.
4. mögen, du magst, er/sie mag / geben, du gibst, er/sie gibt / fahren, du fährst, er/sie fährt / nehmen, du nimmst, er/sie nimmt / schlafen, du schläfst, er/sie schläft
5. 1. Berlin, 2. Circa 30 Euro, 3. Zentrum, 4. S-Bahn, 5. Ja

Lesson 13

3. Brot oder ein Brötchen, Müsli, nur Brot und Butter, einen Löffel, noch einen Teller, mein Messer und meine Gabel, ein Ei, Eier esse ich nicht
4. geschlafen, spät, weg, gleich, Brot, Magst
5. Möchtest, möchtest, mag, mag, mag, möchte
6. mein Bruder, deine Schwester, Meine Schwester, deine Geschwister, deine Eltern, Meine Eltern
8. früh, Frühstück, Mittag, Eltern, Geschwister
9. Test, Ei, Dachwohnung, Eltern, Wort, Sprache
10. kein Auto, keine Uhr, keine Geschwister, keine Zeit, keine Semesterferien, keinen Hunger

11. deine Fahrkarte, dein Handy, dein Kaffee, dein Frühstück, mein Bruder – meinen Bruder, meine Schwester – meine Schwester

12. nicht dein Frühstück – mein Frühstück, nicht deine Schwester – meine Schwester, nicht deine Fahrkarte – meine Fahrkarte, nicht dein Auto – mein Auto, nicht deine Uhr – meine Uhr, nicht dein/mein Problem – mein/dein Problem

13. Niki heißt Bat mit Familiennamen. Er wohnt und arbeitet in Berlin und ist auch hier geboren. Deshalb ist nur der Familienname Chinesisch, nicht der Vorname. Er spricht auch kein Chinesisch. Aber er möchte die Sprache gern lernen. Die Eltern sind 1960 nach Deutschland gekommen. Jetzt haben sie ein chinesisches Restaurant. Das ist das Restaurant in der Hafenstraße. Das Essen dort ist sehr gut, sagt man.

Workbook page 81 / Textbook page 56:
Wörtersalat

Länder und Kontinente: Australien, Spanien, Korea, Polen, Italien, Japan, Europa, Asien, Deutschland

Familie: Tante, Onkel, Sohn, Mädchen, Junge, verheiratet, Großeltern, Eltern, Vater, Mutter, Tochter, Opa, Oma

Jahr, Jahreszeit, Woche und Tag: Frühling, Freitag, Sonnabend, Donnerstag, Sommer, Sonntag, Montag, Wochenende, Mittwoch, Dienstag

Essen und Trinken: Restaurant, Tasse, Milch, Tee, Käse, Kaffee, Marmelade

Berufe: Regisseur, Hausfrau, Hausmann, Maurer, Maler, Arzt

Wohnung: Aufzug, Bad, Wohnzimmer, Balkon, Zimmer, Flur

Stadt: Schule, Tourist, Taxifahrer, Zentrum, Zug, Bahnhof, Auto, Bahn, Flughafen, Hafen, Haltestelle

Test

1. 1. Christian has already left. 2. Tell me ... are you hungry? 3. Jan is still in school. 4. What do you think? 5. By the way ... 6. Really?

2. 1. Vater, 2. Schwester, 3. Opa, 4. Sohn, 5. Tante, 6. Schwiegermutter, 7. Frau

3. 1. dein, 2. dein, 3. dein, 4. dein, 5. deine, 6. deine

4. 1. Möchtest, 2. mag, 3. mag, 4. Möchtest, 5. Magst, 6. mag

Lesson 14

1

Monika Freud (Oma)	Helmut Freud (Opa)
Thomas Bergmann (Vater)	Beatrice Bergmann (Mutter)
Ralf Bergmann (Bruder)	Katrin Bergmann (Schwester) Claudia Bergmann

3 3, 2, 1, 4

4 Wir waren, Das war, Wir hatten, Niki und Claudia waren, Wie war, Hattet ihr

5 1. Katrin ist die Schwester von Claudia. Sie ist Regisseurin. 2. Robert findet eine Regisseurin interessant. 3. Robert spricht gut Englisch, aber nicht perfekt. 4. Robert, Claudia und Niki waren in England. Sie waren in einer Sprachenschule. Sie haben Englisch gelernt. 5. Claudias Mutter hat gekocht.

6 a1, b3, c2, d4, e5

8 Spargel mit Butter und Kartoffeln

9 waren, waren, hatte, war, waren, hatte, war

10 es, ihn, sie, sie, ihn, sie

11 Lieblingsstadt, Lieblingsbruder, Lieblingsschwester, Lieblingsfilm, Lieblingshotel, Lieblingsregisseur, Lieblingszimmer

12 Tschechien - Tschechisch, Polen - Polnisch, Russland - Russisch, Türkei - Türkisch, Japan - Japanisch, Spanien - Spanisch, Italien - Italienisch, China - Chinesisch, Korea - Koreanisch, Österreich - Österreichisch, Schweiz - Schweizerisch, Mexiko - Mexikanisch, Ungarn - Ungarisch, Griechenland - Griechisch

Workbook page 87 / Textbook page 60:
Das mögen wir!

a4, b3, c5, d1, e2, f6

Test

1. 1. Französisch, 2. Polnisch, 3. Österreichisch, 4. Türkisch, 5. Australisch, 6. Chinesisch, 7. Slowenisch, 8. Italienisch

2. 1. hatte, 2. hatte, 3. waren, 4. hatte, 5. war, 6. waren

3. 1. es, 2. sie, 3. es, 4. sie, 5. sie, 6. sie

Lesson 15

1 Robert – Student, Claudia – Medien-Designerin, Claudias Mutter – Malerin, Claudias Vater – Controller, Claudias Schwester – Regisseurin, Claudias Bruder – Schüler

3 1. Er war bei Claudias Eltern. 2. Er ist Ingenieur. 3. Sie ist Malerin. 4. Er geht noch zur Schule. 5. Sie heißt Katrin. 6. Er findet sie interessant.

4 Das ist Claudias Bruder. Das ist Claudias Schwester. Das ist Claudias Mutter. Das ist Claudias Großvater. Das ist Claudias Vater. Das ist Claudias Freund.

5 waren, sind, ist Ingenieur, ist Malerin, ist bald fertig, war auch da, ist Regisseurin

8 *Example:*

Liebe Eltern,

herzliche Grüße aus Rom. Ich bin noch im Hotel, aber ich habe bald eine Wohnung. Sie ist sehr klein, aber das reicht.

Liebe Grüße

Martin

9 Ralfs Mutter, Maxis Eltern, Maries Bruder, Frau Lehmanns Tochter, Herrn Müllers Sohn, Birgits Auto

10 c, d, e, a, b, g, f

11 Regisseur – Regisseurin, Maler – Malerin, Studentin – Studentin, Übersetzerin – Übersetzerin, Ingenieur – Ingenieurin, Frisör – Frisörin, Medien-Designer – Medien-Designerin, Schornsteinfeger – Schornsteinfegerin, Hausmann – Hausfrau, Handwerker – Handwerkerin, Kellner – Kellnerin, Notarzt – Notärztin, Informatiker – Informatikerin, Techniker – Technikerin, Lehrer – Lehrerin, Schüler – Schülerin, Arzt – Ärztin, Taxifahrer – Taxifahrerin, Verkäufer – Verkäuferin, Koch – Köchin, Rechtsanwalt – Rechtsanwältin, Kfz-Mechaniker – Kfz-Mechanikerin, Redakteur – Redakteurin, Busfahrer – Busfahrerin

Workbook page 93 / Textbook page 64:
Berufe

Taxifahrer – Taxifahrerin, Lehrer – Lehrerin, Frisör – Frisörin, Verkäufer – Verkäuferin, Student – Studentin, Politiker – Politikerin, Maurer – ./., Schornsteinfeger – Schornsteinfegerin, Arzt – Ärztin, Hausfrau – Hausmann, Geschäftsmann – Geschäftsfrau

Test

1. 1. Franz ist Übersetzer. 2. Ulrike ist Ärztin. 3. Tommy ist Taxifahrer. 4. Steffi ist Schülerin. 5. Frau Sommer ist Malerin. 6. Herr Gruber ist Verkäufer.

2. 1. die Politikerin, 2. der Geschäftsmann, 3. die Ärztin, 4. der Verkäufer, 5. die Studentin, 6. die Ingenieurin

3. 1. Stefans Vater, 2. Filips Schwester, 3. Frau Meiers Tochter, 4. Annas Tante, 5. Ulrikes Freundin, 6. Katharinas Familie

4. 1. die Studentinnen, 2. die Ärztinnen, 3. die Freundinnen, 4. die Pilotinnen, 5. die Übersetzerinnen, 6. die Politikerinnen

5. 1. sind im Hotel, 2. Abend, 3. um halb acht, 4. eine halbe Stunde, 5. um neun Uhr

Lesson 16

1 1. kein, 2. kein, 3. ein, 4. ein, 5. kein, 6. ein
3 1. im Gäste-Casino, 2. mag gern Fisch, 3. hat 55 Mitarbeiter, 4. einen Service-Techniker, 5. neu, informativ, aktuell
4 Bruckner: d, e, f, j, l; Kühne: b, c, g, h, i, k; Heinrich: a
5 Mitarbeiter, Firma, Leute, Internet-Abteilung, Service-Techniker
7 Mittag, Gespräche, 55 Mitarbeiter, Leute, Abteilung, Techniker
8 unser Computer, unser Auto, unsere Küche, unsere Wohnung, unser Erfolg, unser Handy
9 kein Haus, kein Handy, keine Uhr, kein Auto, keinen Beruf, kein Geld
10 **Wie viel:** Platz, Zeit, Käse, Arbeit, Obst
  Wie viele: Leute, Tische, Mitarbeiter, Monate, Gemüseteller, Techniker, Firmen, Häuser, Lager, Teller, Gäste, Fragen
11 weiß, weißt, weiß
14 das heißt, ich weiß, nach außen, gleich, Automat, Australien, Aufzug, Deutschland, Eier, ein, Häuser, glauben, Haus(frau), Kleinstadt, meinen, Pause, Reise, Raum, Schornsteinfeger, Stau, weit, zu Hause

Workbook page 99 / Textbook page 68:
Würste

a3, b4, c1, d2; Frankfurt, Thüringen, Bayern, Bremen

Test

1. 1. employee, 2. people, 3. You know ..., 4. Have a seat, please. 5. I like that.
  6. since February
2. 1. unsere, 2. unsere, 3. unser, 4. meinen, 5. unsere, 6. Ihren
3. 1. weißt, 2. Kennst, 3. Wissen, 4. kenne, 5. Weißt, 6. weiß
4. 1. Wie viele, 2. Wie viele, 3. Wie viel, 4. Wie viele, 5. Wie viel, 6. Wie viele

Lesson 17

1 3, 4, 2, 5, 7, 1, 6
3 10 Brötchen, 3 Kilo Kartoffeln, 100 Gramm Käse, 200 Gramm Wurst, 1 Flasche Wein, 1 Pfund Weintrauben, 1 Liter Milch, 1 Pfund Kirschen, 2 Flaschen Orangensaft, 3 Salate
4 Trauben, Pfirsiche, Äpfel, Kirschen
5 **Obst:** Äpfel, Kirschen, Pfirsiche, Weintrauben; **Südfrüchte:** Bananen, Ananas, Orangen; **Gemüse:** Tomaten, Kartoffeln, Paprika; **Getränke:** Bier, Milch, Kaffee, Tee, Wein
6 1. Ja, gern. Danke. 2. Ja, Bier trinke ich lieber. 3. Ja, bitte. 4. Was ist das, Apfelschorle?

7   1. Ja, nimm doch den Fisch. 2. Ja, kauf doch 200 Gramm Wurst. 3. Nein, nimm doch lieber Mineralwasser. 4. Nein, kauf lieber Brot und Käse. 5. Kauf doch fünf Stück Kuchen.

8   nimm, kommt, gib, vergesst, sieh, komm, kauft, nehmt

9   Vergiss die Tasche nicht! Vergiss ... das Geld, ... das Mineralwasser, ... die Weintrauben, ... die Tüte, ... die Flaschen, ... den Käse, ... das Handy, ... die Nummer ... nicht!

10 Welchen Wein? Welche Weintrauben? Welchen Käse? Welche Wurst? Welchen Kuchen? Welche Kartoffeln?

Workbook page 105 / Textbook page 72:
Wie finden Sie das?

1c, 2b, 3a, 4f, 5e, 6d

Test

1.   1. What do we need? 2. Stay here. 3. That's enough. 4. What's the matter? 5. Wait here. 6. I've forgotten somerthing.

2.   Singular: 2., 4., 6., 7.
Plural: 1., 3., 8., 10.
Singular + Plural: 5., 9.

3.   1. Vergiss, 2. Komm, 3. Mach, 4. Sieh, 5. Vergessen, 6. Kommen, 7. Nehmen, 8. Sprechen, 9. Hören, 10. Warten

4.   1. Welcher, 2. Welche, 3. Welche, 4. Welches, 5. Welches, 6. Welcher, 7. Welche, 8. Welche

Lesson 18

1   Wein + Mineralwasser, Mineralwasser + Apfelsaft, Orangensaft + Sekt oder Campari, Milch + Bananen, Kaffee + Eis, Bier + Limonade

3   Eis, Kuchen, Euro, Cent, dagegen, zusammen

4   **Dialogue 1**: der junge Mann + die junge Frau
Dialogue 2: das Mädchen + der ältere Mann

5   1. rufe, an, 2. angerufen, 3. rufst, an, 4. angerufen, 5. Rufst du, 6. rufst, an

6   Bitte rufen Sie Frau Schmidt an! Ruf doch Petra an! Ruf doch deine Schwester an! Bitte rufen Sie die Firma Seiblitz an! Ruf bitte zu Hause an! Ruf doch David an!

8   *For example:* Mein Bruder lebt schon 5 Jahre in Griechenland. Er spricht sehr gut Griechisch. Er hat dort ein Haus mit vielen Zimmern und einen Garten mit Blumen. Das Haus liegt direkt am Hafen. Er ist Maler von Beruf.

9   Was trinkst du gern? Möchtest du lieber Bier? Alex trinkt Bier am liebsten / Margit trinkt gern Saft. Magst du Wein lieber als Schorle? – Lieber Schorle. Am liebsten trinke ich Weinschorle / Geht's dir wieder gut? – Ja, besser als gestern. Am besten geht's mir morgens.

10 Das, Die, Das, Das, Der, Die

11 Rufen Sie Frau Fritz zu Hause an? Lädst du auch Familie Wegner ein? Hast du Patrick eingeladen?

12 Morgen rufe ich Karsten an. Heute Abend habe ich Zeit. Jetzt machen wir eine Firmenbesichtigung. Da links ist das Informationszentrum. Dann gehen wir ins Konferenzzimmer. Um zwölf essen wir.

13 Ich bin dagegen. Das ist falsch. Sie haben nicht recht. Das stimmt nicht. Ich gehe nicht nach Hause. Ich rufe Peter nicht an.

15 wissen, weiß, wissen, isst, essen, Essen, Wasser, Großstadt, Großmutter, klasse, Großvater, Spaß, Fuß, Straße, Russland, vergisst, vergessen

16 ist der Preis, Das weiß, wissen nichts, Was ist los?, was vergessen, Saft und Wasser, Wurst und Zwiebeln, Obst und Gemüse

Workbook page 111 / Textbook page 76:
Mögen Sie Obst?

richtig: 1., 3., 4., 6., 7., falsch: 2., 5., 8.

Test

1. 1d, 2h, 3b, 4g, 5a, 6f, 7c, 8i, 9e

2. 1. schlecht, 2. rechts, 3. dagegen, 4. falsch, 5. teuer, 6. groß

3. 1. der – Der, 2. das – Das, 3. der – Den, 4. die – Die, 5. der – Den

4. 1. Martin ruft Alexander an. 2. Petra lädt Familie Müller ein. 3. Herr Wagner fliegt nach Brüssel zurück. 4. Herr Schade ruft die Schule an.

5. Richtig: 2., 3., 5., 6.

Lesson 19

1 a4, b3, c2, d1, e6, f5

3 Nicht richtig: Katrin ist bei Claudia zu Hause. Es ist sehr weit.

4 Bank, Schloss, Kirche, Platz, Schule, Fluss, Post

5 Polizei

8 Niki heißt Bat mit Familiennamen. Er wohnt und arbeitet in Berlin und ist auch hier geboren. Deshalb ist nur der Familienname Chinesisch, nicht der Vorname.
Er spricht auch kein Chinesisch. Aber er möchte die Sprache gern lernen.
Die Eltern sind 1960 nach Deutschland gekommen. Jetzt haben sie ein chinesisches Restaurant. Das ist das Restaurant in der Hafenstraße. Das Essen dort ist sehr gut, sagt man.

9 habe ... angerufen, habe ... erklärt

10 dir den Weg, Ihnen der Kuchen, mir bitte, uns nichts, ihr, Ihnen gefällt

11 An der Post. In der Bank. Am Hotel. Im Restaurant. In der Schule. Am Bahnhof.

12 Zum Bahnhof. Zur Bank. Zum Supermarkt. Zur Schule. Zum Museum. Zur Post.

Workbook page 117 / Textbook page 80:
Mit dem Taxi zur Firma Holz

Den Weg finden Sie bestimmt allein.

Test

1. 1. quite easy, 2. round the square, 3. the third street on the right, 4. past the hotel, 5. as far as the church, 6. straight on to the supermarket
2. 1d, 2b, 3f, 4a, 5e, 6c
3. 1. nach, 2. zum, 3. zum, 4. an, 5. zum, 6. nach, am
4. 1. dritte, 2. zehnte, 3. fünfzehnte, 4. achten, 5. neunte, 6. erste

Lesson 20

1 1 das Kaufhaus, die Kaufhäuser, 2 der Stadtplan, die Stadtpläne, 3 der Pullover, die Pullover, 4 die Tasche, die Taschen, 5 der Schirm, die Schirme, 6 die Postkarte, die Postkarten, 7 das Sandwich, die Sandwich(e)s

3 Karte, Bier, Salat, Gemüsepfanne, Zander, Tomatensuppe, Rindsroulade, Glas Wein, Biergarten

4 die Speisekarte – die Speisekarten, das Brot – die Brote, die Suppe – die Suppen, der Saft – die Säfte, die Kartoffel – die Kartoffeln, der Biergarten – die Biergärten

5 4. Stock: Stadtführer, 3. Stock: Taschen, 2. Stock: Schirme, 1. Stock: Pullover, Erdgeschoss: Postkarten, Untergeschoss: Sandwiches

7 Doch, ich esse gerne Fisch. Doch, ich habe viel Zeit. Doch, ich gehe sofort nach Hause. Doch, ich habe viel Arbeit. Doch, das Essen schmeckt mir gut. Doch, ich habe viele Hobbys.

8 Doch, ich komme mit. Nein, ich habe kein Auto. Doch, ich esse Fleisch. Nein, ich mag keinen Fisch. Doch, ich habe eine Kamera. Doch, wir machen einen Ausflug.

9 1. Übermorgen, 2. am, 3. mit, 4. am, 5. Um, 6. um, 7. im

10 Wir möchten um 12 essen. Ich möchte eine Pause machen. Wir möchten einen Tisch bestellen. Wir möchten die Stadt besichtigen. Ich möchte das Museum sehen. Ich möchte um sechs nach Hause fahren.

12 ↑: Und Ihnen? Wie bitte? Kommen Sie mit?
↓: Wie geht es Ihnen? Es geht. Das Wetter ist so schlecht. Es regnet seit zwei Tagen. Wir möchten die Stadt besichtigen. Gehen Sie doch ins Museum! Warum nicht?

13 ↑: Kommen Sie mit? Erklären Sie mir den Weg? Fahren Sie zum Bahnhof? Fahren Sie geradeaus? Fahren Sie sofort los?
↓: Kommen Sie doch mit! Erklären Sie mir bitte den Weg! Fahren Sie bitte zum Bahnhof! Fahren Sie bitte geradeaus! Fahren Sie sofort los!

Workbook page 123 / Textbook page 84:
Wo isst man das?

Scholle – in Norddeutschland, Schweinebraten – in Süddeutschland, Marillenknödel – in Österreich, Zürcher Geschnetzeltes – in der Schweiz

Test

1. 1. Koffer, 2. Schirme, 3. Stadtpläne, 4. Bonbons, 5. Kuchen, 6. Tische, 7. CDs
2. 1e, 2c, 3a, 4f, 5b, 6d
3. 1. Ja, 2. Nein, 3. Doch, 4. Doch, 5. Nein, 6. Nein
4. 1. am, 2. um, 3. im, 4. im, 5. am, 6. im

Lesson 21

1 a5, b2, c4, d6, e3, f1

3 Blumenkohlsuppe : 3,50 €, Kartoffelsuppeneintopf: 7,50 €, Blattsalate: 8,60 €, Gemischter Salat: 6,90 €, Räucherlachs: 7,60 €, Gebackene Kartoffel: 5,00 €, Penne: 7,60 €, Asiatische Reispfanne: 8,60 €

4 den Salat, das Frühstück (*partly warm*), die Brotzeit, den Kuchen, das Schweinefleisch (*warm and cold*)

6 Rindsroulade mit Kartoffelklößen, Kuchen mit Sahne, Salat mit Thunfisch, Brötchen mit Butter und Marmelade, Tomatensuppe mit Brötchen, Kaffee mit Milch

8 Tomatensuppe, Reispfanne, Blattsalate, Schweinefleisch, Thunfisch, Hühnchenbrust

9 das Telefon + die Nummer, die Kantine + das Essen, die Konferenz + der Raum, das Taxi + der Fahrer, das Gemüse + der Teller, der Garten + das Restaurant

10 mitkommen – er / sie kommt mit, zurückfahren – er / sie fährt zurück, losfahren – er / sie fährt los, einladen – er / sie lädt ein

11 ... Schweinefleisch? – Im Kühlschrank in der Mitte rechts. / ... Wurst? – Unten in der Mitte. / ... Tomaten? – Unten. / ... Salami? – In der Mitte links. / ... Fisch? – Oben rechts. / ... Jogurt? – In der Tür oben. / ... Butter? – Hinten links. / ... Milch? – Unten in der Tür. / ... Käse? – In der Mitte.

12 Weißt du, wo die Wurst ist? ..., wann Christian kommt? ..., wie das Restaurant heißt? ..., was es heute gibt? ..., was Zander ist?

13 1. Tankstelle, 2. Ampel, 3. Hotel, 4. Bank, 5. Schule, 6. Bahnhof

Workbook page 129 / Textbook page 88:
Im Kaufhaus

Kunde / Kundin: 1., 2., 4., 5., 7., 8., 9.; Verkäufer / Verkäuferin: 3., 6., 10.
Lampen im vierten Stock, Schirme im Erdgeschoss, Kaffee im Untergeschoss, Restaurant im Untergeschoss, Kugelschreiber im Erdgeschoss, Videokassetten im dritten Stock

Test

1. 1. Enjoy your meal. 2. What is Rösti?

2. 1. Brot oder Brötchen, 2. Rührei, 3. Sahne, 4. Rösti, 5. Thunfisch, 6. Kartoffeln

3. 1. fahren, 2. losfahren, 3. zurückfahren, 4. einladen, 5. mitkommen

4. 1. ..., wo das Restaurant ist? 2. ..., wann der Zug fährt? 3. ..., wie ich zum Bahnhof komme? 4. ..., wie der Platz hier heißt? 5. ..., wie weit es zum Schloss ist? 6. ..., wo ich Reiseführer finde?

5. 1. einen Schirm, einen Pullover und eine Tasche. 2. einen Reiseführer. 3. im Bahnhof.

Lesson 22

1 Das Brandenburger Tor, Im Bundeskanzleramt, Im Schloss Bellevue, Der Potsdamer Platz

3 gemacht, angerufen, gefahren, geparkt, gelaufen, gefallen, gesehen, ausgesehen, gestanden

4 Wie kommen ...? / Wohin fahren ...? / ... und parken dort. Dann machen ... / ... zu Fuß gehen? / Wir laufen ... / Mittags machen ... / Am Nachmittag gehen ... / Ich möchte ... / Sie stehen ... / Um 8 Uhr sind ...

5 Examples: **rot:** Ärger, Feuer, Wein; **blau:** Himmel, Augen; **grün:** Baum, Wald; **gelb:** Zitrone; **rosa:** Baby; **schwarz:** Gewitter, Angst; **weiß:** Schnee, Papier, Wein, Milch; **braun:** Schokolade, Kaffee

6 Deutschland: Schwarz, Rot und Gold (Schwarz, Rot, Gold); Österreich: Rot und Weiß (Rot, Weiß, Rot)

7 Rot gefällt mir besser als Grün. Am Besten gefällt mir Blau. Alfons trinkt gern Schokolade. Am liebsten trinken alle Cola. Die Wohnung ist schön, aber die Dachwohnung ist noch schöner. Am schönsten ist natürlich ein Haus.

8 Wir sind in die Firma gefahren. Wir haben bis 12 gearbeitet. Dann sind wir in die Kantine gegangen. Wir haben Fisch gegessen. Ich habe die Firma besichtigt. Ich habe viele Abteilungen gesehen.

9 schlafen, machen, fahren, parken, sehen, besichtigen, nehmen, finden, anrufen, zurückfahren

10 *For example:* Letzte Woche haben wir einen Ausflug nach Oberdorf gemacht. Wir haben auf dem Parkplatz geparkt und sind über die große Brücke ins Zentrum gelaufen. Dort sind wir einkaufen gegangen. Zuerst waren wir zwei Stunden im Kaufhaus. Dann haben wir Würstchen mit Kartoffelsalat gegessen. Zuletzt haben wir noch einen Kaffee getrunken. Am Schluss haben wir Markus getroffen und sind nach Hause gefahren.

Workbook page 135 / Textbook page 92:
Rund ums Auto

der Scheinwerfer - die Scheinwerfer, das Rad - die Räder, der Sitz - die Sitze, die Tür - die Türen

Test

1. 1. kommt, 2. parkt, 3. sieht ... aus?, 4. steht, 5. Gefällt 6. fährt, 7. läuft, 8. geht
2. 1. rot, 2. blau/braun, 3. grün/gelb, 4. schwarz, 5. weiß, 6. bunt
3. 1. wohnen, 2. finden, 3. arbeiten, 4. gehen, 5. fliegen, 6. lernen, 7. sehen, 8. anrufen
4. 1. Wir haben im Zentrum geparkt. 2. Wir haben Madeleine und Thomas getroffen. 3. Dann sind wir einkaufen gegangen. 4. Thomas hat ein Eis gekauft. 5. Das hat prima geschmeckt. 6. Madeleine hat lieber Kuchen gegessen.

Lesson 23

3 E, C, D, A, B
4 1. fahren, 2. steigen, 3. schwimmen / fahren (Boot), 4. lesen, 5. spielen, 6. gehen
7 Hallo, Markus,

kommst du mit nach Arraba? Wir fahren am Wochenende nach Südtirol. Zwei Zimmer sind noch frei. Bitte antworte ganz schnell.

Der Schnee ist noch sehr gut. Ich habe mit dem Hotel telefoniert. Dann reserviere ich die Zimmer von Freitag Abend bis Sonntag.

Wir machen am Freitag früher Schluss und fahren schon so um zwei. Geht das bei dir auch?

Wir sind heute zu Hause.

Herzliche Grüße

Arne

8 in den Süden, in die Schweiz, ans Schwarze Meer, an den Rhein, in die Türkei, an den Atlantik, an den Bodensee, ans Mittelmeer
9 1. der, 2. ein, 3. das, 4. ein, 5. eine, 6. das
10 Fahrräder, Hotels, Inseln, Kleinstädte, Gäste, Mitarbeiter
12 **Dialogue B**

Interviewer: Entschuldigung, ich komme von der Zeitschrift *Eltern heute*. Ich möchte Sie etwas fragen.

Armin H.:   Ja, bitte? Ich habe aber nicht viel Zeit.

Interviewer: Nein, nein, es dauert nicht lange. Wir möchten Sie fragen: Bleiben Sie in den Ferien zu Hause oder fahren Sie weg?

Armin H.:   Wir haben im September Urlaub. Wir fahren weg.

Interviewer: Wie lange machen Sie dann Urlaub?

Armin H.:   Im September immer drei Wochen. Wir haben keine Kinder.

Interviewer: Bleiben Sie in Deutschland oder in Europa oder fahren Sie weiter weg?

Armin H.:   Wir möchten nach Spanien.

Interviewer: Fliegen Sie oder fahren Sie mit dem Auto?

Armin H.:   Spanien ist sehr weit. Wir fliegen.

Interviewer.   Haben Sie schon ein Hotel?

Armin H.:   Ja, natürlich.

Interviewer.   Danke schön. Das reicht. Vielen Dank auch.

Workbook page 141 / Textbook page 96:
Welchen Sport betreiben Ihre Freunde?

1e, 2a, 3f, 4c, 5b, 6d

Test

1. 1. go on holiday, 2. stay at home, 3. for example, 4. do sport, 5. go far away, 6. go for a walk, 7. I prefer that. 8. What do you like best?, 9. The bill, please.
2. 1. an, 2. in, 3. auf, 4. auf, 5. in, 6. nach
3. 1. mich, 2. sie, 3. sie, 4. uns, 5. Herrn Mai, 6. ihn
4. 1. ihn, 2. sie, 3. es, 4. sie, 5. es, 6. sie, 7. sie, 8. sie

Lesson 24

3   die Urlaubspläne, der Reiseprospekt, die Rundreise, der Reisetermin, der Wanderweg, das Doppelzimmer
  Answer: die Reise

4   Bergmann 5, Urban 1, Hürlimann 0, Meinert 2, Kunze 3, Weber 4, Erler 6, Bernd 7

5   1 der Herbst, 2 der Winter, 3 der Frühling, 4 der Sommer

6   a1, b3, c4, d5, e6, f2

7   Januar, Februar, März, April, Mai, Juni, Juli, August, September, Oktober, November, Dezember

8   1. Terminkalender, 2. Reiseprospekt, 3. Sportplatz, 4. Doppelzimmer, 5. Abendessen, 6. Autonummer, 7. Rundreise, 8. Flughafen

9   **Nur Singular:** Mai, Wasser, Frühstück, Urlaub, Osten, Glück, Hunger, Sport
  Singular und Plural: Wurst – Würste, Zug – Züge, Wolke – Wolken, Jahr - Jahre

10   1. Pläne, 2. Kartoffeln, 3. Getränke, 4. Kirschen, 5. Kilometer, 6. Weintrauben

11   1. die Auskunft, 2. der Besuch, 3. die Marmelade, 4. die Miete, 5. der Saft, 6. der Mittag

12   1. fahren, 2. treiben, 3. spielen, 4. fahren, 5. fahren, 6. gehen

13   Languages have the ending *-isch.* The male inhabitants of countries have the ending *-e* or *-er.* The female form ends in the singular in *-in* and in the plural in *-innen.*

16   **2 Silben:** Be-ruf; **3 Silben:** Ge-burts-ort, na-tür-lich, be-su-chen, stu-die-ren;
  4 Silben: Wo-chen-en-de, be-sich-ti-gen, ge-gen-ü-ber, ge-ra-de-aus, Au-to-num-mer

Workbook page 147 / Textbook page 100:
Ratespiel: Haben Sie das gewusst?

A 1. Bodensee, 2. Universitätsstadt, 3. Dachwohnung, 4. Urlaubsländer, 5. Urlaubsreise, 6. Großmutter; **B** 1. der See, 2. die Stadt, 3. die Wohnung, 4. das Land, 5. die Reise, 6. die Mutter; **C** *Answer:* So ein Mist!

Test

1. 1. Dänen, 2. Holländer, 3. Japaner, 4. Engländer, 5. Koreaner, 6. Italiener, 7. Franzosen, 8. Griechen, 9. Australier, 10. Chinesen

2. Only singular: 1., 5., 7.

3. 1. die Pläne, 2. die Würste, 3. die Getränke, 4. die Kilometer, 5. die Jahre

4. Frau Ulrich: 3., 6.; Frau Mandl: 8., 9., 14.

Lesson 25

3 Computer, PC-Fortbildung, erklären, Kurs, lernen, müde, Postfach, E-Mail, Freundin, Stipendium

4 ich hoffe, es geht euch gut. Ich bin ..., Ich habe ..., Seid ihr zu Hause? Bitte antwortet mir schnell. ... eure Laura

5 **formell-geschäftlich:** Sie, Ihnen; Sehr geehrter Herr Meyer, Sehr geehrte Frau Schuh, Sehr geehrte Damen und Herren, Mit besten Grüßen Christine Mann, Mit freundlichen Grüßen Regine Merz

persönlich: du, ihr, dich, dir, euch, Liebe Familie Kraus, Liebe Marion, Hallo, Lieber Helmut, Herzliche Grüße eure Rosa, Herzliche Grüße euer Franz, Liebe Grüße Laura, Ciao Fritz

7 kann, kann, können

8 Kannst du, Kann Daniela, Kann Ulrike, Können Sie, Musst du, Patrick muss, Er darf

9 1. Ich muss ein Fortbildung machen. 2. Ich kann dir helfen. 3. Er kann gut erklären. 4. Ich will systematisch lernen. 5. Ich muss nach Hause fahren.

11 1. Bitte, können Sie mir helfen? 2. Bitte, wo ist die Auskunft? 3. Bitte, wo ist der Flughafen-Bus? 4. Bitte, wie komme ich in die Stadt? 5. Bitte, können Sie das wiederholen? 6. Ich verstehe Sie nicht. Bitte sprechen Sie nicht so schnell.
7. Ich habe das Wort nicht verstanden. Bitte wiederholen Sie es. 8. Bitte, buchstabieren Sie Ihren Namen.

Workbook page 153 / Textbook page 104:
Raten Sie

a1, b4, c2, d3

Test

1. 1. Can you help me? 2. You must do a course. 3. He can't explain. 4. I can learn that on my own. 5. Please reply quickly. 6. Dear Sirs 7. Yours sincerely 8. Very best wishes

2. 1. kann, 2. Möchtest, 3. muss, 4. dürft, 5. kann

3. 1. müssen, 2. darf, 3. kann, 4. Können, 5. möchte, 6. muss

Lesson 26

1 1 die Mail, die Mails, 2 die Briefmarke, die Briefmarken, 3 das SMS / die SMS(-Nachricht), die SMS, 4 die Postkarte, die Postkarten, 5 der Brief, die Briefe

3 **Richtig:** 1., 2., 4., 5., 6., 7., 8., 10.

4 4., 5., 6., 2., 3., 1.

7 neu – alt, spannend – langweilig, warm – kalt, schwarz – weiß, groß – klein, zusammen – getrennt, links – rechts, morgens – abends, Wohin? – Woher?, ja – nein, schrecklich – schön, gut – schlecht

8 Liebe Eltern,
herzliche Grüße aus Italien. Mir geht es sehr gut. Das Wetter ist prima. Wir sind hier direkt am Meer. Conny ist schon ganz braun.
Bis bald
euer Timo

9 1. Am, 2. Im, 3. Am, 4. Auf dem, 5. In der, 6. An der, 7. Im, 8. In der, 9. Im 10. In den, 11. In, 12. Auf der

10 mit dem Bus, zum Bahnhof, bei uns, zu den Eltern, von meinem Onkel, zu seinem Freund

11 Freust du dich? Warum freut er sich nicht? Hat sich Tommy gefreut? ... Ich freue mich. ... Er freut sich sehr. ... Wir freuen uns schon.

Workbook page 159 / Textbook page 108:
Herzlichen Glückwunsch

Geburtstag 2, Hochzeit 4, Prüfung 3, Geburt 1
Karte: 2, 4, 1, 3

Test

1. 1. das, 2. die, 3. der, 4. die, 5. die, 6. das/die

2. 1. die PCs, 2. die Mails, 3. die Briefe, 4. die Postkarten, 5. die Notizen, 6. die Grüße

3. 1. bei, 2. zu, 3. mit, 4. mit, 5. von, 6. zum

4. 1. aus dem, 2. im, auf der, 3. auf der, 4. am, 5. in den, 6. an der, 7. an der

Lesson 27

1 1 vor zwei Jahren – 2 letzten Monat – 3 letzte Woche – 4 vorgestern – 5 gestern – 6 heute – 7 morgen – 8 übermorgen – 9 nächste Woche – 10 nächsten Monat – 11 in zwei Jahren

3 **Claudia**: a., b., e., f., h.; **Robert**: c., d., g.

4 1. Eine Argentinierin. Eine Freundin von Claudia. Eine Studentin. 2. Laura soll schnell antworten. Claudia möchte gern planen. 3. Claudia möchte mal nach Argentinien fahren.

5 Schreib, Antworte, Bleib, Gib, Lerne, Mach

6 der Argentinier – die Argentinierin, der Italiener – die Italienerin, der Spanier – die Spanierin, der Chilene – die Chilenin, der Berliner – die Berlinerin, der Hamburger – die Hamburgerin, der Finne – die Finnin, der Österreicher – die Österreicherin, der Franzose – die Französin, der Nürnberger – die Nürnbergerin, der Schweizer – die Schweizerin, der Holländer – die Holländerin

9 ..., ich habe dich ja schon lange nicht mehr gesehen. Was machst du denn so? Ruf doch mal an! Du bist ja ein Musik-Fan. ... Komm doch zu uns! ...

10 1. Meiner Freundin. 2. Meinem Freund. 3. Der Oma. 4. Unserem Vater. 5. Unserer Mutter. 6. Dem Opa.

11 1. euch, 2. Ihnen, 3. dir, 4. deinem Bruder, 5. deiner Schwester, 6. deinen Eltern

12 Schreib doch mal! Hilf uns doch! Bleib doch ruhig! Fahr doch hin! Hör doch auf! Antworte doch mal!

15 1. wächst, 2. Geburtsort, 3. herzliche, 4. warst, 5. gemacht, 6. liebsten, 7. buchstabiere, 8. sprichst, 9. schnell, 10. Tankstelle, 11. fünfte, 12. erste

Workbook page 165 / Textbook Seite 112:
Haben Sie es gewusst?

Berg mit Z: die Zugspitze – Alpen
Stadt mit K: Köln
See mit B: Bodensee – in der Schweiz
Stadt mit W: Wien – Österreich
Schloss mit Neu-: Neuschwanstein – Bayern;
Schweiz: ... und Italienisch
Deutschland: ... ca. 5 Millionen Ausländer. Sie sprechen Türkisch, Italienisch, Serbisch, Griechisch, Polnisch, Kroatisch, Russisch ...
Deutschland: ... Studenten aus: China, Frankreich, Spanien, Polen, Italien, Bulgarien, Ungarn, Russland, England usw.
Österrreich: Österreichisch
EU: europäische Union

Test

1. 1. in ten years, 2. fifty years ago, 3. last year, 4. next week, 5. the day before yesterday, 6. the day after tomorrow

2. 1. mir, 2. uns, 3. mir, 4. deinem Bruder, 5. ihr, 6. deinen Geschwistern

3. 1. a, b; 2. a, c; 3. a, c, d; 4. ./.; 5. a; 6. a, c

Lesson 28

1 *Example*: Ich finde den Jungen oben links unsympathisch. Die Frau in der Mitte sieht nett aus. Das Mädchen oben rechts finde ich sympathisch. Der Junge unten links sieht lustig aus. Das Kind in der Mitte finde ich hübsch. Der Mann unten rechts sieht freundlich aus.

3 **Richtig:** 1., 2., 4., 6., 7., 8., 10.

4 klein, sehr gut, pünktlich, zuverlässig, fast perfekt, absolut perfekt, sehr kompetent, angenehm, sympathisch, zu teuer

5 a4, b1, c3, d2, e5

6 Konkurrenz muss ..., Kontakte müssen ..., Software muss ..., Mitarbeiter müssen ...

7 ... soll sehr kompetent ..., Die Firma soll ..., Die Qualität soll ..., Die Mitarbeiter sollen ..., Sie sollen ...

9 1. mag, 2. kann, 3. darf, 4. soll, 5. weiß, 6. muss

10 4 Verben: die Modalverben und das Verb *wissen*

11 1. Wen? 2. Mit wem? 3. Wen? 4. Wem? 5. Wer? 6. Was?

12 1. Die Firma ist klein, aber die Mitarbeiter sind zuverlässig. 2. Die Software ist ohne Fehler und die Qualität stimmt. 3. Herr Lüders ist sehr kompetent, aber er hat keinen Humor. 4. Die Konkurrenz ist nicht schlecht, aber (sie ist) zu teuer. 5. Wir haben einen guten Eindruck und wir möchten Sie gerne einladen. 6. Die Entfernungen sind groß und persönliche Kontakte müssen sein.

14 **1. Wort:** <u>sehr</u> sympathisch, <u>kei</u>ne Software ohne Fehler; **2. Wort:** <u>Fir</u>ma, <u>wis</u>sen, <u>Zu</u>sammenarbeit, zu <u>teu</u>er, fast per<u>fekt</u>; **3. Wort:** mit der Konkur<u>renz</u>

15 **2. Wort:** Guten <u>Tag</u>, Vielen <u>Dank</u> ...; **3. Wort:** <u>mei</u>ne Firma, <u>ar</u>beitet gut, per<u>fekt</u>, stimmt, <u>sehr</u> kompetent; **4. Wort:** ist <u>klein</u>, nächste <u>Woche</u>, organi<u>sie</u>ren

Workbook page 171 / Textbook page 116:
Ein Spiel

Stimmt das oder stimmt das nicht? – Kaffee, Tee und Wasser sind Getränke – Der Plural von Firma ist Firmen. – Wie viele Tage hat das Jahr? – Können Sie mir helfen? – Herzlichen Glückwunsch zur Hochzeit! – Das Jahr hat zwölf Monate. – In Österreich. – Er hat viel Humor. – Bitte, ruf doch mal an. – Spannend. – Nein, danke. – Berlin ist die Hauptstadt von Deutschland. – Das Gegenteil von „jemand" ist „niemand". – Ich habe es eilig, ich rufe ein Taxi. – Mögen Sie Spaghetti? – Ja, natürlich. – *For example*: Ingenieur, Lehrerin, Maurer, Arzt, Taxifahrer – *For example*: Mineralwasser, Sekt, Bier – Fisch oder Fleisch? – Deutsch, Französisch, Italienisch – Wen möchten Sie sprechen? – Sind Sie verheiratet oder ledig? – Das war kein Taxifahrer, das war eine Taxifahrerin. – Die Wohnung hat 90 Quadratmeter. – Ein Sprichwort sagt: Lieber spät als nie. – das Wetter und der Bericht – falsch – 1 Euro hat 100 Cent. – Doch, das stimmt. – Wir essen mit Messer und Gabel. – Ich habe schon gegessen. – das Wort, die Pause, das Ziel – Norden, Süden, Osten und Westen.

Test

1. 1. Eindruck, 2. Qualität, 3. wissen, Fehler, 4. finde, 5. teuer, 6. Außerdem
2. 1. ... zu weit. 2. sehr gut. 3. ... besonders schnell.
3. 1. wem, 2. Wer, 3. Wen, 4. Was, 5. Was, 6. Wem
4. 1. Er soll Geld haben. 2. Er kann Urlaub machen. 3. Er möchte nach Italien fahren. 4. Er mag nicht fliegen. 5. Er muss mit dem Zug fahren. 6. Er muss in vierzehn Tagen zurück sein.
5. 1. Sie schreibt eine Mail oder ein(e) SMS. 2. Die Qualität stimmt und die Software ist perfekt. 3. Herr Schröder arbeitet zuverlässig, aber er ist nicht besonders schnell.

Lesson 29

1 Die Humboldt-Universität, 34.000 Studenten, Sybille ist Studentin, das Fach Medienkunde, schon drei Semester, studierst, Semesterferien
3 Ja, was ist? / Das ist ganz einfach. Ich bleibe in Berlin. / Nächstes Semester studiere ich hier. Was sagst du dazu? / Genau. Die ist sehr gut in meinem Fach. Nächste Woche fahre ich nach Hause und komme dann in drei Wochen wieder. Zu Semesterbeginn. / Au ja, prima. Ich muss mir bald ein Zimmer oder eine Wohnung suchen. / Und was sagt Niki dazu?
4 Räumen Sie oft um?, ...zuletzt umgeräumt?, ... möchte gern umräumen., ... Er räumt nicht gern um. dann räumen Carolin und Alfons um. Umräumen macht Spaß!
5 5 der Tisch, 9 das Bett, 2 der Sessel, 1 die Blumen, 3 der Schreibtisch, 6 der Stuhl, 7 die Couch, 4 der Schrank, 8 der Vorhang, 10 die Lampe
6

	Couch	Schrank
	Liege	
Tische		
+ Stühle		Bett
	Tür	

8 (an den) – am / in die – (in der) / (an die) – an der / an den – (am) / (auf den) – auf dem / ins – (im)
9 auf den Tisch, auf dem Tisch, in den Flur, In der Küche., ins Wohnzimmer, In den Keller.
10 ... will ich ... . / Ich werde ... / Ich werde ... / Das wird ...

Workbook page 177 / Textbook page 129:
Mein Zimmer

1. Couch, Computertisch, Schrank, Schreibtisch, Tisch, Stühle, Bücherregal, Sessel, Bett
2. *For example*: Mein Zimmer ist groß, aber ich habe nicht viele Möbel. Das Zimmer hat 32 Quadratmeter. Ich habe also viel Platz. In der Mitte stehen Tisch und Stühle. Mein Schreibtisch steht am Fenster. In der Ecke rechts stehen die Couch, zwei Sessel und der Fernseher und das Bücherregal. Links steht der Computertisch mit Computer und Drucker. Mehr brauche ich nicht.

252

Test

1. 1. das Wochenende, 2. der Bahnhof, 3. das Flugzeug, 4. die Studenten, 5. der See, 6. der Schirm, 7. der Einkaufszettel
2. 1. das Semester, 2. die Prüfung, 3. das Fach, 4. der Semesterbeginn, 5. studieren – er/sie studiert, hat studiert, 6. das Studium, 7. der Student, 8. die Studentin, 9. die Semesterferien, 10. die Universität
3. 1. ins, 2. an, 3. nach / in den, 4. auf, 5. zum, 6. nach
4. 1. auf, 2. an, 3. an / in, 4. auf, 5. im, 6. auf

Lesson 30

1 Zusammenarbeit
3 Noch einmal vielen Dank für alles. Wir freuen uns auf die Zusammenarbeit. Und danke für die Einladung gestern. Auf Wiedersehen, ... Und bis bald. Wir wünschen eine gute Reise.
4 **privat:** Tschüs. Mach's gut. Bis bald. Auf Wiedersehen. Gute Besserung. Es war sehr schön bei euch. Danke für die Einladung. Mach(t)'s gut. Gute Reise. Viel Spaß! Ciao.
im Beruf: Besuchen Sie uns bald wieder. Wir freuen uns.
privat und im Beruf: Bis bald. Auf Wiedersehen. Bis zum nächsten Mal. Danke für die Einladung. Gute Reise.
5 meinen Schal, meine Schuhe, meinen Anzug, meine Bluse, meine Brille, mein Portemonnaie, meine Hemden, meine Hosen, meine Jacke, mein Kleid, meinen Pullover, meinen Rock, meinen Schlüssel, meinen Schirm, meine Tasche, mein Ticket, meinen Pass
Männer tragen Anzüge und Hemden, **Frauen** tragen Blusen, Kleider und Röcke.
7 gekommen, Es gibt, werde, werden, dürfen, schläft, haben, müssen, wissen
8 1. nächstes Jahr, 2. nächsten Monat, 3. nächste Woche, 4. nächsten Dienstag, 5. nächstes Wochenende, 6, nächstes Semester
9 dich verletzt, dich noch, mich schon, dich doch, dich beschweren, dich doch, mich schon

Workbook page Seite 183 / Textbook page 124:
Reiseziele

a2, b8, c9, d5, e6, f7, g1, h4, i3

Test

1. 1. in three hours, 2. in a week at the latest, 3. really very nice, 4. send, 5. What are you planning? 6. We'll be glad to come. 7. You know ... 8. The food is not bad either.
2. 1. nächstes Jahr, 2. nächsten Monat, 3. nächste Woche, 4. in einer Woche, 5. in einem Jahr, 6. nächsten Freitag
3. 1. uns, 2. dich, 3. sich, 4. dich, 5. dich, 6. uns
4. am Bahnhof

Quellenverzeichnis

Seite 37:   MHV-Archiv (Heribert Mühldorfer)

Seite 75:   links außen: © PhotoDisc; Mitte links und rechts außen: MHV-Archiv
              (Dieter Reichler); Mitte rechts: MHV-Archiv (Gerd Pfeiffer)

Seite 129:   Renate Luscher, München

Seite 184:   © DB AG / Klee

**Übungsgrammatik
für die Grundstufe
Deutsch als Fremdsprache**
240 Seiten
ISBN 978–3–19–107448–7

Übung macht den Meister!

Die moderne, lehrwerksunabhängige *Übungsgrammatik für die Grundstufe –
Deutsch als Fremdsprache* vermittelt kleinschrittig und klar strukturiert die zentralen
Grammatikthemen der Grundstufe. Abwechslungsreiche Übungen führen Sie zu
soliden Grammatikkenntnissen auf dem Niveau B1.

▶ Abwechslungsreiche Übungen wie Lückentexte, Zuordnungs-,
  Umformungs- und Satzbildungsübungen
▶ Lösungsschlüssel zu den Übungen und eine Liste unregelmäßiger
  Verben im Anhang
▶ Übersichtliches, lernerfreundliches Layout für den schnellen Überblick
▶ Zahlreiche vierfarbige Illustrationen für mehr Spaß am Lernen
▶ Geeignet für den Einsatz im Unterricht und das Selbststudium zu Hause

Auch erhältlich: *Übungsgrammatik für die Mittelstufe – Deutsch als Fremdsprache.*

 **Freude an Sprachen**

Renate Luscher

deutsch kompakt neu

Selbstlernkurs Deutsch für Anfänger

Textbuch

Hueber Verlag

5. 4. 3.   Die letzten Ziffern
2018 17 16 15 14   bezeichnen Zahl und Jahr des Druckes.
Alle Drucke dieser Auflage können, da unverändert,
nebeneinander benutzt werden.
1. Auflage
© 2013 Hueber Verlag GmbH & Co. KG, 85737 Ismaning, Deutschland
Redaktion: Hans Hillreiner, Hueber Verlag, Ismaning
Umschlaggestaltung: creative partners gmbh, München
Coverfotos von links: © Getty Images/Westend61; © Thinkstock/iStockphoto
Satz, Layout und Grafik: Martin Lange, Karlsfeld
Zeichnungen: Marlene Pohle, Stuttgart
Druck und Bindung: Auer Buch + Medien GmbH, Donauwörth
Printed in Germany
ISBN 978-3-19-617480-9

Inhalt

Vorwort

Liebe Deutsch-Lernende,

Sie haben einen Deutsch-Selbstlernkurs erworben und möchten die Sprache lernen, die Muttersprache für 100 Millionen Menschen ist. Damit Sie schnell und fundiert vorankommen, werde ich Ihnen den Kurs kurz vorstellen. In dem Package finden Sie:
1. ein Zweisprachiges Arbeitsbuch,
2. ein Textbuch und
3. drei Audio-CDs.

Das *Arbeitsbuch* ist Ihr Leitfaden, der Sie Schritt für Schritt sicher durch den Kurs führt. Wichtig: Bevor Sie weitermachen, lesen Sie immer zuerst die *Anweisung* im Arbeitsbuch. Wir geben Ihnen Lektion 1 als Muster:

S. 5/6 + S. 5-7

Dialog mit Übungen:
Arbeiten Sie mit dem Textbuch und dem Arbeitsbuch parallel. Im Arbeitsbuch finden Sie die Piktogramme der Höraufnahmen (mit CD- und Tracknummer) und die Übersetzung der Übungsanweisungen.

S. 7-8

Grammatik – Neue Wörter – Übungen:
Arbeiten Sie entsprechend der Nummerierung weiter im Arbeitsbuch. Es vermittelt Ihnen ausführlich die Grammatik, die im Textbuch nur als kurze Notizen dargestellt ist.

S. 9

Aussprache:
Weiter im Arbeitsbuch finden Sie Übungen zur Aussprache.

S. 8 + S. 9

Kulturelle Info:
Zum Abschluss machen Sie eine auflockernde Übung, lösen ein Rätsel oder machen ein Spiel – jeweils im Textbuch auf der letzten Seite einer Lektion. Übersetzungen und Erklärungen dazu finden Sie im Arbeitsbuch.

S. 10

Test:
Der Test am Ende jeder Lektion sagt Ihnen, ob Sie wiederholen und weitermachen können.

Im Anhang finden Sie sämtliche *Lösungen* und das komplette *Glossar*. Sollten Sie ein Wort nicht verstehen oder vergessen haben, schauen Sie bitte im Glossar nach. So lernen Sie am schnellsten. Am Ende werden Sie ca. 1.500 Wörter kennen. Sie werden so viel gelernt haben, dass Sie sich gut im Alltag verständigen, telefonieren und einfache Briefe schreiben können.

Nun also viel Spaß! Und noch ein kleiner Tipp: Hören Sie nicht auf diejenigen, die behaupten, Deutsch sei eine schwere Sprache. Wir überzeugen Sie vom Gegenteil!

Ihre
Renate Luscher

Guten Tag oder Hallo!

1 Ordnen Sie zu.

a. ◯ Guten Tag!

b. ◯ Guten Morgen!

c. ◯ Guten Abend!

d. ◯ Auf Wiedersehen!

e. ◯ Tschüs!

2 Das sind Jürgen Heinrich, Chris Bruckner, Robert und Claudia

Jürgen Heinrich   Chris Bruckner   Robert Klein   Claudia Bergmann

1A
Guten Tag. Sind Sie Herr Heinrich?
Ja, das bin ich.
Mein Name ist Bruckner, Chris Bruckner.
Guten Tag, Frau Bruckner. Herzlich willkommen.

1B
Hallo, Rob.
Hallo, Claudia.
Wie geht's dir?
Danke, gut.

Übungen – und ein bisschen Grammatik

3 Hören Sie. Wie ist die Reihenfolge?

___ Mein Name ist Bruckner, Chris Bruckner.

___ Guten Tag, Frau Bruckner. Herzlich willkommen.

___ Ja, das bin ich.

_1_ Guten Tag, sind Sie Herr Heinrich?

___ Wie geht's dir?

___ Hallo, Claudia.

___ Danke, gut.

___ Hallo, Rob.

4 Was passt zusammen?

Hallo, Rob.   Danke, gut. Und Ihnen?
Wie geht es Ihnen?   Hallo, Claudia.
Guten Tag, ich bin Chris Bruckner.   Gut, danke.
Wie geht's dir?   Guten Tag, Frau Bruckner. Herzlich willkommen.
Sind Sie Herr Heinrich?   Ja, das bin ich.

5 Ergänzen Sie.

Sie

Guten Tag. Sind _____ Herr Heinrich?

Ja, das bin ich.

Mein Name ist Bruckner. Chris Bruckner.

_____ _____, _____ Bruckner, herzlich willkommen.

du

_____, Rob.

_____, Claudia.

Wie geht's?

Danke, gut.

6 Ergänzen Sie.

Sie

_____ Sie Herr Fischer?

Ja, das _____ ich.

Mein Name _____ Graf.

Guten Tag, Frau Graf.

du

_____ du Eva?

Ja, ich _____ Eva.

Ich _____ Markus. Und du?

Tag, Markus. Ich _____ Eva.

sein
ich bin ...
*Mein Name **ist** ...*
***Sind** Sie ...?*

7 Was passt? Hören Sie und markieren Sie.

1. Guten Tag.

☐ Danke, gut.

☐ Guten Tag.

2. Wie geht's?

☐ Danke, gut.

☐ Ich bin Julia.

3. Hallo.

☐ Mein Name ist Schulte.

☐ Hallo.

4. Hallo, ich bin Micha. Und du?

☐ Ich bin Felix.

☐ Hallo, hallo.

8 Was passt? Schreiben Sie.

1.

● Guten Tag, Frau Bruckner.

▶ _____

● Herzlich willkommen.

a. Guten Tag.

b. Tag, Robert.

c. Danke.

2.

● Sind Sie Herr Heinrich?

▶ _____

● Guten Tag, ich bin Chris Bruckner.

a. Hallo, Chris.

b. Tag, Chris.

c. Ja, das bin ich.

3.

● Hallo, Robert.

▶ Hallo, Claudia.

● _____

a. Wie geht's?

b. Wie geht es Ihnen?

c. Danke, gut.

Guten Tag, Servus, Grüezi

Hören Sie.

Norddeutschland = 1
Bayern = 2
Österreich = 3
Schweiz = 4

Schreiben Sie. 1, 2, 3 oder 4?

⌴ Guten Tag.	⌴ Servus.	⌴ Tschüs.
⌴ Grüß Gott.	⌴ Auf Wiedersehen.	⌴ Salut.
⌴ Grüezi.	⌴ Uf Widerluege.	⌴ Auf Wiederschaun.
⌴ Hallo.	⌴ Baba.	⌴ Pfiat di.
⌴2 Griaß di.		

Hören Sie und vergleichen Sie.

Woher kommen Sie?

1 *Wo ist ...?* Suchen Sie die Städte. (Seite 8)

Berlin

München

Wien

Zürich

Salzburg

Bern

Sagen Sie: *Da ist ...*

2 **Herr Heinrich und Frau Bruckner im Auto**

Frau Bruckner: Sind Sie aus Berlin, Herr Heinrich?

Herr Heinrich: Ja, klar. Und Sie, woher kommen Sie?

Frau Bruckner: Aus Österreich, ich bin aus Wien. Aber ich lebe in München. Schon lange.

Herr Heinrich: Sind Sie gern in München?

Frau Bruckner: Ja, sehr gern. Ich wohne schon fünf Jahre dort.

Herr Heinrich: Kennen Sie Berlin?

Frau Bruckner: Ja, aber nicht gut.

Übungen – und ein bisschen Grammatik

3 Markieren Sie die passenden Verben.

Ich **komme** aus Wien
Ich **wohne** / **lebe** in München
Ich **bin** in Berlin.
Ich **kenne** Berlin nicht gut.

1. _____ Sie aus Berlin?
☐ Wohnen   ☐ Sind   ☐ Leben

2. Woher _____ Sie?
☐ kommen   ☐ wohnen   ☐ leben

3. Ich _____ aus Wien.
☐ bin   ☐ wohne   ☐ lebe

4. Aber ich _____ in München.
☐ komme   ☐ lebe   ☐ kenne

5. _____ Sie gern in München?
☐ Kennen   ☐ Sind   ☐ Kommen

6. Ja, ich _____ schon fünf Jahre dort.
☐ komme   ☐ wohne   ☐ kenne

4 Was passt?

Herr Heinrich ist _____ .

Er lebt _____ .

Frau Bruckner kommt _____ .

Sie wohnt aber _____ .

Sie lebt schon _____ .

Sie kennt _____ .

in München

aus Berlin

in Berlin

fünf Jahre dort

Berlin nicht gut

aus Österreich

5 Fragen Sie Chris Bruckner.
Markieren Sie die richtige Antwort.

Woher **kommen** Sie?
Kommen Sie aus ...?

1. Sind Sie aus Berlin?
☐ Ja, klar.
☐ Nein, ich bin aus Wien.

2. Wohnen Sie in München?
☐ Nein, in Berlin.
☐ Ja, schon lange.

3. Kennen Sie Berlin?
☐ Nein.
☐ Ja, aber nicht gut.

6 Antworten Sie. Was ist richtig?

1. Sind Sie aus Köln?   ☐ Ja, ich bin aus München.

☐ Nein, aus München.

☐ Ich wohne in München.

2. Kennen Sie Berlin?   ☐ Ja, gern.

☐ Nein, ich kenne Berlin.

☐ Ja, klar.

3. Sind Sie Herr Schuler?   ☐ Nein, ich bin Herr Schuler.

☐ Ja, das bin ich.

☐ Ja, ich bin Herr Müller.

7 Wir fragen – Sie antworten

Hallo, ...

wie geht's dir? / wie geht's Ihnen?   Danke, gut.
Danke, sehr gut.
Danke, es geht.
Ach, nicht so gut.

geht's dir gut? / geht's Ihnen gut?   Ja, super.
Na ja, es geht.
Ach, nicht so gut.

8 Schreiben Sie.

Herr Heinrich _____ (leben) in Berlin.

Frau Bruckner _____ (wohnen) in München.

Wo _____ (wohnen) Sie?

Frau Bruckner _____ (kommen) aus Wien.

Woher _____ (kommen) Sie?

Frau Bruckner _____ (kennen) Berlin nicht gut.

_____ (kennen) Sie Berlin?

Städte-Quiz

Wie heißt die Stadt?
Schreiben Sie die Städtenamen.

H_____

K_____

L_____

A_____

S_____

B_____

Z_____

G____

Was ist D, A, CH?   D ist _____ .

A ist _____ .

CH ist die _____ .

Im Hotel

1 Ordnen Sie zu.

| | Julian |

a. der Name | | Stuttgart

b. der Vorname

c. der Geburtsort | | Deutschland | d | Berlin

    die Adresse:

    d. der Ort | | 10543

    e. die Postleitzahl | | Groß

    f. die Straße

    g. das Land | | Neue Straße 10 | | *Julian Groß*

h. die Unterschrift

2 Die Hotelanmeldung
    Das ist die Visitenkarte von Frau Bruckner. Schreiben Sie die Hotelanmeldung.

Lernfabrik GmbH

Christine Bruckner
Robert-Koch-Straße 10
81825 München
Deutschland

Tel.: 089 / 439 44 88
Fax: 089 / 439 44 89
E-Mail: bruckner @ lernfabrik.de

Hotelanmeldung

Name	Vorname	Geburtsort

Adresse: Straße

PLZ	Ort	Land

Unterschrift

Übungen – und ein bisschen Grammatik

3 Wie ist Ihr Name?
Schreiben Sie Ihre Hotelanmeldung.

4 Frage und Antwort

a. ◯ Wie heißen Sie?
b. ◯ Wie ist Ihr Name?
c. ◯ Wie ist Ihr Vorname?
d. ◯ Woher kommen Sie?
e. ◯ Wo sind Sie geboren?
f. ◯ Wie ist Ihre Adresse?
g. ◯ Wie heißt die Straße?
h. ◯ Wie heißt der Ort?
i. ◯ Wie ist die Postleitzahl?

Hotelanmeldung

Name ❶   Vorname ❷

Geburtsort ❸

Adresse: ❹

Straße ❺

PLZ ❻   Ort ❼

Land ❽

Unterschrift

5 Was gehört zusammen? Schreiben Sie das Nomen mit Artikel.

_____ _____

_____ _____

_____ _____

_____ _____

_____ _____

_____ _____

_____ _____

der

die   Ort

der   Name

der   Postleitzahl

die   Straße

das   Vorname

die   Adresse   Land

der Name
die Adresse
das Land

6 Wie heißt das Wort?

```
                                              U
                                              N
                                              T
               U    V          D    E    N
          L    N    O    H    A    R    A
          ☐    ☐    ☐    ☐    ☐    ☐    ☐
          N    N    R         C    M
          D    A    R         H
               M              R
               E              I
                              F
                              T
```

7 Ein Formular – Füllen Sie aus.

Familienname _____	Nationalität _____
Vorname/Vornamen _____	Adresse
Geburtsname _____	Straße/Platz/Nummer _____
Geburtsort _____	Postleitzahl/Stadt _____
Geburtsland _____	Land _____
Geburtsdatum _____ _____ _____ Tag Monat Jahr	
Familienstand ☐ ledig ☐ verheiratet ☐ geschieden	Pass-Nummer/Ausweis-Nummer _____
Geschlecht ☐ weiblich ☐ männlich	Datum/Unterschrift

8 Was gehört zusammen?   der Pass der Name der Ort männlich

ledig   das Hotel   der Geburtsort   Datum

das Geburtsjahr   der Vorname   die Postleitzahl   weiblich

das Visum   Unterschrift   verheiratet   die Adresse

9 Schreiben Sie, wie Sie heißen, woher Sie kommen und wo Sie wohnen. Sprechen Sie die Sätze.

Ich _____ .

Ich komme _____ (= Land)

und wohne _____ . (= Stadt)

10 *aus* und *in*

Petra und Jens

leben _____ Leipzig.

wohnen _____ Dresden.

kommen _____ Halle.

sind _____ Berlin.

Ausländer in Deutschland

**Was sagt der Reporter? Was sagt der Mann?
Schreiben Sie den Dialog.**

Aus Deutschland.
Entschuldigen Sie, woher sind Sie?
Özcan Saglem.
Ja klar, ich bin aus Berlin. Ich wohne hier.
Aha.
Aus Deutschland?
Und wie heißen Sie?

Entschuldigen Sie, _____

_____

_____

_____

_____

_____

Jetzt hören Sie zu. Vergleichen Sie.

Smalltalk

1 Ordnen Sie zu.

Wie geht's?   1 2 4   1 Gut, danke.

Wie ist das Wetter?   ☐ ☐   2 Nicht sehr gut. Leider.

Wie ist das Hotel?   ☐ ☐ ☐   3 Das ist prima.

Wie war die Reise?   ☐ ☐ ☐   4 Es geht, danke.

2 Frau Bruckner und Herr Kühne im Büro

4A

Herr Kühne: Guten Tag, Frau Bruckner. Wie geht's? Wie war die Reise?

Frau Bruckner: Guten Tag, Herr Kühne. Danke, gut.

Herr Kühne: Und wie ist das Hotel?

Frau Bruckner: Auch gut. Und nicht weit.
Sie sind ja direkt im Zentrum.

Herr Kühne: Ja, das ist sehr praktisch.

4B

Frau Bruckner: Das Wetter ist auch prima.

Herr Kühne: Ja, es ist schön und sehr warm.
Wie ist es denn in München?

Frau Bruckner: Leider schlecht. Es regnet schon
zwei Tage.

Herr Kühne: Da haben Sie hier Glück. Kennen
Sie die Stadt?

Frau Bruckner: Nicht sehr gut.

Herr Kühne: Dann machen wir eine Stadtrundfahrt. Vielleicht morgen?

Frau Bruckner: Ja, gerne.

Übungen – und ein bisschen Grammatik

3 Hören Sie den Dialog. Markieren Sie die Person.

a. Wie war die Reise? ☐ ☐

b. Danke, gut. ☐ ☐

c. Und wie ist das Hotel? ☐ ☐

d. Das ist sehr praktisch. ☐ ☐

e. Auch gut. ☐ ☐

f. Das Wetter ist auch prima. ☐ ☐

g. Wie ist es denn in München? ☐ ☐

h. Leider schlecht. ☐ ☐

i. Kennen Sie die Stadt? ☐ ☐

j. Dann machen wir eine Stadtrundfahrt. ☐ ☐

4 Was ist richtig (✔)? Was ist falsch (✗)? Markieren Sie.

> Ja. – Nein.
> Ja, das ist gut.
> – Nein, das ist **nicht** gut.

a. Das Hotel ist ☐ gut. ☐ nicht gut.

b. Das Hotel ist ☐ direkt im Zentrum. ☐ nicht im Zentrum.

c. Das ist ☐ praktisch. ☐ nicht praktisch.

d. Das Wetter in Berlin ist ☐ schlecht. ☐ nicht schlecht.

e. Es regnet ☐ in München. ☐ in Berlin.

f. Frau Bruckner kennt Berlin ☐ sehr gut. ☐ nicht sehr gut.

5 Lesen Sie.

Frau A.: Guten Tag. Wie geht's?
Herr B.: Guten Tag. Danke, gut. Und Ihnen?
Frau A.: Danke. Auch gut.
Herr B.: Wie war die Reise?
Frau A.: Es geht.
Herr B.: Wohnen Sie im Hotel Berlin?
Frau A.: Nein, ich bin im Hotel Amsterdam.
Herr B.: Ah, im Amsterdam.
Frau A.: Ja, das ist sehr praktisch. Direkt im Zentrum.
Herr B.: Ja, und sehr schön ist es auch.

6 Was ist richtig?

☐ Frau A. kommt aus Amsterdam.
☐ Frau A. wohnt im Hotel Amsterdam.

☐ Herr B. wohnt im Amsterdam.
☐ Frau A. wohnt im Amsterdam.

☐ Das Hotel ist sehr praktisch.
☐ Das Hotel ist nicht schön.

7 Ein Interview
Lesen Sie zuerst die Antworten. Hören Sie dann und sprechen Sie Ihre Antwort.

☺   ☹

a. Wie geht es Ihnen?   Danke, sehr gut.   Danke, nicht so gut.
b. Wie war die Reise?   Danke, gut.   Es geht.
c. Wie ist das Hotel?   Prima.   Nicht gut.
d. Wie ist das Wetter?   Es ist warm und schön.   Es ist sehr schlecht.
e. Kennen Sie Berlin?   Ja, gut.   Nicht gut.

8 Hören Sie. Schreiben Sie das Adjektiv.

Herr Kühne: Guten Tag, Frau Bruckner.
    Wie geht's? Wie war die Reise?

Frau Bruckner: Guten Tag, Herr Kühne. Danke,
    _____ .

gut – praktisch – weit – schön – schlecht – prima – warm
*Das ist **prima / gut / schön**.*

Herr Kühne: Und wie ist das Hotel?

Frau Bruckner: Auch _____ . Und nicht _____ .
    Sie sind ja direkt im Zentrum.

Herr Kühne: Ja, das ist sehr _____ .

Frau Bruckner: Das Wetter ist auch _____ .

Herr Kühne: Ja, es ist _____ und sehr _____ .
    Wie ist es denn in München?

Frau Bruckner: Leider _____ . Es regnet schon zwei Tage.

Herr Kühne: Da haben Sie hier Glück. Kennen Sie die Stadt?

Frau Bruckner: Nicht sehr _____ .

Herr Kühne: Dann machen wir eine Stadtrundfahrt. Vielleicht morgen?

Frau Bruckner: Ja, gerne.

Ländernamen

Ergänzen Sie die Ländernamen und suchen Sie alle Namen mit -land. Wie viele sind es?

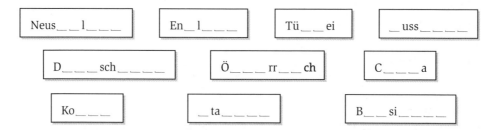

Neus_ _ l _ _ _ _   En_ l _ _ _ _   Tü _ _ ei   _ uss _ _ _ _ _

D _ _ _ sch _ _ _ _ _   Ö _ _ _ rr _ _ ch   C _ _ _ a

Ko _ _ _ _   _ ta _ _ _ _ _   B _ _ si _ _ _ _ _

Erkennen Sie das Land? Ordnen Sie die Ländernamen zu.

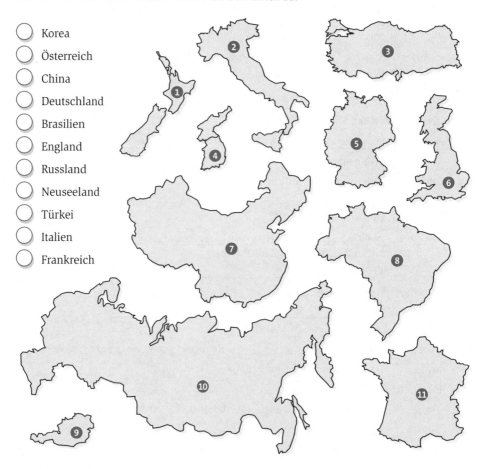

◯ Korea
◯ Österreich
◯ China
◯ Deutschland
◯ Brasilien
◯ England
◯ Russland
◯ Neuseeland
◯ Türkei
◯ Italien
◯ Frankreich

Wie lange fahren wir denn?

1 Wer sagt das?

a. ◯ Oh, das ist schön.

b. ◯ Aha, ich verstehe.

c. ◯ Ja, klar. Ich komme. Noch fünf Minuten.

d. ◯ Nein, nein, das ist nicht richtig.

e. ◯ Na ja, das ist nicht schlimm.

2 Claudia und Robert nehmen die S-Bahn

5A

Robert:	Was kostet die Fahrkarte?
Claudia:	Zwei Euro.
Robert:	Aha. Das habe ich. Wo ist der Automat?
Claudia:	Nein, nein, ich mache das.
Robert:	Das ist nett. Vielen Dank. Wie lange fahren wir denn?
Claudia:	Eine Stunde.
Robert:	Wie bitte?
Claudia:	Ja, eine Stunde und fünf Minuten. Du bist hier in Berlin und nicht in Rosenheim!
Robert:	Ja, ja. Berlin ist eine Großstadt und Rosenheim ist eine Kleinstadt.

5B

Claudia:	Morgen haben wir das Auto. Niki fährt mit der S-Bahn.
Robert:	Super. Wann kommt Niki denn nach Hause?
Claudia:	Heute kommt er spät. Er arbeitet wieder furchtbar viel.
Robert:	Und ich arbeite furchtbar wenig.
Claudia:	Hast du ein Glück!

Übungen – und ein bisschen Grammatik

3 **Lesen Sie den Text. Ergänzen Sie das Fragewort.**

Was / Wo / Wie / Wann / Wie lange

Robert: _____ kostet die Fahrkarte?

Claudia: Zwei Euro.

Robert: Aha. Das habe ich. _____ ist der Automat?

Claudia: Nein, nein, ich mache das.

Robert: Das ist nett. Vielen Dank. _____ fahren wir denn?

Claudia: Eine Stunde.

Robert: _____ bitte?

Claudia: Ja, eine Stunde und fünf Minuten. Du bist hier in Berlin und nicht in Rosenheim!

Robert: Ja, ja. Berlin ist eine Großstadt und Rosenheim ist eine Kleinstadt.

Claudia: Morgen haben wir das Auto. Niki fährt mit der S-Bahn.

Robert: Super. _____ kommt Niki denn nach Hause?

Claudia: Heute kommt er spät. Er arbeitet wieder furchtbar viel.

Robert: Und ich arbeite furchtbar wenig.

Claudia: Hast du ein Glück!

Hören Sie jetzt den Text noch einmal.

4 **Das ist falsch! Korrigieren Sie.**

Das ist falsch.	**Das ist richtig.**
Die Fahrkarte kostet drei Euro.	_____
Robert und Claudia sind in Rosenheim.	_____
Rosenheim ist eine Großstadt.	_____
Berlin ist eine Kleinstadt.	_____
Niki arbeitet nicht viel.	_____
Robert arbeitet viel.	_____

5 *Wie bitte?* **Lesen Sie. Ergänzen Sie.**

B: Ihr Name, bitte.

A: Babecki.

B: Wie bitte?

A: Ich _____ Babecki.

B: Vorname?

A: Bitte?

B: Wie _____ Ihr Vorname?

A: Witold.

B: Danke. Geboren?

A: Wie bitte?

B: Wo _____ Sie geboren?

A: In Warschau.

B: Adresse?

A: Wie bitte?

B: Wie _____ Ihre Adresse?

A: Das Hotel?

B: Ja, bitte.

A: Europa.

B: Das Hotel _____ Europa?

A: Ja, Hotel Europa.

B: Danke sehr.

Hören Sie jetzt und vergleichen Sie.

> Woher kommst du?
> Ich komme aus Deutschland. /
> **Aus Deutschland.**

6 **Ein paar Fragen – Antworten Sie ganz kurz.**

	lang	kurz
Was kostet die Fahrkarte?	Sie kostet zwei Euro.	_____
Wie lange fahren wir?	Wir fahren eine Stunde.	_____
Niki fährt mit der S-Bahn.	Das ist super.	_____
Wie kommt Niki nach Hause?	Er fährt mit der S-Bahn.	_____
Wann kommt Niki nach Hause?	Er kommt spät.	_____
Arbeitest du viel?	Nein, ich arbeite furchtbar wenig.	_____

> eine Stadt – zwei Städte
> ein Land – zwei Länder
> eine Stunde – zwei Stunden

7 **Schreiben Sie den Singular.**

Wie lange fahren wir? – Zwei Stunden.   Eine _____.

Was kosten die Fahrkarten?   Was kostet d____ _____?

Ich habe ein paar Fragen.   Ich habe eine _____.

Sind das Hotels?   Ist das ein _____?

Sind München und Hamburg Großstädte?   Ist Hamburg eine _____?

Sind Hamburg und Bremen Bundesländer?   Ist Bremen ein _____?

Nachbarländer

Welche Länder sind das?
Hören Sie die Ländernamen. Notieren Sie.

_____   _____   _____

_____   _____   _____

_____   _____   _____

Schreiben Sie die Länder in die Landkarte.

6

Wer ist Claudia? Wer ist Robert?

1 Wer ist wer? Ordnen Sie zu.

a. ◯ Robert Klein: 25 Jahre, Student. Hobbys: Reisen, Partys.

b. ◯ Niki Bat: 28 Jahre, Informatiker. Hobbys: Job und Karriere.

c. ◯ Katrin Sommer: 18 Jahre, Schülerin. Hobbys: Facebook, Deutsch, Geschichte.

d. ◯ Wolf Elberfeld: 45 Jahre, Ingenieur. Hobbys: Fußball.

e. ◯ Patrick Neumann: 30 Jahre, Geschäftsmann. Hobbys: Tennis, Ski fahren.

f. ◯ Claudia Bergmann: 23 Jahre, Medien-Designerin. Hobbys: Reisen, Sprachen.

g. ◯ Nanni Köhler: 52 Jahre, Ärztin. Hobbys: Musik.

2   Claudia und Robert

6A

Claudia ist in Berlin geboren.
Sie ist 23 Jahre alt.
Sie ist Medien-Designerin von Beruf.
Sie arbeitet bei Art & Design.
Ihre Hobbys sind Reisen und Sprachen.
Ihre Handy-Nummer ist 0174 – 32 38 66.

6B

Robert kommt aus Rosenheim.
Das ist eine Kleinstadt in Bayern.
Sie liegt südlich von München.
Robert studiert in München Informatik.
Er ist 25 Jahre alt und Student.
Er hat viele Hobbys und immer wenig Zeit.
Seine Handy-Nummer ist 0175 – 34 71 75.
Seine Telefonnummer ist 08031 – 14 05 91.
Robert kennt Claudia und Niki schon ein Jahr.
Er findet Claudia sehr sympathisch.

Übungen – und ein bisschen Grammatik

3 **Woher kommt Robert? Wo studiert Robert? Wo ist er jetzt? Ergänzen Sie die Sätze.**

B_____ :   Hier _____ Claudia und Niki.

R_____ :   Hier _____ Robert.

M_____ :   Hier _____ Robert.

Berlin   München   Rosenheim

4 **Was fehlt?**

_____ ist Claudia?

Claudia ist in Berlin _____ .

Sie ist 23 _____ alt.

Sie ist Medien-Designerin von _____ .

Sie arbeitet _____ Art & Design.

Ihre _____ sind Reisen und Sprachen.

> **Wer** ist das?
> Woher ...? Wo ...?
> Wie (lange) ...? Was ...?

_____ ist Robert?

Robert kommt _____ Rosenheim.

Er studiert in _____ Informatik.

Er ist 25 Jahre und _____ .

Er hat viele Hobbys und immer wenig _____ .

Robert kennt Claudia und Niki schon ein Jahr.

Er _____ sie sehr sympathisch.

5 **Wir fragen – Sie antworten**

Wo ist Claudia geboren?   Sie ist _____

Wie alt ist sie?   Sie ist _____

Was ist sie von Beruf?   Sie ist _____

Wo arbeitet sie?   _____

Was sind Ihre Hobbys?   Ihre Hobbys sind _____

Woher kommt Robert?   _____

6 Wie findest du das?

a. ◯ Das finde ich schön.

b. ◯ Das finde ich schlecht.

c. ◯ Das finde ich nicht richtig.

d. ◯ Das finde ich praktisch.

e. ◯ Das finde ich richtig.

f. ◯ Das finde ich schwer.

1 Er isst viel.

2 Das ist ein Geschenk.

3 Er isst gut.

4 Er übt Grammatik.

5 Das ist verboten!

6 Das ist neu.

7 Wie bitte? Fragen Sie wie im Beispiel.

Beispiel:
● Ich heiße Sebastian Mittler.
▶ Wie bitte? Wie heißen Sie?

1. Ich wohne in Nürnberg.
2. Ich arbeite bei Lernsoft.
3. Ich bin Medien-Designer von Beruf.

4. Ich bin aus Rosenheim.
5. Mein Vorname ist Sebastian.
6. Mittler ist mein Name.

8 Wie finden Sie die? Ergänzen Sie die Person und das Adjektiv.

- Robert / Chris Bruckner / Jürgen Heinrich
- sympathisch / nett / nicht so sympathisch / nicht besonders nett

Ich finde Claudia _____.

Ich finde _____.

Ich finde _____.

Ich finde _____.

Ein Schloss in Bayern

Beantworten Sie die Fragen.

1. Wo liegt Neuschwanstein?
im Süden / München

_____

2. Das sind ...
☐ 500 Kilometer
☐ 150 Kilometer
☐ 1.000 Kilometer
☐ 2.000 Kilometer

3. Was kostet das Ticket?

_____

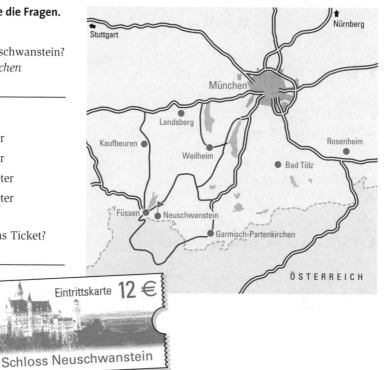

Entschuldigung!

1 Ergänzen Sie.

Was möchten Sie trinken?

_____, bitte.

Mit _____ und _____?

Bitte mit _____.

| Kaffee | Tee | Milch | Zucker |

2 Kaffee trinken im Büro

Herr Heinrich:	Möchten Sie etwas trinken? Kaffee?
Frau Bruckner:	Haben Sie auch Tee?
Herr Heinrich:	Ja, natürlich. – Oh, tut mir leid. Der Tee ist schon kalt.
Frau Bruckner:	Dann nehme ich Kaffee.
Herr Heinrich:	Möchten Sie Milch und Zucker?
Frau Bruckner:	Nur Milch, bitte.
Herr Heinrich:	Entschuldigung ...
Frau Bruckner:	Macht nichts.
Herr Heinrich:	Hier ist eine Serviette.
Frau Bruckner:	Vielen Dank.
Herr Kühne:	Also: Wir arbeiten jetzt bis Mittag. Dann machen wir eine Stunde Pause und gehen in die Kantine. Einverstanden?
Frau Bruckner:	Einverstanden.

Übungen – und ein bisschen Grammatik

3 Wie ist die Reihenfolge?

1 Herr Kühne: Also: Wir arbeiten jetzt bis Mittag. Dann machen wir eine Stunde
                       Pause und gehen in die Kantine. Einverstanden?
   Frau Bruckner: Einverstanden.

2 Herr Heinrich: Möchten Sie etwas trinken? Kaffee?
   Frau Bruckner: Haben Sie auch Tee?
   Herr Heinrich: Ja, natürlich. – Oh, tut mir leid. Der Tee ist schon kalt.

3 Herr Heinrich: Entschuldigung ...
   Frau Bruckner: Macht nichts.
   Herr Heinrich: Hier ist eine Serviette.
   Frau Bruckner: Vielen Dank.

4 Frau Bruckner: Dann nehme ich Kaffee.   Reihenfolge:
   Herr Heinrich: Möchten Sie Milch und Zucker?
   Frau Bruckner: Nur Milch, bitte.   ⌞_⌟ ⌞_⌟ ⌞_⌟ ⌞_⌟

4 Fragen Sie.

1. Entschuldigung, sind ⌞_⌟   **a.** Sie noch Kaffee?

2. Entschuldigung, wo ⌞_⌟   **b.** Sie Herr Heinrich?

3. Entschuldigung, möchten ⌞_⌟   **c.** kommen Sie?

4. Entschuldigung, wie ⌞_⌟   **d.** ist die Kantine?

5. Entschuldigung, woher ⌞_⌟   **e.** kostet die Fahrkarte?

6. Entschuldigung, was ⌞_⌟   **f.** machen wir Pause?

7. Entschuldigung, wann ⌞_⌟   **g.** ist Ihr Name?

5 Kreuzworträtsel

1 senkrecht   Tut mir _____, der Tee ist schon kalt.

2 senkrecht   Wir arbeiten bis _____.

3 waagerecht   Nehmen Sie Zucker? – Ja, _____.

4 waagerecht   Dann gehen wir in die _____.

5 senkrecht   Trinken Sie Kaffee? – Nein, nur _____.

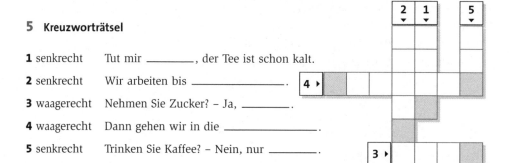

6 **Hören Sie die Frage. Antworten Sie höflich.**
Hören Sie dann die Antwort.

möchten
*Ich **möchte** ...*
***Möchten** Sie ...?*

a. Möchten Sie eine Pause machen? ☐ Ja, gerne. ☐ Ja. ☐ Morgen.

b. Möchten Sie Kaffee oder Tee? ☐ Tee, bitte. ☐ Kaffee. ☐ Nein.

c. Möchten Sie eine Serviette? ☐ Ja. ☐ Ja, danke. ☐ Aha.

d. Möchten Sie auch Zucker? ☐ Nein. ☐ Ja, bitte. ☐ Milch.

e. Möchten Sie Milch und Zucker? ☐ Nur Milch, bitte. ☐ Ja. ☐ Nein.

f. Möchten Sie in die Kantine? ☐ Nein. ☐ Ja. ☐ Ja, gerne.

7 **Was passt nicht? Schreiben Sie.**

a. Frau	Mann	Kind	Fahrkarte	*Fahrkarte*
b. Hobby	Studentin	Student	Universität	
c. Handy	Sprache	Fax	Telefon	
d. Land	Name	Geburtsort	Buchstabe	
e. warm	kalt	schön	sympathisch	
f. Tag	Informatik	Stunde	Minute	

8 **Notizen von Chris Bruckner**

Ergänzen Sie: gut / Beruf / fünf Jahre / alt / Herr / liegt / Chef.

Dienstag, 24.

Firma Europartner: Das Büro _____ direkt im Zentrum. Die Adresse ist

sehr _____. Die Firma ist schon _____ _____ dort. Herr Kühne und _____

Heinrich sind sehr sympathisch.

Herr Kühne ist der _____, 40 Jahre _____, von Beruf Informatiker.

Herr Heinrich ist der Marketing-Chef. Er ist von _____ Ingenieur.

Kaffee trinken

Wo sind wir? In Deutschland, in der Schweiz oder in Österreich?

In _____.

- ● Bitte eine Tasse Kaffee.
- ► Möchten Sie Kaffee, Espresso oder Cappuccino?
- ● Kaffee, bitte, mit Milch und Zucker.

Wo sind wir? In Deutschland, in der Schweiz oder in Österreich?

In _____.

- ● Bitte eine Tasse Kaffee.
- ► Möchten Sie Milchkaffee, einen großen Braunen, einen kleinen Braunen oder ...?
- ● Oh, kann ich bitte die Karte haben?
- ► Bitte sehr.
- ● Bitte einen Kaffee mit Milch.
- ► Gern.

Wo sind wir? In Deutschland, in der Schweiz oder in Österreich?

In _____.

- ● Bitte eine Tasse Kaffee.
- ► Möchten Sie Kaffee oder eine Schale?
- ● Eine Schale?
- ► Das ist Milchkaffee.
- ● Ah ja, gerne.

Zu Hause

1 Hier fehlt was. Ergänzen Sie die Vokale.

i
e
a
ei
e
o
e
e
e
e
a
e

_ rb _ _ t _ n

k _ ch _ n

tr _ nk _ n

_ ss _ n

spr _ ch _ n

f _ hr _ n

2 Zu Hause bei Claudia und Niki

Niki: Hallo, Robert!

Robert: Hallo, Niki. Du bist ja zu Hause!

Niki: Na klar. Ich bin extra früher gegangen.

Robert: Das ist prima. Und? Wie geht's?

Niki: Gut. Alles bestens.

Robert: Claudia sagt, du arbeitest viel.

Niki: Ach was! Von nichts kommt nichts, sagt man. Die Arbeit macht auch Spaß.

Claudia: Aber jetzt machen wir Pause.

Niki: Du hast recht, Claudia.

Claudia: Und jetzt essen wir was. Robert, hast du Hunger?

Robert: Immer.

Niki: Nun bin ich dran. Ich habe nämlich eine Überraschung! Es gibt heute Spaghetti und Salat. Ich habe gekocht!

Claudia: Bah, klasse. Und was trinken wir?

Übungen – und ein bisschen Grammatik

3 Ergänzen Sie. Hören Sie dann noch einmal und korrigieren Sie.

> Hunger / prima / Spaß / Pause / zu Hause / Überraschung / recht / Salat

Niki: Hallo, Robert!

Robert: Hallo, Niki. Du bist ja _____ _____!

Niki: Na klar. Ich bin extra früher gegangen.

Robert: Das ist _____. Und? Wie geht's?

Niki: Gut. Alles bestens.

Robert: Claudia sagt, du arbeitest viel.

Niki: Ach was! Von nichts kommt nichts, sagt man. Die Arbeit macht auch _____.

Claudia: Aber jetzt machen wir _____.

Niki: Du hast _____, Claudia.

Claudia: Und jetzt essen wir was. Robert, hast du _____?

Robert: Immer.

Niki: Nun bin ich dran. Ich habe nämlich eine _____! Es gibt heute

            Spaghetti und _____. Ich habe gekocht!

Claudia: Bah, klasse. Und was trinken wir?

4 **Buchstabensalat**

Suchen Sie die Wörter H_ _ _ _ _ und D_ _ _ _ .

Z	E	W	Q	C	V	Z	T
T	Z	V	Q	W	E	Z	N
C	H	U	N	G	E	R	T
A	N	D	U	R	S	T	E
B	B	E	E	R	B	T	Z
A	B	C	D	E	F	G	H
H	G	F	E	D	C	B	A
Ö	Ä	Ü	S	E	Ü	Ä	Ö

5 **Was sagen Robert, Niki und Claudia? Markieren Sie.**

a. Robert:	Du bist ja	☐ zu Hause.	☐ im Büro.		
b. Niki:	Ich bin extra	☐ später gegangen.		☐ früher gegangen.	
c. Robert:	Du arbeitest	☐ viel.	☐ nicht.	☐ wenig.	
d. Niki:	Du hast	☐ recht.	☐ nicht recht.		
e. Claudia:	Robert, hast du	☐ Hunger?	☐ Zeit?	☐ Glück?	
f. Niki:	Es gibt	☐ nichts.	☐ Kaffee und Tee.	☐ Spaghetti und Salat.	

6 Ergänzen Sie.

Er _____ (sein) früher nach Hause gegangen.

Er _____ (sein) mit dem Auto gefahren.

Er _____ (haben) viel gearbeitet.

Die Arbeit _____ (haben) Spaß gemacht.

Er _____ (haben) Spaghetti gekocht.

Wir _____ (haben) nichts gegessen.

Wir _____ (haben) nichts getrunken.

	sein	haben
ich	bin	habe
du	bist	hast
er/sie	ist	hat
wir	sind	haben
ihr	seid	habt
Sie/sie	sind	haben

7 Was sagen Sie?

a. Es gibt eine Überraschung! ___*Klasse!*___ | klasse | | prima | | schade |

b. Habt ihr schon ein Hotel? _____ | na klar | | macht nichts | | ach was |

c. Studierst du noch? _____ | bestens | | ach was | | na klar |

d. Wie geht's zu Hause? _____ | na ja | | bestens | | schade |

e. Du arbeitest zu viel! _____ | prima | | na klar | | na ja |

f. Robert hat immer recht. _____ | ach was | | klasse | | na klar |

g. Ich komme heute nicht. _____ | schade | | prima | | macht nichts |

8 Tagebuch von Robert

Ergänzen Sie: gekommen / Hause / recht / arbeitet / und / gemacht / fahren / fährt

Dienstag, 24.

Bei Claudia und Niki: Ich bin bei Claudia und Niki zu _____. Niki ist heute

extra früher nach Hause _____. Claudia sagt, er _____ viel.

Das stimmt. Sie hat _____.

Niki hat gekocht. Wir haben Spaghetti _____ Salat gegessen. Das hat Spaß

_____. Morgen _____ wir in die Stadt. Claudia hat das Auto.

Niki _____ mit der S-Bahn.

Sprichwörter

Ergänzen Sie die Wörter.

studieren / Rat / Zeit / Ton / Apfel / probieren / Musik / Likör / Sorgen / Stamm

Kommt _____ , kommt _____ .

Der _____ fällt nicht weit vom _____ .

_____ geht über _____ .

Der _____ macht die _____ .

Wer _____ hat, hat auch _____ .

Sorgen

Ton

Rat

Stamm

Musik

probieren

Zeit

Apfel

Likör

studieren

Die Wohnung ist schön

1 Wo ist was?

das Wohnzimmer

das Schlafzimmer

die Küche

das Bad

die Toilette

der Flur

der Balkon

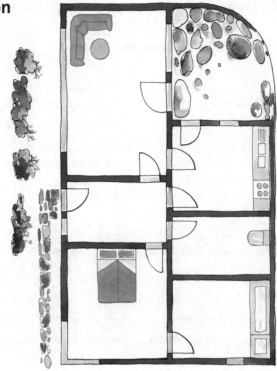

2 Zwei Zimmer, Küche und Bad

Die Wohnung von Claudia und Niki ist nicht groß. Sie ist aber sehr gemütlich. Ein Zimmer mit Bad, das reicht, hat Niki immer gesagt. Und jetzt haben sie zwei Zimmer, eine Küche und ein Bad. Auch für Besuch ist Platz. Robert schläft im Wohnzimmer.
Claudia hat lange zu Hause gewohnt und die Miete gespart. Niki hat im Zentrum gewohnt. Dann haben sie die Wohnung im Norden von Berlin gefunden.

Claudia hat die Anzeige gelesen.

Berlin-Frohnau
Dachwohnung mit Balkon, 45 qm, 2 Zimmer, Küche, Bad, 550 Euro monatlich warm, ab sofort frei. Telefon: 030 – 884421.

Übungen – und ein bisschen Grammatik

3 Was ist richtig? Markieren Sie.

1. Niki hat
☐ zu Hause
☐ im Zentrum
gewohnt.

2. Die Wohnung von
Claudia und Niki hat
☐ ein Zimmer mit Bad.
☐ zwei Zimmer mit Bad.
☐ drei Zimmer.

3. Es ist
☐ eine Dachwohnung.
☐ eine 3-Zimmer-Wohnung.
☐ eine 1-Zimmer-Wohnung.

4. Robert schläft
☐ im Wohnzimmer.
☐ im Hotel.
☐ im Schlafzimmer.

5. Die Miete ist
☐ 500 Euro kalt.
☐ 550 Euro warm.
☐ 750 Euro kalt.

6. Die Wohnung ist
☐ im Norden
☐ im Osten
☐ im Westen
von Berlin.

4 Sie sind jetzt Claudia. Sagen Sie *ich* und *wir*.

Die Wohnung ist nicht groß. Sie ist aber sehr gemütlich. Ein Zimmer mit Bad, das reicht,

hat Niki immer gesagt. Und jetzt _____ ____ sogar zwei Zimmer, eine Küche und ein

Bad. Auch für Besuch ist Platz. Robert schläft im Wohnzimmer.

____ _____ lange zu Hause gewohnt und die Miete gespart. Niki hat im Zentrum ge-

wohnt. Dann _____n ___ die Wohnung gefunden. _____ ____e die Anzeige gelesen.

5 *Mieten, Mieten, Mieten ...* Ordnen Sie zu.

a. ◯ 3-Zimmer-Wohnung, 90 m², neu,
S-Bahn, 900 Euro kalt

b. ◯ 4-Zimmer-Wohnung in Landsberg,
sehr schön, 104 m², ab sofort,
600 Euro kalt

c. ◯ Dachwohnung mit 2 Zimmern,
500 Euro monatlich

d. ◯ Garage, 100 Euro monatlich

e. ◯ 1-Zimmer-Appartement, 37 m²,
mit Balkon, Bad/WC, 400 Euro
monatlich

f. ◯ Einfamilienhaus, 190 m², 2 Bäder,
1.300 Euro

6 Wir rechnen.

1. Das Schlafzimmer hat drei mal vier
Meter. Das sind _____
Quadratmeter.

2. Der Balkon hat fünf mal ein Meter.
Das sind _____ Quadratmeter.

3. Das Wohnzimmer hat 16 Quadratmeter, das Schlafzimmer 12 Quadratmeter, das Bad 6,
die Küche 5, der Flur 6: Die Wohnung hat also _____ Quadratmeter.

4. Miete 450 €, Quadratmeter 45: Das sind 450 durch 45 gleich _____ € pro
Quadratmeter. Gehalt 1.500 € minus Miete. Bleiben _____ €.

$3 + 3 = 6$ drei **plus** drei **gleich** sechs
$3 - 3 = 0$ drei **minus** drei **gleich** null
$3 \times 3 = 9$ drei **mal** drei **gleich** neun
$3 : 1 = 3$ drei **(geteilt) durch** eins **gleich** drei

7 Ergänzen Sie die Verben.

Bad: _____ | arbeiten | baden | Wohnzimmer: _____

Küche: _____ | fahren | kochen | Arbeit: _____

Schlafzimmer: _____ | wohnen | schlafen | Fahrkarte: _____

8 Wie finden Sie das?

Wie finden Sie die Wohnung? – Super.   Ich _____

Wie finden Sie das Bad? – Praktisch.   _____

Wie finden Sie den Balkon? – Schön.   _____

Wie finden Sie den Kaffee? – Gut.   _____

Wie finden Sie das Hotel? – Schlecht.   _____

Hören Sie und antworten Sie.

9 Ergänzen Sie das Adjektiv.

Das Bad ist praktisch.   Das _____ Bad.

Markus ist nett.   Der _____ Markus.

Das Hotel ist schlecht.   Das _____ Hotel.

Daniela ist sympathisch.   Die _____ Daniela.

Die Lösung ist richtig.   Die _____ Lösung.

schön
der schöne Flur
das schöne Bad
die schöne Wohnung

Rätsel

Ergänzen Sie die Zahlen.

Ein Hufeisen

Ein Fliegenpilz

Ein Schornsteinfeger

A	=	eins
B	=	zwei
C	=	drei
D	=	_____
E	=	_____
F	=	_____
G	=	_____
H	=	_____
I	=	neun
J	=	zehn
K	=	_____
L	=	_____
M	=	_____
N	=	_____
O	=	_____

P	=	_____
Q	=	siebzehn
R	=	_____
S	=	_____
T	=	_____
U	=	_____
V	=	_____
W	=	_____
X	=	_____
Y	=	_____
Z	=	sechsundzwanzig
Ä	=	siebenundzwanzig
Ö	=	achtundzwanzig
Ü	=	neunundzwanzig
ß	=	dreißig

Ein Schwein

Ein Kleeblatt

... bringt Glück.

Schreiben Sie die Buchstaben.

22   9   5   12   7   12   29   3   11

⌞_⌟ ⌞_⌟ ⌞_⌟ ⌞_⌟   ⌞_⌟ ⌞_⌟ ⌞_⌟ ⌞_⌟ ⌞_⌟ !

Viel Verkehr!

1 Uhren – Ordnen Sie zu.

Es ist halb zwölf.

a. ◯ Die Bahnhofsuhr zeigt zwölf Uhr einunddreißig.

b. ◯ Die Küchenuhr zeigt elf Uhr zwanzig.

c. ◯ Die Armbanduhr zeigt elf Uhr neunundzwanzig.

d. ◯ Die Taschenuhr zeigt drei Uhr.

e. ◯ Die Digitaluhr zeigt elf Uhr dreißig.

f. ◯ Die Kuckucksuhr zeigt ein Uhr.

2 Chris Bruckner fährt mit dem Taxi zur Firma Europartner

Frau Bruckner:	Bitte in die Potsdamer Straße Nummer 205.
Taxifahrer:	Heute ist viel Verkehr. Haben Sie es sehr eilig?
Frau Bruckner:	Ja, ich habe einen Termin um 10 Uhr.
Taxifahrer:	Kein Problem.
Frau Bruckner:	Wie weit ist es? Wie lange brauchen wir?
Taxifahrer.	Ungefähr 40 Minuten. Wir nehmen die Stadtautobahn.
Frau Bruckner:	Berlin hat viel Wasser. Man sieht viele Kanäle und Häfen.
Taxifahrer:	Wie in Venedig.
Frau Bruckner:	Fast.

Frau Bruckner:	... 78 34 ... Herr Heinrich? Bruckner hier. Ich komme leider eine Viertelstunde später. Der Verkehr .... Danke. Bis gleich.
Taxifahrer:	Tut mir leid. Morgens ist immer Stau.
Frau Bruckner:	In München auch: morgens, mittags, abends. Schrecklich!
	...
Taxifahrer:	Nummer 205? Da sind wir. 26 Euro, bitte.
Frau Bruckner:	Und bitte eine Quittung.

Übungen – und ein bisschen Grammatik

3 Wer hat das gesagt? Frau Bruckner oder der Taxifahrer? Markieren Sie.

a. Bitte in die Potsdamer Straße. ☐ ☐

b. Haben Sie es sehr eilig? ☐ ☐

c. Wie lange brauchen wir? ☐ ☐

d. Ich komme leider eine Viertelstunde später. ☐ ☐

e. Morgens ist immer Stau. ☐ ☐

f. Bitte eine Quittung. ☐ ☐

4 Ergänzen Sie.

> Verkehr / Straße / Nummer / Quittung / Viertelstunde / Termin /
> Minuten / Wasser / Stau / Euro

Frau Bruckner: Bitte in die Potsdamer _____ Nummer 205.

Taxifahrer: Heute ist viel _____. Haben Sie es sehr eilig?

Frau Bruckner: Ja, ich habe einen _____ um 10 Uhr.

Taxifahrer: Kein Problem.

Frau Bruckner: Wie weit ist es? Wie lange brauchen wir?

Taxifahrer: Ungefähr 40 _____. Wir nehmen die Stadtautobahn.

Frau Bruckner: Berlin hat viel _____. Man sieht viele Kanäle und Häfen.

Taxifahrer: Wie in Venedig.

Frau Bruckner: Fast.

Frau Bruckner: ... 78 34 ... Herr Heinrich? Bruckner hier. Ich komme leider eine
_____ später. Der Verkehr ... Danke. Bis gleich.

Taxifahrer: Tut mir leid. Morgens ist immer _____.

Frau Bruckner: In München auch: morgens, mittags, abends. Schrecklich!

Taxifahrer: _____ 205? Da sind wir. 26 _____, bitte.

Frau Bruckner: Und bitte eine _____.

5 Wie spät ist es?

a. ◯ Es ist 10 vor 10 (Uhr).   **c.** ◯ Es ist Viertel nach 10.

b. ◯ Es ist 10 nach 10 (Uhr).   **d.** ◯ Es ist halb elf.

6 Sprechübung
Sie nehmen jetzt ein Taxi. Hören Sie zuerst das Beispiel.
Antworten Sie, wir korrigieren.

Beispiel:

● Bitte in die Potsdamer Straße.

▶ Es ist viel Verkehr. Haben Sie es eilig?

● Ja, ich habe einen Termin um 10 Uhr.

1. Münchner Straße – 9 Uhr
2. Berliner Straße – 3 Uhr
3. Wiener Straße – 11 Uhr
4. Hamburger Straße – 1 Uhr

7 Ich möchte ...
Sie träumen von einer Reise. Sie sehen Fotos mit vielen Reisezielen.
Schreiben Sie: *Ich möchte nach XY fahren / fliegen.*

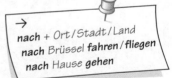

→
nach + Ort / Stadt / Land
nach Brüssel **fahren / fliegen**
nach Hause **gehen**

_____

_____

_____

Wien   Frankfurt   Rom   Paris   Athen   Sydney   Rio

Sie können die Übung auch noch mündlich machen. Antworten Sie ganz kurz.

Beispiel:

Wohin möchten Sie?   (Wien) → Nach Wien.

1. Wohin fahren Sie?   (Frankfurt)   **4.** Wohin fliegen Sie?   (Sydney)
2. Wohin fliegen Sie?   (Athen)   **5.** Wohin fahren Sie?   (Paris)
3. Wohin möchten Sie?   (Rom)   **6.** Wohin möchten Sie?   (Rio)

Wie weit ist das von Frankfurt?

10 Länder – 10 Hauptstädte

Notieren Sie die Hauptstädte.

| Athen | Lissabon | Stockholm |

| Bern | Brüssel | Madrid | Oslo |

| Wien | Warschau | Moskau |

Wie weit ist das von Frankfurt?

1.892 km	363 km
316 km	1.447 km
598 km	2.023 km
1.803 km	892 km
1.099 km	1.188 km

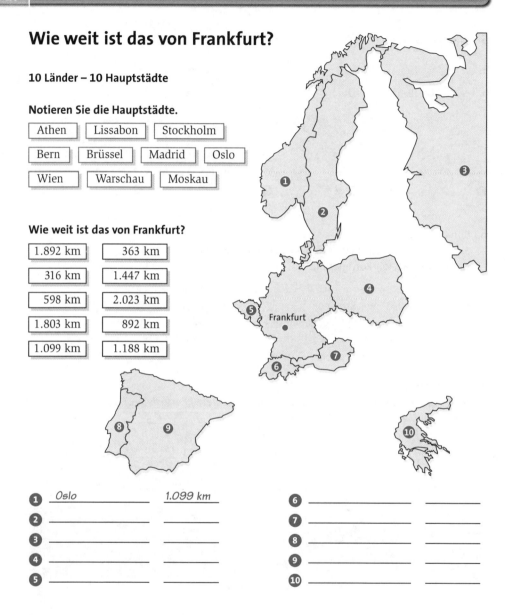

1   _Oslo_____   1.099 km
2   _____   _____
3   _____   _____
4   _____   _____
5   _____   _____

6   _____   _____
7   _____   _____
8   _____   _____
9   _____   _____
10 _____   _____

Ergänzen Sie.

Nach Moskau ist es _____ als nach Madrid.

Nach Madrid ist es weiter _____ nach O_____.

Nach Athen ist es _____ als nach B_____.

Die Firmenbesichtigung, Teil 1

1   Markieren Sie. Sagen Sie warum.

Fahren Sie gern	ja, sehr gern	nein, nicht so gern	nein, nicht gern
mit dem Auto?	☐	☐	☐
mit dem Zug?	☐	☐	☐
mit dem Bus?	☐	☐	☐
mit der S-Bahn?	☐	☐	☐
mit dem Taxi?	☐	☐	☐
Fliegen Sie gern?	☐	☐	☐

Warum? Warum nicht?

Auto fahren ..., Taxi fahren, Fliegen ...

ist (sehr) teuer / billig / geht schnell / dauert sehr lange / macht Spaß.

... ist sehr langsam / sehr gemütlich / praktisch ...

2   Eine Einladung zum Essen und eine Besichtigung

11A

Herr Heinrich:	Es ist 11 Uhr. Mein Vorschlag: Wir machen jetzt eine Firmenbesichtigung und um 12 Uhr gehen wir in die Kantine.
Herr Kühne:	Gut. Ich komme um 12 in die Kantine.
	Eine Frage, Frau Bruckner: Haben Sie heute Abend Zeit? Wir möchten Sie zum Essen einladen.

Frau Bruckner:	Gerne.
Herr Kühne:	Ist sieben Uhr in Ordnung?
Frau Bruckner:	Geht auch halb acht?
Herr Kühne:	Gut, um halb acht. – Wann fliegen Sie zurück?
Frau Bruckner:	Morgen. Das heißt, ich fahre mit dem Zug. Das sind nur sechseinhalb Stunden.

11B

Herr Heinrich:	So, hier ist also der Vertrieb: Die Geschäftsleitung und das Sekretariat sind hier geradeaus. Wir nehmen jetzt den Aufzug.
	Hier ist ... Oh, Entschuldigung, das ist der Keller ... Einen Moment ...
Frau Bruckner:	Und was gibt es im Keller?
Herr Heinrich:	Nur das Archiv.

Übungen – und ein bisschen Grammatik

3 **Ergänzen Sie den Text. Hier fehlen die Zeitangaben.**

> morgen / halb acht / sieben Uhr / um halb acht / heute Abend /
> um 12 / 11 Uhr / um 12 Uhr

Herr Heinrich: Es ist _____. Mein Vorschlag: Wir machen jetzt eine
Firmenbesichtigung und _____ gehen wir in die Kantine.

Herr Kühne: Gut. Ich komme _____ in die Kantine.
Eine Frage, Frau Bruckner: Haben Sie _____ Zeit?
Wir möchten Sie zum Essen einladen.

Frau Bruckner: Gerne.

Herr Kühne: Ist _____ in Ordnung?

Frau Bruckner: Geht auch _____?

Herr Kühne: Gut, _____. – Wann fliegen Sie zurück?

Frau Bruckner: _____. Das heißt, ich fahre mit dem Zug. Das sind nur 6 einhalb
Stunden.

4 **Was ist richtig? Markieren Sie.**

1. Wer isst um zwölf in der Kantine?
☐ Herr Heinrich und Frau Bruckner
☐ Herr Heinrich, Frau Bruckner und
Herr Kühne
☐ Frau Bruckner und Herr Kühne

2. Wer lädt ein?
☐ Herr Heinrich
☐ Frau Bruckner
☐ Herr Kühne

3. Was sagt Herr Kühne?
☐ Wir möchten Sie zum Essen einladen.
☐ Wir laden Sie zum Essen ein.
☐ Möchten Sie heute Abend essen?

4. Wann ist das Essen heute Abend?
☐ Um zwölf.
☐ Um acht.
☐ Um halb acht.

5. Wie fährt Frau Bruckner nach
München?
☐ Sie fliegt.
☐ Sie fährt mit dem Zug.
☐ Sie fährt mit dem Auto.

6. Wie lange fährt sie?
☐ Zehn Stunden.
☐ Sechseinhalb Stunden.
☐ Sechs Stunden.

5 Antworten Sie mit *Nein*.

Haben Sie ein Auto? *Nein, ich habe kein Auto* .

Haben Sie eine Firma? _____ .

Haben Sie einen Aufzug? _____ .

Haben Sie einen Keller? _____ .

Haben Sie ein Archiv? _____ .

Haben Sie ein Sekretariat? _____ .

einen – keinen
*Habt ihr **einen** Balkon?*
*Nein, wir haben **keinen** Balkon.*

6 Was passt nicht? Markieren Sie.

nehmen	☐ den Zug	☐ das Auto	☐ die Bahn	☐ den Aufzug	☐ den Vertrieb
möchten	☐ einen Salat	☐ ein Zimmer	☐ eine Serviette	☐ einen Tag	☐ einen Kaffee
haben	☐ einen Beruf	☐ ein Haus	☐ ein Hobby	☐ eine Frage	☐ einen Bahnhof
kennen	☐ das Wort	☐ die Stadt	☐ die Stunde	☐ die Hausnummer	☐ den Namen
mieten	☐ eine Wohnung	☐ ein Büro	☐ eine Straße	☐ ein Haus	☐ ein Zimmer

7 Üben Sie den Dialog wie im Beispiel. Hören Sie dann zu.

Beispiel:
● Hast du heute Abend Zeit?
▶ Ja, wann?
● Um 7 Uhr.

1. heute Abend / 18 Uhr
2. heute Abend / 8 Uhr
3. heute Abend / 20 Uhr
4. morgen / 15 Uhr

8 Notizen von Chris Bruckner

Ergänzen Sie: Uhr / halb / mit / wenig / mittags / Essen

Dienstag, 24.

Firma Europartner: 10 _____ bis 15 in der Firma, Gespräch _____ Herrn Kühne.

Wir haben nur _____ Zeit. 11 Uhr Firmenbesichtigung. _____ in der Kantine.

Einladung zum _____ heute Abend um _____ acht.

Buchstaben-Labyrinth

Der Weg ist das Ziel

Auf Sie wartet eine Überraschung. Starten Sie bei START. Suchen Sie den Weg ins Ziel.
Die Buchstaben ergeben zwei Sätze. Wie heißen die Sätze?
Viel Spaß!

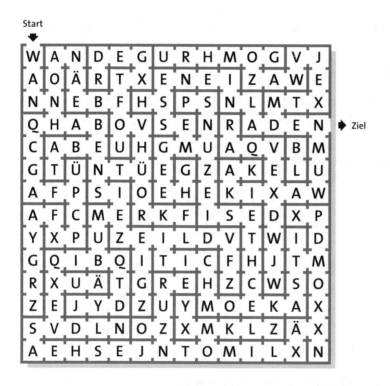

Start

Ziel

⌐ ⌐ ⌐ ⌐ ⌐ ⌐ ⌐ ⌐ ⌐ ⌐ ⌐ ⌐ ⌐ ⌐ ⌐ ⌐ ⌐ ⌐ ?

⌐ ⌐ ⌐ ⌐ ⌐ ⌐ ⌐ ⌐ ⌐ ⌐ ⌐ ⌐ ⌐ ⌐ ⌐ ⌐ ⌐ ⌐ ⌐

⌐ ⌐ ⌐ ⌐ ⌐ ⌐ ⌐ ⌐ ⌐ ⌐ ⌐ ⌐ ⌐ ⌐ .

Die Firmenbesichtigung, Teil 2

1 Was sehen Sie? Ordnen Sie zu.

○ der Empfang
○ die IT-Abteilung
○ die Buchhaltung
○ die Redaktion
○ das Lager
○ das Informationszentrum
○ die Kantine
○ der Konferenzraum

 ①
 ②
 ③
 ④
 ⑤
 ⑥
 ⑦
 ⑧

2 Links, rechts, geradeaus

geradeaus
links ⬅ ➡ rechts

12A

Herr Heinrich: Wir sind jetzt im Erdgeschoss. Hier links ist das Informationszentrum. Hier ist auch der Konferenzraum.

Frau Bruckner: Schön! Da macht die Arbeit Spaß.

Herr Heinrich: Den Empfang und die Redaktionen haben Sie schon gesehen.
Wir gehen nach rechts. Da ist die Buchhaltung und die IT-Abteilung.
Gegenüber ist das Controlling. Da geradeaus ist die Kantine.

Frau Bruckner: Und wo haben Sie das Lager?

Herr Heinrich: Das ist nicht hier. Hier ist kein Platz.

Frau Bruckner: Ich verstehe.

Herr Heinrich: Möchten Sie das Lager besichtigen? Das ist eine Viertelstunde zu Fuß.

Frau Bruckner: Nein, ich glaube nicht.

Herr Heinrich: Dann gehen wir in die Kantine. Da kommt schon Herr Kühne ... Wir gehen in Raum 1.

12B

Kantine Selbstbedienung		Gäste-Casino:	Raum 1
		Anmeldung:	Frau Gartner
Geöffnet von:	7.30 bis 9 Uhr		Telefon 366
	11.30 bis 14 Uhr	Kantinenleitung:	Telefon 365

Übungen – und ein bisschen Grammatik

3 **Wie ist die Reihenfolge? Hören Sie den Text und notieren Sie B bis F.**

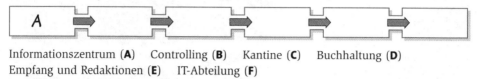

Informationszentrum (**A**)   Controlling (**B**)   Kantine (**C**)   Buchhaltung (**D**)
Empfang und Redaktionen (**E**)   IT-Abteilung (**F**)

4 **Das ist die Firma Europartner. Lesen Sie den Text und zeichnen Sie dann den Weg in die Skizze.**

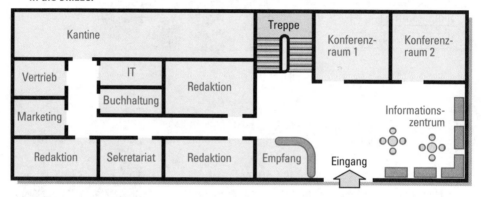

Hier ist der Empfang. Bitte nach **rechts**. Das ist das Informationszentrum und das sind die Konferenzräume. Bitte in Raum Nummer 1.

Wir gehen jetzt zurück. Das ist wieder der Empfang. Dann haben wir **links** und **rechts** die Redaktionen. **Links** sitzt Frau Bäumler. „Guten Tag, Frau Bäumler!" Frau Bäumler macht die Zeitschrift „Märkte". Wir gehen nach rechts. Dann kommt **links** die Marketing-Abteilung und der Vertrieb. Rechts sind Buchhaltung und die IT-Abteilung. **Geradeaus** kommen wir in die Kantine.

5 **Frau Bruckner erzählt Herrn Kühne, was sie alles gesehen hat. Schreiben Sie die richtige Form: *haben* oder *sind*, *habe* oder *bin*.**

Wir _____ den Vertrieb gesehen.

Dann _____ wir den Aufzug genommen.

Wir _____ plötzlich in den Keller gefahren.

Dann _____ ich das Erdgeschoss besichtigt.

Das Lager _____ ich nicht gesehen.

Um 12 _____ wir in die Kantine gegangen.

6 Ordnen Sie zu.

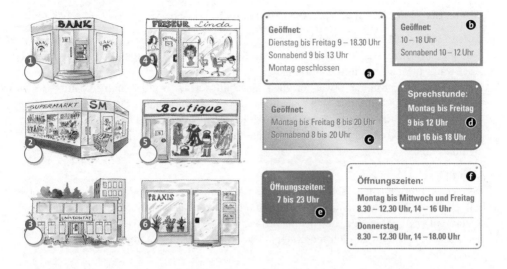

7 Sprechübung. Was möchten Sie alles sehen? Hören Sie zuerst das Beispiel.
    Antworten Sie dann.

Beispiel:

Was möchten Sie gern sehen?   (die Redaktion) → *Ich möchte die Redaktion sehen.*

1. Was möchten Sie besichtigen?   (das Brandenburger Tor)
2. Was möchten Sie sehen?   (die Kanäle)
3. Was möchten Sie besichtigen?   (die Stadt)
4. Was möchten Sie besichtigen?   (den Reichstag)
5. Was möchten Sie kennenlernen?   (die Firma)
6. Was möchten Sie sehen?   (das Informationszentrum)

8 Schreiben Sie die Wochentage in den Kalender.

Samstag / Sonnabend / Sonntag / Donnerstag / Dienstag / Freitag / Mittwoch

K A L E N D E R	7 ▪
4 ▪ *Montag*	8 ▪
5 ▪	9 ▪
6 ▪	10 ▪

Kleine Tipps

Was mache ich da? Was sage ich? **Lesen Sie den Text.**

Guten Tag und Auf Wiedersehen

Man gibt sich meistens die Hand, wenn man *Guten Tag* sagt oder auch *Auf Wiedersehen*. Aber wann tut man das und wann nicht?

Hände schütteln ist immer etwas förmlich. Geschäftspartner begrüßt man so. Gute Freunde oder Kollegen sehen sich täglich, sie tun es natürlich nicht. Sie sagen *Hallo, Guten Tag* oder *Grüß Gott* im Süden, oft auch mit dem Namen, und das ist es.

Bei Festen und Geburtstagen werden auch Freunde und Kollegen förmlich und schütteln sich die Hand.

Mahlzeit

Mittags im Büro hört man sehr oft den Gruß *Mahlzeit*. Man sagt *Mahlzeit* und antwortet mit *Mahlzeit*. Dann geht man in die Kantine oder isst etwas im Büro. Zu Hause oder im Restaurant sagt man es nie, nur bei der Arbeit.

Viele sagen, der Gruß ist nicht besonders elegant. Sie sagen extra immer nur *Guten Tag* oder *Hallo*.

Hilfe! Ich komme zu spät!

In Deutschland ist Pünktlichkeit wichtig. Wer im Geschäftsleben sehr unpünktlich ist, macht einen schlechten Eindruck. Aber manchmal passiert es doch. Dann können Sie anrufen und sagen: *Ich komme leider eine halbe Stunde später* oder Sie entschuldigen sich mit dem Satz: *Tut mir leid, dass ich zu spät komme.*

Haben Sie alles verstanden? Die Übersetzung finden Sie im Arbeitsbuch.

Was ist richtig?

1. ☐ Man schüttelt sich immer die Hand.
   ☐ Gute Freunde schütteln sich die Hand.
   ☐ Man schüttelt sich die Hand bei Geburtstagen und Festen.
   ☐ Geschäftspartner schütteln sich die Hand.

2. ☐ Der Gruß *Mahlzeit* ist „in".
   ☐ Mittags kann man *Mahlzeit* sagen.
   ☐ *Mahlzeit* sagt man nur im Restaurant und zu Hause.
   ☐ *Mahlzeit* sagt man nur mittags bei der Arbeit.
   ☐ Der Gruß *Mahlzeit* ist hässlich, sagen viele.

3. ☐ Pünktlichkeit ist in Deutschland wichtig.
   ☐ Man sagt: Tut mir leid, dass ich zu spät komme.
   ☐ Man sagt: Ich komme zu spät.
   ☐ Man sagt: Ich komme leider ein paar Minuten zu spät.

Das Frühstück

1 Ordnen Sie zu.

das Brötchen

die Butter

das Brot

der Tee

das Ei

der Teller

die Tasse

die Marmelade

das Messer

der Löffel

die Gabel

der Käse

das Obst

die Serviette

Hören Sie zu und sprechen Sie nach.

2 Es gibt Frühstück

Claudia: Hast du gut geschlafen, Robert?

Robert: Ja, sehr gut. Wie spät ist es denn?

Claudia: Acht Uhr. Niki ist schon weg. Es gibt gleich Frühstück.
Was möchtest du? Müsli, Brötchen oder Brot, Kaffee oder Tee?

Robert: Keinen Tee, ich mag lieber Kaffee.
Und dann ein Brötchen mit Butter und Marmelade.

Claudia: Eier sind auch da. Magst du ein Ei?

Robert: Ja, gern. Sag mal, Claudia, deine Eltern, wo wohnen die eigentlich?

Claudia: Ganz in der Nähe. Übrigens, meine Schwester ist da. Sie ist gestern aus Sidney gekommen. Sie hat dort ein paar Monate gearbeitet.

Robert: So? Was ist sie denn von Beruf?

Claudia: Regisseurin.

Robert: Interessant!

Claudia: Mein Bruder Ralf geht noch zur Schule. Er wohnt natürlich zu Hause.
Wir besuchen heute meine Eltern. Was meinst du?

Robert: Super, dann lerne ich endlich deine Geschwister kennen.

Übungen – und ein bisschen Grammatik

3 Ergänzen Sie.

Magst du lieber Brot oder ein Br_____?

Wer isst Mü_____? Robert, du?

Isst du Marmelade? – Nein, bitte nur Brot und Bu_____.

Ich brauche einen L_____.

Brauchst du noch einen T_____?

Wo ist mein M_____ und meine G_____?

Hier sind Eier. Magst du ein _____?

Nein, _____ esse ich nicht, aber du isst bestimmt zwei.

4 Schreiben Sie das richtige Wort.

Claudia: Hast du gut _____ (gearbeitet / geschlafen / gegessen), Robert?

Robert: Ja, sehr gut. Wie _____ (früh / spät / eilig) ist es denn?

Claudia: Acht Uhr. Niki ist schon _____ (weg / da / aus). Es gibt _____ (später / um 11 / gleich) Frühstück. Was möchtest du? Müsli, Brötchen oder _____ (Butter / Brot / Marmelade), Kaffee oder Tee?

Robert: Keinen Tee, ich mag lieber Kaffee. Und dann ein Brötchen mit Butter und Marmelade.

Claudia: Eier sind auch da. _____ (Magst / Möchten / Kennst) du ein Ei?

Robert: Ja, gern.

5 Ergänzen Sie.

_____ du jetzt frühstücken? (möchten)

Was _____ du trinken? (möchten)

Ich _____ heute kein Frühstück. (mögen)

Ich _____ keine Eier. (mögen)

Ich _____ morgens kein Brot. (mögen)

Ich _____ heute in der Stadt frühstücken. (möchten)

Kommst du mit?

mögen
Ich **mag** Kaffee.
Magst du lieber Tee?
Möchtest du noch einen Tee?

6 Ergänzen Sie.

Ralf, das ist _____ Bruder.

Wie heißt _____ Schwester?

_____ Schwester heißt Katrin.

Und wie heißen _____ Geschwister?

Wo wohnen _____ Eltern?

_____ Eltern wohnen ganz in der Nähe.

> *mein* und *dein*
> *mein / dein* Bruder
> *meine / deine* Schwester
> *meine / deine* Eltern

7 Sprechübung
   Was mögen Sie lieber?
   Hören Sie die Frage. Lesen Sie dann die Stichwörter und antworten Sie.
   Das Bild gibt die Antwort.

Beispiel:
Was mögen Sie lieber? Kaffee oder Tee?   → *Ich mag lieber Kaffee.*

Was mögen Sie lieber?

    Kaffee oder Tee?   Zucker oder Milch?

    Brot oder Brötchen?   Butter oder keine Butter?

    Müsli oder Brot?   Zucker oder keinen Zucker?

8 Das Tagebuch von Robert. Hier fehlen ein paar wichtige Wörter.

> früh / Mittag / Geschwister / Eltern / Frühstück

Mittwoch, 25.

Bei Claudia und Niki: Ich habe heute sehr _____ gefrühstückt. Niki habe ich

nicht gesehen. Claudia hat _____ gemacht.

Heute _____ besuchen wir die _____ und _____ von Claudia.

Wörtersalat

Suchen Sie die Wörter. Wir haben 7 Oberbegriffe. Notieren Sie auch den Artikel.

Frühling	Restaurant	Schule	Tasse	Tourist	Taxifahrer	Zentrum	Zug
Tante	Onkel	Sohn	Mädchen	Aufzug	Junge	Australien	Bahnhof
verheiratet	Großeltern	Bad	Wohnzimmer	Freitag	Sonnabend	Balkon	
Spanien	Zimmer	Auto	Milch	Bahn	Regisseur	Donnerstag	Tee
Sommer	Sonntag	Korea	Montag	Polen	Italien	Japan	Eltern	Vater
Europa	Mutter	Asien	Tochter	Deutschland	Wochenende	Mittwoch	
Dienstag	Käse	Flughafen	Hafen	Hausfrau	Haltestelle	Hausmann	
Flur	Kaffee	Maurer	Marmelade	Maler	Opa	Oma	Arzt

Länder und Kontinente:

Familie:

Jahr, Jahreszeit, Woche und Tag:

Essen und Trinken:

Berufe:

Wohnung:

Stadt:

Wir besuchen meine Familie

1 Hören Sie, was Claudia erzählt.
Schreiben Sie die Namen in die Skizze.

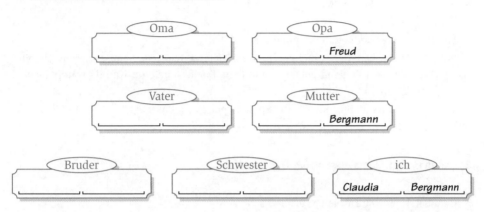

Oma

Opa
Freud

Vater

Mutter
Bergmann

Bruder

Schwester

ich
Claudia   Bergmann

2 Die Familie

Claudia: Hallo, Katrin, lange nicht gesehen.

Katrin: Hallo, Claudia.
Du bist sicher Robert. Claudia hat
schon viel von dir erzählt.

Robert: So? Wirklich?

Claudia: Tag, Mama, Tag, Papa. Das ist
Robert.

Vater: Wie gefällt Ihnen Berlin, Robert?

Robert: Sehr gut.

Vater: Und woher kennen Sie Claudia
und Niki?

Robert: Das war in der Sprachenschule in England. Ich hatte Semesterferien. Da bin
ich nach England gefahren und habe Englisch gelernt. Und da waren auch
Claudia und Niki.

Vater: Und jetzt sprechen Sie die Sprache perfekt, nicht wahr?

Robert: Nicht perfekt, aber nicht schlecht.

Mutter: Kinder, ihr habt bestimmt Hunger. Ich habe dein Lieblingsessen gekocht,
Claudia.

Robert: Was ist denn dein Lieblingsessen?

Claudia: Das siehst du gleich.

Übungen – und ein bisschen Grammatik

3 Wie ist die Reihenfolge?

1 Vater: Wie gefällt Ihnen Berlin, Robert?

Robert: Sehr gut.

Vater: Woher kennen Sie Claudia und Niki?

Robert: Das war in der Sprachenschule in England. Ich hatte Semesterferien. Da bin ich nach England gefahren und habe Englisch gelernt. Und da waren auch Claudia und Niki.

Vater: Und jetzt sprechen Sie die Sprache perfekt, nicht wahr?

Robert: Nicht perfekt, aber nicht schlecht.

2 Claudia: Tag, Mama, Tag, Papa. Das ist Robert.

3 Claudia: Hallo, Katrin, lange nicht gesehen.

Katrin Hallo, Claudia.

Du bist sicher Robert. Claudia hat schon viel von dir erzählt.

Robert: So? Wirklich?

4 Mutter: Kinder, ihr habt bestimmt Hunger. Ich habe dein Lieblingsessen gekocht, Claudia.

Robert: Was ist denn dein Lieblingsessen?

Claudia: Das siehst du gleich.

Reihenfolge:

⌐ ⌐ ⌐ ⌐

4 Ergänzen Sie.

Wir _____ in England.

Das _____ in der Sprachenschule.

Wir _____ Semesterferien.

Niki und Claudia _____ auch da.

Wie _____ das Wetter in England?

_____ ihr Glück?

hatte – war

ich habe – ich **hatte**

ich bin – ich **war**

5 **Was ist richtig? Markieren Sie.**

1. ☐ Katrin ist die Schwester
von Claudia.

☐ Sie hat in Amerika
gearbeitet.

☐ Sie ist Regisseurin.

2. ☐ Robert kennt Katrin.

☐ Robert hat Katrin in
England kennengelernt.

☐ Robert findet eine
Regisseurin interessant.

3. ☐ Robert spricht perfekt Englisch.

☐ Robert spricht gut Englisch, aber nicht perfekt.

☐ Robert lernt Englisch.

4. ☐ Robert, Claudia und Niki waren in England.

☐ Sie waren in einer Sprachenschule.

☐ Sie haben Englisch gelernt.

5. ☐ Claudias Mutter hat gekocht.

☐ Sie hat ein Abendessen gemacht.

☐ Sie möchte noch kochen.

6 **Wir haben fünf Personen. Wer hat was gesagt?**

a. ◯ Tag, Mama, Tag, Papa.

b. ◯ Wie gefällt Ihnen Berlin?

c. ◯ Ihr habt bestimmt Hunger.

d. ◯ Das war in der Sprachenschule in England.

e. ◯ Du bist sicher Robert. Claudia hat schon viel von dir erzählt.

① ② ③ ④ ⑤

7 **Sprechübung**
Lesen Sie zuerst das Beispiel und die Stichwörter.
Hören Sie dann die Frage und antworten Sie.

Beispiel:

● Wo warst du denn in den Semesterferien?

▶ (Frankreich – Französisch) → *Ich war in Frankreich und habe Französisch gelernt.*

1. England – Englisch
2. Italien – Italienisch
3. Spanien – Spanisch
4. Holland – Holländisch
5. Deutschland – Deutsch

Q	S	W	B	U	Z	M	I	P	Ü
S	P	R	U	L	M	I	Z	O	V
K	A	R	T	O	F	F	E	L	N
W	R	M	T	L	K	N	B	Z	T
Y	G	I	E	Z	I	P	Ü	M	X
W	E	V	R	E	Z	U	A	V	G
H	L	J	K	A	D	L	K	N	C

8 **Buchstabensalat**

Suchen Sie das Lieblingsessen von Claudia. _____ mit _____ und _____

Das mögen wir!

Hier sind sechs Zeichnungen. Ordnen Sie die sechs Texte den richtigen Zeichnungen zu.

a. ◯ Deine Lieblingsfilme kommen aus Frankreich, nicht wahr?

b. ◯ Ich nehme den Spargel mit Butter und Kartoffeln.

c. ◯ Dortmunder Bier ist mein Lieblingsbier. – So? Und das Bier aus Bayern?

d. ◯ Sie ist meine Lieblingsschwester.

e. ◯ Ist das dein Lieblingsrestaurant?

f. ◯ Wie heißt die Stadt? Sie hat einen Hafen. Das Wetter ist oft schlecht. Die Leute sind nett und freundlich.

Eine Mail von Robert

1 Ordnen Sie die Berufe zu.
Was ist er oder sie von Beruf?

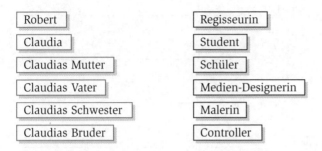

Robert	Regisseurin
Claudia	Student
Claudias Mutter	Schüler
Claudias Vater	Medien-Designerin
Claudias Schwester	Malerin
Claudias Bruder	Controller

2 Robert schreibt eine E-Mail an seinen Freund Jonas

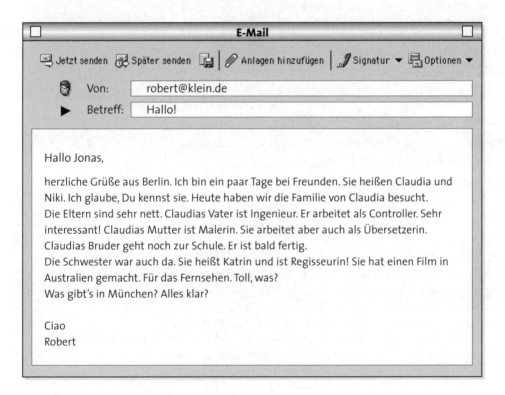

```
╔══════════════════════ E-Mail ══════════════════════╗

🖳 Jetzt senden  🖳 Später senden  🖳  ∅ Anlagen hinzufügen  |  ✐ Signatur ▼  🖳 Optionen ▼

   🖳   Von:      robert@klein.de
   ▶   Betreff:  Hallo!
```

Hallo Jonas,

herzliche Grüße aus Berlin. Ich bin ein paar Tage bei Freunden. Sie heißen Claudia und
Niki. Ich glaube, Du kennst sie. Heute haben wir die Familie von Claudia besucht.
Die Eltern sind sehr nett. Claudias Vater ist Ingenieur. Er arbeitet als Controller. Sehr
interessant! Claudias Mutter ist Malerin. Sie arbeitet aber auch als Übersetzerin.
Claudias Bruder geht noch zur Schule. Er ist bald fertig.
Die Schwester war auch da. Sie heißt Katrin und ist Regisseurin! Sie hat einen Film in
Australien gemacht. Für das Fernsehen. Toll, was?
Was gibt's in München? Alles klar?

Ciao
Robert

Übungen – und ein bisschen Grammatik

3   Beantworten Sie die Fragen.

1. Wo war Robert?

| war | bei | Claudias Eltern. | Er | _____

2. Was ist Claudias Vater von Beruf?

| Er | Ingenieur. | ist | _____

3. Was ist Claudias Mutter von Beruf?

| Malerin. | Sie | ist | _____

4. Was macht Claudias Bruder?

| Er | zur Schule. | geht | noch | _____

5. Wie heißt Claudias Schwester?

| Katrin. | Sie | heißt | _____

6. Wie findet Robert Claudias Schwester?

| sie | interessant. | Er | findet | _____

4   Claudias Familie

Wer ist Jan?	– Das ist _____ Bruder.
Wer ist Katrin?	– Das ist _____ .
Wer ist Beatrice Bergmann?	– _____ .
Wer ist Helmut Freund?	– _____ .
Wer ist Thomas Bergmann?	– _____ .
Wer ist Robert Klein?	– _____ Freund.

> Claudias Eltern
> = die Eltern von Claudia

5   Robert erzählt. Unterstreichen Sie die richtige Form.

Wir *sind/waren* bei Claudias Eltern. Die Eltern *sind/waren* sehr nett. Claudias Vater *ist/war* Ingenieur. Er arbeitet als Controller. Sehr interessant! Claudias Mutter *ist/war* Malerin. Sie arbeitet aber auch als Übersetzerin.
Claudias Bruder geht noch zur Schule. Er *ist/war* bald fertig.
Die Schwester *ist/war* auch da. Sie heißt Katrin und *ist/war* Regisseurin! Sie hat einen Film in Australien gemacht. Für das Fernsehen. Das finde ich toll.

6 Sprechübung – Lesen Sie zuerst die Stichwörter.
Hören Sie die Frage und antworten Sie wie im Beispiel. Sie hören dann die Antwort
von der CD.

Beispiel:
● Was sind Sie von Beruf?
▶ (Ingenieur / Ingenieurin) → Ich bin Ingenieur. / Ich bin Ingenieurin.

1. Lehrer / Lehrerin
2. Designer / Designerin
3. Arzt / Ärztin

4. Student / Studentin
5. Was ist Ihr Beruf?

7 Sprechübung
Antworten Sie wie im Beispiel. Hören Sie dann die Antwort von der CD.

Beispiel:
● Was sind Sie von Beruf?
▶ (Maler / Übersetzer) → Ich bin Maler / Malerin, aber ich arbeite
als Übersetzer / Übersetzerin.

1. Lehrer / Verkäufer
2. Ingenieur / Lehrer
3. Lehrer / Controller

4. Student / Übersetzer
5. Techniker / Taxifahrer

8 *Ich schreibe eine Mail.*
Schreiben Sie eine Mail nach Hause. Setzen Sie die E-Mail aus den Textbausteinen
zusammen.

Lieber … (Anton), Liebe … (Anna, Eltern), Hallo …,

herzliche Grüße aus … viele Grüße aus …

Ich bin noch im Hotel …,
aber ich habe bald eine Wohnung.
Ich habe jetzt eine Wohnung.
Ich habe jetzt eine Wohnung gefunden.

Sie ist klein, aber sehr gemütlich.
Sie ist klein und kostet nicht viel.
Sie ist groß und kostet ziemlich viel.
Sie ist sehr klein, aber das reicht.
Sie gefällt mir gut / sehr gut.

Liebe Grüße / Herzliche Grüße

Euer … (Martin, Philipp …) / Eure … (Martina, Laura …)

Berufe

Wie heißen die Berufe? Notieren Sie auch die männliche bzw. die weibliche Form.

er	fahr	Geschäfts	stein	feger	Haus
frau	mann	Mau	Fri	Schorn	Taxi
Ärzt	in	rer	Leh	Stu	Ver
rer	käufer	sör	dent	Poli	tiker

männlich – weiblich _____

männlich – weiblich _____

_____

_____

_____

_____

_____

_____

_____

_____

_____

_____

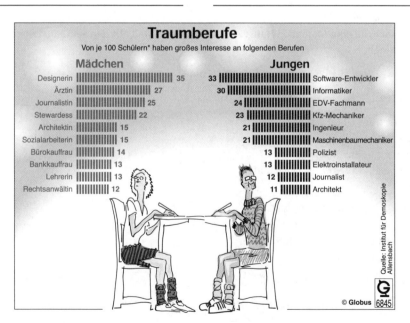

Traumberufe

Von je 100 Schülern* haben großes Interesse an folgenden Berufen

Mädchen		Jungen	
Designerin	35	33	Software-Entwickler
Ärztin	27	30	Informatiker
Journalistin	25	24	EDV-Fachmann
Stewardess	22	23	Kfz-Mechaniker
Architektin	15	21	Ingenieur
Sozialarbeiterin	15	21	Maschinenbaumechaniker
Bürokauffrau	14	13	Polizist
Bankkauffrau	13	13	Elektroinstallateur
Lehrerin	13	12	Journalist
Rechtsanwältin	12	11	Architekt

Quelle: Institut für Demoskopie Allensbach

© Globus 6845

16

In der Kantine

1 Welcher Beruf ist ein Internet-Beruf? Ergänzen Sie *ein* oder *kein*.

❶ Das ist _____ Internet-Beruf.

❷ Das ist _____ Internet-Beruf.

❸ Das ist _____ Internet-Beruf.

❹ Das ist _____ Internet-Beruf.

❺ Das ist _____ Internet-Beruf.

❻ Das ist _____ Internet-Beruf.

① der Service-Techniker ② der Taxifahrer ③ der Medien-Designer ④ die Informatikerin ⑤ der Verkäufer ⑥ der Internet-Redakteur

2 Gespräch in der Kantine

Herr Kühne:	Kommen Sie. Unser Tisch ist dahinten. Bitte nehmen Sie Platz.
Frau Müller:	Wer bekommt den Fisch? Und wer hat den Gemüseteller?
Herr Heinrich:	Frau Bruckner, Sie haben den Fisch bestellt, nicht wahr? Danke, Frau Müller.
Frau Bruckner:	Wie viele Mitarbeiter haben Sie hier?
Herr Kühne:	Im Moment sind wir 55. Hier im Haus und im Lager zusammen. Und Sie?

Frau Bruckner: Sie wissen ja, unsere Firma ist klein. Wir sind sechs Leute. Wir geben viel nach außen.

Herr Kühne: Das tun wir auch. Wir suchen aber trotzdem Leute. Unsere Internet-Abteilung wächst. Unsere Homepage ist neu. Seit Februar haben wir zwei Internet-Redakteurinnen. Einen Service-Techniker brauchen wir auch.

Frau Bruckner: Ihre Homepage gefällt mir sehr gut. Sie ist informativ und immer aktuell.

Herr Kühne: Das ist auch wichtig. Qualität und Schnelligkeit machen den Unterschied.

Frau Bruckner: Und der Preis.

Übungen – und ein bisschen Grammatik

3 **Was ist richtig? Markieren Sie.**

1. Chris Bruckner, Herr Kühne und Herr Heinrich essen
☐ im Restaurant.
☐ im Gäste-Casino.
☐ zu Hause.

2. Chris Bruckner
☐ mag gern Fisch.
☐ isst nur Gemüse.
☐ hat keinen Hunger.

3. Die Firma von Herrn Kühne
☐ ist sehr groß.
☐ hat 55 Mitarbeiter.
☐ hat auch ein Lager.

4. Die Firma braucht noch
☐ einen Service-Techniker.
☐ Internet-Redakteurinnen.
☐ sechs Leute.

5. Die Homepage ist
☐ neu.
☐ informativ.
☐ aktuell.

4 **Wer sagt was?**
Lesen Sie zuerst die Sätze.
Hören Sie dann und markieren Sie.

> ein Tisch – **unser/Ihr** Tisch
> eine Firma – **unsere/Ihre** Firma
> ein Lager – **unser/Ihr** Lager

a. Sie haben den Fisch bestellt, nicht wahr?	☐	☐	☐
b. Im Moment haben wir 55 Mitarbeiter.	☐	☐	☐
c. Das sind auch die Mitarbeiter im Lager.	☐	☐	☐
d. Unsere Firma ist klein.	☐	☐	☐
e. Wir sind nur sechs Leute.	☐	☐	☐
f. Ihre Homepage gefällt mir sehr gut.	☐	☐	☐
g. Wir suchen Leute.	☐	☐	☐
h. Die Internet-Abteilung wächst noch.	☐	☐	☐
i. Wir brauchen einen Service-Techniker.	☐	☐	☐
j. Ihre Homepage ist sehr informativ.	☐	☐	☐
k. Qualität und Schnelligkeit sind wichtig.	☐	☐	☐
l. Und der Preis.	☐	☐	☐

5 **Hier fehlen ein paar Wörter. Ergänzen Sie.**

Leute / Internet-Abteilung / Mitarbeiter / Service-Techniker / Firma

Frau Bruckner: Wie viele _____ haben Sie hier?

Herr Kühne:　　 Im Moment sind wir 55. Hier im Haus und im Lager zusammen. Und Sie?

Frau Bruckner: Sie wissen ja, unsere _____ ist klein. Wir sind sechs Leute.

　　　　　　　　Wir geben viel nach außen.

Herr Kühne:　　 Das tun wir auch. Wir suchen aber trotzdem _____. Unsere

　　　　　　　　_____ wächst. Unsere Homepage ist neu. Seit Februar

　　　　　　　　haben wir zwei Internet- Redakteurinnen. Einen _____

　　　　　　　　brauchen wir auch.

6 **Sprechübung**
   Hören Sie, was der Manager sagt.
   Ihre Firma ist klein. Lesen Sie die Stichwörter und antworten Sie.

Beispiel:
Unsere Firma ist sehr groß.　　　　　　　(sehr klein) → *Unsere Firma ist sehr klein.*

1. Sie hat 1000 Mitarbeiter.　　　　　　　(nur 5 Mitarbeiter)
2. Unsere Firma arbeitet in Europa und Asien. (sein, nur Stuttgart)
3. Wir brauchen noch Mitarbeiter.　　　　　(auch)
4. Wir haben viele Lager.　　　　　　　　　(kein Lager)
5. Der Vertrieb hat fast 100 Mitarbeiter.　　(1 Mitarbeiter, machen, Vertrieb)
6. Unsere Firma wächst um 10 %.　　　　　(20 %)

7 **Notizen von Chris Bruckner**

Ergänzen Sie: Mittag / Gespräche / 55 Mitarbeiter / Leute / Abteilung / Techniker

Mittwoch, 25.

Firma Europartner: Heute _____ in der Kantine mit Herrn Kühne und Herrn

Heinrich gegessen. Gute _____. Die Firma hat _____ (Haus + Lager).

Firma sucht _____. Internet-_____ wächst. Zwei neue Internet-

Redakteurinnen. Service-_____ gesucht.

Würste

Ordnen Sie zu.

a. ◯ Original Frankfurter

b. ◯ Thüringer Bratwurst

c. ◯ Bayerische Weißwürste

d. ◯ Bremer Grünkohl mit Pinkel

Wo isst man die Würste?
Notieren Sie die Stadt oder das Bundesland.
Sie finden die Lösung im Namen der Wurst.

Original Frankfurter:

F _____

Thüringer Bratwurst:

T _____

Bayerische Weißwürste:

B _____

Bremer Grünkohl mit Pinkel:

B _____

Im Supermarkt

1 Wie heißen die Getränke? Ordnen Sie zu.

○ der Wein
○ das Bier
○ das Mineralwasser
○ der Sekt
○ die Milch
○ der Orangensaft
○ der Apfelsaft

Hören Sie dann und sprechen Sie nach.

2 Claudia und Robert im Supermarkt

Claudia: Robert, komm! Nimm einen Wagen. Wir
          kaufen zuerst die Getränke.

Robert: Was brauchen wir denn? … Saft, Wasser …
          Wein oder Bier?

Claudia: 3 Flaschen Mineralwasser. Trinkst du Saft?

Robert: Ja, ich mag Schorle, Apfelschorle. Also drei
          Flaschen Apfelsaft.

Claudia: Nicht so viel. Der bleibt nur übrig. Nimm
          auch Orangensaft. Wie teuer ist der Wein?
          Das ist Wein aus Franken.

Robert: 4 Euro. Der ist aber gut. Da bin ich Spezialist.

Claudia: Gut, nimm zwei Flaschen. Da hinten links sind
          die Salate. Da bekommen wir auch Brötchen, Käse und Wurst.
          Wie viel Wurst brauchen wir? Isst du gern Wurst?

Robert: Ja. Nimm 200 Gramm. Das ist genug. – Brauchen wir Obst?

Claudia: Natürlich: Weintrauben und Kirschen.

Robert: Claudia, was ist los? Warum bleibst du stehen?

Claudia: Ich habe was vergessen. Kartoffeln und Zwiebeln.

Robert: Bleib hier! Ich gehe schnell. 1 Kilo Kartoffeln und 1 Pfund Zwiebeln?

Claudia: Ja, genau.

Übungen – und ein bisschen Grammatik

3 Ergänzen Sie.

> Pfund / Kilo / Gramm / – / Flasche / Pfund / Liter / – / Flaschen / – / Gramm

10	_____	Brötchen
3	K_____	Kartoffeln
100	_____	Käse
200	_____	Wurst
1	F_____	Wein
1	P_____	Weintrauben
1	L_____	Milch
1	P_____	Kirschen
2	F_____	Orangensaft
3	_____	Salate

kg = das Kilo(gramm)
g = das Gramm
Pf. = das Pfund
l = der Liter
Stück (das)
*   (1 Stück Kuchen)*
die Flasche, die Flaschen

4 Was wächst in Deutschland?
Wir sind auf dem Markt. Schauen Sie sich das Obst an. Was kommt aus Deutschland, was aus dem Ausland? Notieren Sie, was in Deutschland wächst.

5 Was gehört wohin? Ordnen Sie ein.

> Bananen / Tomaten / Bier / Kartoffeln / Milch / Äpfel / Kirschen / Kaffee /
> Pfirsiche / Ananas / Tee / Orangen / Weintrauben / Paprika / Wein

Obst: _____ , _____ , _____ , _____

Südfrüchte: _____ , _____ , _____

Gemüse: _____ , _____ , _____

Getränke: _____ , _____ , _____ , _____ , _____

6 Was antworten die Gäste?
Auf einer Party kommen viele Leute zusammen. Lesen Sie die Fragen und markieren
Sie die passende Antwort. Hören Sie dann zu und antworten Sie.

1. Trinken Sie Wein?
☐ Ja, gern. Danke.
☐ Warum?
☐ Nein danke, ich trinke kein Bier.

3. Wer trinkt Saft?
☐ Ja, bitte.
☐ Kein Sekt, nur Orangensaft.
☐ Kein Alkohol, bitte.

2. Mögen Sie lieber Bier?
☐ Nein, nein, kein Wasser.
☐ Ja, Bier trinke ich lieber.
☐ Ja, ich habe Durst.

4. Trinkst du eine Apfelschorle?
☐ Ich esse jetzt nichts.
☐ Das ist Mineralwasser.
☐ Was ist das, Apfelschorle?

7 Im Supermarkt – Antworten Sie.
Sie sind im Supermarkt. Ihr Freund / Ihre Freundin
fragt, Sie antworten.
Bringen Sie die Satzteile in die richtige Reihenfolge.

holen   **Hol** doch den Wein!
kaufen   **Kauf** doch den Wein!
nehmen   **Nimm** doch den Wein!

1. Magst du Fisch?
Ja, | Fisch. | den | nimm doch   _____

2. Isst du Wurst?
Ja, | Wurst. | 200 Gramm | kauf doch   _____

3. Trinkst du Orangensaft?
Nein, | lieber | nimm doch | Mineralwasser.   _____

4. Magst du Salate?
Nein, | und | Brot | kauf lieber | Käse.   _____

5. Nehmen wir Kuchen oder Eis?
Kauf doch | Stück | fünf | Kuchen.   _____

Wie finden Sie das?

Es geht immer ums Essen und Trinken. Hören Sie zu und notieren Sie das passende Bild.

1. • Wie finden Sie das Restaurant?   Bild ◯
   ▸ Nicht schlecht. Das Essen schmeckt gut.

2. • Was gibt es heute?   Bild ◯
   ▸ Nichts. Ich habe nicht gekocht.
   • Was?

3. • Schmeckt Ihnen der Fisch in der Kantine?   Bild ◯
   ▸ Na ja, es geht. Der Gemüseteller ist besser.

4. • Nimm ein Pfund Kirschen! Die sind gut.   Bild ◯

5. • Essen Sie gern Fleisch?   Bild ◯
   ▸ Ich esse alles. Aber lieber esse ich Fisch.

6. • Sieh mal, der Sekt kostet hier fünf Euro.   Bild ◯
   ▸ Das ist Prosecco. Nimm zwei Flaschen!

Was ist mit Eis?

1 **Mixen Sie ein Getränk.**

Hier sind die Zutaten.

Mineralwasser   Apfelsaft   Bananen   Sekt oder Campari   Eis   Limonade

Wein + _____	(= Weinschorle)
Mineralwasser + _____	(= Apfelschorle)
Orangensaft + _____	
Milch + _____	
Kaffee + _____	
Bier + _____	(= Radler, Alsterwasser)

2 **Robert, Claudia und Katrin**

Robert: Sieh mal die Schlange!

Claudia: Nicht so schlimm. Das geht schnell.
Gib mal zwei Tüten. Danke!

Robert: Was ist mit Eis?

Claudia: Eis? Kauf drei Packungen.
Oder magst du lieber Kuchen?

Robert: Nein, nein, ich esse lieber Eis. Der Kuchen im Supermarkt schmeckt nicht.

Kasse: 35 Euro fünfzig. Haben Sie fünfzig Cent?

Claudia: Ja, bitte sehr.
…

Claudia: So, und jetzt fahren wir schnell nach Hause und dann in die Stadt.

Robert: Du, Claudia, hast du was dagegen?

Claudia: Was heißt das? … dagegen …?

Robert: Katrin möchte auch in die Stadt. Ich rufe sie jetzt an, dann treffen wir sie zu
Hause und dann fahren wir zusammen.

Claudia: So? Na gut, dann ruf gleich an. Nimm mal die Tüten, die sind so schwer.

Übungen – und ein bisschen Grammatik

3 Hier fehlen Informationen. Ergänzen Sie die Wörter.

Kuchen / Eis / Cent / dagegen / zusammen / Euro

Robert:	Sieh mal, die Schlange!
Claudia:	Nicht so schlimm. Das geht schnell. Gib mal zwei Tüten. Danke!
Robert:	Was ist mit _____?
Claudia:	Eis? Kauf drei Packungen. Oder magst du lieber _____?
Robert:	Nein, nein, ich esse lieber Eis. Der Kuchen im Supermarkt schmeckt nicht.
Kasse:	35 _____ fünfzig. Haben Sie fünfzig _____?
Claudia:	Ja, bitte sehr.
	...
Claudia:	So, und jetzt fahren wir schnell nach Hause und dann in die Stadt.
Robert:	Du, Claudia, hast du was _____?
Claudia:	Was heißt das? ... dagegen ...?
Robert:	Katrin möchte auch in die Stadt. Ich rufe sie jetzt an, dann treffen wir sie zu Hause und dann fahren wir _____.
Claudia:	So? Na gut, dann ruf gleich an. Nimm mal die Tüten, die sind so schwer.

Hören Sie jetzt den Text noch einmal und vergleichen Sie.

4 Wer ist wer? Hören Sie zuerst zwei Dialoge.
Wer spricht in Dialog 1 und wer in Dialog 2? Wie sehen die Leute wohl aus?
Markieren Sie.

Dialog 1	☐	☐	☐	☐
Dialog 2	☐	☐	☐	☐

5   2 Wörter oder 1 Wort – Präsens oder Perfekt

1. Ich _____ Kerstin morgen _____.

2. Hast du Sigi schon _____?

3. Warum _____ du Frau Sommer nicht _____?

4. Ich habe sie schon _____.

5. _____ du Martin an?

6. Wann _____ du Sandra _____?

anrufen
ich rufe an
ich habe angerufen

Ruf an!
Ruf doch an!
Bitte rufen Sie an!

6   Ruf an! Schreiben Sie die Imperative.

bitte	anrufen	Sie	Frau Schmidt	_____
doch	anrufen	Petra		_____
doch	anrufen	deine Schwester		_____
bitte	anrufen	die Firma Seiblitz		_____
bitte	anrufen	zu Hause		_____
doch	anrufen	David		_____

7   Sprechübung
Hören Sie zu und antworten Sie mit den Stichwörtern.

1. Was machst du heute noch?   (nach Hause fahren)
2. Und dann?   (dann – Benedikt anrufen)
3. Was ist mit Benedikt?   (möchten – ihn treffen)
4. Was macht ihr dann?   (wir – in die Stadt fahren)
5. Kann ich mitkommen?   (natürlich – du kannst mitkommen)
6. Wann treffen wir uns?   (um 7 – bei mir)

8   Mein Bruder Alex
Erzählen Sie eine Geschichte. Wir geben Ihnen die Stichwörter. 5 bis 6 Sätze genügen.

Bruder	Griechenland	5 Jahre	leben
sprechen	Griechisch	sehr gut	fast perfekt
haben	Haus	viele Zimmer	Garten	Blumen	Hafen
Maler	von Beruf

Mögen Sie Obst?

1. Hören und lesen Sie die beiden Dialoge. Welcher gefällt Ihnen besser?

Dialog A

- ● Mögen Sie Obst?
- ▶ Ja, sehr.
- ● Was mögen Sie besonders?
- ▶ Ich esse gern Weintrauben.
- ● Haben Sie einen Garten?
- ▶ Nein, wir haben leider keinen Garten.
  Aber meine Eltern haben einen Garten.
- ● Und was wächst dort?
- ▶ Ich glaube, sie haben Äpfel und Kirschen.
- ● Aber keine Weintrauben, oder?
- ▶ Leider nicht.

☐ Mir gefällt Dialog A besser.
☐ Mir gefällt Dialog B besser.

Dialog B

- ● Mögen Sie Obst?
- ▶ Nein, nicht so sehr.
- ● Und warum?
- ▶ Ich weiß nicht. Obst schmeckt mir nicht.
- ● Und was ist mit Säften, zum Beispiel Apfelsaft?
- ▶ Apfelsaft mag ich. Säfte finde ich nicht schlecht.
- ● Und was essen Sie gern?
- ▶ Käse, Spaghetti, Eis ...
- ● Aha, Sie essen also gern italienisch.
- ▶ Ja, das stimmt. Und ich trinke gern Wein aus Italien.

2. Was ist richtig? Was ist falsch? Kreuzen Sie an.

	richtig	falsch
1. Die Frau in Dialog A isst gern Obst.	☐	☐
2. Sie hat einen Garten.	☐	☐
3. Die Eltern haben Obstbäume.	☐	☐
4. Sie haben aber keine Weintrauben.	☐	☐
5. Der Mann in Dialog B isst auch gern Obst.	☐	☐
6. Er trinkt auch gern Säfte.	☐	☐
7. Er isst gern Italienisch.	☐	☐
8. Er mag aber keine Spaghetti.	☐	☐

3. Sprechen Sie jetzt Ihren Text nach.

19

Wo bist du denn?

1 Ordnen Sie zu. Die Vokabeln finden Sie im Leitfaden.

a. ◯ am Fluss entlang

b. ◯ über die Brücke

c. ◯ zur Bank

d. ◯ zum Bahnhof

e. ◯ am Sportplatz vorbei

f. ◯ an der Ampel

2 Robert telefoniert mit Katrin

Robert: Hallo, Katrin, wir fahren jetzt in die Stadt. Kommst du mit?

Katrin: Ja, wo bist du denn?

Robert: Na, bei Claudia zu Hause.

Katrin: Ich war noch nicht bei ihr. Die Adresse habe ich aber.

Robert: Ich erkläre dir den Weg. Das ist ganz einfach und nicht weit.

Katrin: Okay. Ich komme mit dem Auto. Schieß los!

Robert: Du fährst in Richtung Stadt. Circa fünf Kilometer. Dann kommt eine Kreuzung mit Ampel. Da fährst du nach rechts. Das ist die Oranienburger Straße.

Katrin: Was hast du gesagt? Nach links in die Oranienburger …?

Robert: Nein, nein, nach rechts. Entschuldigung, links, du hast recht. Dann wieder circa drei Kilometer, da ist ein Platz. Du fährst um den Platz herum und geradeaus weiter. Dann fährst du die dritte Straße nach links. Das Haus Nummer 14 ist dann gleich rechts. Wir sind hier im dritten Stock. Das ist eine Dachwohnung. Das weißt du ja.

Katrin: Prima. Ich habe alles notiert. Ich fahre sofort los. Bis gleich.

Robert: Bis gleich.

Übungen – und ein bisschen Grammatik

3 **Welche Sätze sind nicht richtig? Markieren Sie, was nicht stimmt.**

☐ Robert ruft Katrin an.

☐ Er möchte mit Katrin und Claudia
   in die Stadt fahren.

☐ Katrin ist bei Claudia zu Hause.

☐ Robert erklärt ihr den Weg.

☐ Sie kommt mit dem Auto.

☐ Es ist sehr weit.

☐ Katrin notiert alles.

☐ Dann fährt sie sofort los.

4 **Suchen Sie 7 Wörter.
   Die Wörter sind Orte und Ziele in der Stadt.
   Lesen Sie zuerst die Wegbeschreibung im
   Leitfaden Nr. 13.**

	1	2	3	4	5	6	7	8	9
1	E	N	U	O	B	A	N	K	T
2	U	D	S	C	H	L	O	S	S
3	E	D	O	G	Q	X	Y	B	N
4	U	P	K	I	R	C	H	E	G
5	U	K	Ä	N	P	L	A	T	Z
6	Ö	S	C	H	U	L	E	E	T
7	F	L	U	S	S	S	T	G	B
8	S	I	K	C	Ü	P	O	S	T

5 **Notieren Sie 7 Buchstaben aus dem Rätsel Übung 4.
   Wie heißt das Lösungswort?**

Reihe: | 5 | 1 | 6 | 4 | 5 | 6 | 8 |
Buchstabe: | 5 | 4 | 6 | 4 | 9 | 7 | 2 |

Lösungswort: ⎵ ⎵ ⎵ ⎵ ⎵ ⎵ ⎵

6 **Hören Sie zu. Zwei Kollegen sprechen über einen Wochenendausflug
   in eine kleine Stadt. Gehen Sie den Weg.**

> **von** der Autobahn
> **(nach)** rechts / links – geradeaus
> **an** der Kirche **(vorbei)**
> **(bis) zum** Museum / **zur** Kirche
> **über** die Brücke

7 Sprechübung
   Die Leute fragen Sie. Sie kennen die Wege genau. Hören Sie die Frage. Lesen Sie die Stichwörter und antworten Sie mit den Stichwörtern.

Beispiel:
Bitte, wo ist hier eine Bank?   (gehen, hier, links, dann, geradeaus, da, sehen, die Bank) → *Gehen Sie hier links, dann geradeaus. Da sehen Sie die Bank.*

1. Bitte, wo ist der Bahnhof?   (gehen, über die Brücke, rechts, geradeaus, kommen, zum Bahnhof)

2. Entschuldigung, wo fährt hier der Bus Nummer 3?   (sehen, Bushaltestelle, da links? da, fahren, der Bus Nummer 3)

3. Wann fährt der Bus ab?   (3 Uhr 40)

4. Kennen Sie hier ein Schnellrestaurant?   (Tut mir leid, hier, gibt es, kein)

5. Wie weit ist es zur Post?   (gehen, am Hotel vorbei, gleich rechts)

6. Wie komme ich zum Museum?   (fahren, über die Brücke, an der Kirche vorbei, dann, kommen, direkt zum Museum)

8 **Wie ist die Reihenfolge? Schreiben Sie den Text.**

Niki heißt Bat mit Familiennamen.
Aber er möchte die Sprache gern lernen.
Die Eltern sind 1980 nach Deutschland gekommen. Jetzt haben sie ein chinesisches Restaurant.
Das ist das Restaurant in der Hafenstraße. Das Essen dort ist sehr gut, sagt man.
Er wohnt und arbeitet in Berlin und ist auch hier geboren.
Deshalb ist nur der Familienname Chinesisch, nicht der Vorname. Er spricht auch kein Chinesisch.

9 Roberts Tagebuch
   Markieren Sie die Perfektformen.

Mittwoch, 24.

Ich habe Katrin angerufen. Sie kommt gleich. Sie hat die Adresse, war aber noch nie hier. Ich habe ihr alles genau erklärt. Jetzt warte ich. Sie hat gesagt, sie fährt sofort los! Das war um eins. Sie ist bestimmt gleich da. Dann fahren wir in die Stadt.

Mit dem Taxi zur Firma Holz

Sie sind jetzt ein Taxifahrer und haben einen Gast im Auto. Sie fahren und er sagt Ihnen
den Weg.
Hören Sie zu und fahren Sie den Weg auf der Karte.
Lesen Sie zur Kontrolle den Text.

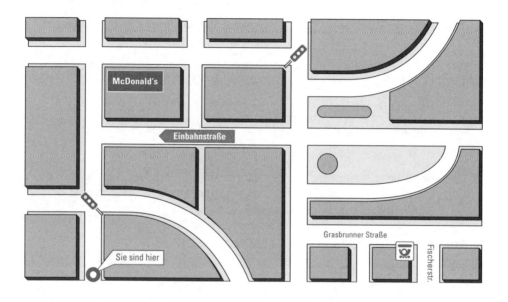

Sie fahren jetzt immer geradeaus. Weiter geradeaus.
Jetzt kommt rechts ein McDonald's. Da fahren Sie nach rechts.
Jetzt wieder immer geradeaus. Ungefähr fünf Kilometer bis zur Ampel.
So, ... an der Ampel fahren Sie wieder rechts. Die vierte Straße dann bitte links. Das ist die Grasbrunner Straße.
Und wieder geradeaus. Bis zur zweiten Straße rechts. Da ist ein Briefkasten. Und das ist die Fischerstraße 4.

Im Restaurant, Teil 1

1 **Das Bildwörterbuch**
Bild plus Wort: Machen Sie Ordnung und schreiben Sie die passenden Wörter.

❶ _____

❷ _____

❸ _____

❹ _____

❺ _____

❻ _____

❼ _____

das Kaufhaus, ⸚er	der Stadtplan, ⸚e
der Pullover, –	die Tasche, -n
die Postkarte, -n	der Schirm, -e	das Sandwich, -es

2 **Im Restaurant direkt an der Spree**

Frau Bruckner:	Schön ist es hier! Direkt an der Spree.
Herr Heinrich (zum Ober):	Die Karte, bitte!
Ober:	Was möchten Sie trinken?
Herr Kühne:	Was trinken Sie? Ich nehme zuerst ein Bier.
Frau Bruckner:	Ja, ich auch.
Herr Heinrich:	Bitte drei Bier.
	...

Ober:	Möchten Sie jetzt bestellen?
Frau Bruckner:	Ja, bitte einen Salat und die Gemüsepfanne.
Herr Kühne:	Ich nehme den Zander ... und auch einen Salat.
Herr Heinrich:	Ich esse die Tomatensuppe und eine Rindsroulade.
Herr Kühne:	Wie schmeckt Ihnen das Bier in Berlin?
Frau Bruckner:	Gut. Es ist nicht sehr stark. Zu Hause trinken wir gern ein Glas Wein.
Herr Kühne:	Keine Maß Bier?
Frau Bruckner:	Doch, die trinken wir im Sommer im Biergarten. Am liebsten abends nach der Arbeit.
Herr Heinrich:	Ja ja, die Münchner Biergärten sind berühmt.

Übungen – und ein bisschen Grammatik

3 **Hier fehlen wichtige Wörter. Ergänzen Sie. Suchen Sie die passenden Wörter.**

> Kartoffeln / Karte / Biergarten / Brot / Zander / Salat / Apfelsaft /
> Gemüsepfanne / Rindsroulade / Fisch / Bier / Glas Wein / Tomatensuppe

Frau Bruckner:	Schön ist es hier! Dirckt an der Spree.
Herr Heinrich (zum Ober):	Die _____ bitte!
Ober:	Was möchten Sie trinken?
Herr Kühne:	Was trinken Sie? Ich nehme zuerst ein _____.
Frau Bruckner:	Ja, ich auch.
Herr Heinrich:	Bitte drei Bier.
	...
Ober:	Möchten Sie jetzt bestellen?
Frau Bruckner:	Ja, bitte einen _____ und die _____.
Herr Kühne:	Ich nehme den _____ ... und auch einen Salat.
Herr Heinrich:	Ich esse die _____ und eine _____.
Herr Kühne:	Wie schmeckt Ihnen das Bier in Berlin?
Frau Bruckner:	Gut. Es ist nicht sehr stark. Zu Hause trinken wir gern ein _____.
Herr Kühne:	Keine Maß Bier?
Frau Bruckner:	Doch, die trinken wir im Sommer im _____. Am liebsten abends nach der Arbeit.
Herr Heinrich:	Ja ja, die Münchner Biergärten sind berühmt.

Hören Sie dann den Text zur Kontrolle noch einmal.

4 **Ergänzen Sie den Artikel und den Plural.**

_____	Speisekarte	die	*Speisekarten*
_____	Brot	die	_____
_____	Suppe	die	_____
_____	Saft	die	_____
_____	Kartoffel	die	_____
_____	Biergarten	die	_____

5 Das Kaufhaus – Hören Sie die Dialoge. Ordnen Sie zu.

6 Sie arbeiten in einem Kaufhaus und beantworten täglich viele Fragen.
Hören Sie die Fragen und antworten Sie wie im Beispiel.

Beispiel:
Wo gibt es Getränke? (Untergeschoss.)
→ *Die gibt es im Untergeschoss.*

1. Entschuldigen Sie, wo gibt es hier Taschen? (3. Stock)
2. Ich brauche einen Stadtplan. (4. Stock)
3. Wo finde ich hier Pullover? (1. Stock)
4. Guten Tag, ich möchte eine Postkarte kaufen. (Erdgeschoss)
5. Bitte, wo gibt es hier Schirme? (2. Stock)
6. Wir haben Hunger. Gibt es hier Sandwiches? (Untergeschoss)

7 Schreiben Sie die Antwort mit *doch*.
Lesen Sie zuerst das Beispiel.

> *Essen Sie kein Obst? – Nein, nicht so gern.*
> *Essen Sie kein Obst? – Doch, natürlich.*

Beispiel:
● Essen Sie kein Eis? (gerne) ▶ Doch, ich esse gerne Eis.
● Essen Sie keinen Fisch? (gerne) ▶ Doch, _____
● Haben Sie keine Zeit? (viel) ▶ _____.
● Gehen Sie nicht nach Hause? (sofort) ▶ _____.
● Haben Sie keine Arbeit? (viel) ▶ _____.
● Schmeckt Ihnen das Essen nicht? (gut) ▶ _____.
● Haben Sie keine Hobbys? (viele) ▶ _____.

Wo isst man das?

Was isst man gern in Norddeutschland und was in Süddeutschland, in Österreich und der Schweiz?

Süddeutschland   Österreich   Schweiz   Norddeutschland

Ordnen Sie das Land bzw. die Region der Spezialität zu.

- Scholle mit Bratkartoffeln isst man in _____.
  (Eine Scholle ist ein Fisch.)

- Schweinebraten mit Kartoffelknödel isst man in _____.

- Marillenknödel isst man in _____.
  (Marillen = Aprikosen)

- Zürcher Geschnetzeltes mit Rösti isst man in der _____.

Die Speisekarte

1 Kartoffelgerichte
Was ist das? Was meinen Sie? Notieren Sie den richtigen Buchstaben.

a. ◯ Pellkartoffeln
b. ◯ Kartoffelknödl
c. ◯ Rösti
d. ◯ Salzkartoffeln
e. ◯ Bratkartoffeln
f. ◯ Kartoffelsuppe

2 Essen im Zug
Sie sitzen im Zug und möchten etwas essen. Lesen Sie die Speisekarte.
Die Übersetzung finden Sie im Leitfaden.

Guten Appetit!

Blumenkohlsuppe	
Brot oder Brötchen	3,50 €
Kartoffelsuppeneintopf	
mit Eisbeinfleisch	
Brot oder Brötchen	7,50 €

Salat & Co.

Verschiedene frische Blattsalate	
mit Tomate, Gurke und Streifen	
von der Hühnchenbrust	8,60 €
Frischer gemischter Salat	
mit Thunfisch und	
Zwiebelringen	6,90 €

Snacks & Speisen

Räucherlachs mit Rührei	
und Salatbouquet	
Butter, Brot oder Brötchen	7,60 €
Gebackene Kartoffel	
mit Sauerrahm	
und Salatgarnitur	5,00 €
Penne mit Tomatensoße	7,60 €
Asiatische Reispfanne	
mit Gemüse und Schweinefleisch	8,60 €
Kuchen	
Auf Wunsch mit Sahne	2,45 €

Übungen – und ein bisschen Grammatik

3 **Hören Sie zu und notieren Sie die Preise.**
Hier sitzen zwei Personen in einem Zugrestaurant. Es gibt nur eine Speisekarte.

Blumenkohlsuppe: _____ €   Räucherlachs mit Rührei: _____ €

Kartoffelsuppeneintopf: _____ €   Gebackene Kartoffel: _____ €

Blattsalate mit Hühnchenbrust: _____ €   Penne: _____ €

Gemischter Salat mit Thunfisch: _____ €   Asiatische Reispfanne: _____ €

4 **Was isst man kalt? Markieren Sie.**

der Salat ☐

das Frühstück ☐

die Brotzeit ☐

der Kuchen ☐

das Schweinefleisch ☐

der Reis ☐

der Eintopf ☐

die Suppe ☐

5 **Sprechübung**
Antworten Sie wie im Beispiel.

Beispiel:
• Was ist Zander?   (Fisch) → *Das ist Fisch.*

1. Was ist Räucherlachs?   (Fisch)
2. Was ist Eisbein?   (Schweinefleisch)
3. Was ist Eintopf?   (Suppe mit Gemüse)
4. Was ist Hähnchen?   (Geflügel)
5. Was ist eine Gurke?   (Gemüse)

6 Das ist Ihr Menü. Was passt zusammen? Schreiben Sie die Wörter.

Sahne / Kartoffelklößen / Thunfisch / Brötchen / Milch / Butter und Marmelade

Rindsroulade mit _____   Brötchen mit _____

Kuchen mit _____   Tomatensuppe mit _____

Salat mit _____   Kaffee mit _____

7 Sprechübung
Sie möchten bestellen. Hören Sie zuerst zu und antworten Sie dann mit den Stichwörtern.

Beispiel:
● Was möchten Sie bestellen?
▶ (nehmen/ein Mineralwasser) → *Ich nehme ein Mineralwasser.*

1. (nehmen/die Tomatensuppe)   **4.** (trinken/ein Glas Wein)
2. (trinken/ein Bier)   **5.** (nehmen/der Zander)
3. (essen/ein Salat)   **6.** (essen/ein Fisch)

8 Nomen + Nomen
Was passt zusammen? Schreiben Sie die Wörter.

fisch / brust / fleisch / suppe / salate / pfanne

die Kartoffel + *der* Eintopf
= *der* Kartoffeleintopf

Tomaten_____   Schweine_____

Reis_____   Thun_____

Blatt_____   Hühnchen_____

9 Notieren Sie die beiden Nomen mit Artikel.

	Nomen 1		Nomen 2
die Telefonnummer	_____	+	_____
das Kantinenessen	_____	+	_____
der Konferenzraum	_____	+	_____
der Taxifahrer	_____	+	_____
der Gemüseteller	_____	+	_____
das Gartenrestaurant	_____	+	_____

Im Kaufhaus

Wer sagt was? Markieren Sie.

	Kunde/Kundin	Verkäufer/Verkäuferin
1. Entschuldigung, wo finde ich hier Schirme?	☐	☐
2. Bitte, wo gibt es hier Kaffee?	☐	☐
3. Kann ich Ihnen helfen?	☐	☐
4. Entschuldigung, können Sie mir helfen?	☐	☐
5. Vielen Dank.	☐	☐
6. Nichts zu danken.	☐	☐
7. Gibt es hier ein Restaurant?	☐	☐
8. Wo finde ich hier Kugelschreiber?	☐	☐
9. Ich suche Videokassetten.	☐	☐
10. Wie bitte?	☐	☐

Wo finden Sie das? Ordnen Sie zu.

Lampen

Schirme

Kaffee

Restaurant

Kugelschreiber

PC-Spiele

4 Bettwaren / Bettwäsche
Teppiche / Bilder / Lampen

3 Elektrogeräte / Multimedia / Foto
TV / DVD & Audio / Computer / Games

2 Kinderkonfektion / Baby-Wäsche
Schuhe / Sportbekleidung / Sportgeräte
Fahrräder / Camping
Reisebüro

1 Damenbekleidung / Damenwäsche / Bademoden
Herrenbekleidung / Herrenwäsche

EG Information / Lederwaren / Schreibwaren
Bücher / Zeitungen / Zeitschriften / Tabak
Schirme / Handschuhe / Strümpfe
Uhren / Schmuck

UG Restaurant / Lebensmittel / Kosmetik / Spielwaren

Was habt ihr heute gemacht?

1 Das Zentrum von Berlin. Sie sehen vier wichtige Sehenswürdigkeiten.

Brandenburger Tor   Schloss Bellevue   Potsdamer Platz   Bundeskanzleramt

Ergänzen Sie die Sätze.

Das _____ _____ ist das Wahrzeichen von Berlin.

Im _____ wohnt und arbeitet der Bundeskanzler.

Im _____ _____ ist der Bundespräsident zu Hause.

Der _____ _____ ist der modernste und schönste Platz in Berlin.

2 Claudia und Robert erzählen

Niki: Erzählt mal! Was habt ihr heute gemacht? Ihr habt mich gar nicht angerufen.

Claudia: Entschuldige, aber … Also: Wir sind ins Zentrum gefahren. Am Brandenburger Tor haben wir geparkt und sind dann gelaufen.

Robert: Zuerst zum Reichstag. Die Kuppel ist großartig. Die hat mir sehr gefallen. Das Gebäude ist alt, aber die Kuppel ist ganz modern. Im Westen sieht man das Kanzleramt und dahinter das Schloss Bellevue.

Niki: Da wohnt der Bundespräsident.

Robert: Genau. Dann sind wir durch den Tiergarten gelaufen. Und von da zum Potsdamer Platz.

Claudia: Die Restaurants waren sehr voll. Aber unter dem Dach sitzt man sehr schön. Wir haben da einen Aperitif getrunken.

Robert: Dann waren wir Unter den Linden und sind zur Humboldt-Universität gelaufen.

Claudia: Auf der Straße stehen im Augenblick Bären-Plastiken. Bestimmt zwanzig Bären. Die Bären sind ganz bunt, rot, blau oder grün. Das sieht lustig aus. Ein Bär steht sogar auf dem Kopf.

Robert: Und was machen wir morgen?

Übungen – und ein bisschen Grammatik

3 Hier fehlen wichtige Verben. Ergänzen Sie.

> gemacht / geparkt / gefallen / angerufen / gestanden / gelaufen /
> gesehen / ausgesehen / gefahren

Was habt ihr _____?

Ihr habt nicht _____.

Wir sind ins Zentrum _____.

Am Brandenburger Tor haben wir _____.

Wir sind zuerst zum Reichstag _____.

Die Kuppel hat mir sehr _____.

Unter den Linden haben wir die Bären-Plastiken _____.

Die haben sehr lustig _____.

Wir haben dort lange _____.

> *laufen – ich bin **ge**laufen*
> *st**e**hen – ich habe dort **ge**standen*
> ***an**rufen – ich habe dich **an**gerufen*

4 Sie sind zum ersten Mal in Berlin und möchten die Stadt besichtigen. Dann können Sie diese Sätze bestimmt gut gebrauchen. Ergänzen Sie.

Wie k_ _ _ _ _ _ wir in die Stadt? Fahren wir mit dem Auto oder mit der S-Bahn?

Wohin f_ _ _ _ _ _ wir zuerst?

Wir fahren zuerst ins Zentrum und p_ _ _ _ _ _ dort.

Dann m_ _ _ _ _ _ wir eine Stadtrundfahrt.

Oder möchtest du lieber zu Fuß g_ _ _ _ _ ?

Wir l_ _ _ _ _ _ zuerst zum Reichstag, dann zum Potsdamer Platz.

Mittags m_ _ _ _ _ _ wir eine Pause.

Am Nachmittag g_ _ _ _ _ wir zur Humboldt-Universität.

Ich m_ _ _ _ _ _ die Bären-Plastiken sehen. Sie s_ _ _ _ _ _ alle auf der

Allee *Unter den Linden*.

Und 8 Uhr s_ _ _ _ wir wieder zu Hause.

5 Sie lesen das Wort *rot*. Was haben Sie vor Augen?
Schreiben Sie die Wörter hinter die Farbe.

| Schnee | Gewitter | Ärger | Zitrone | Himmel | Baby | Feuer | Papier |

| Baum | Wald | Wein | Schokolade | Augen | Angst | Milch | Kaffee |

rot: _____   rosa: _____

blau: _____   schwarz: _____

grün: _____   weiß: _____

gelb: _____   braun: _____

6 Landesfarben – Ergänzen Sie.

Die Landesfarben von Deutschland sind _____, _____ und _____.

Die Landesfarben von Österreich sind _____ und _____.

Die Schweiz hat ein weißes Kreuz auf Rot.

| Gold | Schwarz | Weiß | Rot |

7 *Schöner* und *besser* – Schreiben und hören Sie. Was passt?

Rot gefällt mir _____ als Grün.

Am _____ gefällt mir Blau.

Alfons trinkt _____ Schokolade.

Am _____ trinken alle Cola.

Die Wohnung ist schön, aber die

Dachwohnung ist noch _____.

Am _____ ist natürlich ein Haus.

schön – schöner (als) – *am schönsten*
gern – *lieber (als)* – *am liebsten*
gut – *besser (als)* – *am besten*

8 Was haben Sie heute gemacht? Schreiben Sie die Sätze richtig.

| in die Firma | Wir | gefahren | sind | _____

| haben | bis 12 | Wir | gearbeitet | _____

| Dann | wir | in die Kantine | sind | gegangen | _____

| Fisch | Wir | haben | gegessen | _____

| habe | Ich | die Firma | besichtigt | _____

| habe | Ich | gesehen | viele Abteilungen | _____

Rund ums Auto

Claudia und Robert waren mit dem Auto in der Stadt.
Hier sind wichtige Vokabeln rund ums Auto.

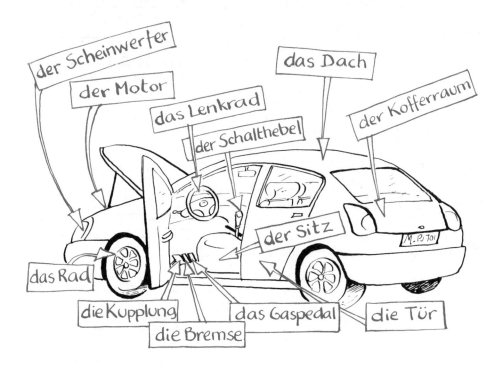

Was gibt es nicht nur ein Mal? Schreiben Sie die Wörter mit Plural.

_____

_____

_____

_____

_____

Im Restaurant, Teil 2

1 **Haben Sie Urlaubspläne? Hier ist unser Fragebogen.**

Machen Sie bald Urlaub? ☐ Ja. ☐ Nein. ☐ Weiß nicht.

1. Wenn *ja*:

a. Wann machen Sie Urlaub?
☐ Im Sommer.
☐ Im Winter.
☐ Im Sommer und im Winter.

c. Möchten Sie
☐ ganz weit weg?
☐ nicht so weit weg?
☐ zu Hause bleiben?

b. Was mögen Sie am liebsten?
☐ Eine Stadt besichtigen.
☐ Ins Gebirge fahren.
☐ Ans Meer fahren.

d. Wohin möchten Sie fahren?
☐ In die Tropen.
☐ Ans Mittelmeer.
☐ Nach Deutschland, Österreich oder in die Schweiz.

2. Ihre Antwort ist *Nein*: Machen Sie die Übung in einem Jahr noch einmal.

3. Ihre Antwort ist *Weiß nicht*: Machen Sie zuerst Lektion 23 fertig. Beantworten Sie
dann die Fragen noch einmal.

2 **Smalltalk im Restaurant**

Herr Kühne: Was macht der Urlaub?

Frau Bruckner: Wir gehen immer im August in Urlaub.
Da ist das Geschäft sehr ruhig.

Herr Heinrich: Haben Sie schon ein Ziel?

Frau Bruckner: Ja, wir bleiben zu Hause. Das heißt in
Deutschland. Wir fahren zwei Tage an
den Bodensee, dann ein Wochenende
nach Dresden und ein paar Tage an
die Ostsee.

Herr Kühne: Im August ist das Wetter meistens schön.

Frau Bruckner: In Dresden war ich zum Beispiel noch nie. Dort gibt es so viel zu
besichtigen. Und Sie, was machen Sie?

Herr Kühne: Wir machen immer im Winter Urlaub. Da hat man zwei Möglichkeiten.
Entweder wir fahren in die Berge oder wir fahren weit weg. Ich treibe
viel Sport: Ski fahren, Rad fahren – auch mit dem Mountainbike –,
Fußball spielen, schwimmen, alles. Auch Motorrad fahren.

Frau Bruckner: Das finde ich zu gefährlich. Da gehe ich lieber spazieren. Was meinen
Sie, Herr Heinrich?

Herr Heinrich: Sie haben recht. Sport ist ungesund. Am liebsten lese ich oder ich
faulenze. ... Da kommt unser Espresso. ... Bitte zahlen. Zusammen.

Übungen – und ein bisschen Grammatik

3 **Hören Sie den Text noch einmal. Notieren Sie die richtige Reihenfolge.**

A Frau Bruckner: Das finde ich zu gefährlich. Da gehe ich lieber spazieren. Was meinen Sie, Herr Heinrich?

Herr Heinrich: Sie haben recht. Sport ist ungesund. Am liebsten lese ich oder ich faulenze.

B Herr Heinrich: Da kommt unser Espresso.
Bitte zahlen. Zusammen.

C Frau Bruckner: Ja, wir bleiben zu Hause. Das heißt in Deutschland. Wir fahren zwei Tage an den Bodensee, dann ein Wochenende nach Dresden und ein paar Tage an die Ostsee.

Herr Kühne: Im August ist das Wetter meistens schön.

Frau Bruckner: In Dresden war ich zum Beispiel noch nie. Dort gibt es so viel zu besichtigen. Und Sie, was machen Sie?

D Herr Kühne: Wir machen immer im Winter Urlaub. Da hat man zwei Möglichkeiten. Entweder wir fahren in die Berge oder wir fahren weit weg. Ich treibe viel Sport: Ski fahren, Rad fahren – auch mit dem Mountainbike –, Fußball spielen, schwimmen, alles. Auch Motorrad fahren.

E Herr Kühne: Was macht der Urlaub?

Frau Bruckner: Wir gehen immer im August in Urlaub.   Reihenfolge:
Da ist das Geschäft sehr ruhig.

Herr Heinrich: Haben Sie schon ein Ziel?   ⌐⌐ ⌐⌐ ⌐⌐ ⌐⌐ ⌐⌐

4 **Man kann am Wochenende so viel machen. Ergänzen Sie die passenden Verben.**

> gehen / spielen / steigen / fahren / lesen / schwimmen

1. Wir _____ Boot.

2. Wir _____ auf einen Berg.

3. Wir _____ über den See.

4. Wir _____ ein Buch.

5. Wir _____ Fußball.

6. Wir _____ spazieren.

5 Sagen Sie Ihren Freunden, was Sie lieber tun. Hören Sie zuerst zu. Antworten Sie dann mit den Stichwörtern.

Beispiel: Wir essen gern Italienisch. (ich – Griechisch – essen) → *Ich esse lieber Griechisch.*

1. Wir gehen gern in die Berge.   (wir – an einen See – fahren)
2. Ich fahre gern Motorrad.   (ich – Fahrrad – fahren)
3. Wir spielen gern Fußball.   (wir – im Garten – arbeiten)
4. Ich schwimme gern.   (ich – spazieren – gehen)
5. Ich reise gern.   (ich – zu Hause – bleiben)
6. Wir gehen gern ins Restaurant.   (wir – zu Hause – essen)

6 Ihre Meinung ist uns wichtig. Leider gefällt Ihnen überhaupt nichts.
   Hören Sie zuerst die Frage. Antworten Sie dann mit dem Stichwort und *zu*.

Beispiel: Wie findest du den Wein?   (süß) → *Ich finde den Wein zu süß.*

1. Wie findest du die Suppe?   (kalt)
2. Wie findest du den Urlaub?   (kurz)
3. Wie findest du das Restaurant?   (teuer)
4. Wie findest du den See?   (kalt)
5. Wie findest du den Sport?   (gefährlich)
6. Wie findest du die Wohnung?   (klein)

Das Wasser ist **kalt**.
Das Wasser ist **zu kalt**.

7 Eine E-Mail. Schreiben Sie die Teile in der richtigen Reihenfolge ab.

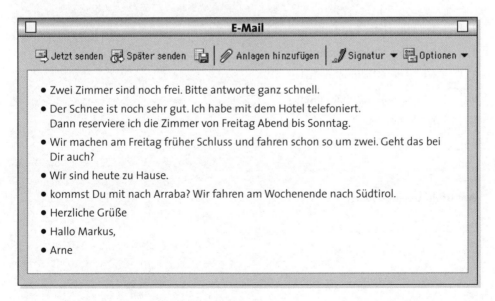

E-Mail
🖥 Jetzt senden 🖥 Später senden 🖥	📎 Anlagen hinzufügen	✏ Signatur ▾ 🖥 Optionen ▾

- Zwei Zimmer sind noch frei. Bitte antworte ganz schnell.
- Der Schnee ist noch sehr gut. Ich habe mit dem Hotel telefoniert.
  Dann reserviere ich die Zimmer von Freitag Abend bis Sonntag.
- Wir machen am Freitag früher Schluss und fahren schon so um zwei. Geht das bei Dir auch?
- Wir sind heute zu Hause.
- kommst Du mit nach Arraba? Wir fahren am Wochenende nach Südtirol.
- Herzliche Grüße
- Hallo Markus,
- Arne

Welchen Sport betreiben Ihre Freunde?

**Sie möchten wissen, welchen Sport Ihre Freunde und die Kinder betreiben.
Hören Sie zu. Ordnen Sie dann die Zeichnungen zu.**

1. ◯ Ich lerne jetzt Rad fahren.
2. ◯ Ich lerne Motorrad fahren.
3. ◯ Ich lerne schwimmen.
4. ◯ Ich lerne Motorboot fahren.
5. ◯ Ich lerne klettern.
6. ◯ Wir lernen Ski fahren.

Was ist Ihr Lieblingssport?

_____

Der Reiseprospekt

Zwei Kollegen, Julio und Walter, sitzen in der Kantine. Sie unterhalten sich über ein grammatisches Problem, aber auch über den Urlaub.

1 Lesen Sie zuerst ein paar Anzeigen in einem Reiseprospekt.

REISEMARKT

Ferien in der Schweiz? Herzlich willkommen!
Tessin
Bestellen Sie den neuen Katalog von Schweiz Tourismus.
Internet: www.MySwitzerland
Die ersten Besteller erhalten eine Flasche Schweizer Wein.
Endlich Ferien. Ihre Schweiz.
❶

Malediven
vom Spezialisten

Der neue Katalog ist da!

Oca Reisen GmbH
info@oca.com
❷

Wien mit Wachau
6-tägige Rundreise
Reisetermine 24. Mai – 29. Mai und
13. September – 18. September

Preise pro Person
Im Doppelzimmer   655 €
❸

Erholung auf der Sonneninsel
im Schwarzwald auf 720 m Höhe
Hotel Funk in Dobel
Hallen- und Freibad, Sauna,
Wanderwege, Fahrradverleih
5 Tage Vollpension
Pro Person   320 €
❹

Rotalis
Reisen per Rad
Europas Nummer Eins
in der Radtouristik
❺

FLÜGE & REISEN & LAST MINUTE
Täglich über 2,5 Mio. Top-Angebote
www.goek.co
Reisekompetenz seit 1987
❻

Abenteuer pur
Wir segeln in der Karibik.
Wer fährt mit?
Telefon: 0049–89–9901
❼

2 Haben Sie Urlaubspläne?

Julio: Wie heißen die Einwohner von Spanien?

Walter: Spanier.

Julio: Ja. Und in der Schweiz heißen sie Schweizer und in Österreich Österreicher. Die Wörter haben alle -er am Ende. Genauso wie die Einwohner von Städten: *die Berliner, die Münchner, die Nürnberger* usw. Aber was ist mit den Bayern und Franken?

Walter: Das sind die Einwohner auf -n. Da gibt es auch *die Franzosen, die Schweden, die Finnen* usw. Sagen Sie mal, haben Sie Grammatik-Probleme oder Urlaubspläne?

Julio: Ich habe drei Tage frei.

Walter: Und da möchten Sie wegfahren, nicht wahr? Wohin geht's denn?

Julio: Ich weiß noch nicht. Das ist ja mein Problem. Haben Sie eine Idee?

Walter: Keine Idee, aber einen Reiseprospekt. Hier: ...

Übungen – und ein bisschen Grammatik

3 Hier sind sechs Wörter versteckt. Suchen Sie die Wörter und notieren Sie sie mit Artikel.

1. ____ _____
2. ____ _____
3. ____ _____
4. ____ _____
5. ____ _____
6. ____ _____

X	U	R	L	A	U	B	S	P	L	Ä	N	E
R	E	I	S	E	P	R	O	S	P	E	K	T
A	C	B	R	U	N	D	R	E	I	S	E	B
H	Z	R	E	I	S	E	T	E	R	M	I	N
Z	U	M	W	A	N	D	E	R	W	E	G	G
A	D	O	P	P	E	L	Z	I	M	M	E	R

Es gibt ein Teilwort, das 3-mal vorkommt. Wie heißt es?

Lösung: _____

4 Reisewünsche

Ihre Kolleginnen und Kollegen haben viele Wünsche für den nächsten Urlaub. Machen Sie Ihnen Vorschläge.

• Lesen Sie zuerst unseren Reiseprospekt (Seite 97).
• Lesen Sie dann den ersten Reisewunsch und suchen Sie ein Reiseziel aus. Ordnen Sie zu.
• Dann lesen Sie den nächsten Reisewunsch usw. Achtung: Jemand braucht keine Vorschläge und keinen Reiseprospekt.

Ingo Bergmann: Ich möchte im Urlaub viel Sport treiben. Das gefällt mir am besten.

Karin Urban: Ich möchte nicht weit weg. Am liebsten fahre ich ein paar Stunden mit dem Auto. Und da bleibe ich dann. Das reicht.

Urs Hürlimann: Bei uns ist es so schön. Ich bleibe zu Hause und mache ein paar Ausflüge.

Petra Meinert: Nur weg. Keine Arbeit, kein Büro mehr, ich fahre in den Süden. Am liebsten ans Meer.

Kurt Kunze: Meine Familie hat schon viele Pläne. Sie möchten in eine Großstadt, viel sehen und besichtigen, Wien, Rom, Athen oder so.

Maria Weber: Meine Eltern kommen mit. Ich möchte ins Mittelgebirge, ein bisschen wandern, gut essen und viel schlafen.

Fritz Erler: Meine Freunde fahren zum Bergsteigen, vielleicht nach Südamerika. Klasse, was?

Evi Bernd: Meine Freunde segeln gern. Sie haben aber kein Schiff. Ich möchte auch gern segeln gehen.

5 Vier Zeichnungen + vier Jahreszeiten
Notieren Sie die Jahreszeit.

❶ Das ist der _____ .   ❸ Das ist der _____ .
❷ Das ist der _____ .   ❹ Das ist der _____ .

6 Welcher Sport ist das? Wir zeigen Ihnen ein paar Piktogramme. Ordnen Sie den passenden Text zu.

a. ◯ Segeln Sie?
b. ◯ Alle spielen Fußball.
c. ◯ In Deutschland wandert man viel.
d. ◯ Im Sommer fahren viele Motorrad.
e. ◯ Im Winter fahren viele Ski.
f. ◯ Schwimmen Sie gern?

7 In diesem Kalender fehlen noch die Monatsnamen. Bringen Sie sie in die richtige Reihenfolge.

| Dezember | März | August | Februar | November | April |

| Juni | Mai | Januar | September | Juli | Oktober |

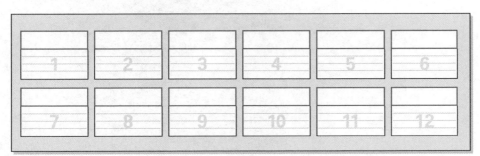

Ratespiel: Haben Sie das gewusst?

A **Im Deutschen gibt es viele zusammengesetzte Wörter. Beantworten Sie zuerst unsere Fragen.**

1. Ein See mit B. Wie heißt er? B_ _ _ _ _ _ _ _ .

2. Heidelberg ist eine Universitäts_ _ _ _ _ _ .

3. Eine Wohnung unter dem Dach ist eine _ _ _ _ _ _ _ _ _ _ _ _ _ .

4. Der Plural von „Urlaubsland" ist Urlaubs_ _ _ _ _ _ _ .

5. Im Urlaub machen wir eine Urlaubs_ _ _ _ _ _ .

6. Meine Mutter hat eine Mutter. Das ist meine _ _ _ _ _ _ _ _ _ _ _ .

B **Notieren Sie jetzt den zweiten Wortteil. Ergänzen Sie den Artikel.**
Achtung: Nomen schreibt man groß.

1. _der_ _S_____   **4.** _____ _____

2. _____ _____   **5.** _____ _____

3. _____ _____   **6.** _____ _____

C **Die Lösung sind drei Wörter. Sie finden etwas gar nicht gut oder Sie haben Pech gehabt, dann können Sie diesen Ausdruck sagen.**
Suchen Sie jetzt die Buchstaben aus Ihren Nomen zusammen (ohne den Artikel).

Wort:	1	3		1	5	4		6	5	2	6
Buchstabe:	1	2		2	3	3		1	3	1	3

Lösung: ⌴ ⌴   ⌴ ⌴ ⌴   ⌴ ⌴ ⌴ ⌴ !

Mein Computer spinnt

1 **Ein paar Fragen an Sie – Antworten Sie ganz schnell.**

1. Haben Sie zu Hause einen Computer?
☐ Ja. ☐ Nein.

2. Ist Ihr Computer alt oder neu?
☐ Alt. ☐ Nicht so alt.
☐ Neu. ☐ Ganz neu.

3. Haben Sie eine PC-Fortbildung
gemacht?
☐ Ja. ☐ Nein.

4. Haben Sie allein gelernt?
☐ Ja. ☐ Nein.

5. Hat Ihnen ein Freund / eine Freundin
geholfen?
☐ Ja. ☐ Nein.

6. Bekommen Sie viele Mails?
☐ Ja, viele. ☐ Nein, nicht so viele.

2 **Kannst du mir helfen?**

Claudia: Robert, kannst du mir helfen? Mein
Computer spinnt.

Robert: Der spinnt nicht, du bist nur nervös.
Jetzt gib deine PIN ein. Okay.
Na bitte, er kommt.

Claudia: Ich muss unbedingt eine PC-Fortbildung
machen.

Robert: Warum? Du bist doch schon fit.
Außerdem kann dir Niki alles erklären.
Da braucht man keinen Kurs. Das
kannst du allein lernen.

Claudia: Nein, nein. Ich möchte das systematisch lernen. Niki ist abends müde. Und gut
erklären kann er auch nicht.

Robert: Das darf er aber nicht hören!

Claudia: Sieh mal: Ich ruf die Mail mal auf. Eine Mail von Laura aus Argentinien. Das ist
eine Freundin von mir.
Liebe Claudia, lieber Niki,
ich hoffe, es geht Euch gut. Ich bin nächsten Monat in Deutschland. Ich habe ein
Stipendium bekommen. Seid Ihr zu Hause? Bitte antwortet schnell.
Liebe Grüße
Eure Laura

Übungen – und ein bisschen Grammatik

3 **In diesem Text fehlen wichtige Wörter. Ergänzen Sie.**

> PC-Fortbildung / lernen / Postfach / erklären / Computer /
> müde / Stipendium / Kurs / E-Mail / Freundin

Claudia: Robert, kannst du mir helfen? Mein _____ spinnt.

Robert: Der spinnt nicht, du bist nur nervös. Jetzt gib deine Pin ein. Okay.
         Na bitte, er kommt.

Claudia: Ich muss unbedingt eine _____ machen.

Robert: Warum? Du bist doch schon fit. Außerdem kann dir Niki alles _____.
         Da braucht man keinen _____. Das kannst du allein _____.

Claudia: Nein, nein. Ich möchte das systematisch lernen. Niki ist abends _____.
         Und gut erklären kann er auch nicht.

Robert: Das darf er aber nicht hören!

Claudia: Sieh mal: Ich ruf die Mail mal auf. Eine Mail von Laura aus Argentinien. Das ist
         eine _____ von mir.
         Liebe Claudia, lieber Niki,
         ich hoffe, es geht Euch gut. Ich bin nächsten Monat in Deutschland. Ich habe ein
         _____ bekommen. Seid Ihr zu Hause? Bitte antwortet schnell.

4 **Rekonstruieren Sie die Mail.**

```
┌─────────────────────────────────────────────────────────────────────┐
│ □                            E-Mail                               □   │
├───────────────────────────────────────────────────────────────────────┤
│ 🖃 Jetzt senden  🖃 Später senden  🖫 │ 🖉 Anlagen hinzufügen │ 🖉 Signatur ▼ 🖼 Optionen ▼ │
├───────────────────────────────────────────────────────────────────────┤
│  Liebe Claudia, lieber Niki,                                          │
│  _____ hoffe, _____ geht _____ gut. _____ bin nächsten Monat in │
│  Deutschland. _____ habe ein Stipendium bekommen. Seid _____ zu Hause? │
│  Bitte antwortet _____ schnell.                                    │
│  Liebe Grüße                                                          │
│  _____ Laura                                                       │
└───────────────────────────────────────────────────────────────────────┘
```

5 **Sie schreiben an Freunde und Geschäftspartner. Was ist formell-geschäftlich?**
   Was ist persönlich?
   Lesen Sie zuerst Übung 12 im Leitfaden.

   formell-geschäftlich ☐   ☐ persönlich

1. Du, Ihr, Dich, Dir, Euch ☐ ☐   **3.** Herzliche Grüße
   Sie, Ihnen ☐ ☐   Eure Rosa ☐ ☐

               Herzliche Grüße
               Euer Franz ☐ ☐

2. Sehr geehrter Herr Meyer, ☐ ☐   Mit besten Grüßen
   Liebe Familie Kraus, ☐ ☐   Christine Mann ☐ ☐
   Sehr geehrte Frau Schuh, ☐ ☐   Mit freundlichen Grüßen
   Sehr geehrte Damen und Herren, ☐ ☐ Regine Merz ☐ ☐
   Liebe Marion, ☐ ☐   Liebe Grüße
   Hallo, ☐ ☐   Laura ☐ ☐
   Lieber Helmut, ☐ ☐   Ciao
               Fritz ☐ ☐

6 **Sprechübung: Du musst nicht, aber du kannst.**
   Lesen Sie zuerst das Beispiel.

Beispiel: • Muss ich schreiben?
   ► Du musst nicht, aber du kannst.

Ich muss das lernen.
Ich muss (nicht).

1. Muss ich das lernen?   **4.** Müssen wir Karsten besuchen?
2. Muss Peter eine Fortbildung machen?   **5.** Musst du nach Madrid fliegen?
3. Muss Maria die Mail beantworten?   **6.** Müsst ihr schon nach Hause fahren?

7 **Roberts Tagebuch**
   Ergänzen Sie *kann* und *können*.

Donnerstag, 24.

Es ist schön bei Niki und Claudia. Ich _____ bestimmt noch bleiben. Niki hat
auch nichts dagegen. Aber ich habe nur noch 100 €! Da _____ ich Claudia zum
Essen einladen und was dann?
Zum Glück habe ich die Bahnfahrt schon bezahlt. Vielleicht _____ die Eltern
helfen. Übermorgen rufe ich sie an. Oder lieber nicht? Das entscheide ich morgen!

Raten Sie

Wer unterhält sich hier? Was meinen Sie?

a. ◯
- ● Haben Sie ein Hobby?
- ► Na klar. Mein Hobby ist Lesen. Ich lese gern.
- ● Was lesen Sie denn?
- ► Krimis. Und Sie?
- ● Krimis sehe ich im Fernsehen. Mein Hobby ist Fußball. Ich spiele viel Fußball.
- ► Na ja, Sie sind ja noch jung ...

b. ◯
- ● Was ist denn Ihr Hobby?
- ► Ich reise gern. Und Sie?
- ● Ich auch. Wohin fahren Sie denn da?
- ► Nach Norden. ... Wir fahren immer nach Norden. Am liebsten nach Skandinavien.
  Wir waren schon mit dem Schiff in Norwegen und in Spitzbergen.
- ● Interessant. Da war ich noch nicht. Wir fahren immer in den Süden zum Baden.

c. ◯
- ● Sag mal, hast du Hobbys?
- ► Klar. Inlineskaten.
- ● Und sonst?
- ► Im Internet surfen.
- ● Aha, das mache ich auch.

d. ◯
- ● Was machst du so lange?
- ► Kochen braucht Zeit. Das ist mein Hobby.
- ● Ja, aber ... Es ist schon neun.
- ► Lies doch die Zeitung! Ich rufe dich dann.

Postkarte oder SMS?

1 Lesen Sie zuerst die Wörter. Suchen Sie dann das passende Bild.

der Brief, die Briefe	die Postkarte, die Postkarten (= die Karte, die Karten)

die Mail, die Mails	das / die SMS, die SMS (= Short Message System)

die Briefmarke, die Briefmarken

❶ _____
_____

❷ _____
_____

❸ _____
_____

❹ _____
_____

❺ _____
_____

2 Herzliche Grüße aus der Hauptstadt

Robert: Ich habe eine Postkarte an meine Eltern geschrieben. Hast du eine Briefmarke?

Claudia: Habe ich. Hier, extra für dich. Sag mal, sind Postkarten eigentlich altmodisch oder nicht?

Robert: Nein, überhaupt nicht. Viele schreiben Postkarten aus dem Urlaub und alle freuen sich. Dir schreibe ich natürlich ein SMS: *Hallo, Berlin ist klasse, Wetter ist gut. Robert*

Claudia: Super, nur der Inhalt ist so langweilig. ... Schreib mir mal was. Ich warte.

Robert: *Hallo, heute Abend gibt's eine Überraschung für dich. Robert*

Claudia: Hör auf, Robert. Ich habe jetzt keine Zeit mehr.

Robert: Finde ich aber spannend. Und macht Spaß!

Claudia: Übrigens, sag mal, bleibst du noch? Laura kann auch bei meinen Eltern schlafen.

Robert: Das ist nett von dir. Aber ich muss ja wieder nach Hause. Mal sehen.

> *Liebe Eltern,*
>
> *herzliche Grüße aus der Hauptstadt. Das Wetter ist gut, die Stadt ist interessant. Gestern waren wir im Reichstag auf der Kuppel. Das war ein Erlebnis!*
>
> *Liebe Grüße*
> *Euer Robert*

Übungen – und ein bisschen Grammatik

3 Was ist richtig? Kreuzen Sie an.

1. ☐ Robert schreibt einen Brief an seine Eltern.
2. ☐ Er hat aber keine Briefmarke.
3. ☐ Claudia hat auch keine Briefmarke.
4. ☐ Viele schreiben Postkarten aus dem Urlaub.
5. ☐ Robert möchte an Claudia ein SMS schreiben.
6. ☐ Claudia findet den Inhalt langweilig.
7. ☐ Robert sagt, er hat eine Überraschung.
8. ☐ Claudia hat keine Zeit mehr.
9. ☐ SMS schreiben macht Robert keinen Spaß.
10. ☐ Robert muss nach München fahren.

4 Mit Roberts Kartengruß ist etwas passiert. Bringen Sie die Teile wieder in die richtige Reihenfolge.

1. Euer Robert
2. Das war ein Erlebnis!
3. Liebe Grüße
4. Liebe Eltern,
5. herzliche Grüße aus der Hauptstadt.
6. Das Wetter ist gut, die Stadt ist interessant.
Gestern waren wir im Reichstag auf der Kuppel.

Reihenfolge:

⌐⌐ ⌐⌐ ⌐⌐ ⌐⌐ ⌐⌐ ⌐⌐

5 Sprechübung
Lisa telefoniert mit Freunden. Was fragt sie zuerst? Natürlich *Hallo, wo bist du denn?* Hören Sie die Frage. Lesen Sie dann das Stichwort und antworten Sie.

1. Fernsehturm – auf
2. Berge – in
3. Bodensee – an
4. Italien – in
5. Schweiz – in

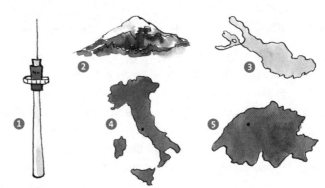

6 **Sprechübung**

Die Eltern sind immer unzufrieden und fragen: *Warum habt ihr nicht angerufen?*
Anworten Sie. Wir geben Ihnen die Stichwörter.

1. wir | doch | gefahren | sind | in die Schweiz
2. wir | doch | waren | Urlaub | im
3. wir | waren | doch | Katrin | bei
4. essen | wir | doch | waren
5. doch | wir | haben | gemacht | einen Ausflug

7 **Wie heißt das Gegenteil? Ordnen Sie zu.**

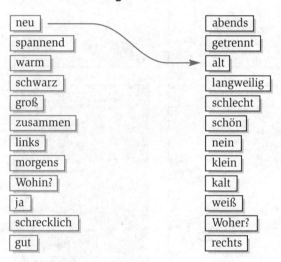

neu — alt

spannend — getrennt

warm

schwarz — langweilig

groß — schlecht

zusammen — schön

links — nein

morgens — klein

Wohin? — kalt

ja — weiß

schrecklich — Woher?

gut — rechts

abends

8 **Hier stimmt was nicht mit der Postkarte. Timo ist in Italien und schreibt seinen Eltern eine ganz besondere Karte. Schreiben Sie die Karte richtig.**

Liebeeltern,   _____

herzlichegrüßeausitalien.   _____

Mirgehtessehrgut.   _____

Daswetteristprima.   _____

Wirsindhierdirektammeer.   _____

Connyistschonganzbraun.   _____

Bisbald   _____

Euertimo   _____

Herzlichen Glückwunsch

Welche Karte verschicken Sie? Suchen Sie die passende Karte aus.

Karte

zum Geburtstag ◯

zur Hochzeit ◯

zur Prüfung ◯

zur Geburt ◯

Was schreiben Sie? Suchen Sie jetzt den passenden Glückwunsch.

Karte

Herzlichen Glückwunsch zum Geburtstag und alles Gute. ◯

Herzlichen Glückwunsch zur Hochzeit. Wir wünschen Euch viel Glück. ◯

Herzlichen Glückwunsch zur Geburt von … (Tim / Tina) und alles Gute. ◯

Herzlichen Glückwunsch zur bestandenen Prüfung und alles Gute für die Zukunft. ◯

Ich antworte gleich

1 **Wann war das? Wann ist das? Wann wird das sein?**
Ordnen Sie die Zeitangaben in der richtigen Reihenfolge.

❶ ❷ ❸ ❹ ❺ ❻ ❼ ❽ ❾ ⑩ ⑪

○ in zwei Jahren   ○ gestern

○ vor zwei Jahren   ○ nächsten Monat

○ letzte Woche   ○ morgen

○ nächste Woche   ○ vorgestern

○ letzten Monat   ○ übermorgen

○ heute

2 **Claudia schreibt eine Mail**

Claudia: Ich antworte gleich und schreibe Laura
eine Mail.

Wem gehören eigentlich die Zettel hier
und das Buch?

Robert: Mir.

Claudia: Das habe ich mir gedacht. Mach doch mal
ein bisschen Ordnung! Das ist ja schrecklich!

Robert: Bleib ganz ruhig. Das dauert nur eine
Sekunde. So, schon fertig!

Claudia: *Liebe Laura, vielen Dank für Deine Mail. Das ist ja prima. Wann warst Du das*
letzte Mal da? War das vor zwei Jahren? Nächsten Monat sind wir zu Hause.
Wann kommst Du? Antworte schnell. Dann können wir weiter planen.
Liebe Grüße auch von Niki
Deine Claudia

Robert: Wann kommt deine Freundin?

Claudia: Nächsten Monat. Genau weiß ich es nicht.

Robert: Ist deine Freundin Argentinierin?

Claudia: Ja, sie ist in Buenos Aires geboren.

Robert: Warst du schon mal da?

Claudia: Nein, noch nicht. Aber ich möchte gern mal hinfahren.

Übungen – und ein bisschen Grammatik

3 Wer hat das gesagt, Claudia oder Robert?
Markieren Sie.

a. Wem gehören eigentlich die Zettel hier? ☐ ☐

b. Das ist ja schrecklich! ☐ ☐

c. Bleib ganz ruhig! ☐ ☐

d. Wann kommt deine Freundin? ☐ ☐

e. Nächsten Monat. ☐ ☐

f. Sie ist in Buenos Aires geboren. ☐ ☐

g. Warst du schon mal da? ☐ ☐

h. Nein, noch nicht. ☐ ☐

4 Wir stellen Ihnen jetzt ein paar Fragen.
Was meinen Sie, welche Antworten sind richtig? Markieren Sie.

1. Wer ist Laura?
☐ Eine Argentinierin.
☐ Eine Freundin von Claudia.
☐ Eine Studentin.

2. Was steht in der Mail?
☐ Laura soll schnell antworten.
☐ Claudia und Niki sind nicht zu Hause.
☐ Claudia möchte gern planen.

3. Was plant Claudia?
☐ Laura kann bei Freunden wohnen.
☐ Laura muss bei den Eltern wohnen.
☐ Claudia möchte mal nach Argentinien fahren.

5 Hier fehlt das Verb. Ergänzen Sie.

> Mach / Schreib / Bleib / Antworte / Gib / Lerne

_____ mir eine Karte!

_____ mir schnell, bitte!

_____ ruhig!

_____ deine PIN ein!

_____ systematisch!

_____ ein bisschen Ordnung!

> geben – Gib!
> machen – Mach!
> antworten – Antwort**e**!
> lernen – Lern(**e**)!

6 Ergänzen Sie. Länder, Sprachen und Bewohner haben Sie schon in Lektion 24 gelernt.
   Schlagen Sie dort nach und wiederholen Sie.

der Argentinier	die Argentinierin	der Finne	_____
_____	die Italienerin	_____	die Österreicherin
_____	die Spanierin	der Franzose	_____
der Chilene	_____	der Nürnberger	_____
der Berliner	_____	_____	die Schweizerin
_____	die Hamburgerin	der Holländer	_____

7 Sprechübung – Wiederholen Sie die Sätze mit *ja*.
   Hören Sie zuerst das Beispiel.

Beispiel: Das ist prima. Das ist ja prima.

1. Das ist schrecklich.
2. Du bist nervös.
3. Er ist fit.

4. Der Computer spinnt.
5. Ich komme.
6. Ich helfe dir.

8 Sprechübung – Wiederholen Sie die Sätze mit *mal*.
   Hören Sie zuerst das Beispiel.

Beispiel: Mach Ordnung! Mach mal Ordnung!

1. Schreib!
2. Sieh!
3. Komm!

4. Sag!
5. Fahr hin!
6. Ruf an!

9 Eine E-Mail – Ergänzen Sie: *ja / doch / denn / mal*

```
┌─┐                          E-Mail                              ┌─┐
└─┘                                                              └─┘
┌──────────────────────────────────────────────────────────────────┐
│  Hallo Anja,                                                       │
│  ich habe Dich _____ schon lange nicht mehr gesehen. Was machst Du _____ so? │
│  Ruf _____ _____ an! Du bist _____ ein Musik-Fan. Morgen ist bei uns die │
│  Nacht der Musik. Da spielen Musiker und Bands auch auf der Straße. Hast Du Zeit? │
│  Komm _____ zu uns! Ich habe ein paar Freunde eingeladen.       │
│  Liebe Grüße                                                       │
│  Patrick                                                           │
└──────────────────────────────────────────────────────────────────┘
```

Haben Sie es gewusst?

Raten Sie und ergänzen Sie die Erklärung.

Ein Berg mit Z: die _____ Sie liegt in den _____ .

Eine Stadt mit K: Sie liegt am Rhein. _____

Ein See mit B: _____

Er liegt in Deutschland, Österreich und _____ _____ _____ .

Eine Stadt mit W: _____ Sie ist die Hauptstadt von _____ .

Ein Schloss mit Neu-: _____ Es liegt in _____ .

Schloss   Bodensee   Köln   Zugspitze   Wien
Neuschwanstein

In der Schweiz spricht man Deutsch, Französisch und _____ .

In Deutschland leben ca. _____ Millionen Ausländer. Sie sprechen Tü_____ ,

It_____ , Serb_____ , Grie_____ , Po_____ ,

Kroa_____ Russ_____ und andere Sprachen.

In Deutschland studieren Studenten aus Ch_____ , Fr_____ ,

Sp_____ , Po_____ , It_____ , Bul_____ ,

U_____ , Ru_____ , En_____ usw.

In Österreich spricht man _____ .

Die EU ist die _____ _____ .

Das Ergebnis finden Sie im Arbeitsbuch.

Fast perfekt

1 Wie finden Sie die / den / das ...? Beschreiben Sie die Personen.

Ich finde die Frau, den Mann, das Mädchen, den Jungen, das Kind ...
Die Frau / Der Mann ... rechts / links / in der Mitte / oben / unten ... sieht ... aus.

❶ _____

❷ _____

❸ _____

❹ _____

❺ _____

❻ _____

| hübsch | hässlich | gesund | krank |

| freundlich | unfreundlich |

| nett | nicht besonders nett |

| alt | jung | dumm | intelligent | sympathisch | unsympathisch | lustig | traurig |

2 Wie ist Ihr Eindruck?

Herr Kühne: Wie ist Ihr Eindruck, Herr Heinrich? Wie finden Sie die Firma?

Herr Heinrich: Die Firma ist klein, aber sie arbeitet sehr gut. Sie soll pünktlich und zuverlässig sein. Das sind meine Informationen.

Herr Kühne: Aber nicht besonders schnell, oder?

Herr Heinrich: Doch, doch. Und die Qualität stimmt auch. Die Software ist fast perfekt.

Herr Kühne: Was heißt hier „fast"? Sie muss absolut perfekt sein.

Herr Heinrich: Herr Kühne, Sie wissen doch. Es gibt keine Software ohne Fehler.

Herr Kühne: Schon gut. Und wie gefällt Ihnen Frau Bruckner?

Herr Heinrich: Ich finde sie sehr kompetent. Und Humor hat sie auch. Die Zusammen-arbeit mit ihr ist sehr angenehm.

Herr Kühne: Ja, ich finde sie auch sehr sympathisch. Was ist mit der Konkurrenz? Sie haben doch mit der Konkurrenz gesprochen.

Herr Heinrich: Die ist zu teuer. Außerdem sind die Konkurrenzfirmen zu weit entfernt.

Herr Kühne: Entfernungen spielen heute keine Rolle. Aber persönliche Kontakte, die müssen sein. Das haben wir jetzt erlebt.

Übungen – und ein bisschen Grammatik

3 Markieren Sie, was richtig ist.

1. ☐ Herr Heinrich findet die Firma von Frau Bruckner zuverlässig.
2. ☐ Herr Kühne ist nicht sicher. Er fragt Herrn Heinrich.
3. ☐ Herr Heinrich hat keine Informationen.
4. ☐ Die Software der Firma ist fast perfekt.
5. ☐ Frau Bruckner ist nicht kompetent, aber sie hat Humor.
6. ☐ Herr Heinrich arbeitet gern mit ihr.
7. ☐ Er hat auch mit der Konkurrenz gesprochen.
8. ☐ Die ist nicht teuer, aber zu weit entfernt.
9. ☐ Entfernungen sind heute wichtig.
10. ☐ Die persönlichen Kontakte spielen eine Rolle.

4 Hier fehlen wichtige Informationen. Rekonstruieren Sie den Text.

> zu teuer / sehr gut / klein / fast perfekt / sympathisch /
> pünktlich und zuverlässig / absolut perfekt / sehr kompetent / angenehm

Herr Kühne: Wie ist Ihr Eindruck, Herr Heinrich? Wie finden Sie die Firma?

Herr Heinrich: Die Firma ist _____, aber sie arbeitet _____ _____. Sie soll
_____ und _____ sein. Das sind meine Informationen.

Herr Kühne: Aber nicht besonders schnell, oder?

Herr Heinrich: Doch, doch. Und die Qualität stimmt auch. Die Software ist _____
_____.

Herr Kühne: Was heißt hier „fast"? Sie muss _____ _____ sein.

Herr Heinrich: Herr Kühne, Sie wissen doch. Es gibt keine Software ohne Fehler.

Herr Kühne: Schon gut. Und wie gefällt Ihnen Frau Bruckner?

Herr Heinrich: Ich finde sie _____ _____. Und Humor hat sie auch. Die
Zusammenarbeit mit ihr ist sehr _____.

Herr Kühne: Ja, ich finde sie auch sehr _____. Was ist mit der
Konkurrenz? Sie haben doch mit der Konkurrenz gesprochen.

Herr Heinrich: Die ist _____ _____. Außerdem sind die Konkurrenzfirmen zu
weit entfernt.

Herr Kühne: Entfernungen spielen heute keine Rolle. Aber persönliche Kontakte, die
müssen sein. Das haben wir jetzt erlebt.

5 Sie wollen einen Videofilm drehen und machen ein Casting, das heißt, Sie suchen Ihre Schauspieler aus. Zusammen mit Kollegen sehen Sie die Fotos an. Ordnen Sie die Texte den Fotos zu.

a. ( ) • Wie finden Sie den?
　　　▶ Na ja, es geht.

b. ( ) • Wie finden Sie den Mann?
　　　▶ Der sieht sympathisch aus.

c. ( ) • Wie finden Sie die Frau?
　　　▶ Das ist bestimmt eine Geschäftsfrau.

d. ( ) • Und das Kind hier?
　　　▶ Das ist nett.

e. ( ) • Und die Frau?
　　　▶ Die gefällt mir nicht so gut.

6 Hier fehlen die Formen von *müssen*.

Konkurrenz _____ sein.　　Software _____ perfekt sein.

Kontakte _____ sein.　　Mitarbeiter _____ zuverlässig sein.

7 Die Firma kennt keiner genau. – Setzen Sie *sollen* ein.

Der Leiter Markus Münch _____ sehr kompetent sein.

Die Firma _____ klein und zuverlässig sein.

Die Qualität _____ stimmen.

Die Mitarbeiter _____ sehr gut sein.

Sie _____ viele Kontakte haben.

er soll Geld haben
sie soll hübsch sein

8 Sprechübung
Sie wissen es nicht genau. Antworten Sie mit *sollen*.

Beispiel:
• Ist die Firma zuverlässig?
▶ Sie soll zuverlässig sein.

1. Hat die Firma genug Geld?
2. Sind die Mitarbeiter zufrieden?
3. Gibt es Fortbildung für die Mitarbeiter?
4. Hat die Firma eine Kantine?
5. Arbeitet die Firma im Ausland?
6. Liegt die Firma im Zentrum?

Ein Spiel

START	Stimmt das oder stimmt das ...?	Kaffee, Tee und Wasser sind	Der Plural von Firma ist	Wie ... Tage hat das Jahr?
Können Sie ... helfen?	1 Feld vor	Herzlichen ... zur Hochzeit!	Das Jahr hat zwölf	Wo liegt Salzburg?
1 Feld vor	Welches Wort fehlt? Er ist lustig. Er hat viel	Bitte, ... doch mal an.	Wie heißt das Gegenteil von „langweilig"?	Möchten Sie ein Glas Wasser? – ..., danke.
Berlin ist die Hauptstadt ... Deutschland.	Das Gegenteil von „jemand" ist	Ich habe es eilig, ich ... ein Taxi.	3 Felder vor	Mögen Sie Spaghetti? – ..., natürlich.
Nennen Sie fünf Berufe.	Nennen Sie drei Getränke.	Was möchten Sie? Fisch oder ... ?	Welche Sprachen spricht man in der Schweiz?	... möchten Sie sprechen?
2 Felder vor	Sind Sie verheiratet oder ...?	Das war kein Taxifahrer, das war eine	Die Wohnung hat 90	Ein Sprichwort sagt: Lieber spät als ... .
Wie heißen die zwei Wörter in „Wetterbericht"?	Was ist das Gegenteil von „richtig"?	5 Felder vor	1 ... hat 100 Cent.	Stimmt das nicht? – ..., das stimmt.
Wir essen mit Messer und	Isst du was? – Ich habe schon	Wie heißen die Artikel? ... Wort ... Pause ... Ziel	Norden, Süden, Osten und	**ZIEL**

Ich studiere hier

1 Welches Wort passt?

| Studenten | Studentin | Universität | Semesterferien | Fach | Semester | studierst |

- Die Humboldt-_____ in Berlin ist alt. Sie ist sehr berühmt.
- Über 29.000 _____ lernen dort.
- Max ist Student, Sybille ist _____.
- Sie studieren das _____ Medienkunde.
- Studierst du schon lange hier? – Ja, schon drei _____.
- Und du, wie lange _____ du schon?
- Sie arbeiten in den _____.

2 Fährst du oder bleibst du noch?

Claudia: Robert, hör mal!

Robert: Ja, was ist?

Claudia: Sag mal, willst du nun fahren oder bleibst du noch? Ich muss das jetzt unbedingt wissen.

Robert: Das ist ganz einfach. Ich bleibe in Berlin.

Claudia: Das habe ich mir fast gedacht.

Robert: Nächstes Semester studiere ich hier. Was sagst du dazu?

Claudia: Finde ich nicht schlecht. Warum nicht? Na ja ... und meine Schwester hat bestimmt auch nichts dagegen ... Habe ich recht? ... Willst du an die TU?

Robert: Genau. Die ist sehr gut in meinem Fach. Nächste Woche fahre ich nach Hause und komme dann in drei Wochen wieder. Zu Semesterbeginn.

Claudia: Deine Sachen kannst du hier lassen.

Robert: Au ja, prima. Ich muss mir bald ein Zimmer oder eine Wohnung suchen.

Claudia: Aber zuerst kommst du zu uns. Da räumen wir ein bisschen um. Wir haben eine Liege. Die stellen wir ins Wohnzimmer. Dann bleibt Laura auch hier. Das geht für ein paar Tage.

Robert: Und was sagt Niki dazu?

Claudia: Kein Problem!

Übungen – und ein bisschen Grammatik

3 Lesen, was Claudia alles sagt. Suchen Sie dann die Antwort von Robert.

Claudia: Robert, hör mal!

Robert: _____

Claudia: Sag mal, willst du nun fahren oder bleibst du noch? Ich muss das jetzt unbedingt wissen.

Robert: _____

Claudia: Das habe ich mir fast gedacht.

Robert: _____

Claudia: Finde ich nicht schlecht. Warum nicht? Na ja ... und meine Schwester hat bestimmt auch nichts dagegen ... Habe ich recht? ...
Willst du an die TU?

Robert: _____

Claudia: Deine Sachen kannst du hier lassen.

Robert: _____

Claudia: Aber zuerst kommst du zu uns. Da räumen wir ein bisschen um. Wir haben eine Liege. Die stellen wir ins Wohnzimmer. Dann bleibt Laura auch hier. Das geht für ein paar Tage.

Robert: _____

Claudia: Kein Problem!

- Und was sagt Niki dazu?
- Ja, was ist?
- Au ja, prima. Ich muss mir bald ein Zimmer oder eine Wohnung suchen.
- Das ist ganz einfach. Ich bleibe in Berlin.
- Nächstes Semester studiere ich hier. Was sagst du dazu?
- Genau. Die ist sehr gut in meinem Fach. Nächste Woche fahre ich nach Hause und komme dann in drei Wochen wieder. Zu Semesterbeginn.

4 *umräumen* ist ein trennbares Verb. Das wollen wir jetzt üben. Ergänzen Sie die Sätze.

_____ Sie oft _____?

Wann haben Sie zuletzt _____?

Carolin möchte gern _____.

Aber Alfons ist dagegen. Er _____ nicht gern _____.

Bald kommt Klaus. Dann _____ Carolin und Alfons _____.

_____ macht Spaß!

5 Sie sitzen zu Hause in Ihrem Wohnzimmer. Wissen Sie, wie die Gegenstände auf
Deutsch heißen? Nein, nicht alle? Dann wollen wir das jetzt üben.
Welches Bild passt zu welchem Wort?

○ der Tisch   ○ der Stuhl

○ das Bett   ○ die Couch

○ der Sessel   ○ der Schrank

○ die Blumen   ○ der Vorhang

○ der Schreibtisch   ○ die Lampe

6 Hören Sie jetzt, was Claudia sagt.
Sie räumt um und Sie helfen ihr
dabei. Notieren Sie in der Skizze,
welche Möbelstücke wohin
kommen.

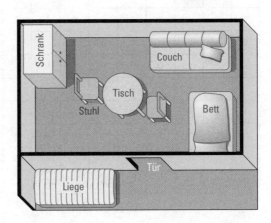

7 Sprechübung – Ein paar Fragen an einen Studenten
Antworten Sie mit den Stichwörtern.

ich / er / sie **will**
du willst
wir / sie / Sie **wollen**
ihr wollt

1. Was machen Sie jetzt? | ich | studieren | wollen |

2. Wo? | ich | wollen | in Leipzig | studieren |

3. Ab wann? | ich | wollen | ab nächstem Semester | studieren |

4. Welches Fach? | ich | wollen | Interkulturelle Studien | studieren |

5. Fahren Sie bald nach Leipzig? | ich | wollen | in zwei Wochen | fahren |

6. Sie fahren doch jetzt nach Hause. | ich | wollen | in vier Wochen | wieder hier sein |

  Wann kommen Sie wieder?

Mein Zimmer

**1. Suchen Sie die Möbel. Schreiben Sie sie auf und ergänzen Sie die Artikel und die Plural-
oder Singularformen.**

C	O	U	C	H	B	T	U	M
O	S	F	A	S	Ü	S	T	L
M	C	L	C	A	C	C	B	T
P	H	A	B	R	H	H	I	M
U	R	M	M	N	E	R	T	B
T	A	P	P	E	R	E	S	E
E	N	E	A	Ö	R	I	Ü	T
R	K	M	U	T	E	B	M	T
T	I	S	C	H	G	T	X	R
I	Z	M	A	L	A	I	M	O
S	E	S	S	E	L	S	Ä	M
C	T	Z	Q	W	G	C	H	M
H	Ö	O	S	T	Ü	H	L	E

_____

_____

_____

_____

_____

_____

_____

_____

**2. Wie sieht Ihr Arbeitszimmer zu Hause aus? Schreiben Sie. Einen Mustertext
finden Sie in den Lösungen.**

_____

_____

_____

_____

_____

Bis bald!

1 In diesem Text gibt es ein Schlüsselwort. Wie heißt es?
Setzen Sie die Silben richtig zusammen.

| sam | Zu | beit | ar | men |

die _____

2 Auf Wiedersehen

Frau Bruckner: So, mein Taxi ist da.

Herr Heinrich: Hatten Sie einen Mantel?

Frau Bruckner: Nein, eine Jacke. Das ist sie.
Und einen Schal.

Herr Heinrich: Wann geht der Zug?

Frau Bruckner: In einer Stunde. Da habe ich
genug Zeit. Noch einmal vielen
Dank für alles. Sie hören sofort
von mir. Ich schicke Ihnen das
Angebot spätestens in einer
Woche.

Herr Kühne: Prima. Wir freuen uns auf die
Zusammenarbeit.

Frau Bruckner: Und danke für die Einladung
gestern. Das Restaurant war
wirklich sehr schön.

Herr Heinrich: Ja, man isst dort sehr gut.

Frau Bruckner: Und wann kommen Sie nach München?

Herr Kühne: Vielleicht zum Vertragsabschluss. Wir kommen gern. Besonders nach
München.

Frau Bruckner: Sie wissen ja, da ist die Küche auch nicht schlecht. Auf Wiedersehen,
Herr Kühne, auf Wiedersehen, Herr Heinrich. Und bis bald.

Herr Kühne: Bis bald! Wir wünschen eine gute Reise.

Übungen – und ein bisschen Grammatik

3 In diesem Text fehlen ein paar wichtige Sätze. Man sagt sie zum Abschied.
Hören Sie den Text noch einmal und setzen Sie die fehlenden Sätze wieder ein.

Herr Heinrich:	Wann geht der Zug?
Frau Bruckner:	In einer Stunde. Da habe ich genug Zeit. _____. Sie hören sofort von mir. Ich schicke Ihnen das Angebot spätestens in einer Woche.
Herr Kühne:	Prima. _____.
Frau Bruckner:	_____. Das Restaurant war wirklich sehr schön.
Herr Heinrich:	Ja, man isst dort sehr gut.
Frau Bruckner:	Das stimmt! Und wann kommen Sie nach München?
Herr Kühne:	Vielleicht zum Vertragsabschluss. Wir kommen gern. Besonders nach München.
Frau Bruckner:	Sie wissen ja, da ist die Küche auch nicht schlecht. _____, Herr Kühne, auf Wiedersehen, Herr Heinrich. _____.
Herr Kühne:	Bis bald. _____.

- Wir freuen uns auf die Zusammenarbeit.
- Und bis bald.
- Wir wünschen eine gute Reise.
- Noch einmal vielen Dank für alles.
- Auf Wiedersehen
- Und danke für die Einladung gestern.

4 Auf *Wiedersehen* oder *Tschüs*?
Was sagen Sie, privat und / oder im Beruf? Ordnen Sie ein.

Tschüs. | Mach's gut. | Bis bald. | Auf Wiedersehen.

Bis zum nächsten Mal. | Gute Besserung. | Es war sehr schön bei euch.

Danke für die Einladung. | Besuchen Sie uns bald wieder.

Gute Reise. | Viel Spaß! | Wir freuen uns. | Ciao.

privat _____

im Beruf _____

privat und im Beruf _____

**5 Ich packe meinen Koffer. An was muss ich alles denken?
Ergänzen Sie die Endungen.**

Ich darf meinen Mantel nicht vergessen.

...

mein___ Schal	mein___ Portemonnaie	mein___ Rock
mein___ Schuhe	mein___ Hemden	mein___ Schlüssel
mein___ Anzug	mein___ Hosen	mein___ Schirm
mein___ Bluse	mein___ Jacke	mein___ Tasche
mein___ Brille	mein___ Kleid	mein___ Ticket
mein___ Kamera	mein___ Pullover	mein___ Pass

Was tragen Männer?_____   **Was tragen Frauen?**_____

_____   _____

**6 Hier verabschieden sich mehrere Personen von Ihnen. Hören Sie, was die Personen
sagen. Antworten Sie dann mit unseren Stichwörtern.**

1. Wann möchten Sie ein Taxi? | 12 Uhr | | bitte | | nicht später |

2. Wohin fahren Sie? | Bahnhof |

3. Wann geht Ihr Zug? | 13 Uhr 20 |

4. Hatten Sie einen Mantel? | Nein | | Jacke |

5. Wir wünschen gute Reise. | danke | | bis bald | | und |

7 Notizen von Chris Bruckner

Ergänzen Sie: werde / werden / schläft / müssen / wissen / haben / es gibt /
gekommen / dürfen

Donnerstag, 26.

Firma Europartner: Ende gut, alles gut! Drei Tage sehr gute Gespräche mit der Firma
Europartner. Wir sind weit _____. _____ _____ keine Probleme.
Nächste Woche _____ ich den Vertrag schicken. Die Partner _____
uns bald in München besuchen. Wir _____ keine Zeit verlieren. Zeit ist Geld!
Die Konkurrenz _____ nicht. Unsere Firmen _____ viel Erfahrung.
Und wir _____ schnell sein. Das _____ beide Parteien.

Reiseziele

**Jede Stadt hat etwas Typisches. So hat Paris den Eiffelturm oder Rom das Kolosseum.
Wir haben neun Sehenswürdigkeiten für Sie ausgesucht. Raten Sie, welche Stadt das ist.**

a. ◯ „Wir haben Karten für das Festspielhaus bekommen und
„Die Zauberflöte" gesehen."

b. ◯ „Wir sind über die alte Holzbrücke gelaufen."

c. ◯ „Wir haben eine Hafenrundfahrt gemacht."

d. ◯ „Wir haben Goethes Gartenhaus besichtigt."

e. ◯ „Wir haben den Reichstag gesehen."

f. ◯ „Wir haben uns die Frauenkirche angeschaut."

g. ◯ „Wir waren auf dem Oktoberfest."

h. ◯ „Wir haben das Schloss Sanssouci von Friedrich dem Großen gesehen."

i. ◯ „Wir waren im Stephansdom."

① München
② Salzburg
③ Wien
④ Potsdam
⑤ Weimar
⑥ Berlin
⑦ Dresden
⑧ Luzern
⑨ Hamburg

Bildquellenverzeichnis

Ideal zum Lernen unterwegs!

Kleines Format, kleiner Preis, großer Inhalt! Mit der Reihe *deutsch üben – Taschentrainer* können Sie anhand von alltagsbezogenen Übungen gezielt Wortschatz- und Grammatik-kenntnisse trainieren.

Die handlichen Titel eignen sich besonders zum Selbstlernen, sind aber auch als Ergänzung zu jedem Lehrbuch einsetzbar.

www.hueber.de/deutsch-lernen

Hueber Freude an Sprachen